Shojo Beat

Fushigi Yûgi

Genbu Kaiden

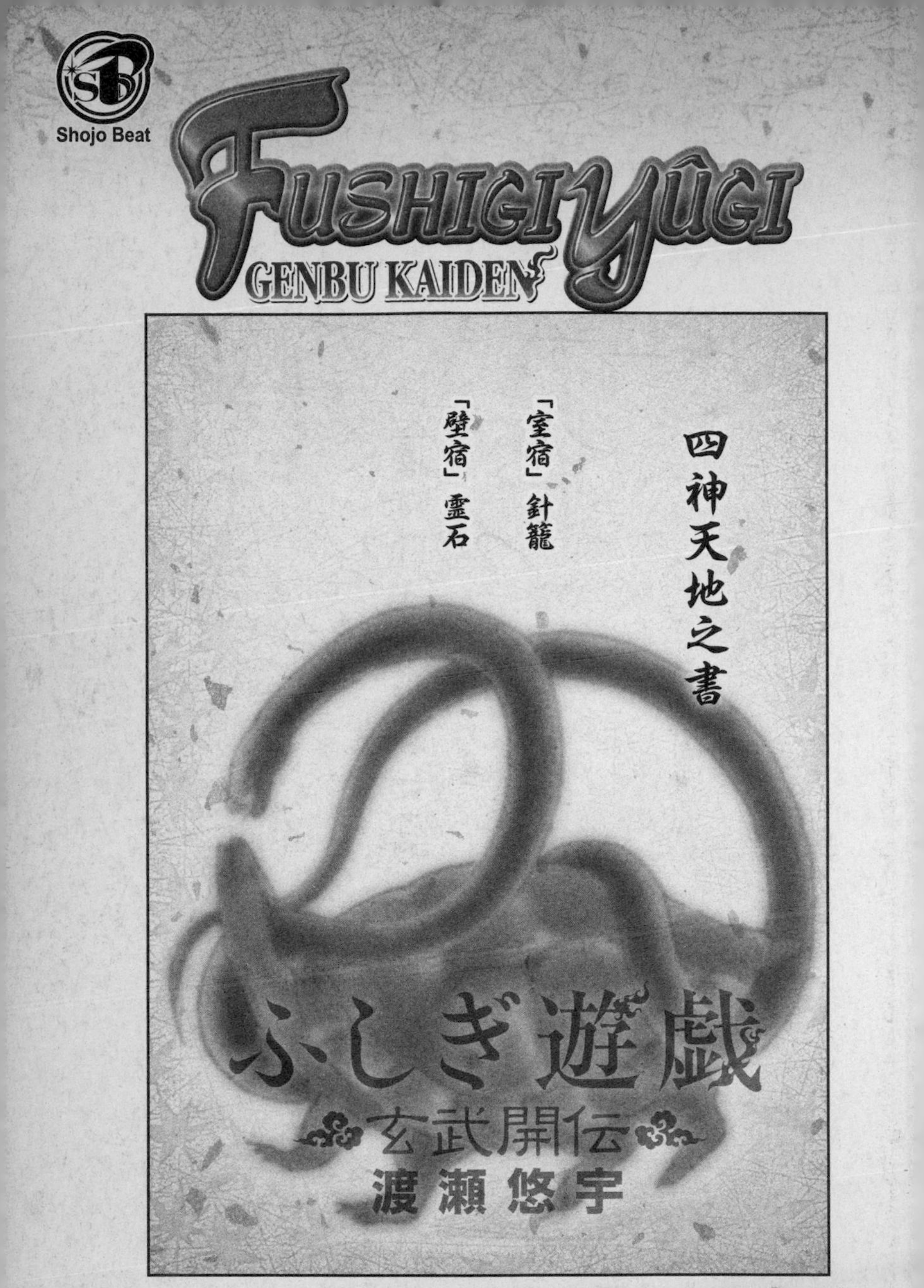
四神天地之書
「室宿」針籠
「壁宿」霊石
ふしぎ遊戯
玄武開伝
渡瀬悠宇

story and art by YUU WATASE

Vol. 6

CONTENTS

TRANSLATION OF "THE UNIVERSE OF
THE FOUR GODS"

Hatsui: Needle Cage
Namame: Spirit Stone

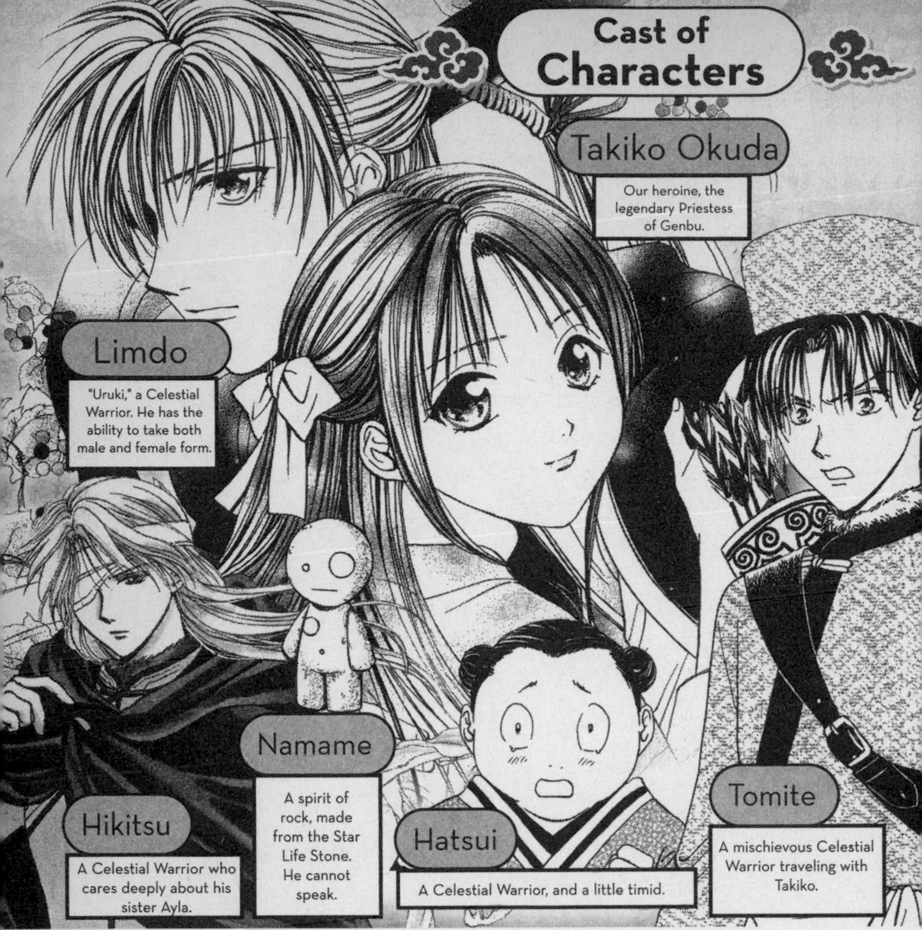
Cast of Characters
Takiko Okuda
Our heroine, the legendary Priestess of Genbu.
Limdo
"Uruki," a Celestial Warrior. He has the ability to take both male and female form.
Tomite
A mischievous Celestial Warrior traveling with Takiko.
Hatsui
A Celestial Warrior, and a little timid.
Namame
A spirit of rock, made from the Star Life Stone. He cannot speak.
Hikitsu
A Celestial Warrior who cares deeply about his sister Ayla.

The Story Thus Far

The year is 1923. Takiko is drawn into the pages of *The Universe of the Four Gods*, a book her father has translated from Chinese. There, she is told that she is the legendary Priestess of Genbu, destined to save the country of Bêi-jîa. She must find the seven Celestial Warriors who will help her on her quest.

Takiko has now been joined by five Celestial Warriors: Uruki, Tomite, Hatsui, Namame and Hikitsu. Together, they travel to Hong-nan to look for the sixth warrior, Inami. Takiko infiltrates a brothel disguised as a prostitute. The madam challenges her to a duel, and in the heat of battle the mark of Inami is revealed on her body!

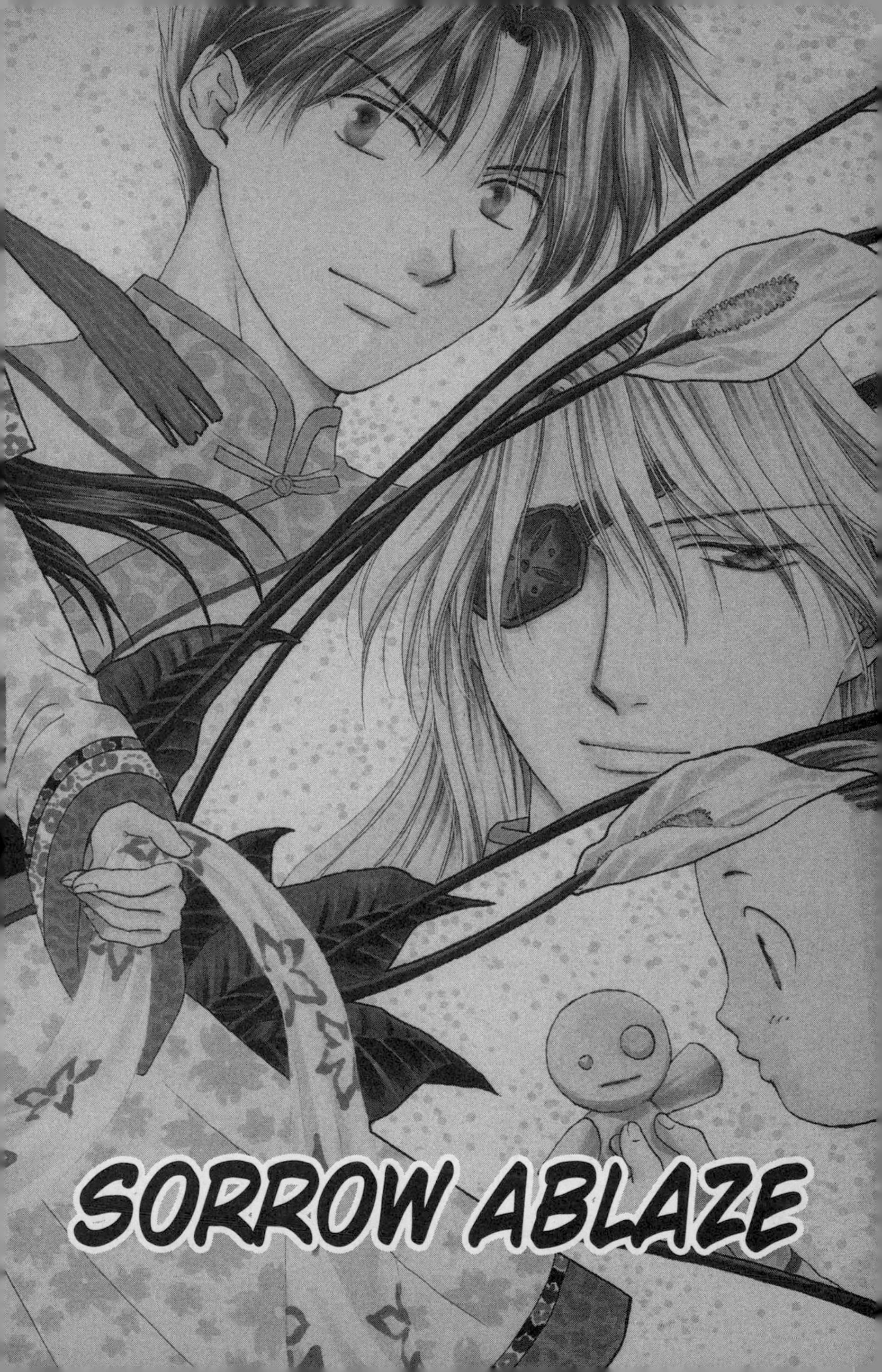
SORROW ABLAZE

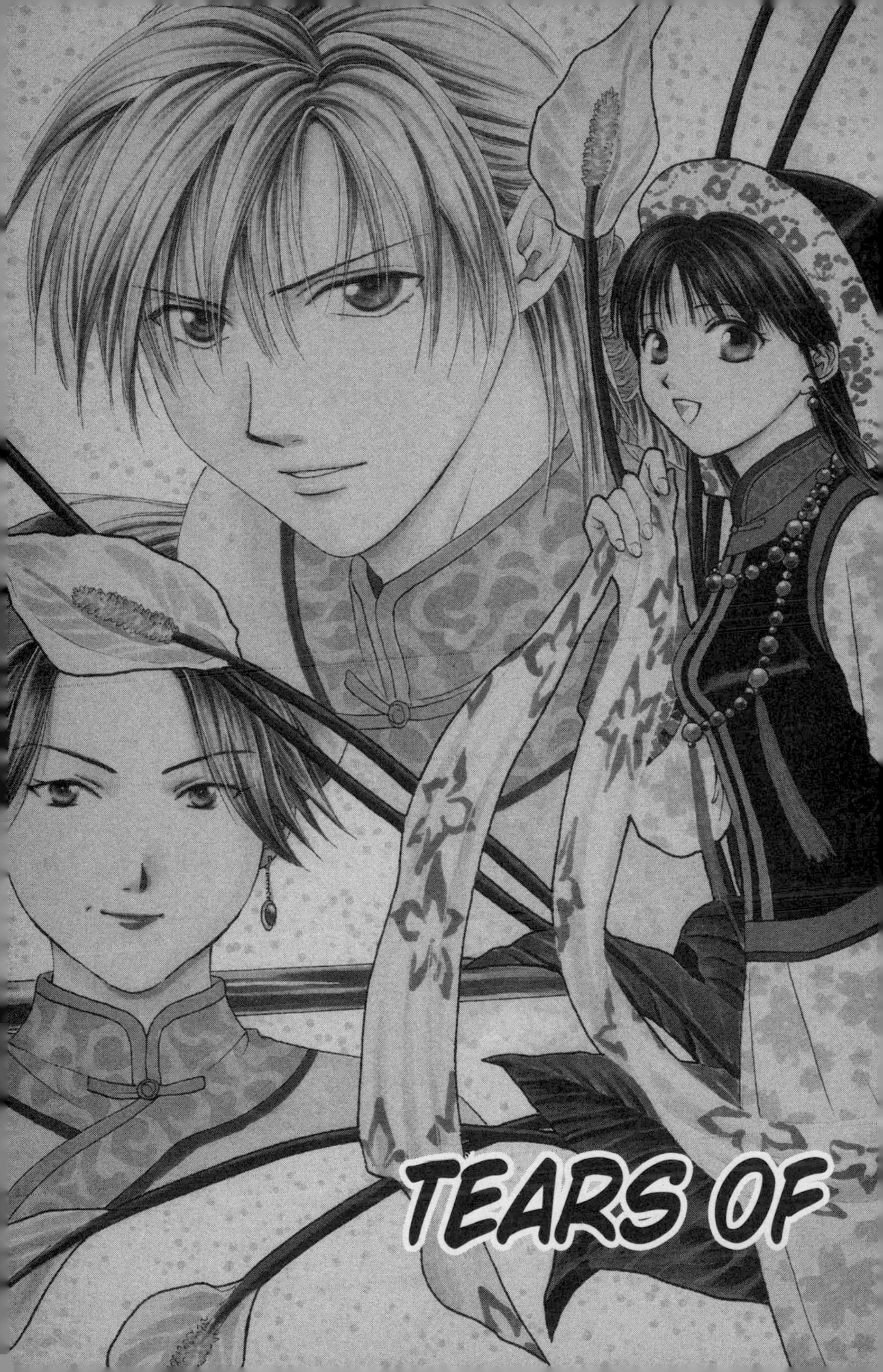
TEARS OF

Hi, everyone. I apologize for the long delay...◊The next volume is finally out!
_{I'm sorry. ◊}
I took some time off from Aug. 2005 to June 2006 to recover from various health issues. The magazine *Fushigi Yugi: Perfect World* made its return in September 2006, and I expect it to start coming out every three months again. Previously, two issues of the magazine made enough content for one graphic novel, but we were a bit wary about going back to the same pace right away. Then there weren't enough pages for volume 6, so we included a one-shot side story from *Ceres: Celestial Legend*. Even though I had my chance when they produced a pocket edition of *Ceres*, I totally forgot to include this episode,◊ and it would've never been seen again if not for this. ◊◊ I hope you enjoy it. All the graphic novels are supposed to be around 180 pages.

The fifth CD drama (oops, I mean "drama CD" ◊) is coming out this summer! And I think there's going to be another PSP game!⊙‿⊙It probably won't be about *Genbu* this time. What does that mean? I don't know the details myself at this point, so please keep checking for news in the magazine. Issue 9 will be out at the same time as volume 6, and issue 10 should be out at the end of June, according to the schedule.

So many things happened during my hiatus◊ I moved (again!) after I got back to work, so that was an ordeal as well. Okay, it's only a 15-minute walk away from my previous place, so it's not all that different.

Around the same time, Yu, my beloved Yorkie, passed away. He was 13 years and 7 months old, so he died of old age. He was healthy up to the very end-- such a "good little doggie" (I often praised him that way) and so kind to his owner.
_{He really was very smart.}
When I was burnt out from work, I'd pet him and feel so much better. I still miss him...◡̈ I'll probably miss him for the rest of my life. It's so sad that pets have such short lives. My mom took it very hard, too. She said, "I'll never get another pet if I have to feel this way!" Yu, get reincarnated and come see us again! I'll smoosh your little head.
_{It comes to this?}
Let's turn the topic back to *Genbu*.
_{It's getting too depressing.}
Inami showed up in the previous volume. There was a lot of, "What? This middle-aged woman is a Celestial Warrior?" in the reader reactions. There have been requests from time to time for a female Celestial Warrior (Uruki doesn't count). The normal thing to do would be to make her a cute girl, but I'm contrary, and I thought that would be too boring. So I opted for someone more advanced in years. There were some comments that "she doesn't have the face to be in the main cast." ◡̈◊Huh? A face doesn't make a Celestial Warrior! I put a lot of thought into her looks and her entrance. I've always liked cool older women, and I also wanted a motherly Celestial Warrior for hard-working Takiko and rebellious Uruki.

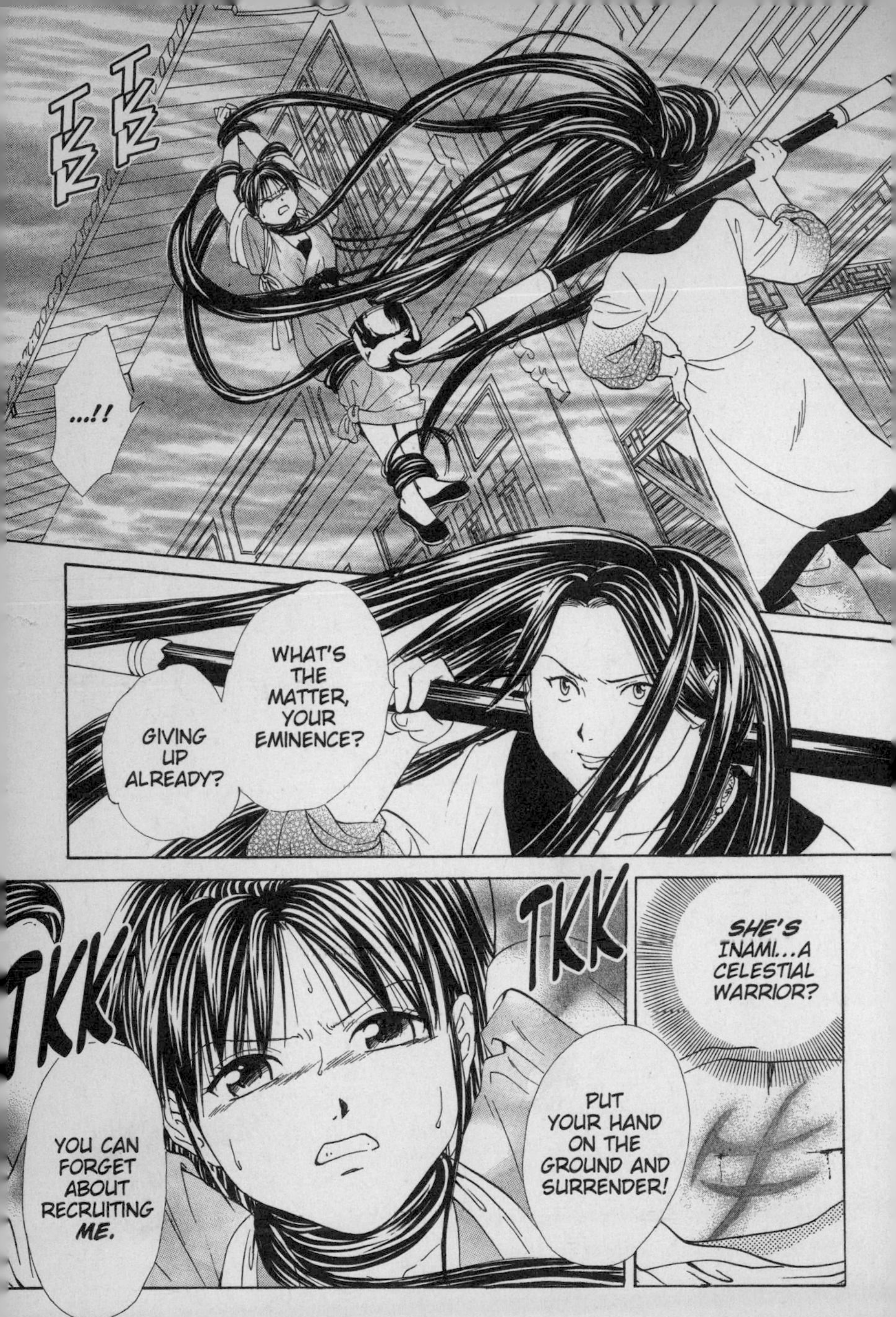
TKK
TKK
...!!
WHAT'S THE MATTER, YOUR EMINENCE?
GIVING UP ALREADY?
SHE'S INAMI...A CELESTIAL WARRIOR?
TKK
PUT YOUR HAND ON THE GROUND AND SURRENDER!
TKK
YOU CAN FORGET ABOUT RECRUITING ME.

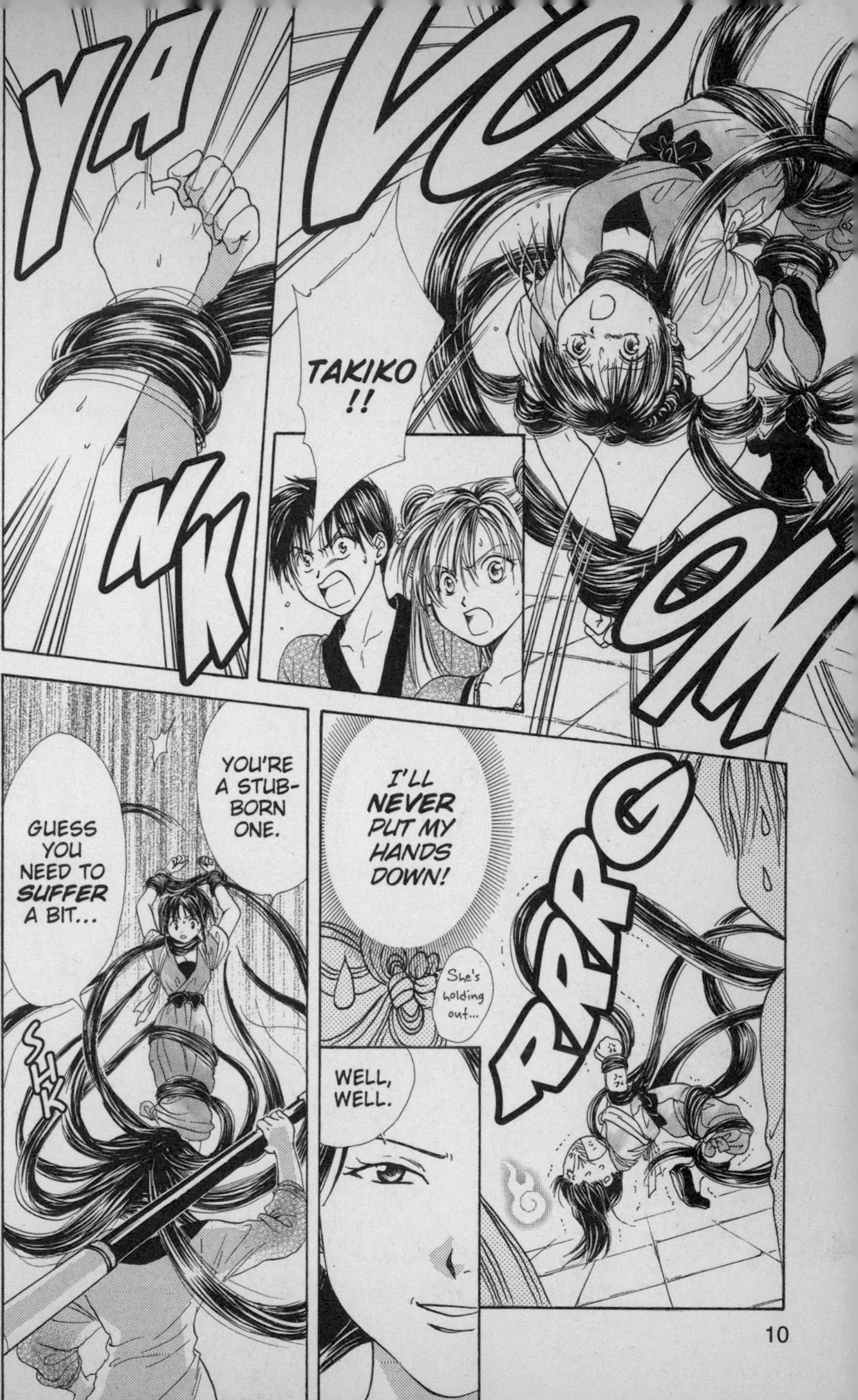
YA
VO
OM
TAKIKO !!
NNK
RRRG
I'LL NEVER PUT MY HANDS DOWN!
She's holding out...
WELL, WELL.
YOU'RE A STUB-BORN ONE.
GUESS YOU NEED TO SUFFER A BIT...
SHK

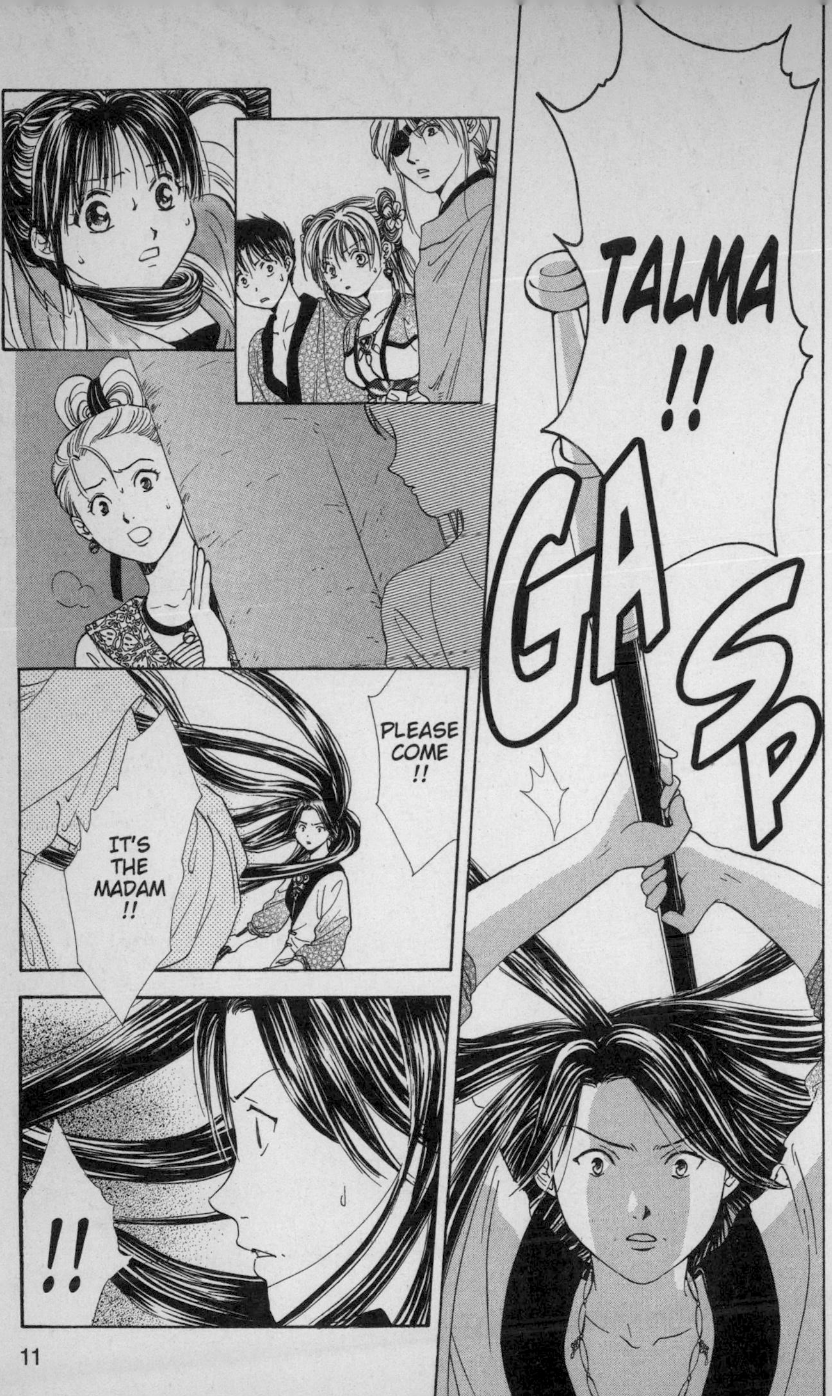
TALMA !!
GASP
PLEASE COME !!
IT'S THE MADAM !!
!!

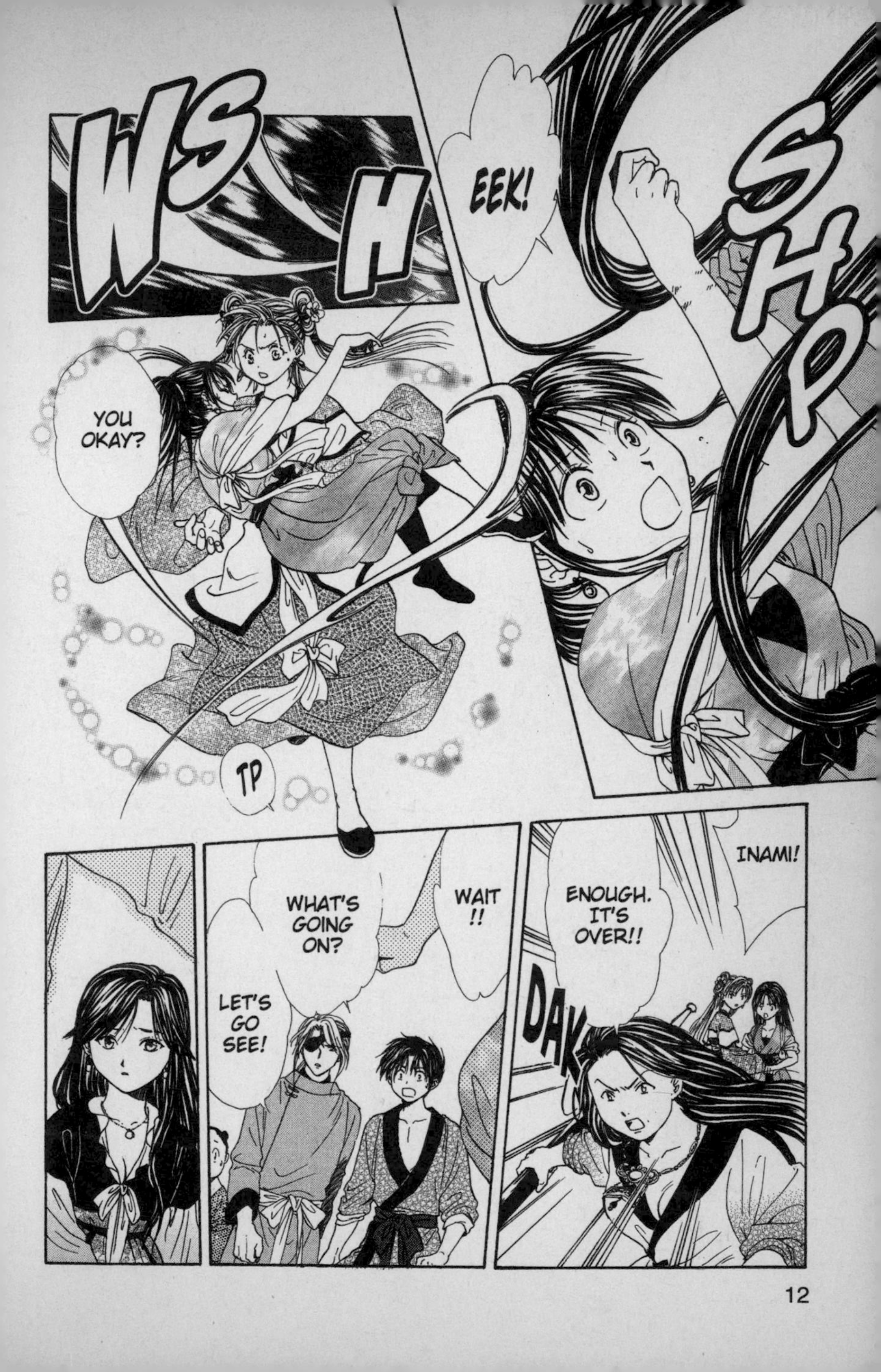
SHP
EEK!
WSH
YOU OKAY?
TP
INAMI!
ENOUGH. IT'S OVER!!
DAK
WAIT !!
WHAT'S GOING ON?
LET'S GO SEE!

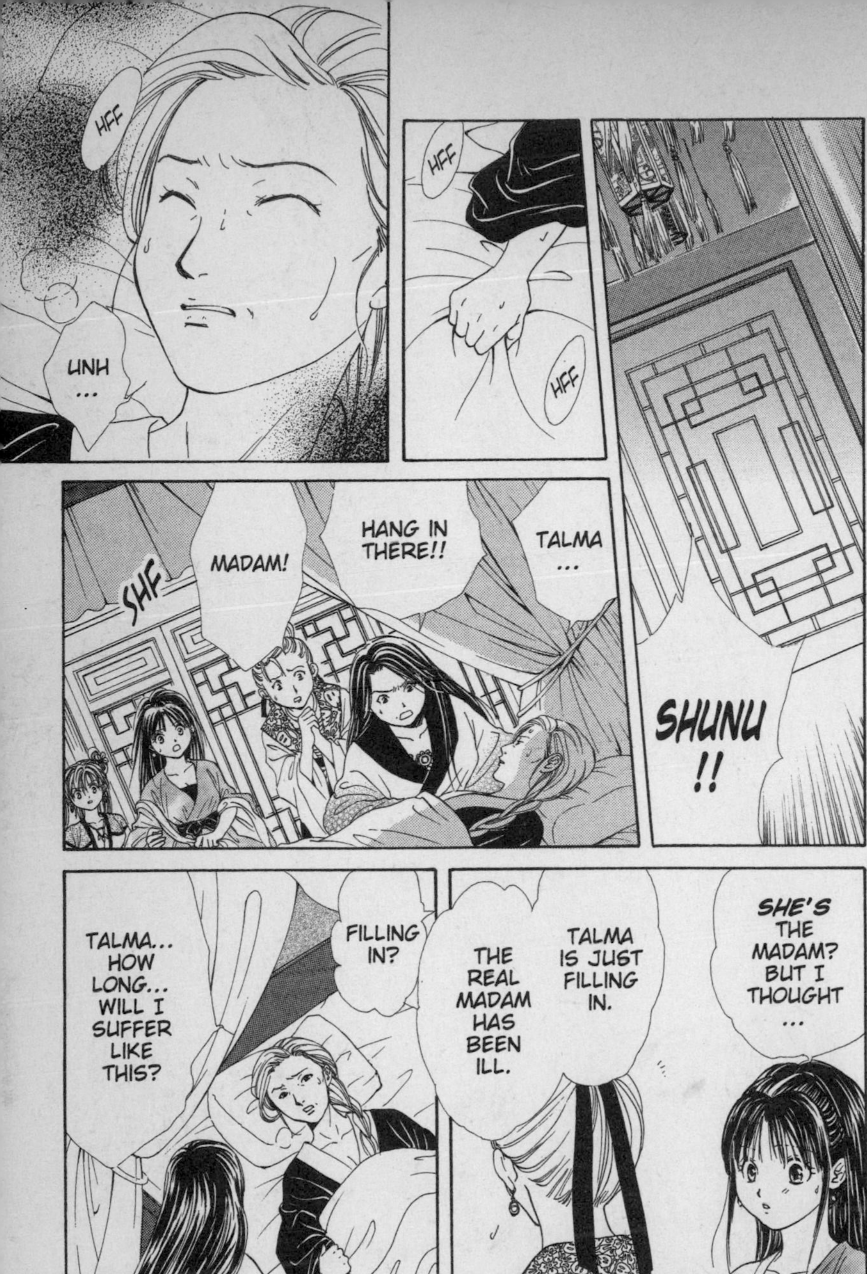
SHUNU!!
HFF
HFF
HFF
UNH...
TALMA...
HANG IN THERE!!
SHF
MADAM!
SHE'S THE MADAM? BUT I THOUGHT...
TALMA IS JUST FILLING IN.
THE REAL MADAM HAS BEEN ILL.
FILLING IN?
TALMA... HOW LONG... WILL I SUFFER LIKE THIS?

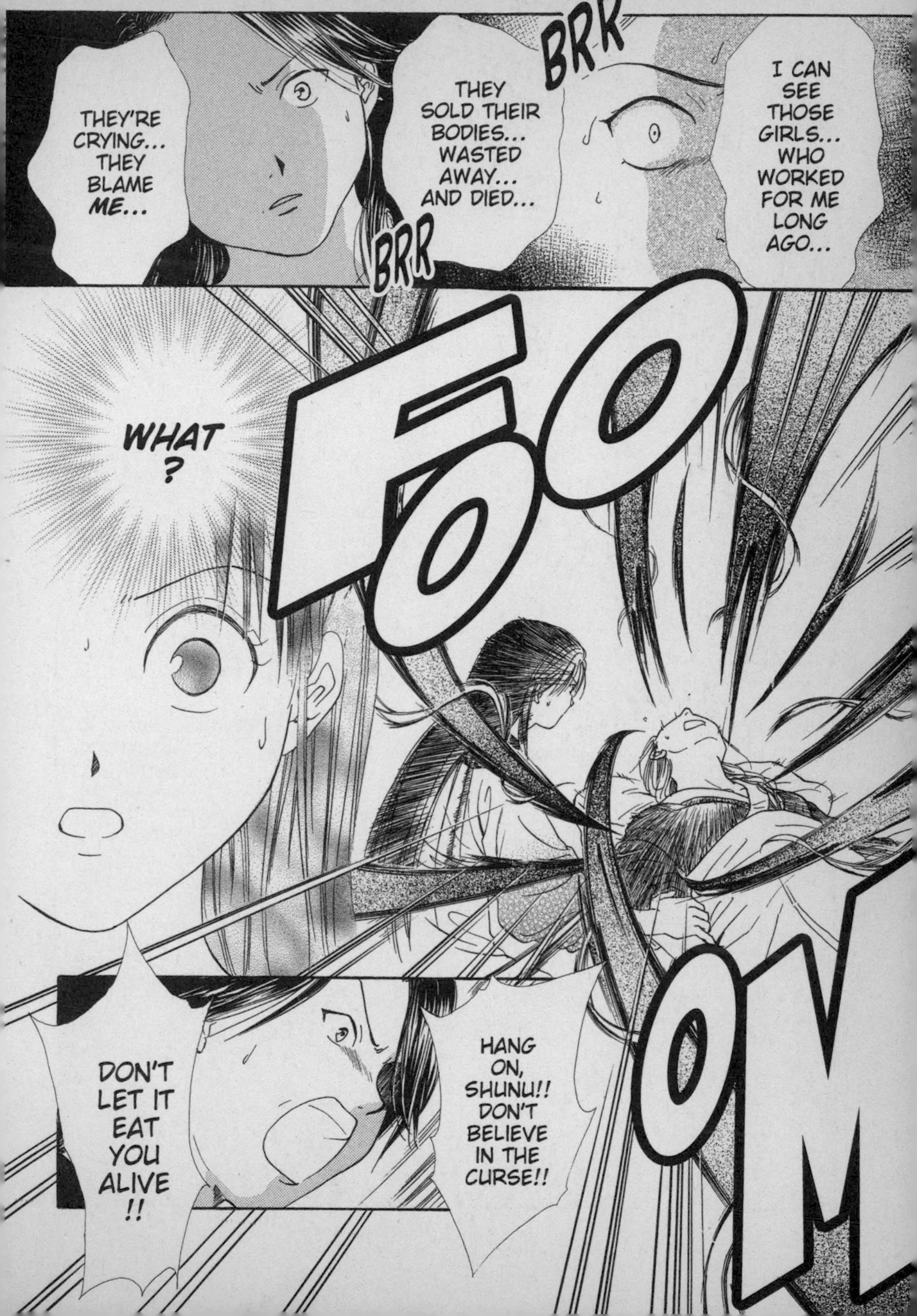
I CAN SEE THOSE GIRLS... WHO WORKED FOR ME LONG AGO...
BRR
THEY SOLD THEIR BODIES... WASTED AWAY... AND DIED...
BRR
THEY'RE CRYING... THEY BLAME ME...
FOOOM
WHAT ?
HANG ON, SHUNU!! DON'T BELIEVE IN THE CURSE!!
DON'T LET IT EAT YOU ALIVE !!

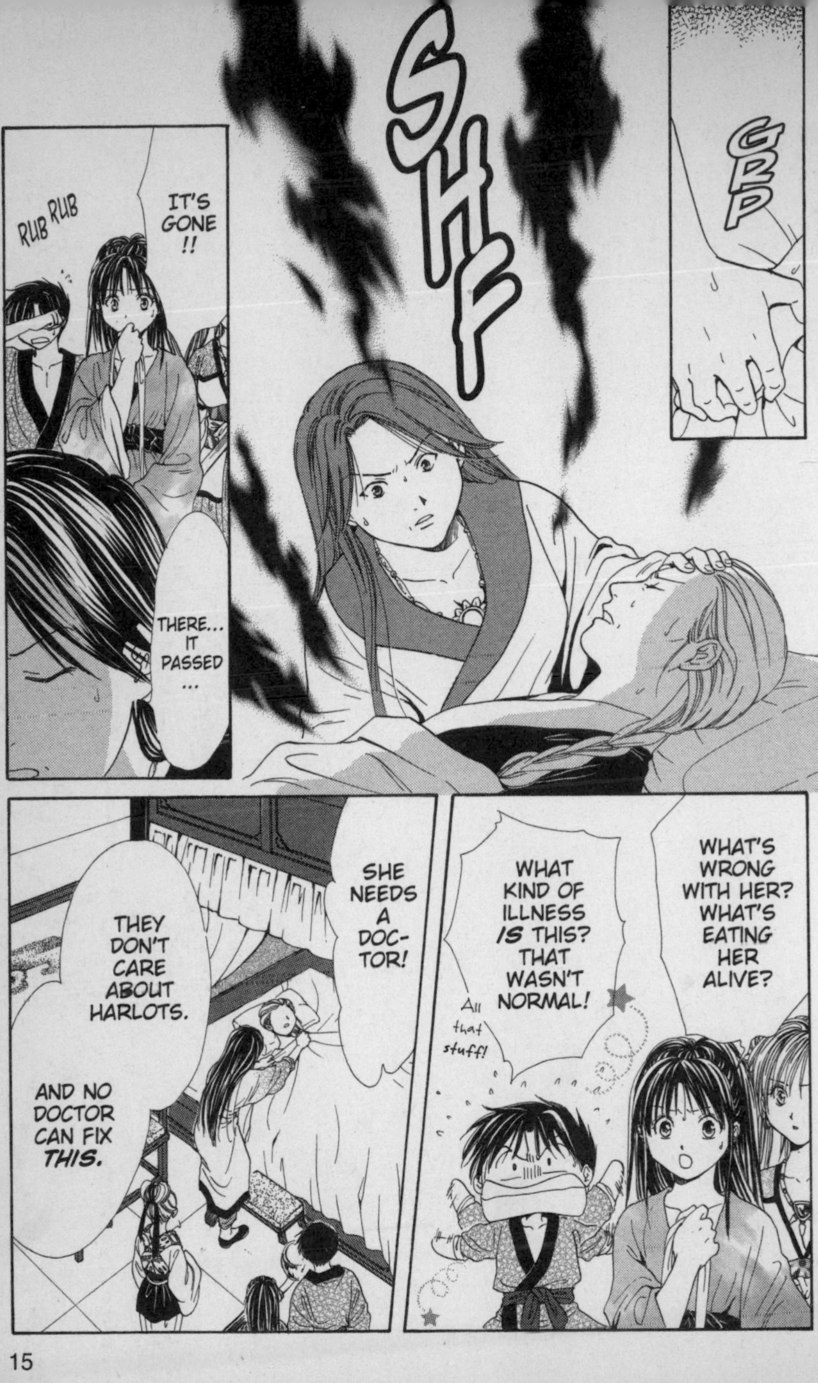
GRP
SHF
IT'S GONE !!
RUB RUB
THERE... IT PASSED ...
WHAT'S WRONG WITH HER? WHAT'S EATING HER ALIVE?
WHAT KIND OF ILLNESS *IS* THIS? THAT WASN'T NORMAL!
All that stuff!
SHE NEEDS A DOC-TOR!
THEY DON'T CARE ABOUT HARLOTS.
AND NO DOCTOR CAN FIX *THIS.*

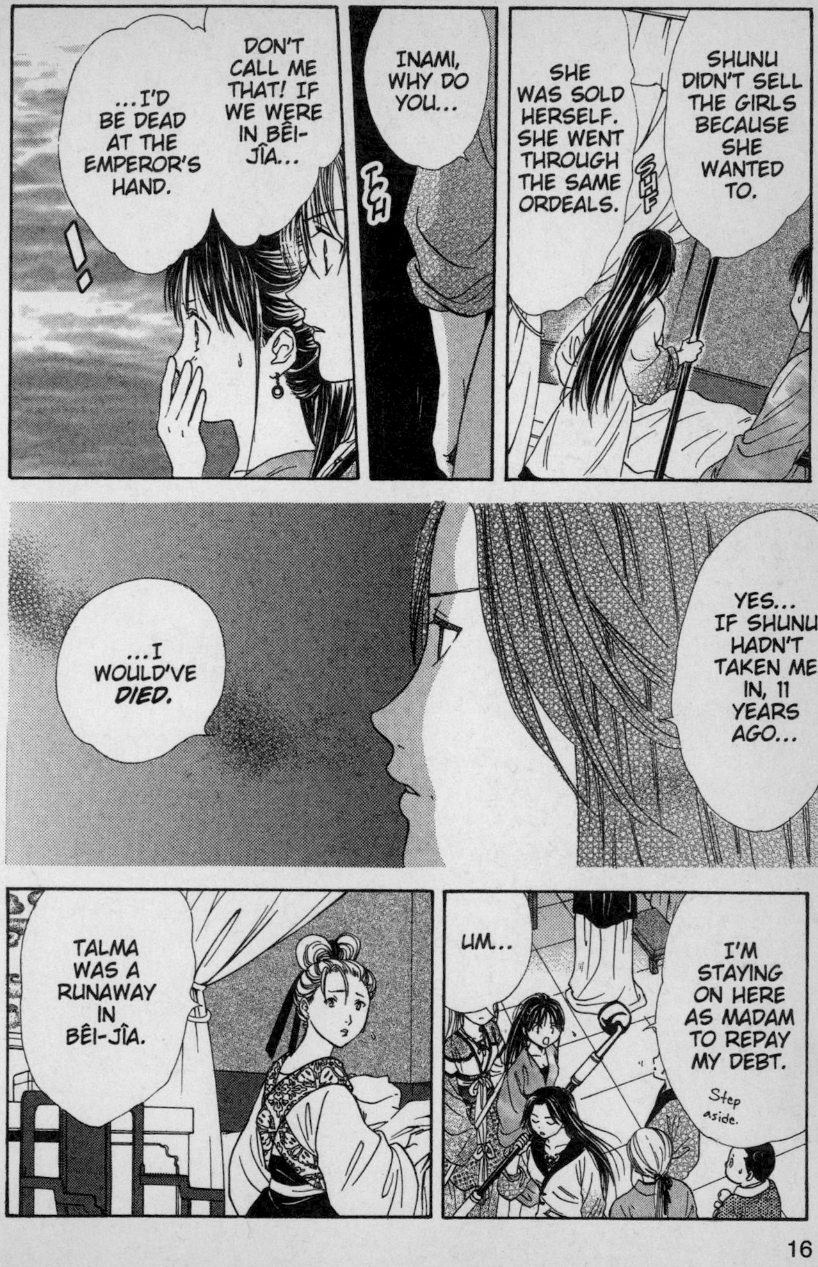
SHUNU DIDN'T SELL THE GIRLS BECAUSE SHE WANTED TO.
SHF
SHE WAS SOLD HERSELF. SHE WENT THROUGH THE SAME ORDEALS.
INAMI, WHY DO YOU...
TCH
DON'T CALL ME THAT! IF WE WERE IN BÊI-JÎA...
...I'D BE DEAD AT THE EMPEROR'S HAND.
!
YES... IF SHUNU HADN'T TAKEN ME IN, 11 YEARS AGO...
...I WOULD'VE *DIED.*
I'M STAYING ON HERE AS MADAM TO REPAY MY DEBT.
Step aside.
UM...
TALMA WAS A RUNAWAY IN BÊI-JÎA.

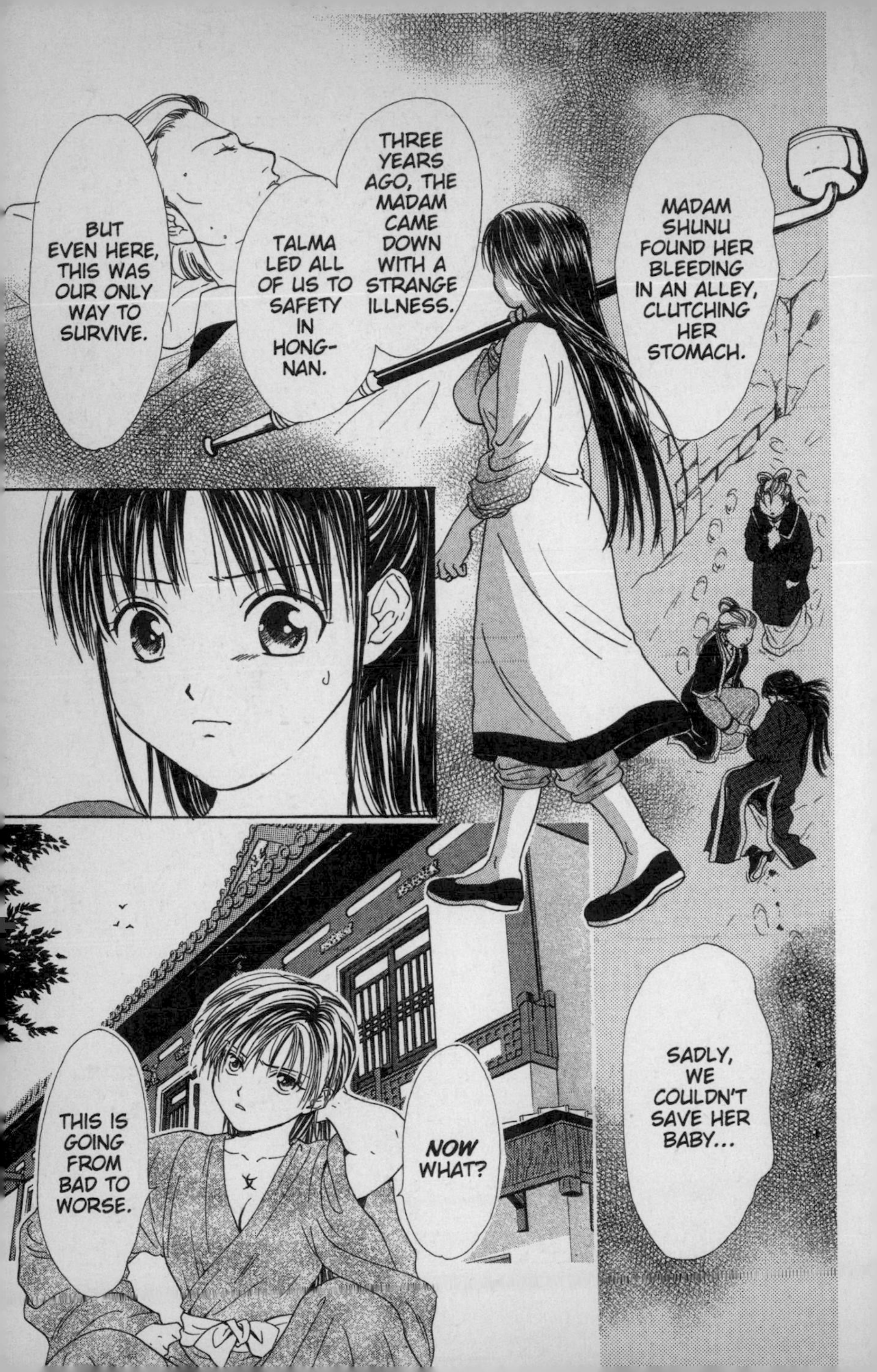
MADAM SHUNU FOUND HER BLEEDING IN AN ALLEY, CLUTCHING HER STOMACH.
THREE YEARS AGO, THE MADAM CAME DOWN WITH A STRANGE ILLNESS.
TALMA LED ALL OF US TO SAFETY IN HONG-NAN.
BUT EVEN HERE, THIS WAS OUR ONLY WAY TO SURVIVE.
SADLY, WE COULDN'T SAVE HER BABY...
NOW WHAT?
THIS IS GOING FROM BAD TO WORSE.

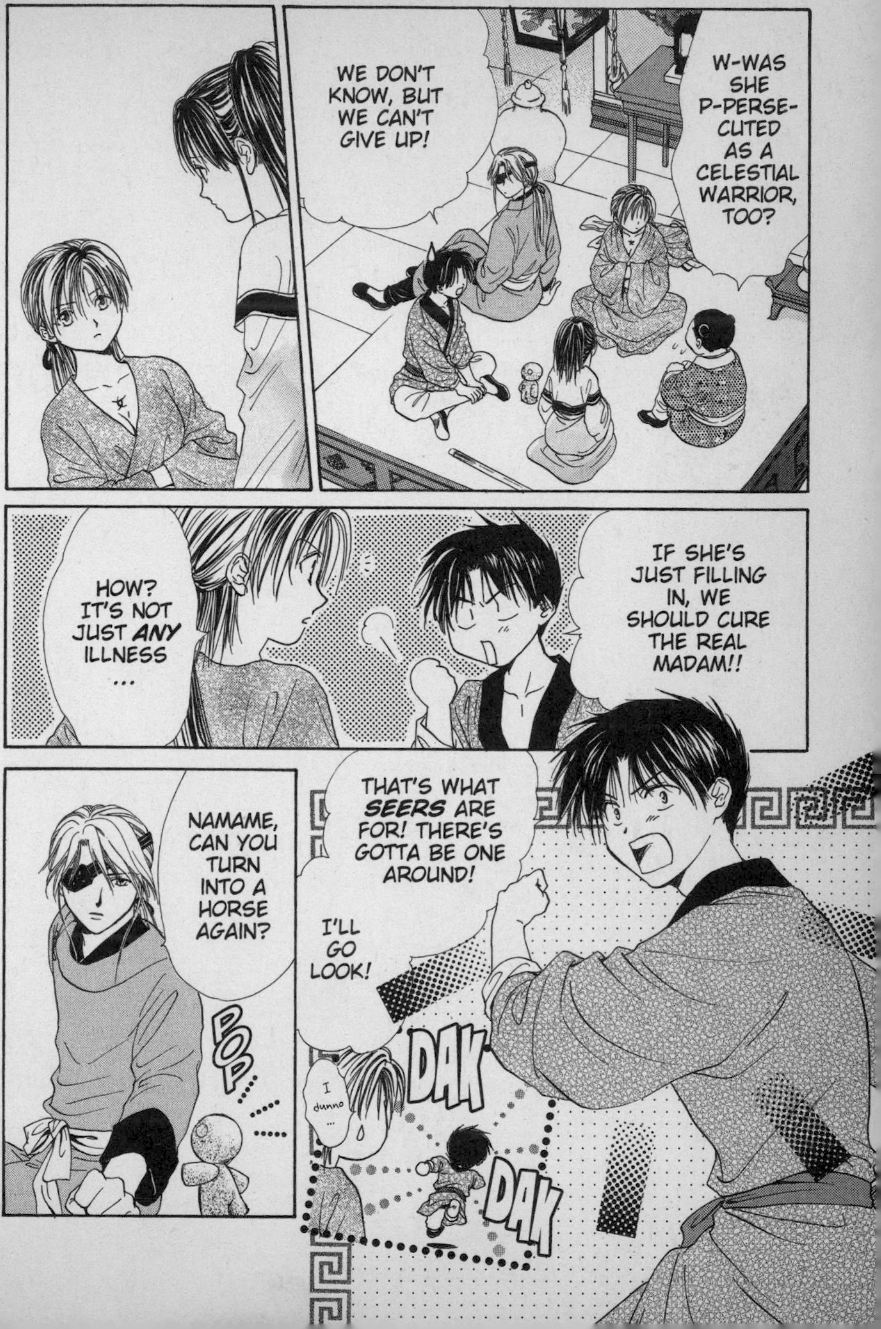
W-WAS SHE P-PERSE-CUTED AS A CELESTIAL WARRIOR, TOO?
WE DON'T KNOW, BUT WE CAN'T GIVE UP!
IF SHE'S JUST FILLING IN, WE SHOULD CURE THE REAL MADAM!!
HOW? IT'S NOT JUST ANY ILLNESS ...
THAT'S WHAT SEERS ARE FOR! THERE'S GOTTA BE ONE AROUND!
I'LL GO LOOK!
DAK
DAK
I dunno ...
NAMAME, CAN YOU TURN INTO A HORSE AGAIN?
POP

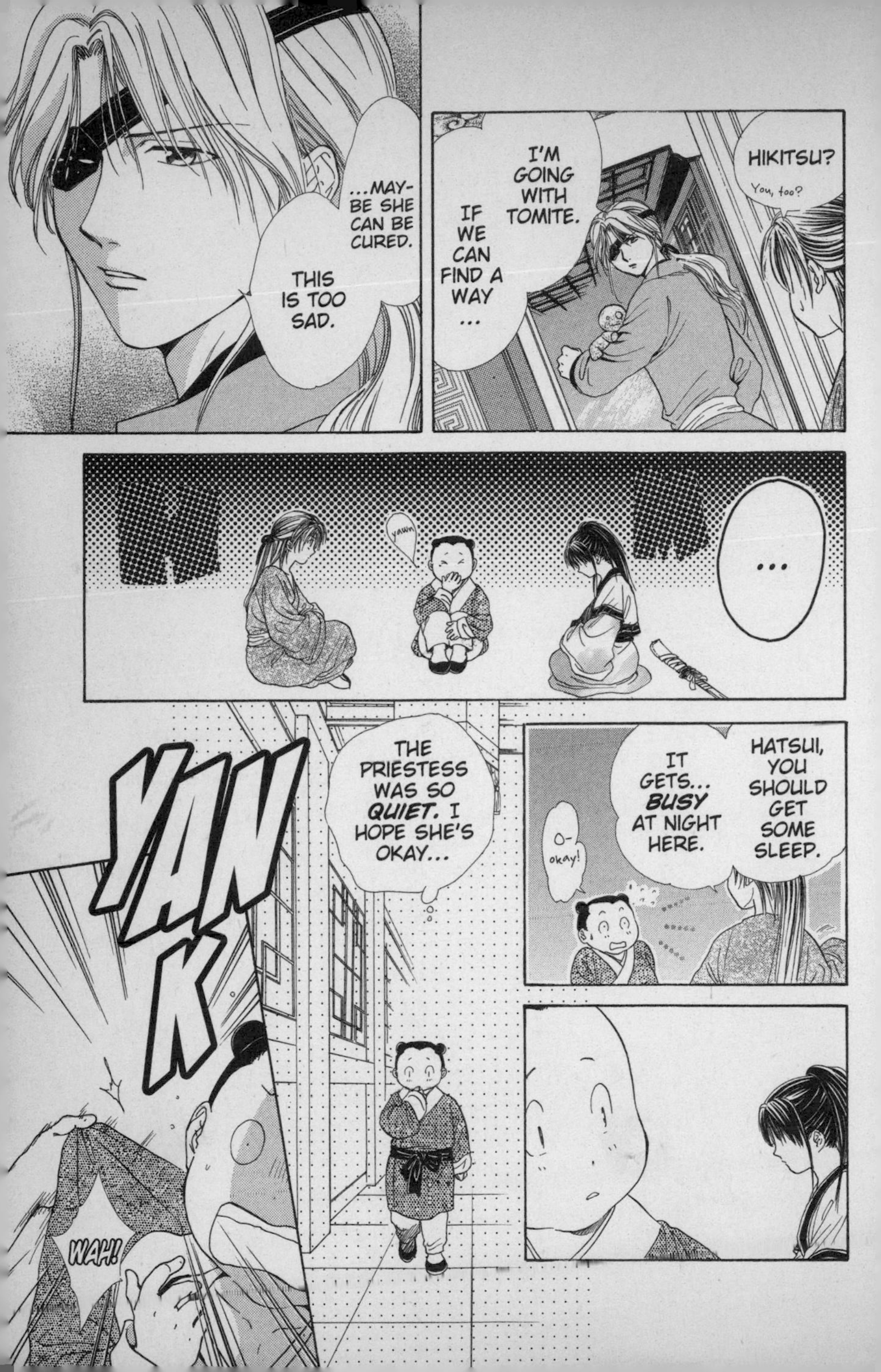
HIKITSU?
You, too?
I'M GOING WITH TOMITE.
IF WE CAN FIND A WAY ...
...MAY-BE SHE CAN BE CURED.
THIS IS TOO SAD.
...
yawn
HATSUI, YOU SHOULD GET SOME SLEEP.
IT GETS... **BUSY** AT NIGHT HERE.
O-okay!
THE PRIESTESS WAS SO **QUIET**. I HOPE SHE'S OKAY...
YANK
WAH!

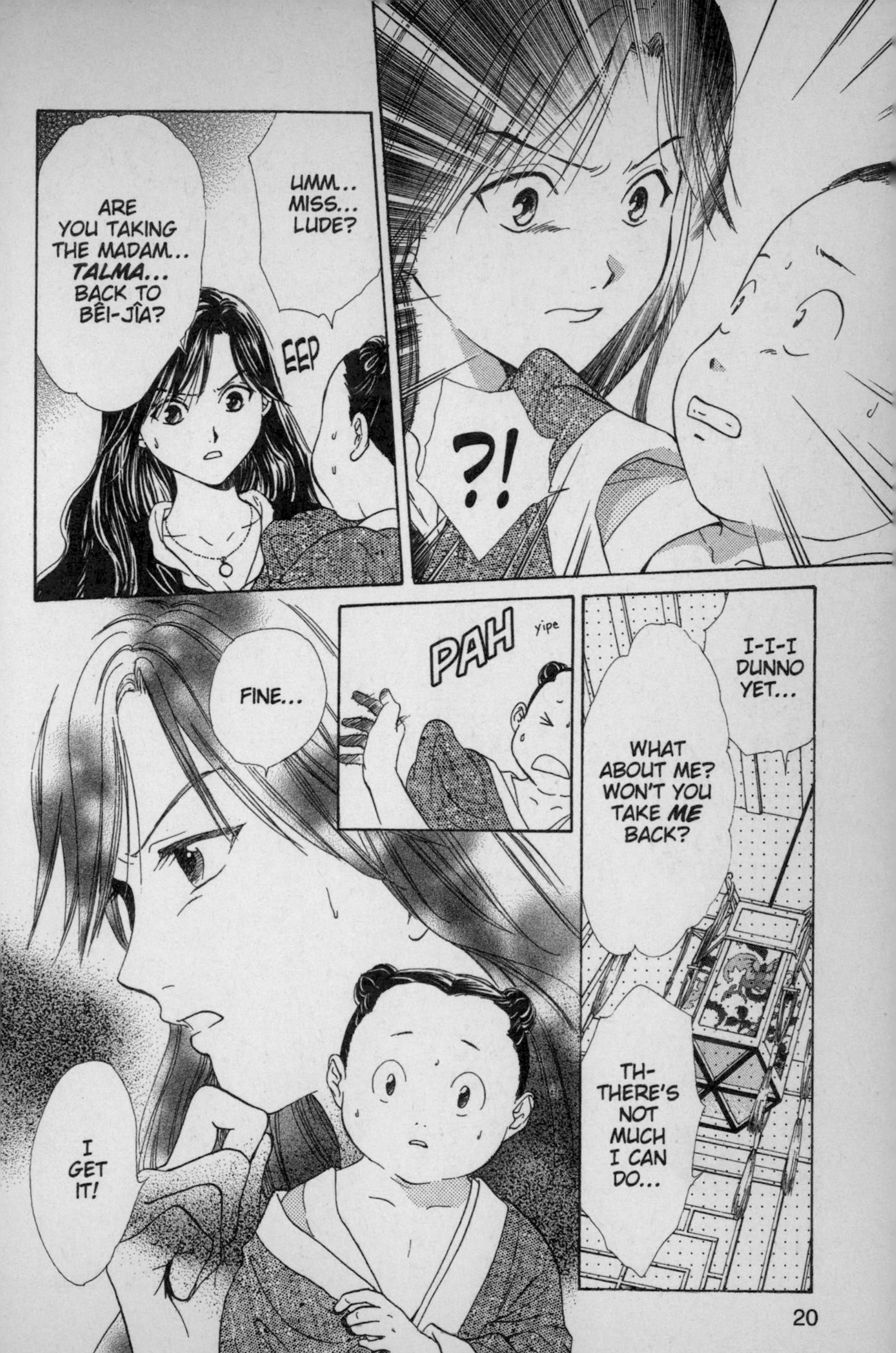
?!
UMM... MISS... LUDE?
EEP
ARE YOU TAKING THE MADAM... *TALMA*... BACK TO BÊI-JÎA?
I-I-I DUNNO YET...
WHAT ABOUT ME? WON'T YOU TAKE *ME* BACK?
TH- THERE'S NOT MUCH I CAN DO...
PAH
yipe
FINE...
I GET IT!

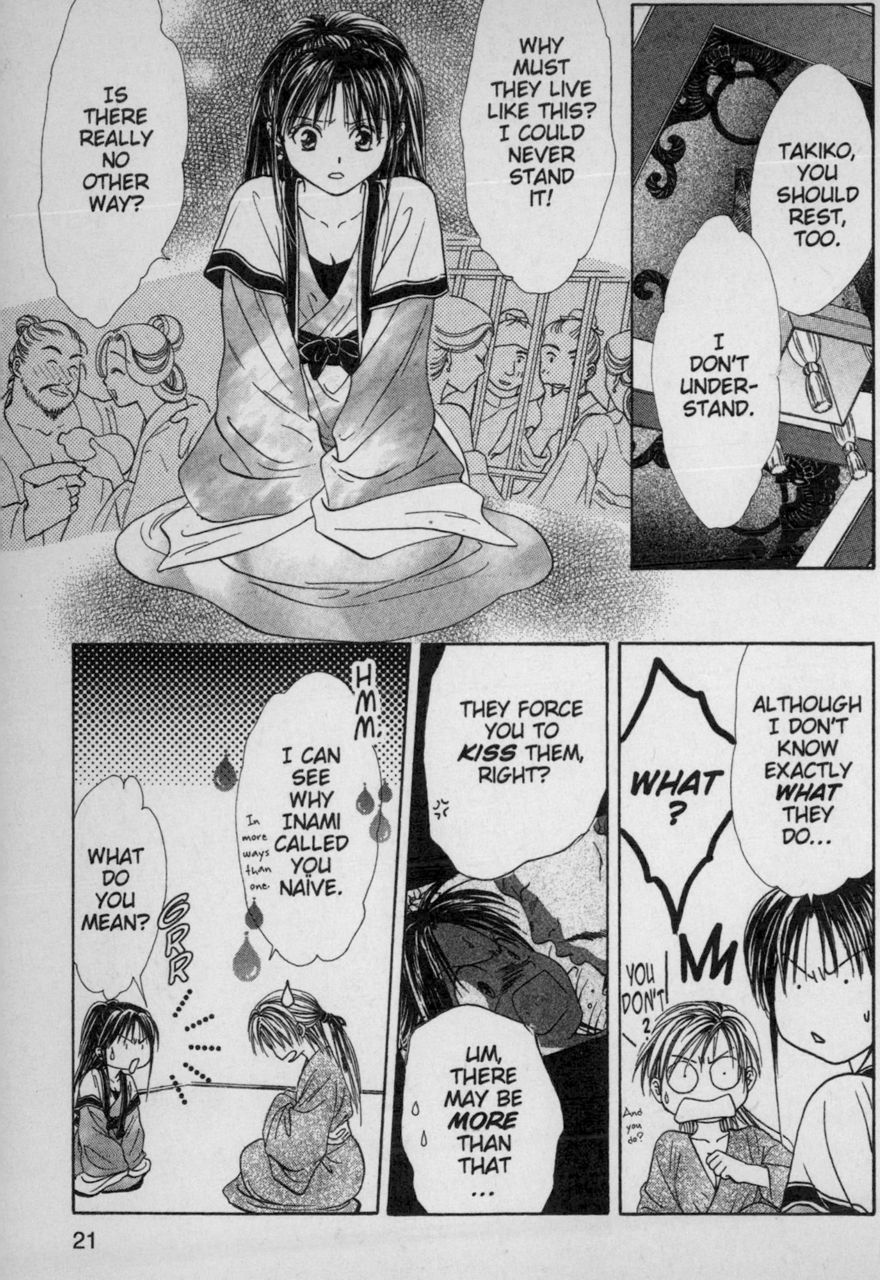
TAKIKO, YOU SHOULD REST, TOO.
I DON'T UNDER-STAND.
WHY MUST THEY LIVE LIKE THIS? I COULD NEVER STAND IT!
IS THERE REALLY NO OTHER WAY?
ALTHOUGH I DON'T KNOW EXACTLY WHAT THEY DO...
WHAT?
MM
YOU DON'T?
And you do?
THEY FORCE YOU TO KISS THEM, RIGHT?
UM, THERE MAY BE MORE THAN THAT...
HMM.
I CAN SEE WHY INAMI CALLED YOU NAÏVE.
In more ways than one.
GRR
WHAT DO YOU MEAN?

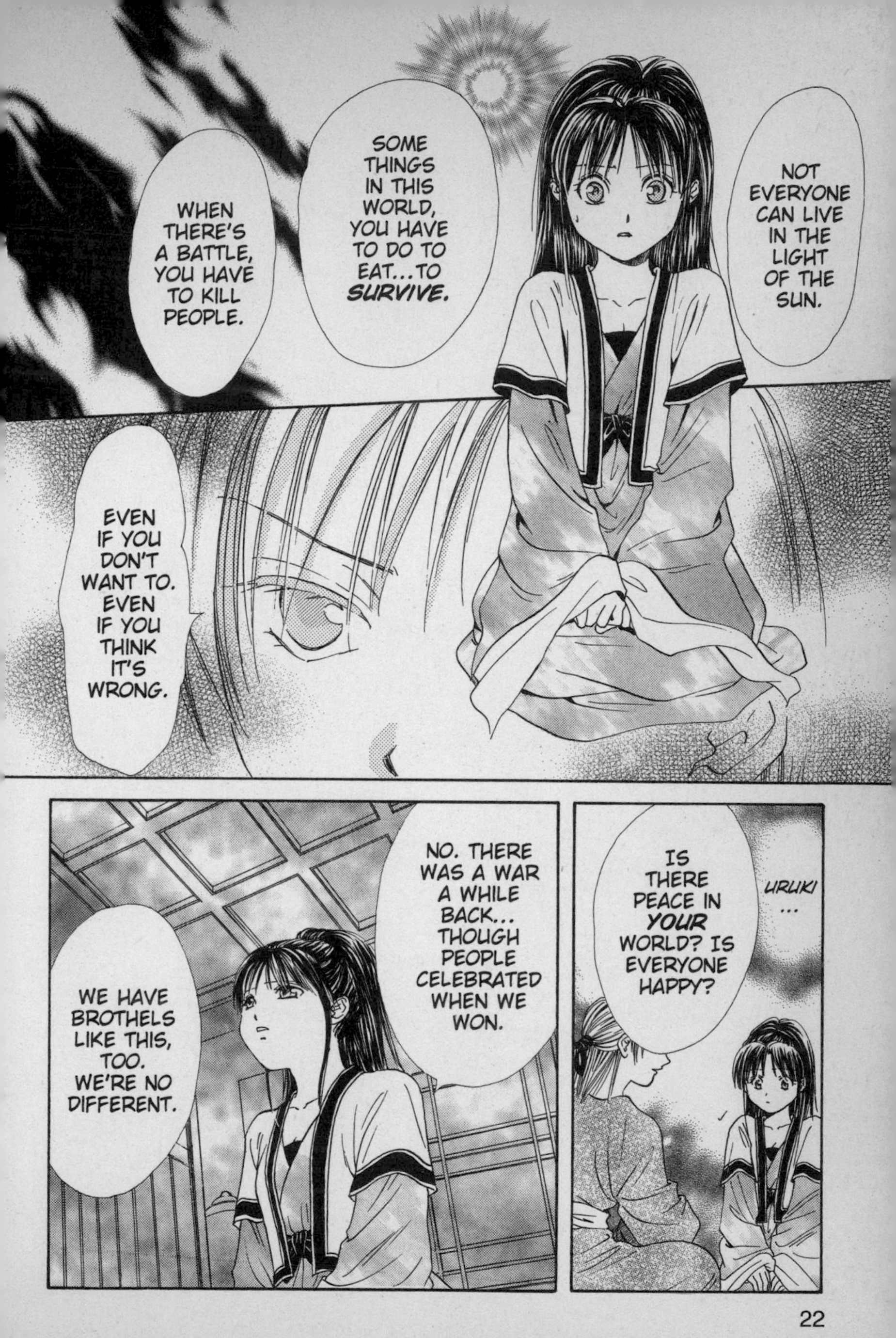
NOT EVERYONE CAN LIVE IN THE LIGHT OF THE SUN.
SOME THINGS IN THIS WORLD, YOU HAVE TO DO TO EAT...TO **SURVIVE.**
WHEN THERE'S A BATTLE, YOU HAVE TO KILL PEOPLE.
EVEN IF YOU DON'T WANT TO. EVEN IF YOU THINK IT'S WRONG.
URUKI ...
IS THERE PEACE IN **YOUR** WORLD? IS EVERYONE HAPPY?
NO. THERE WAS A WAR A WHILE BACK... THOUGH PEOPLE CELEBRATED WHEN WE WON.
WE HAVE BROTHELS LIKE THIS, TOO. WE'RE NO DIFFERENT.

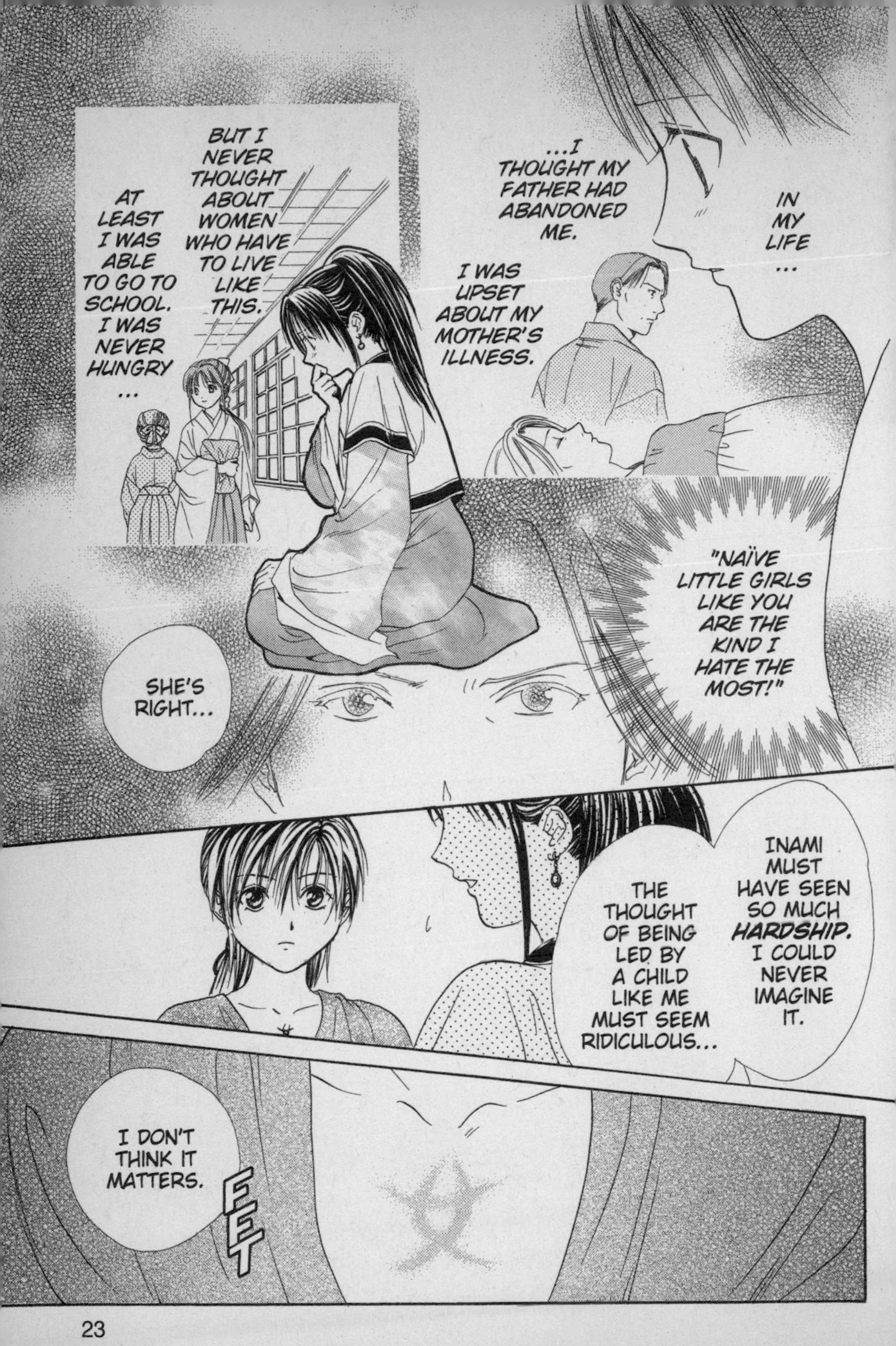
IN MY LIFE ...
...I THOUGHT MY FATHER HAD ABANDONED ME.
I WAS UPSET ABOUT MY MOTHER'S ILLNESS.
BUT I NEVER THOUGHT ABOUT WOMEN WHO HAVE TO LIVE LIKE THIS.
AT LEAST I WAS ABLE TO GO TO SCHOOL. I WAS NEVER HUNGRY ...
"NAÏVE LITTLE GIRLS LIKE YOU ARE THE KIND I HATE THE MOST!"
SHE'S RIGHT...
INAMI MUST HAVE SEEN SO MUCH **HARDSHIP**. I COULD NEVER IMAGINE IT.
THE THOUGHT OF BEING LED BY A CHILD LIKE ME MUST SEEM RIDICULOUS...
I DON'T THINK IT MATTERS.
FET

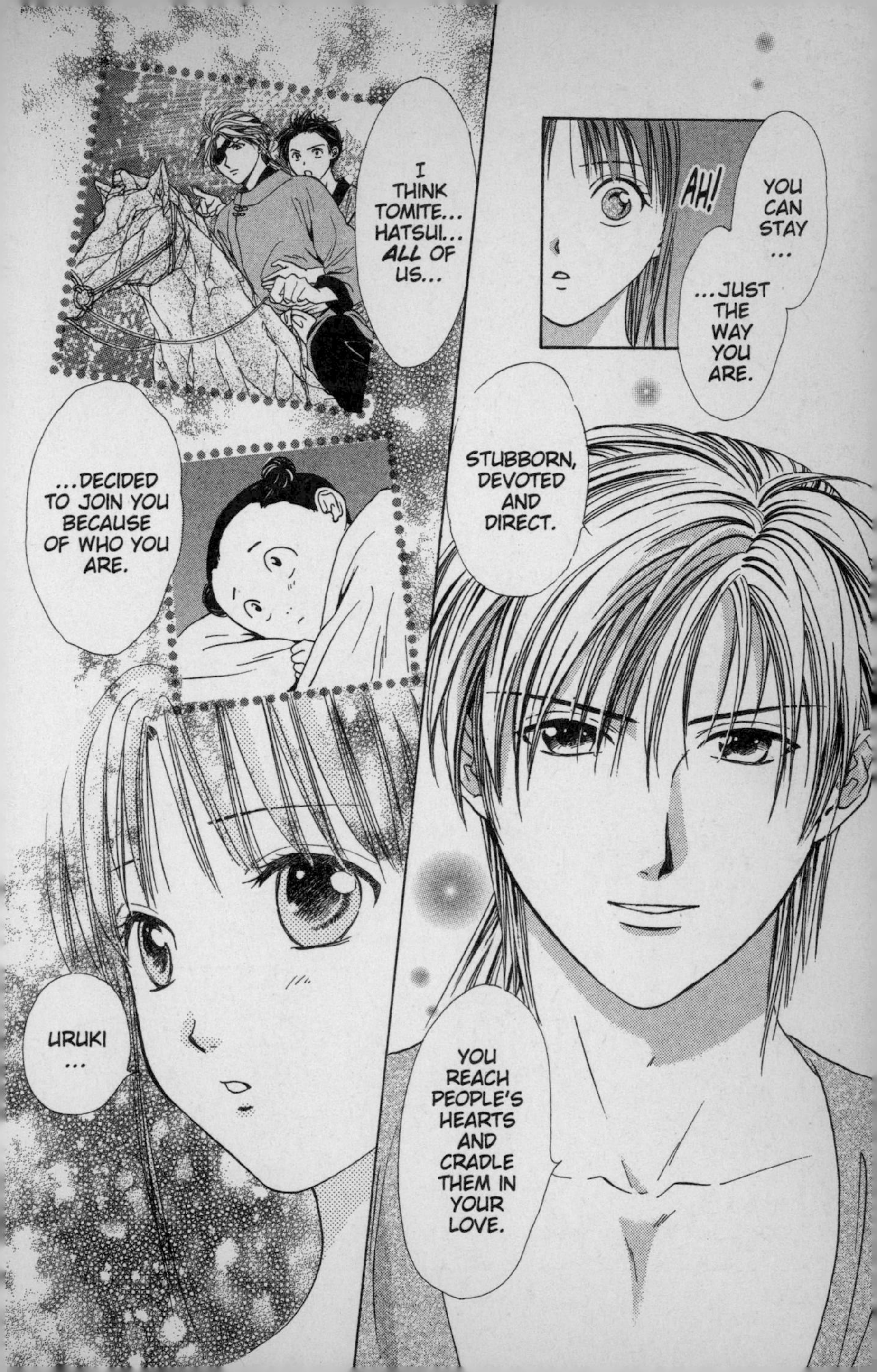
YOU CAN STAY ...
AH!
...JUST THE WAY YOU ARE.
STUBBORN, DEVOTED AND DIRECT.
YOU REACH PEOPLE'S HEARTS AND CRADLE THEM IN YOUR LOVE.
I THINK TOMITE... HATSUI... ALL OF US...
...DECIDED TO JOIN YOU BECAUSE OF WHO YOU ARE.
URUKI ...

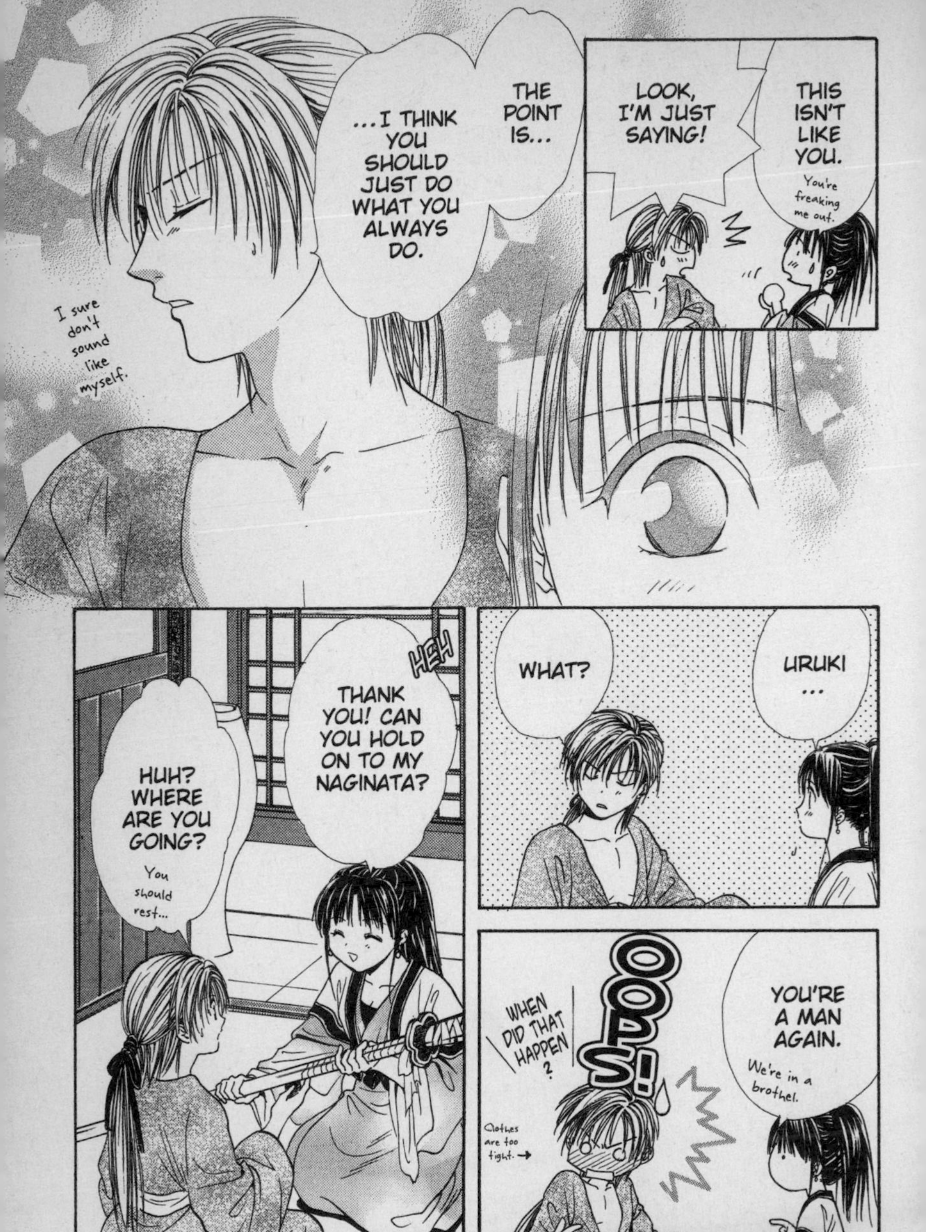
THIS ISN'T LIKE YOU.
You're freaking me out.
LOOK, I'M JUST SAYING!
THE POINT IS...
...I THINK YOU SHOULD JUST DO WHAT YOU ALWAYS DO.
I sure don't sound like myself.
URUKI ...
WHAT?
YOU'RE A MAN AGAIN.
We're in a brothel.
OOPS!
WHEN DID THAT HAPPEN?
Clothes are too tight.
HEH
THANK YOU! CAN YOU HOLD ON TO MY NAGINATA?
HUH? WHERE ARE YOU GOING?
You should rest...

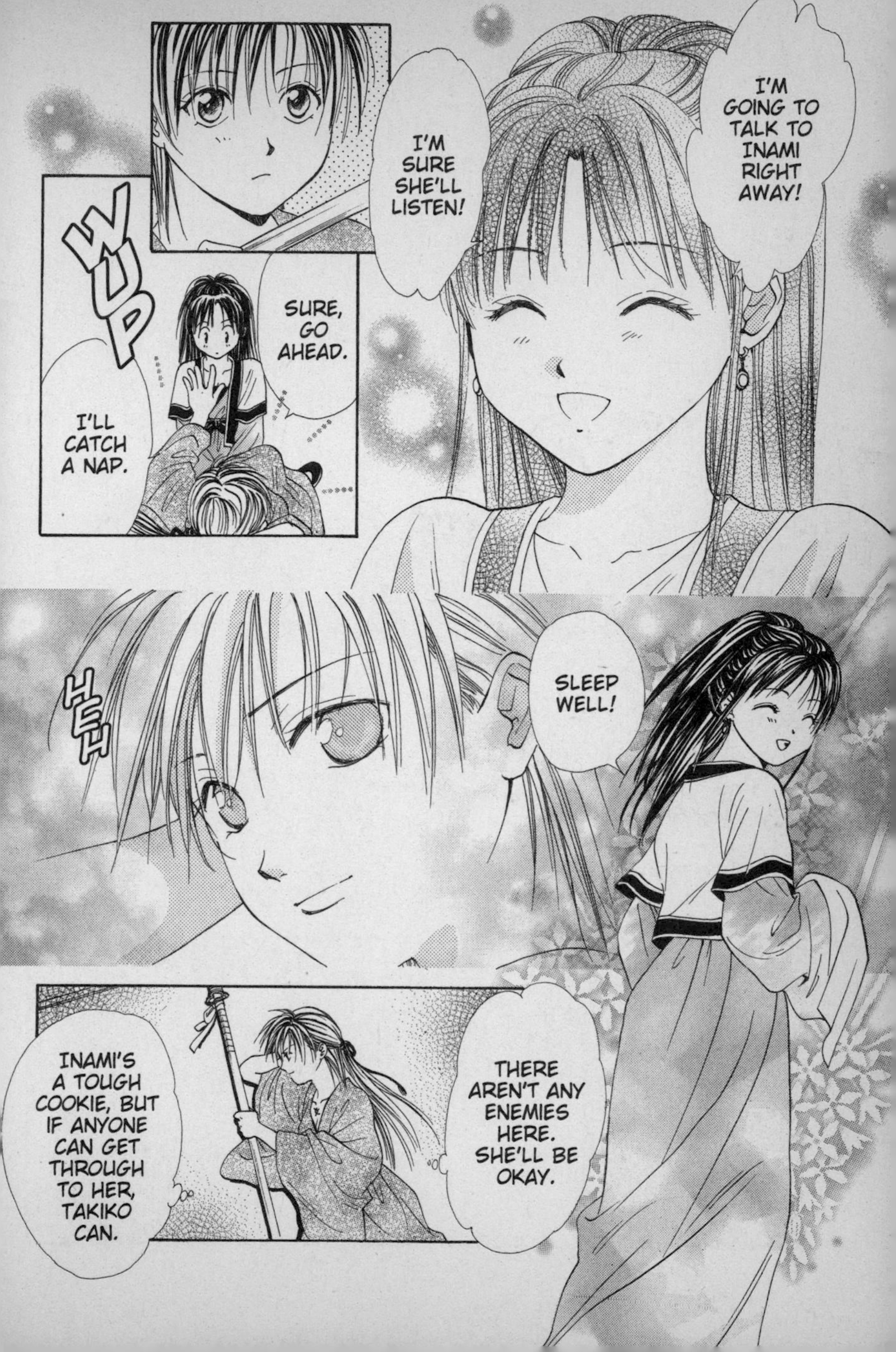
I'M GOING TO TALK TO INAMI RIGHT AWAY!
I'M SURE SHE'LL LISTEN!
SURE, GO AHEAD.
WUP
I'LL CATCH A NAP.
SLEEP WELL!
HEH
THERE AREN'T ANY ENEMIES HERE. SHE'LL BE OKAY.
INAMI'S A TOUGH COOKIE, BUT IF ANYONE CAN GET THROUGH TO HER, TAKIKO CAN.

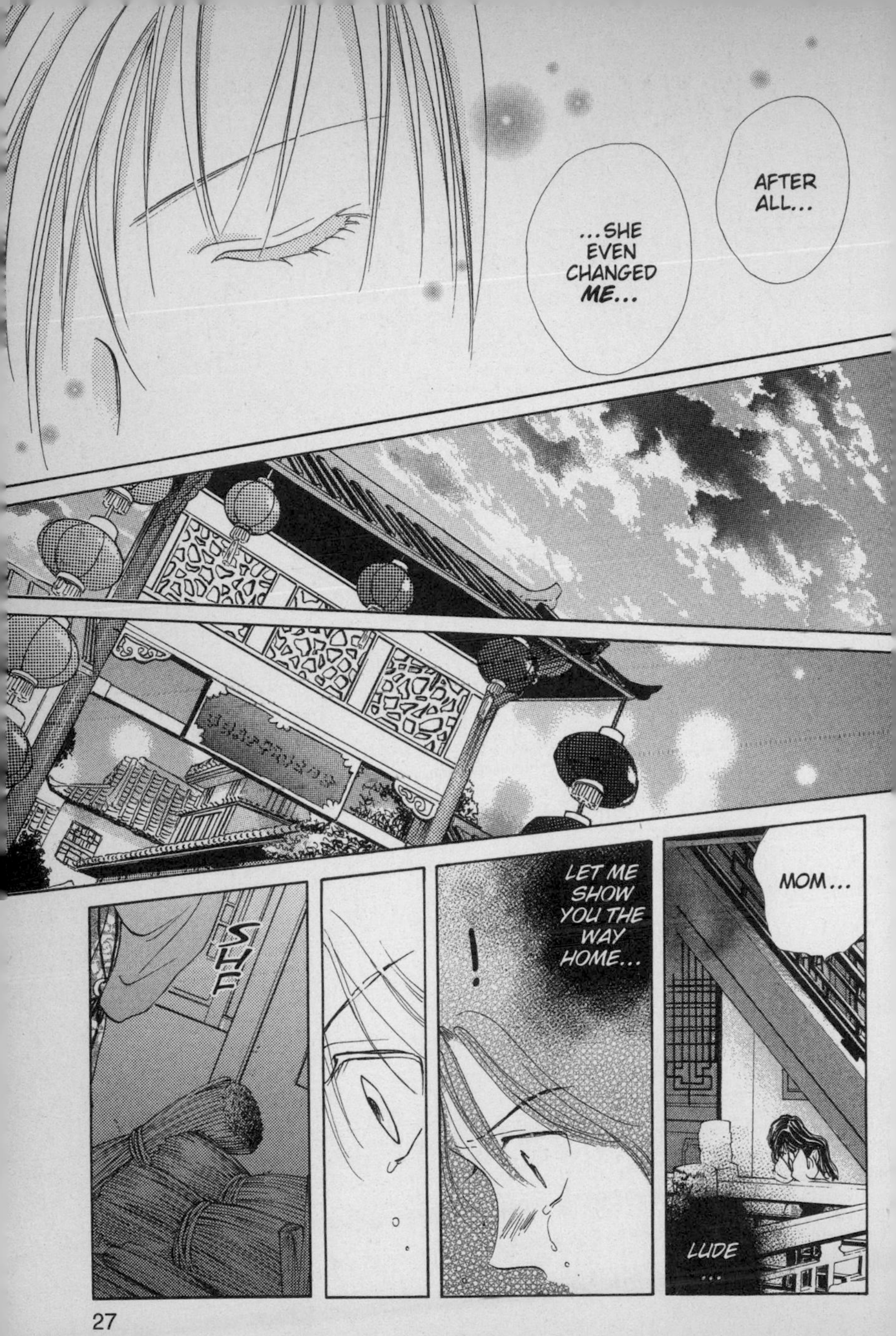
AFTER ALL...
...SHE EVEN CHANGED ME...
MOM...
LUDE ...
LET ME SHOW YOU THE WAY HOME...
!
SHF

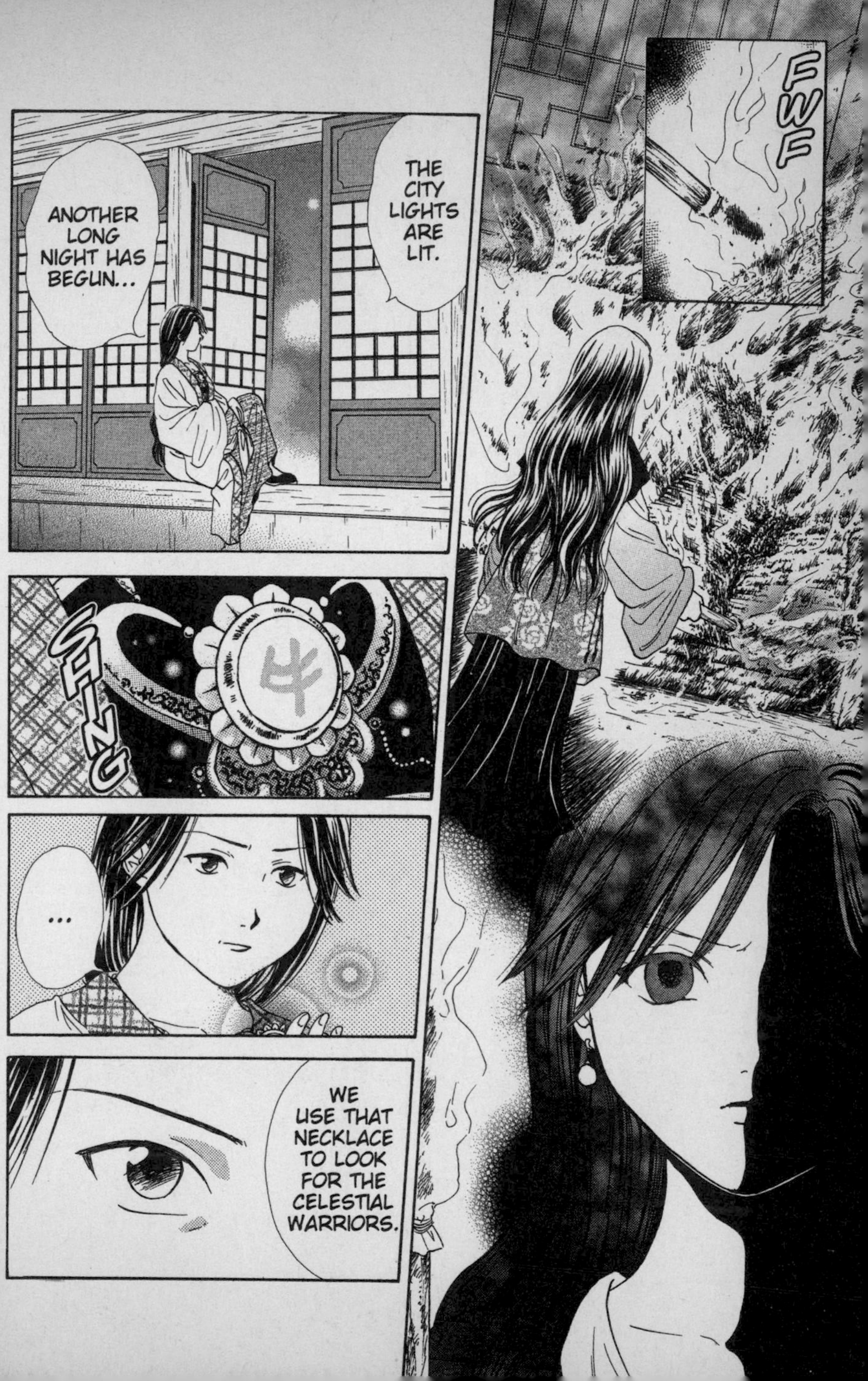
FWF
THE CITY LIGHTS ARE LIT.
ANOTHER LONG NIGHT HAS BEGUN...
SHING
...
WE USE THAT NECKLACE TO LOOK FOR THE CELESTIAL WARRIORS.

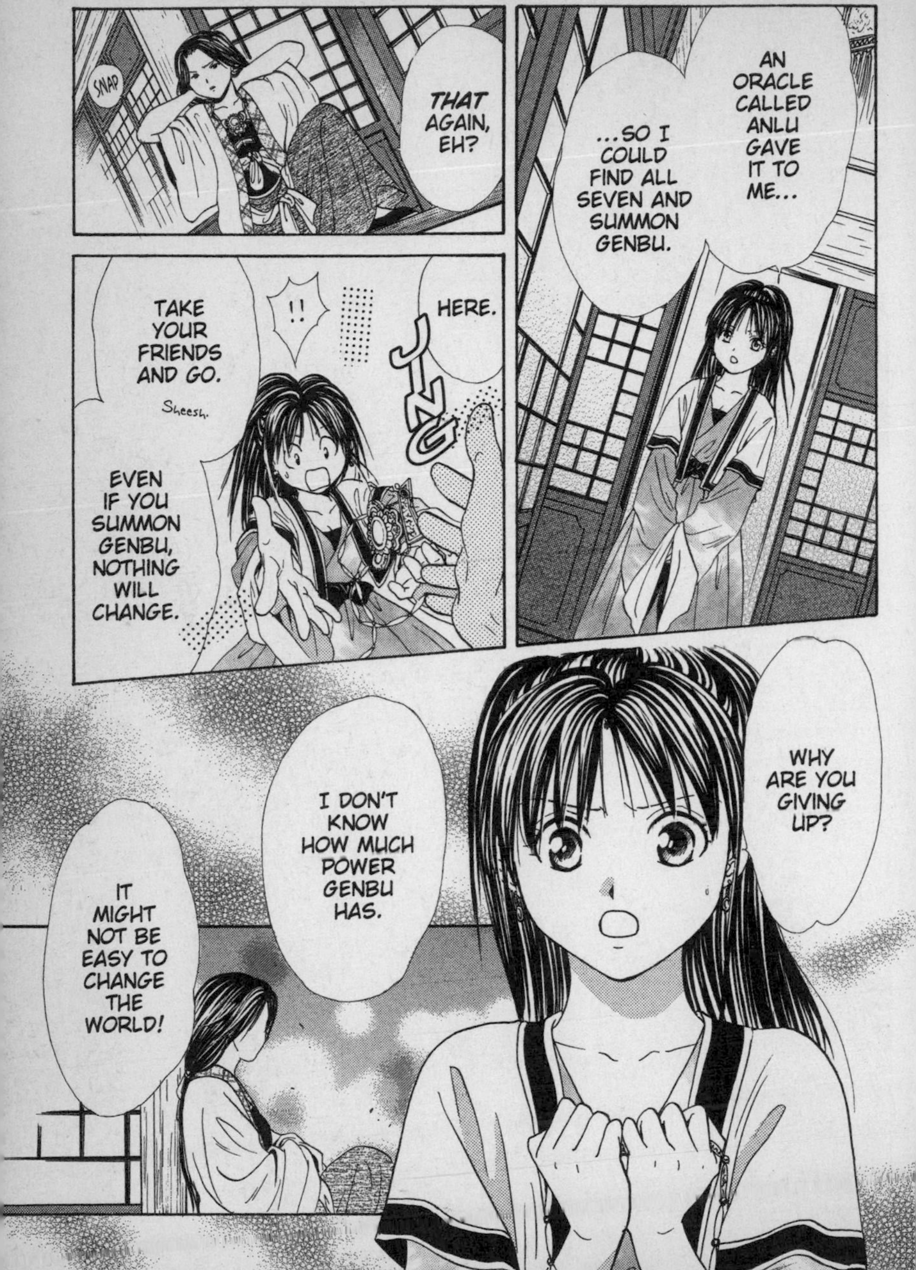
AN ORACLE CALLED ANLU GAVE IT TO ME...
...SO I COULD FIND ALL SEVEN AND SUMMON GENBU.
SNAP
THAT AGAIN, EH?
HERE.
JING
!!
TAKE YOUR FRIENDS AND GO.
Sheesh.
EVEN IF YOU SUMMON GENBU, NOTHING WILL CHANGE.
WHY ARE YOU GIVING UP?
I DON'T KNOW HOW MUCH POWER GENBU HAS.
IT MIGHT NOT BE EASY TO CHANGE THE WORLD!

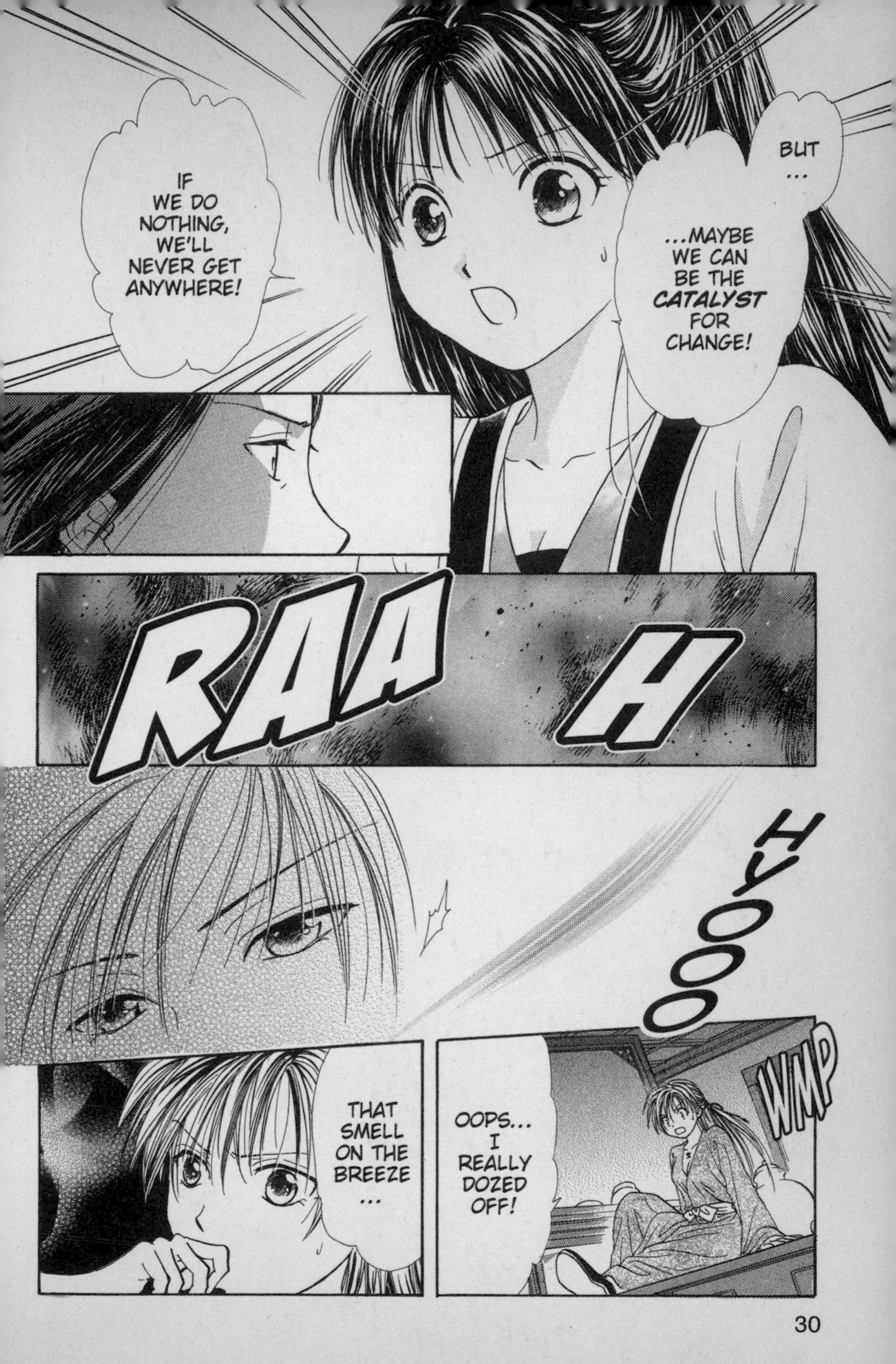
BUT ...
...MAYBE WE CAN BE THE CATALYST FOR CHANGE!
IF WE DO NOTHING, WE'LL NEVER GET ANYWHERE!
RAAH
HYOOOO
WMP
OOPS... I REALLY DOZED OFF!
THAT SMELL ON THE BREEZE ...

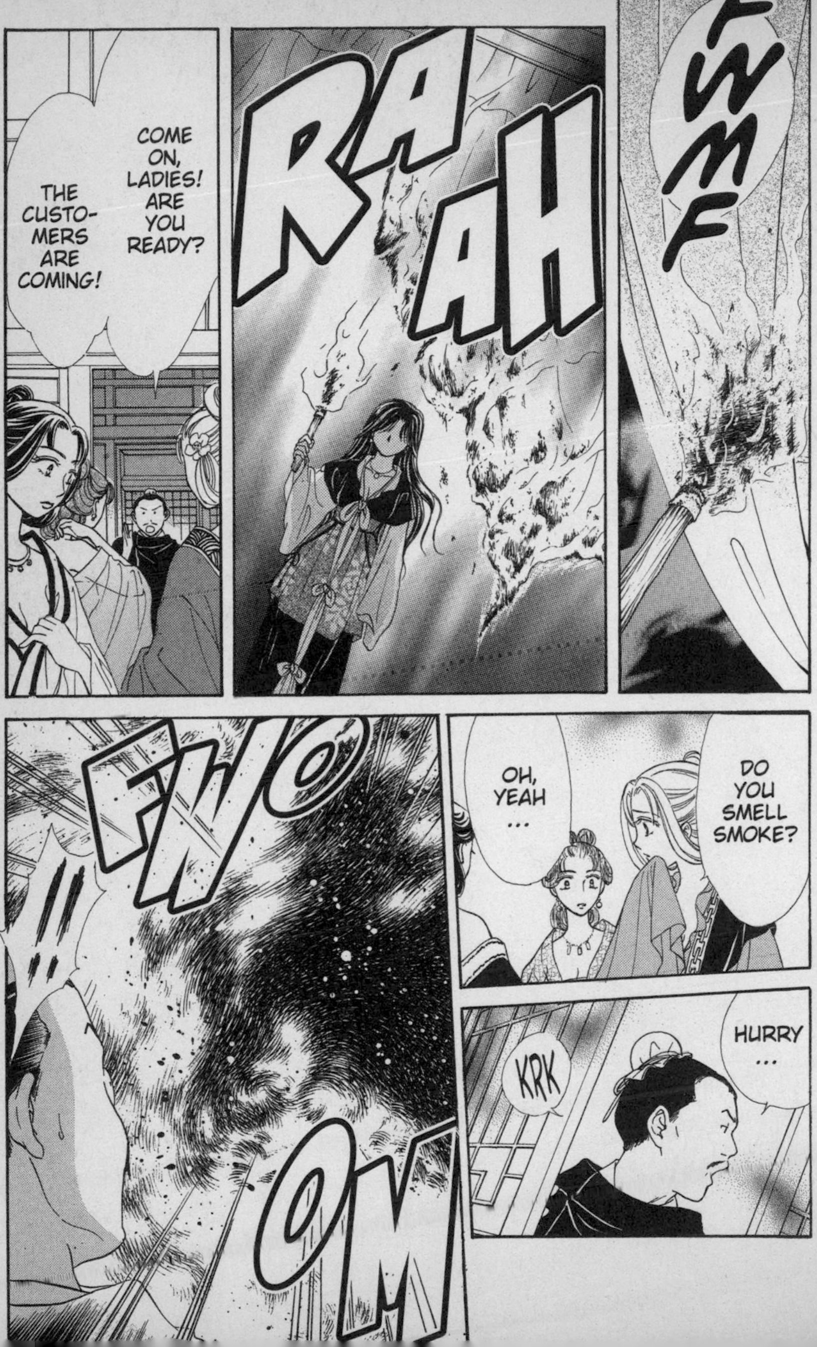
FWMF
RA AH
COME ON, LADIES! ARE YOU READY?
THE CUSTOMERS ARE COMING!
DO YOU SMELL SMOKE?
OH, YEAH ...
HURRY ...
KRK
FWOOM
!!

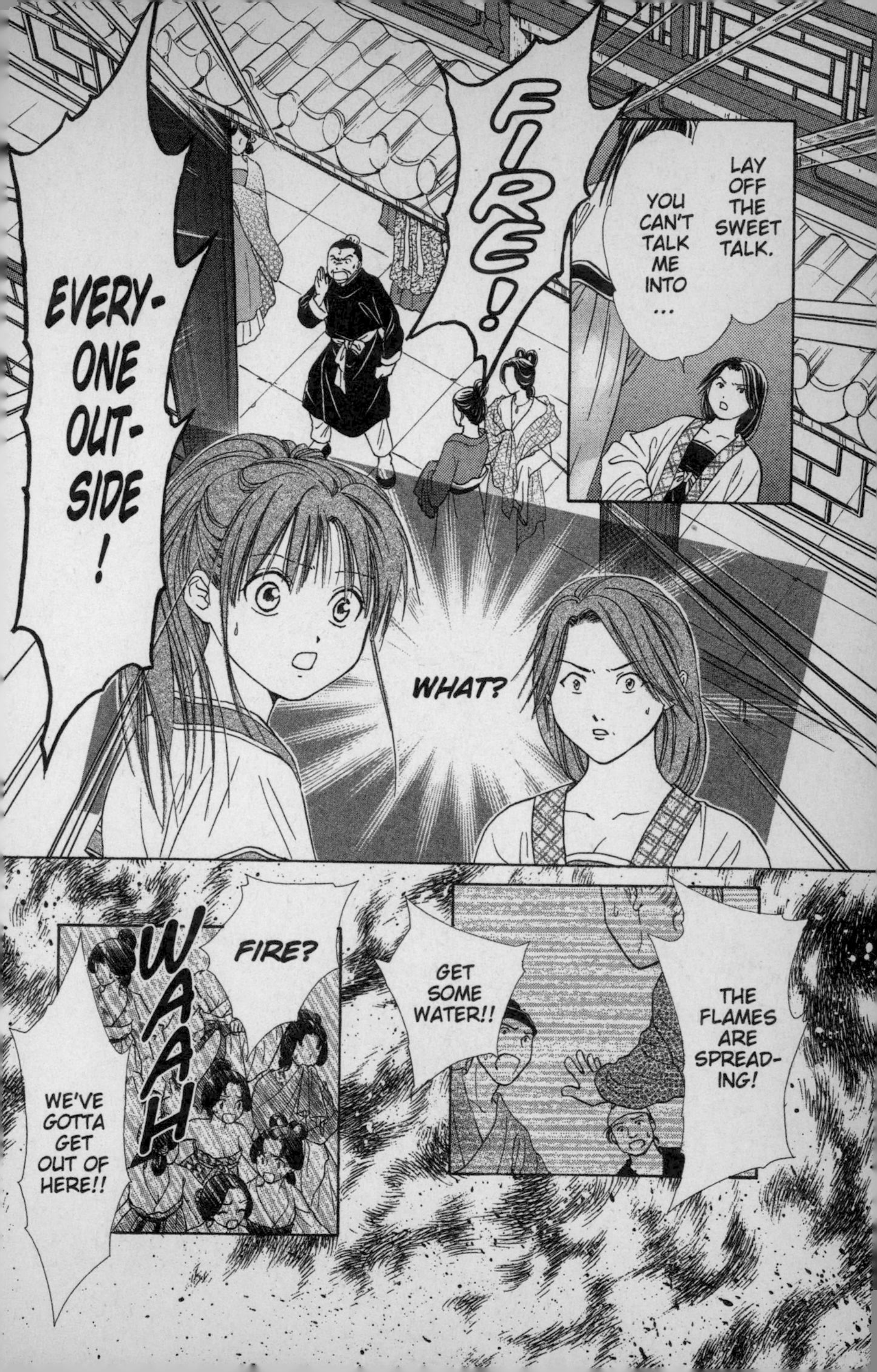
LAY OFF THE SWEET TALK.
YOU CAN'T TALK ME INTO ...
FIRE!
EVERY-ONE OUT-SIDE!
WHAT?
THE FLAMES ARE SPREAD-ING!
GET SOME WATER!!
FIRE?
WAAH
WE'VE GOTTA GET OUT OF HERE!!

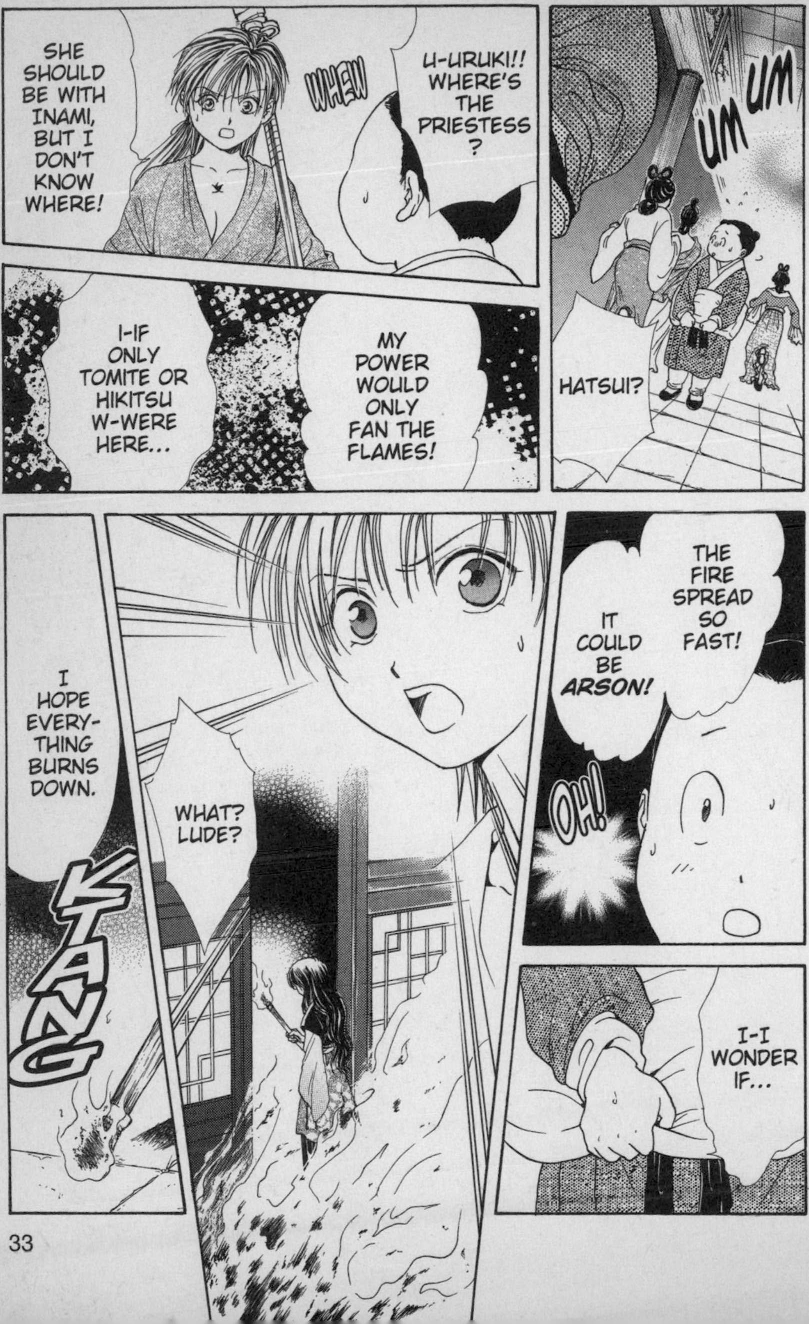
UM UM
HATSUI?
U-URUKI!! WHERE'S THE PRIESTESS?
WHEW
SHE SHOULD BE WITH INAMI, BUT I DON'T KNOW WHERE!
MY POWER WOULD ONLY FAN THE FLAMES!
I-IF ONLY TOMITE OR HIKITSU W-WERE HERE...
THE FIRE SPREAD SO FAST!
IT COULD BE ARSON!
OH!
I-I WONDER IF...
WHAT? LUDE?
I HOPE EVERY-THING BURNS DOWN.
KLANG

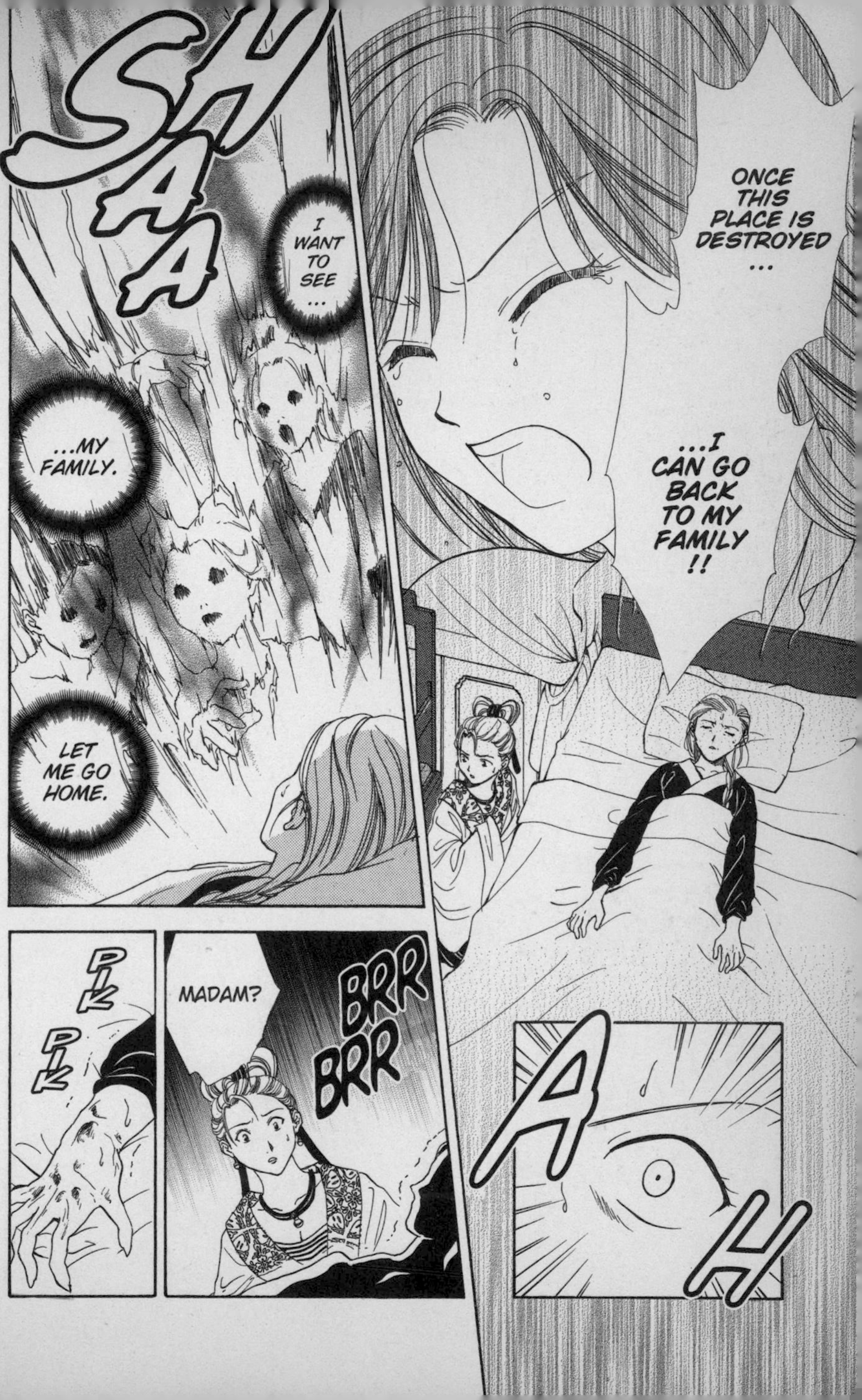
ONCE THIS PLACE IS DESTROYED ...
...I CAN GO BACK TO MY FAMILY !!
SHAA
I WANT TO SEE ...
...MY FAMILY.
LET ME GO HOME.
AH
BRR BRR
MADAM?
PIK PIK

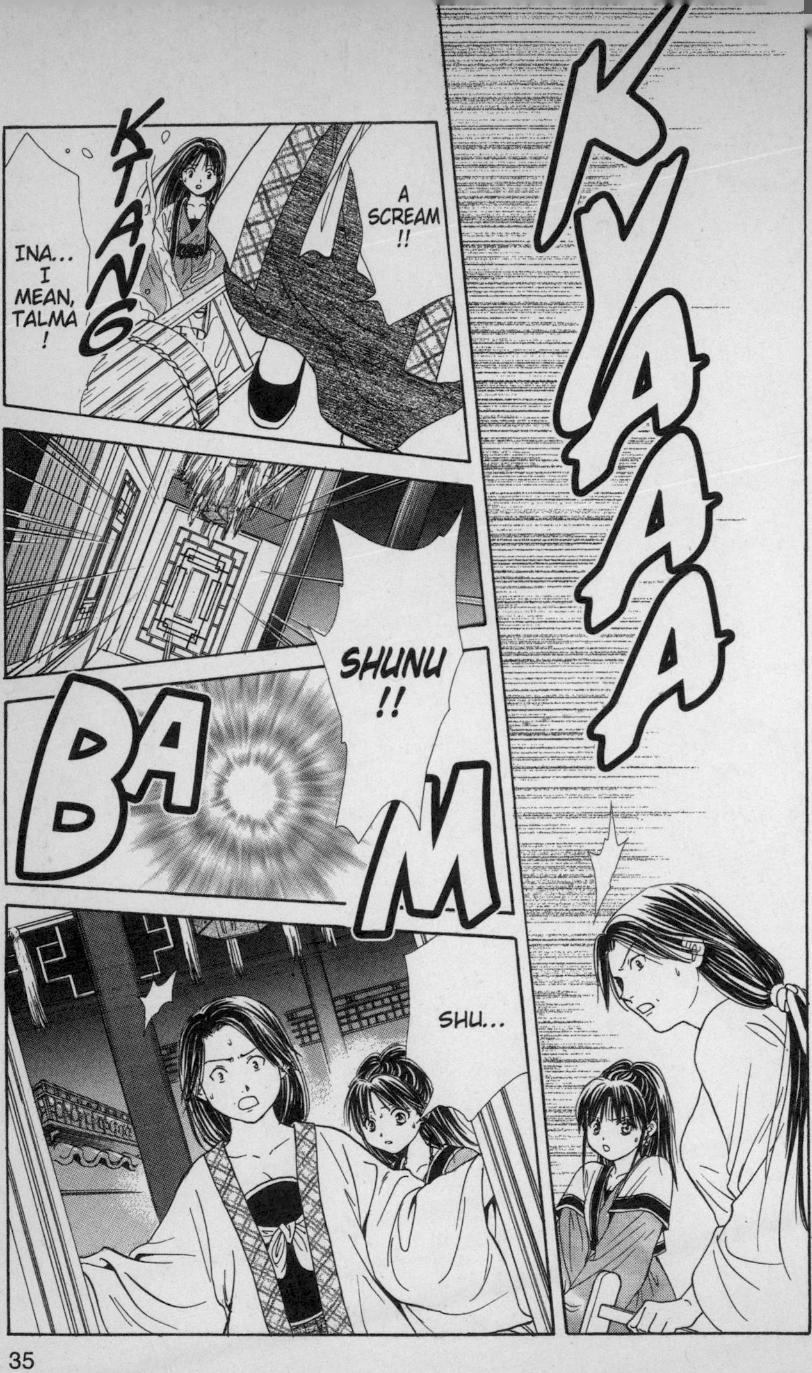
KYAAAA
KTANG
A SCREAM !!
INA... I MEAN, TALMA !
SHUNU !!
BAM
SHU...

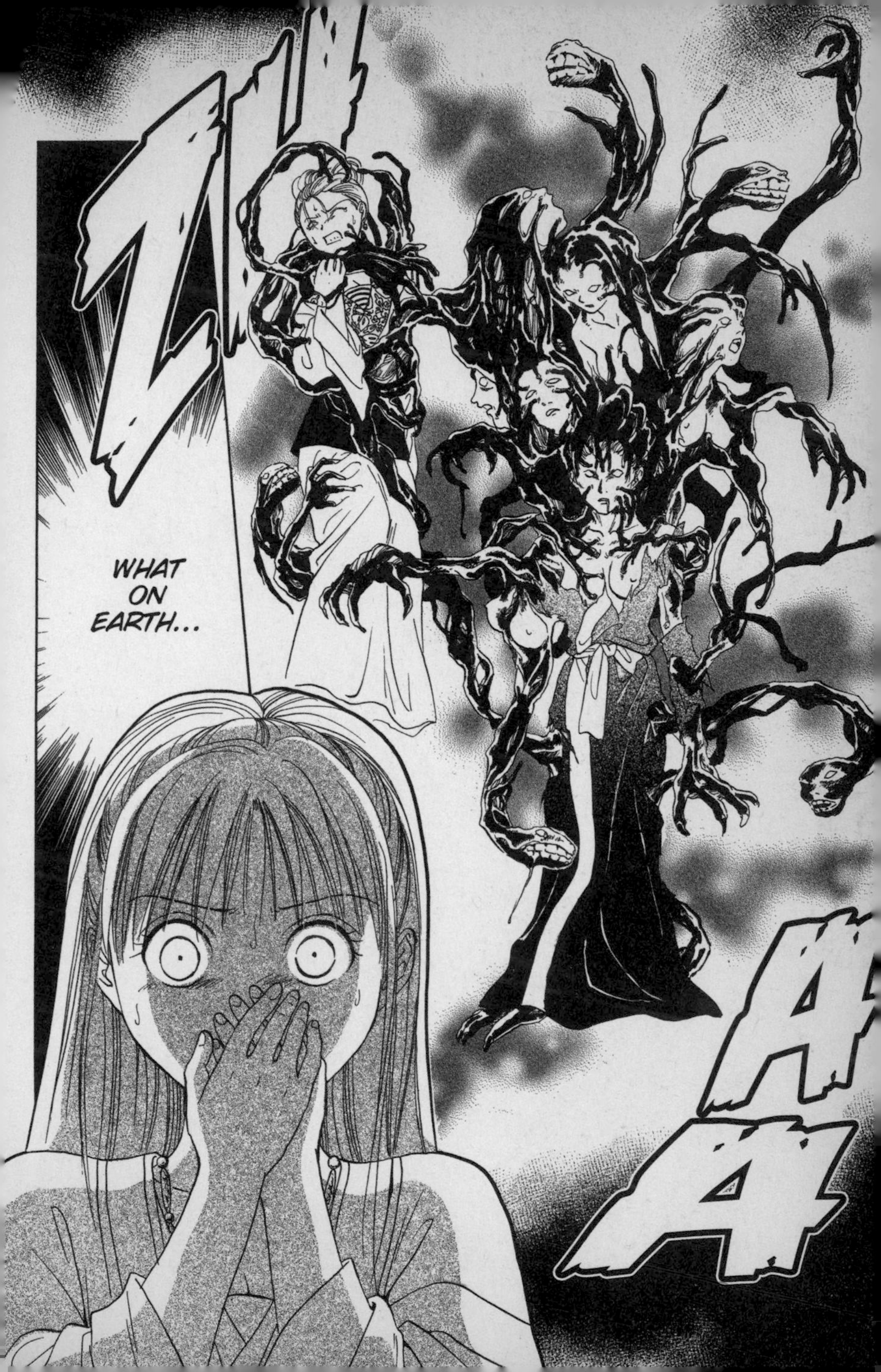
WHAT ON EARTH...

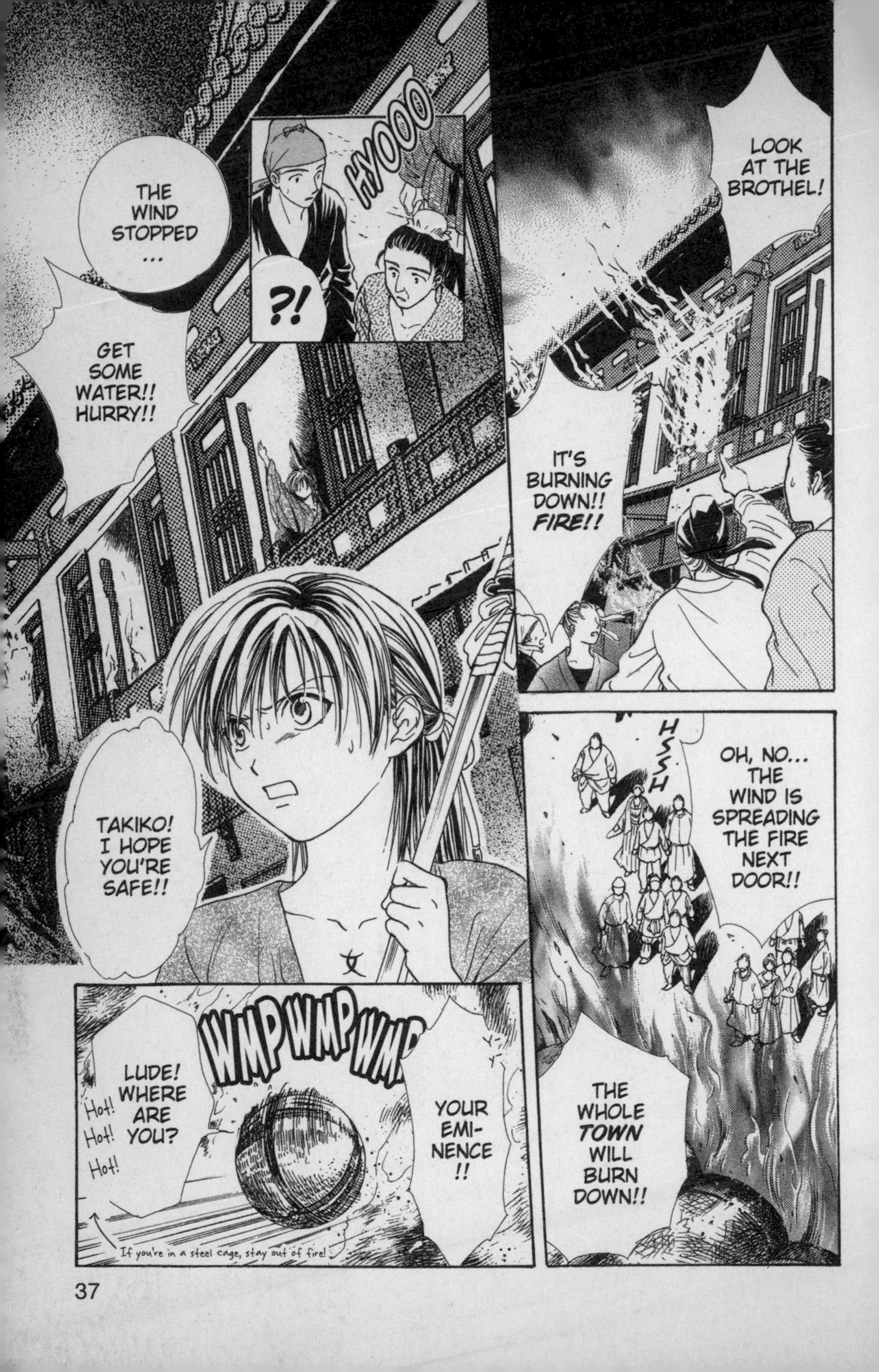
LOOK AT THE BROTHEL!
IT'S BURNING DOWN!! FIRE!!
HYOOO
?!
THE WIND STOPPED ...
GET SOME WATER!! HURRY!!
TAKIKO! I HOPE YOU'RE SAFE!!
HSSH
OH, NO... THE WIND IS SPREADING THE FIRE NEXT DOOR!!
THE WHOLE TOWN WILL BURN DOWN!!
YOUR EMINENCE!!
WMP WMP WMP
LUDE! WHERE ARE YOU?
Hot! Hot! Hot!
If you're in a steel cage, stay out of fire!

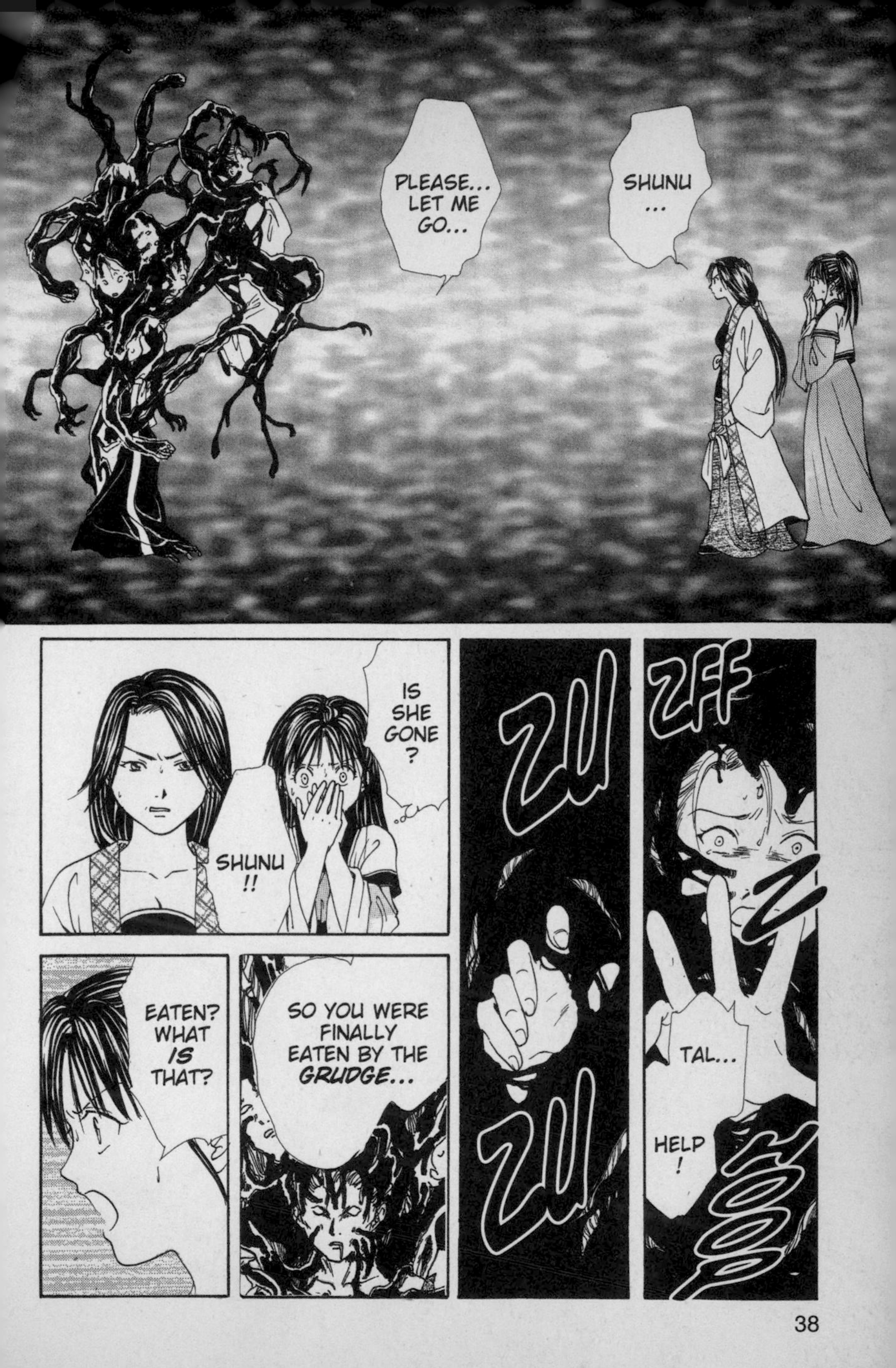
SHUNU...
PLEASE... LET ME GO...
ZFF
TAL...
HELP!
ZU
ZU
IS SHE GONE?
SHUNU!!
SO YOU WERE FINALLY EATEN BY THE *GRUDGE*...
EATEN? WHAT *IS* THAT?

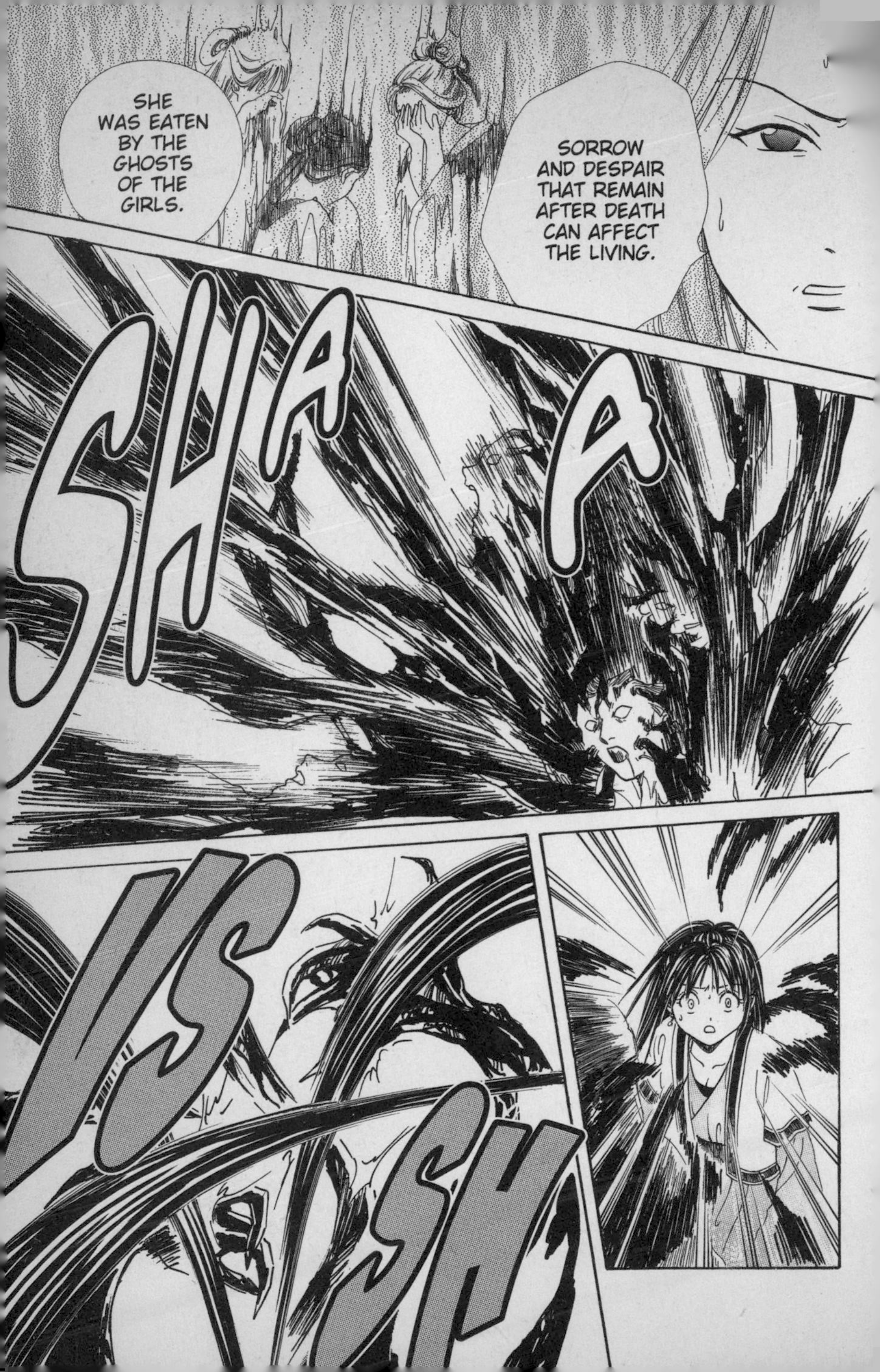
SORROW AND DESPAIR THAT REMAIN AFTER DEATH CAN AFFECT THE LIVING.
SHE WAS EATEN BY THE GHOSTS OF THE GIRLS.
SHAAA
SHSH
SHSH

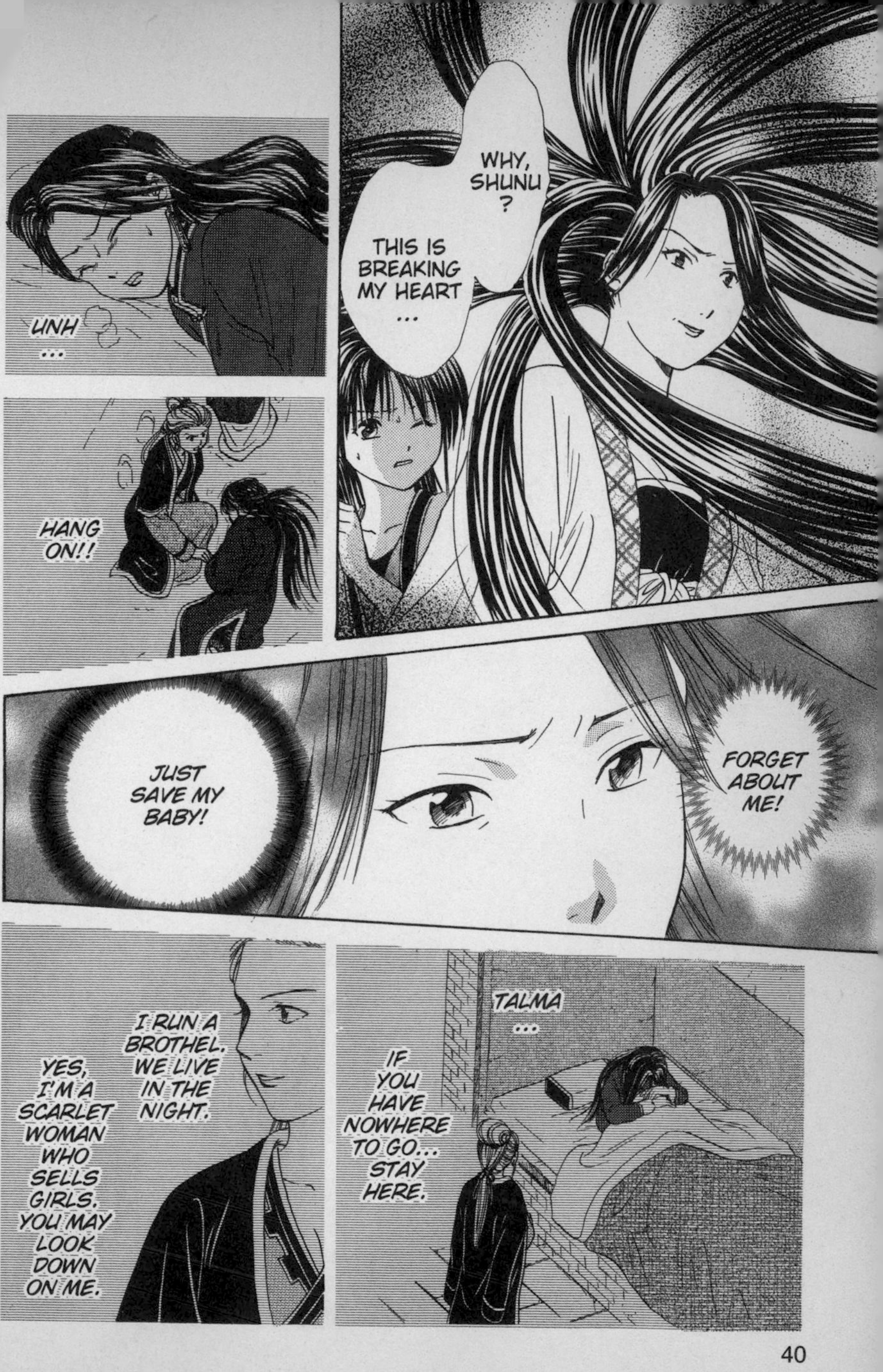
WHY, SHUNU?
THIS IS BREAKING MY HEART...
UNH...
HANG ON!!
FORGET ABOUT ME!
JUST SAVE MY BABY!
TALMA...
IF YOU HAVE NOWHERE TO GO... STAY HERE.
I RUN A BROTHEL. WE LIVE IN THE NIGHT.
YES, I'M A SCARLET WOMAN WHO SELLS GIRLS. YOU MAY LOOK DOWN ON ME.

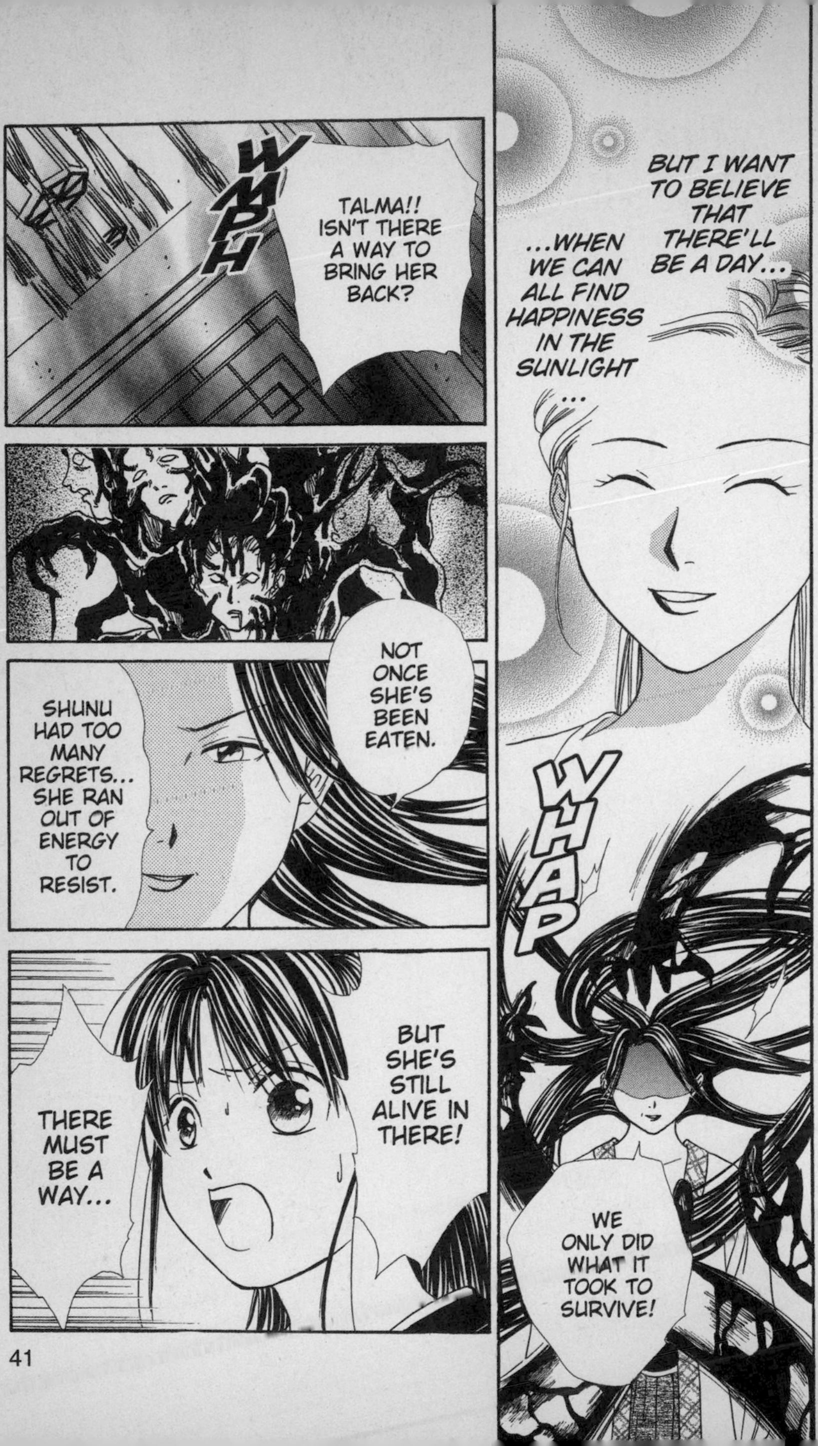
BUT I WANT TO BELIEVE THAT THERE'LL BE A DAY...
...WHEN WE CAN ALL FIND HAPPINESS IN THE SUNLIGHT...
WHAP
WE ONLY DID WHAT IT TOOK TO SURVIVE!
TALMA!! ISN'T THERE A WAY TO BRING HER BACK?
WMPH
NOT ONCE SHE'S BEEN EATEN.
SHUNU HAD TOO MANY REGRETS... SHE RAN OUT OF ENERGY TO RESIST.
BUT SHE'S STILL ALIVE IN THERE!
THERE MUST BE A WAY...

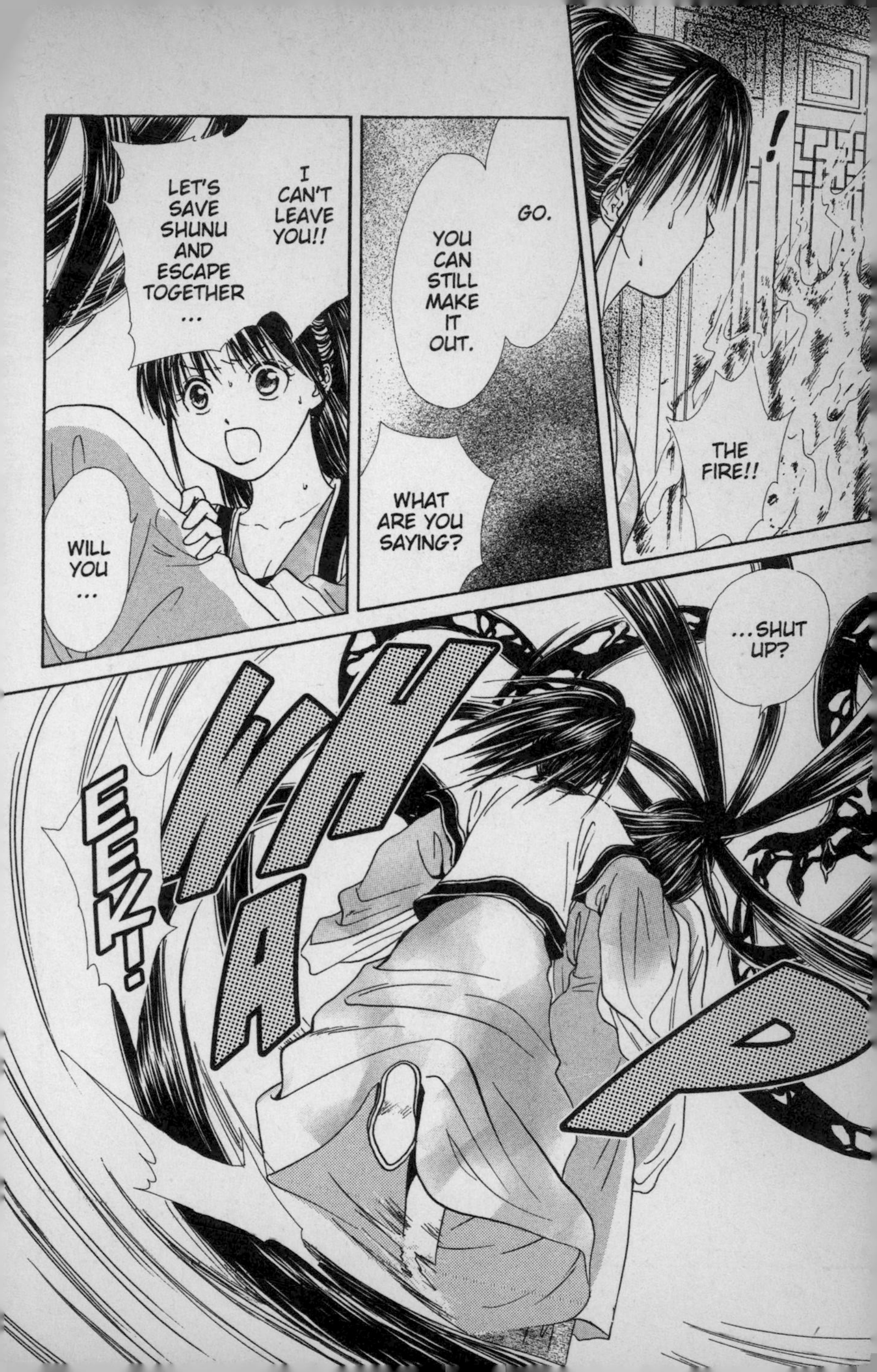
!
THE FIRE!!
GO.
YOU CAN STILL MAKE IT OUT.
WHAT ARE YOU SAYING?
I CAN'T LEAVE YOU!!
LET'S SAVE SHUNU AND ESCAPE TOGETHER...
WILL YOU...
...SHUT UP?
WHAP
EEK!

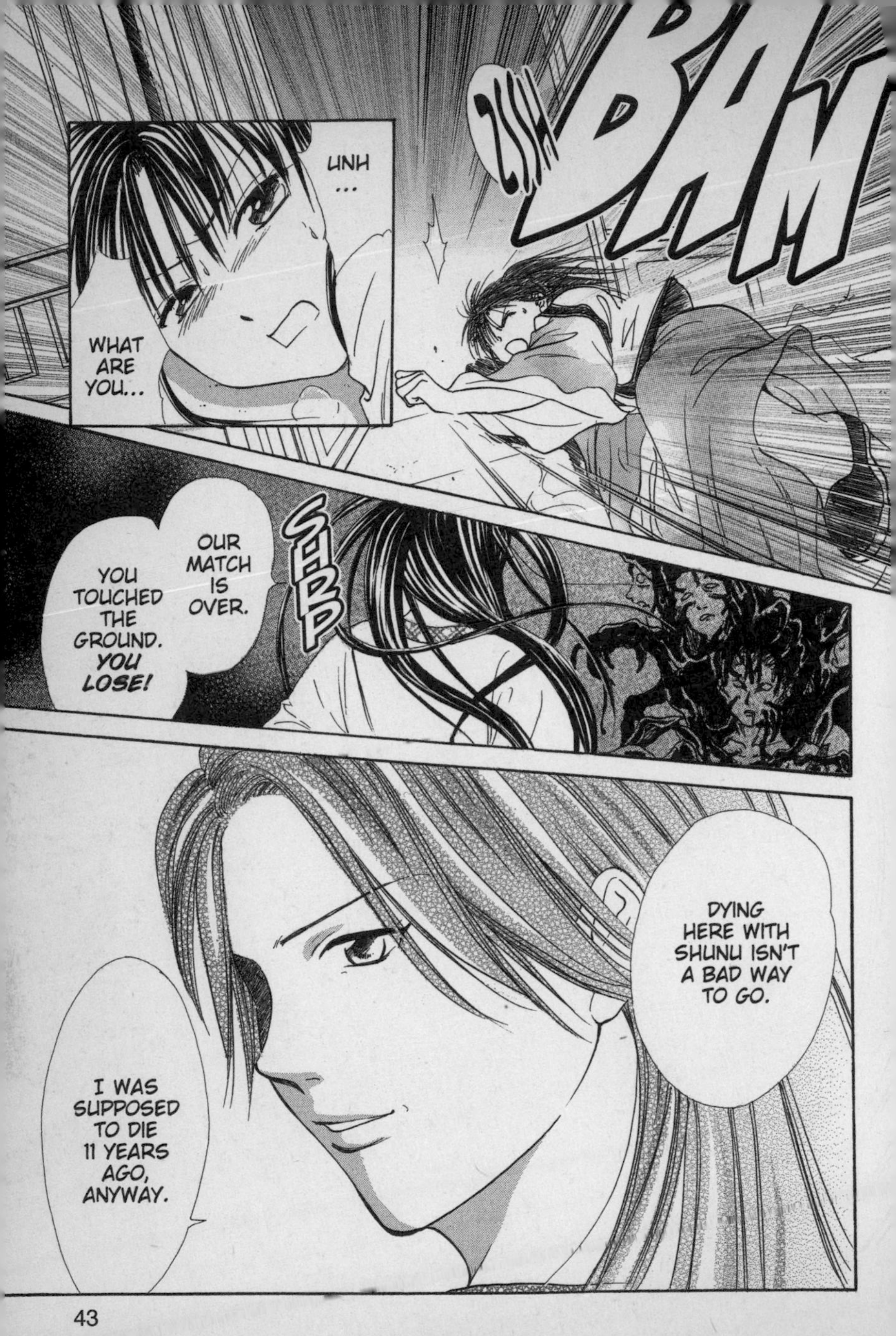
BAM
ZSH
UNH ...
WHAT ARE YOU...
SHPP
OUR MATCH IS OVER.
YOU TOUCHED THE GROUND. YOU LOSE!
DYING HERE WITH SHUNU ISN'T A BAD WAY TO GO.
I WAS SUPPOSED TO DIE 11 YEARS AGO, ANYWAY.

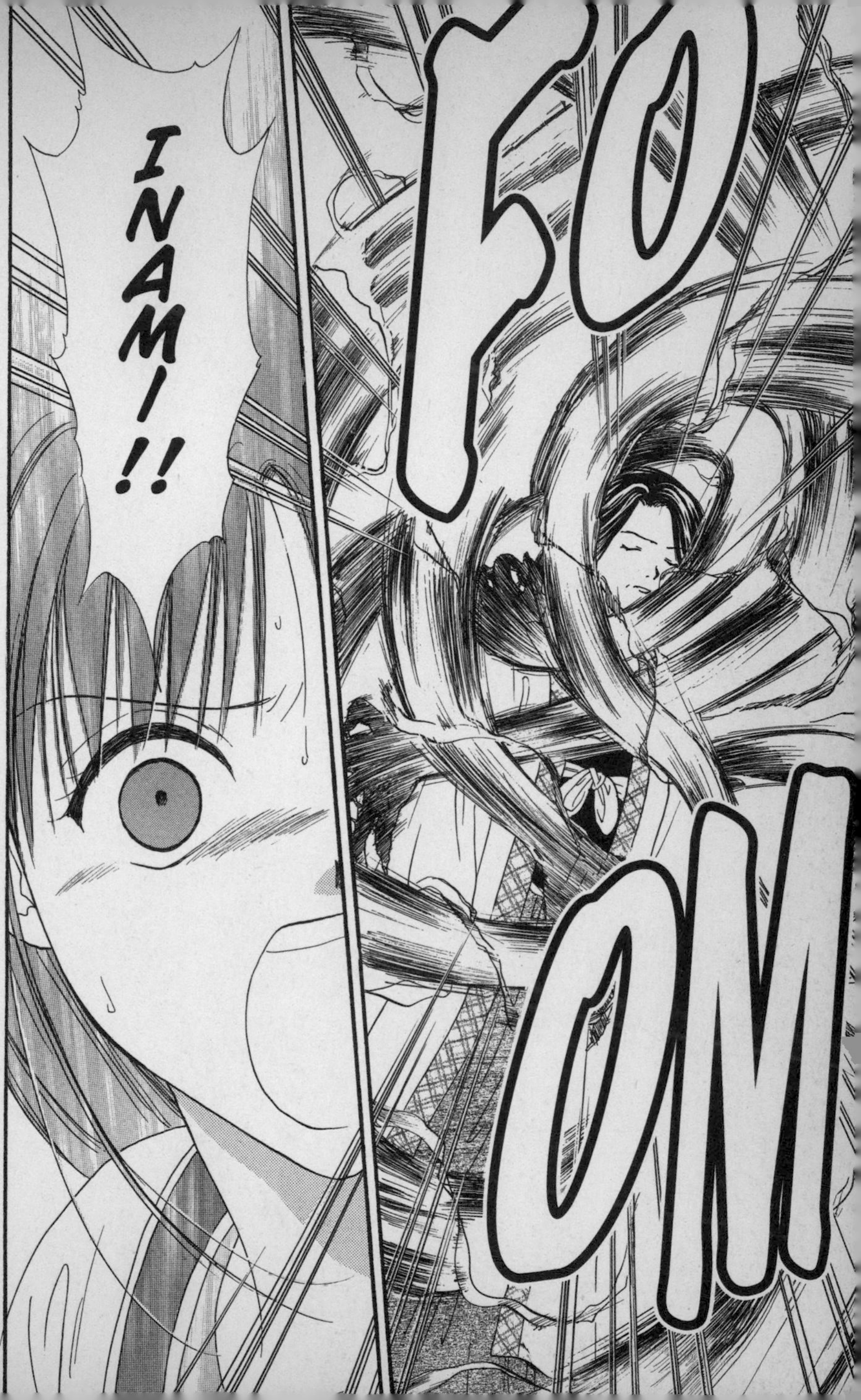
FOOM
INAMI!!

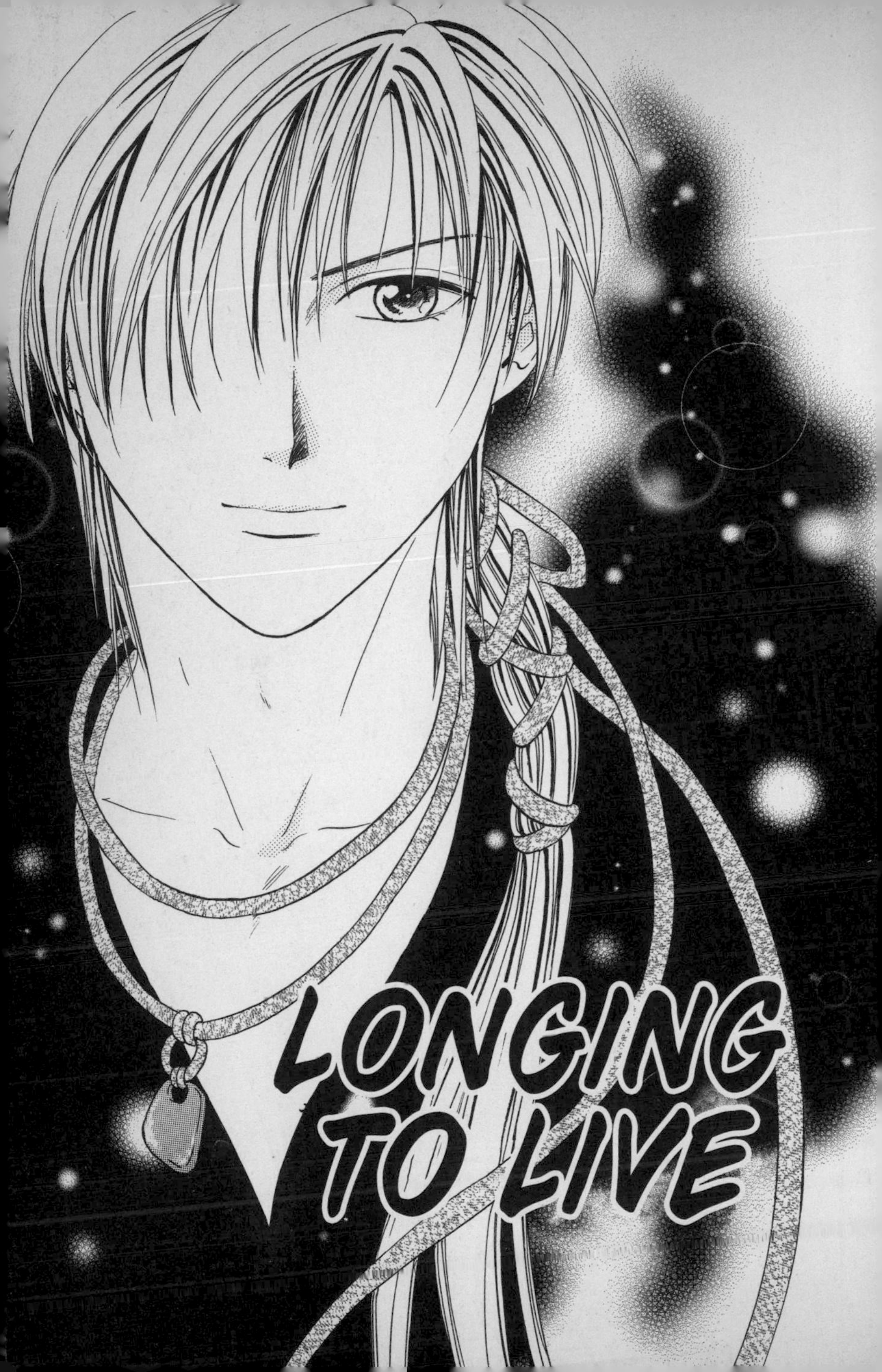
LONGING TO LIVE

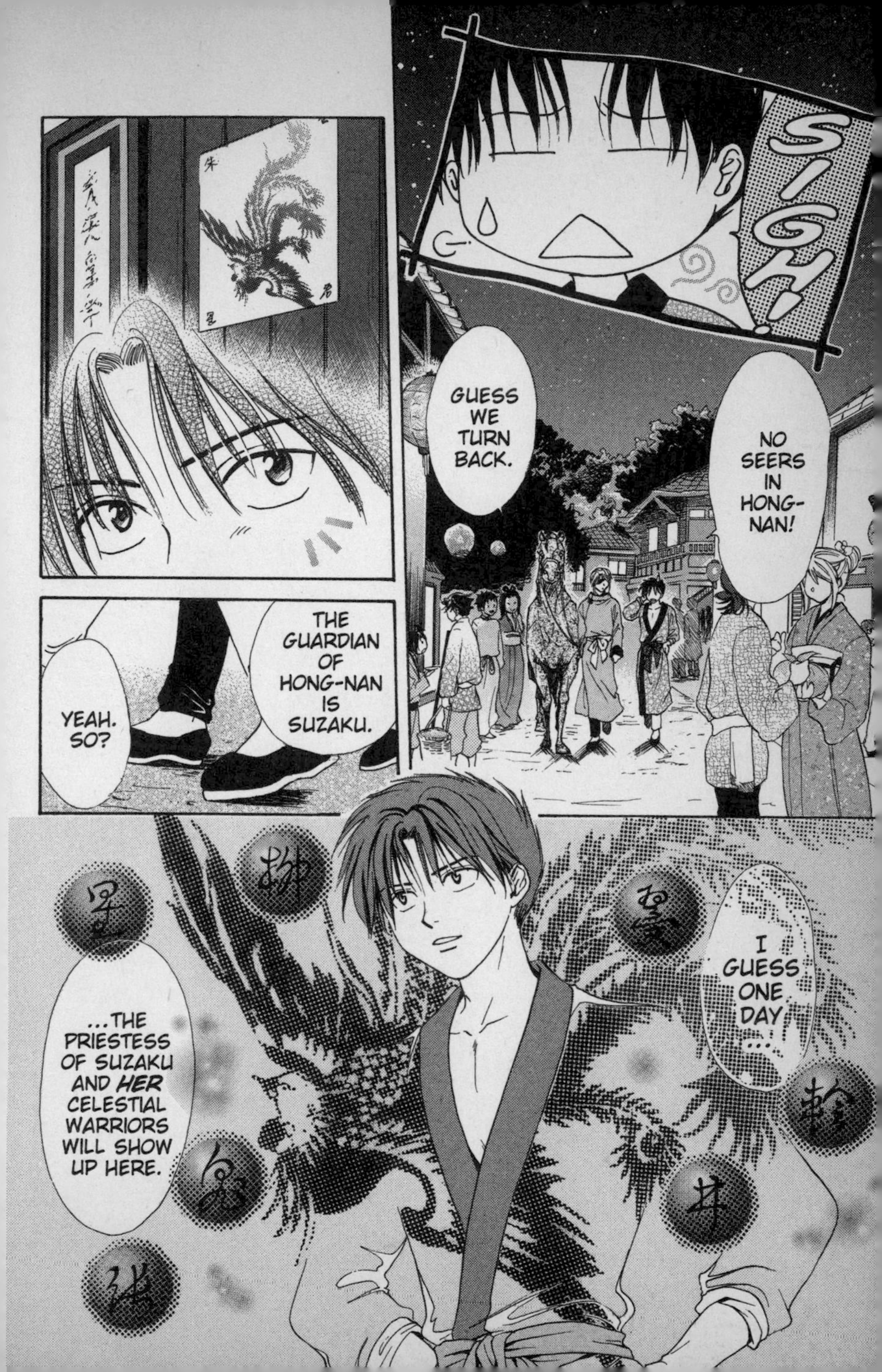
SIGH!
NO SEERS IN HONG-NAN!
GUESS WE TURN BACK.
THE GUARDIAN OF HONG-NAN IS SUZAKU.
YEAH. SO?
I GUESS ONE DAY...
...THE PRIESTESS OF SUZAKU AND ***HER*** CELESTIAL WARRIORS WILL SHOW UP HERE.

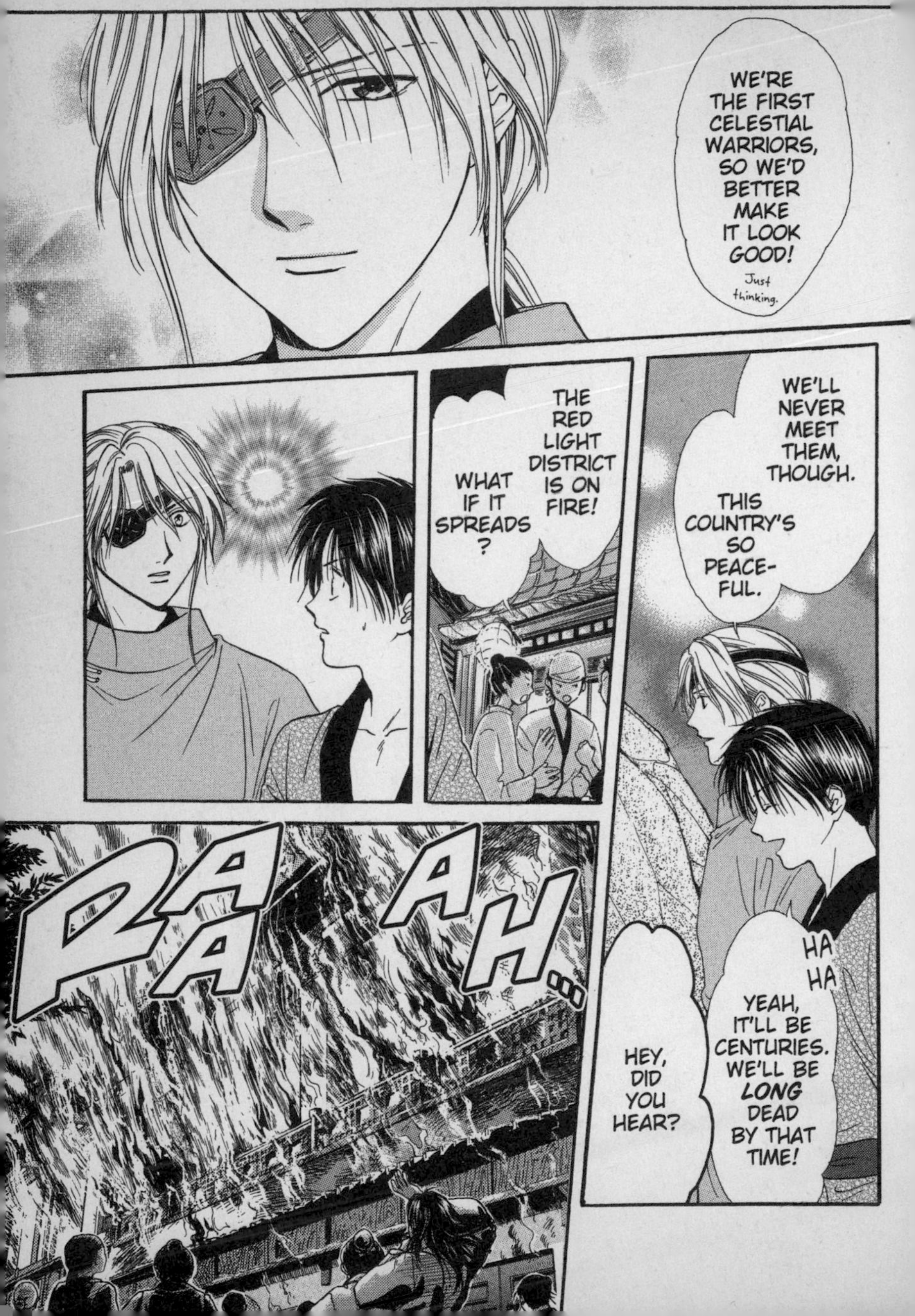
WE'RE THE FIRST CELESTIAL WARRIORS, SO WE'D BETTER MAKE IT LOOK GOOD!
Just thinking.
WE'LL NEVER MEET THEM, THOUGH.
THIS COUNTRY'S SO PEACE-FUL.
HA HA
YEAH, IT'LL BE CENTURIES. WE'LL BE **LONG** DEAD BY THAT TIME!
HEY, DID YOU HEAR?
THE RED LIGHT DISTRICT IS ON FIRE!
WHAT IF IT SPREADS?
RAAAH...

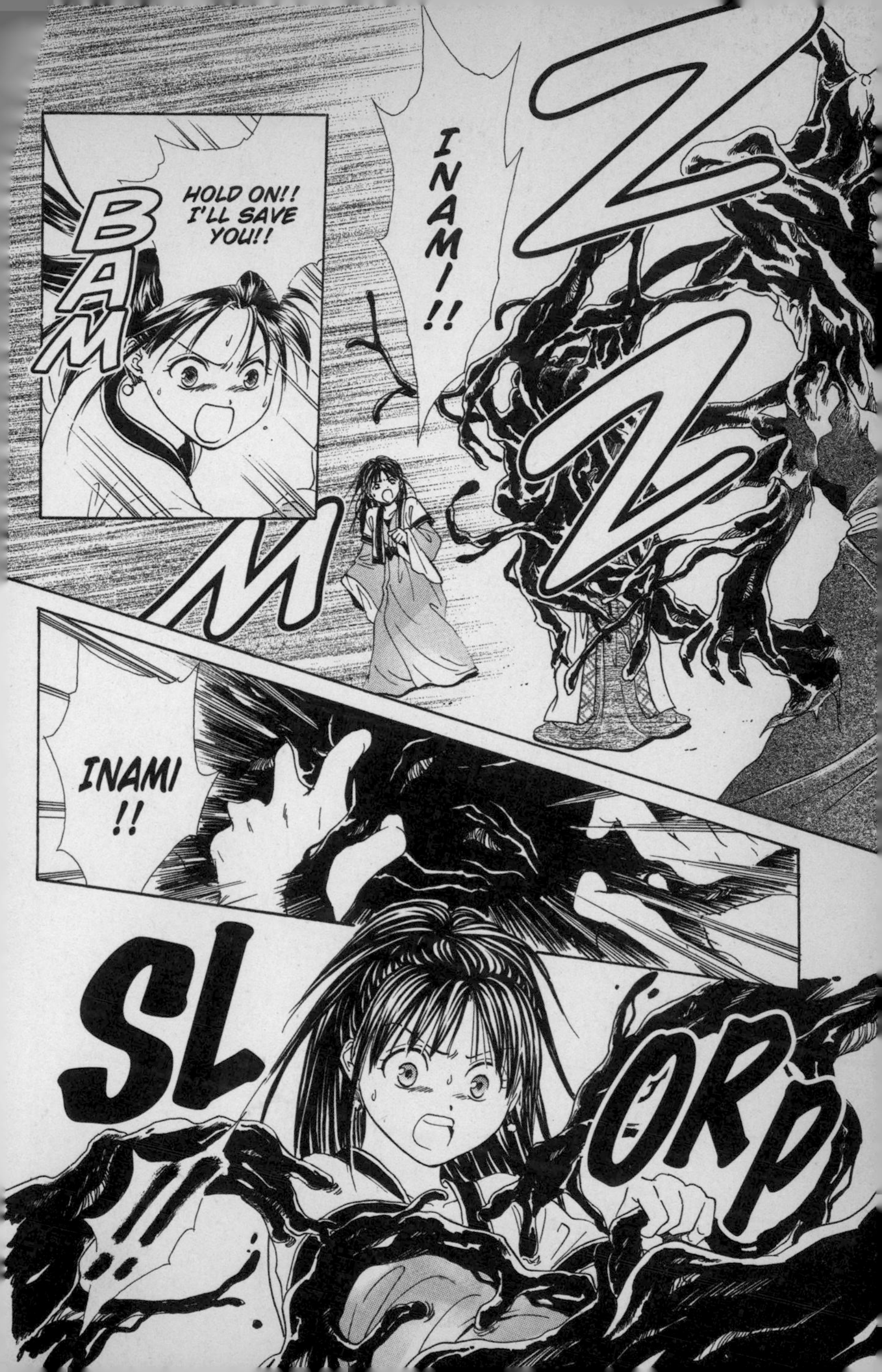
ZZ
INAMI!!
BAM
HOLD ON!! I'LL SAVE YOU!!
M
INAMI!!
SL ORP
!!

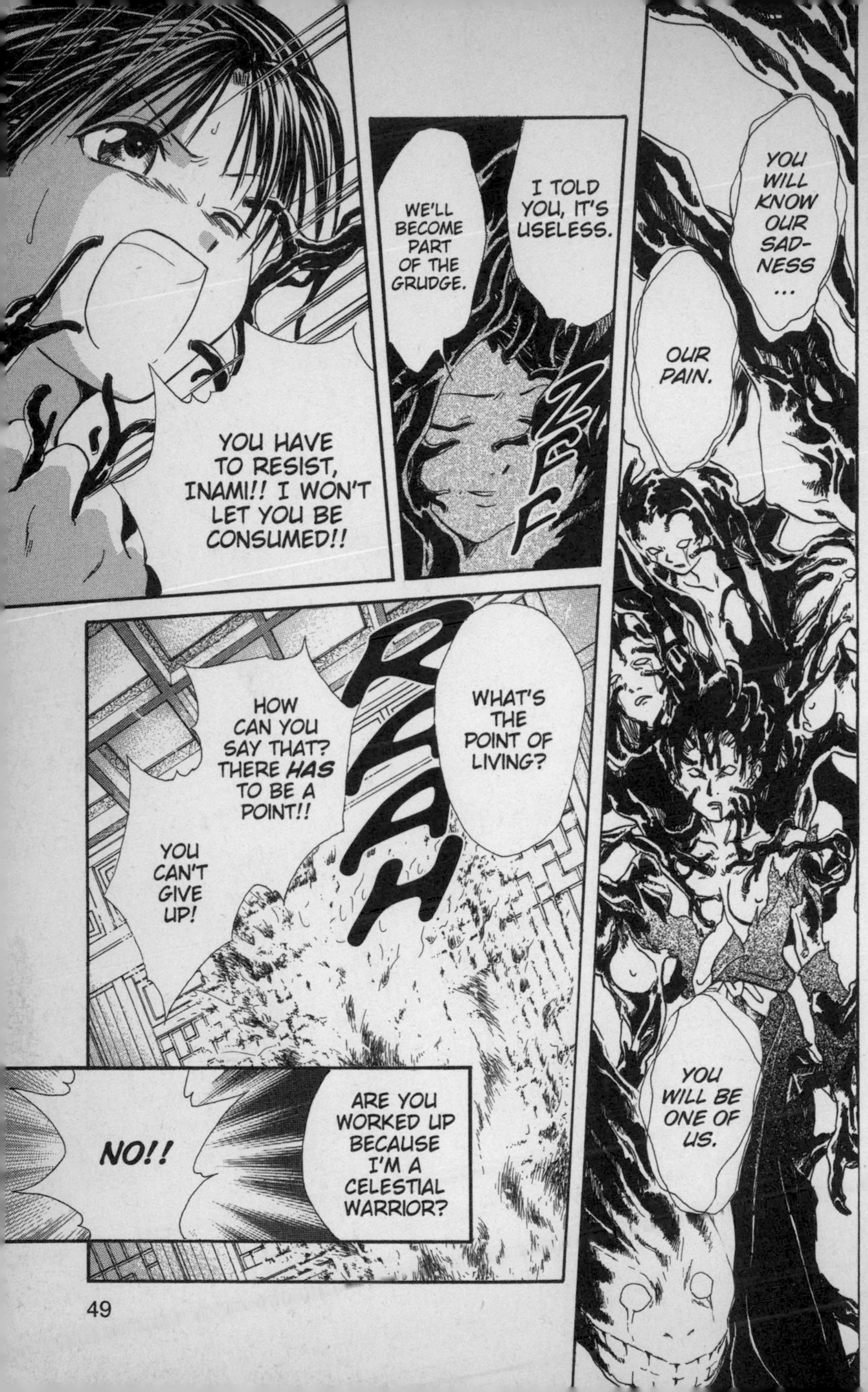
YOU WILL KNOW OUR SAD-NESS ...
OUR PAIN.
YOU WILL BE ONE OF US.
I TOLD YOU, IT'S USELESS.
WE'LL BECOME PART OF THE GRUDGE.
YOU HAVE TO RESIST, INAMI!! I WON'T LET YOU BE CONSUMED!!
WHAT'S THE POINT OF LIVING?
HOW CAN YOU SAY THAT? THERE *HAS* TO BE A POINT!!
YOU CAN'T GIVE UP!
ARE YOU WORKED UP BECAUSE I'M A CELESTIAL WARRIOR?
NO!!

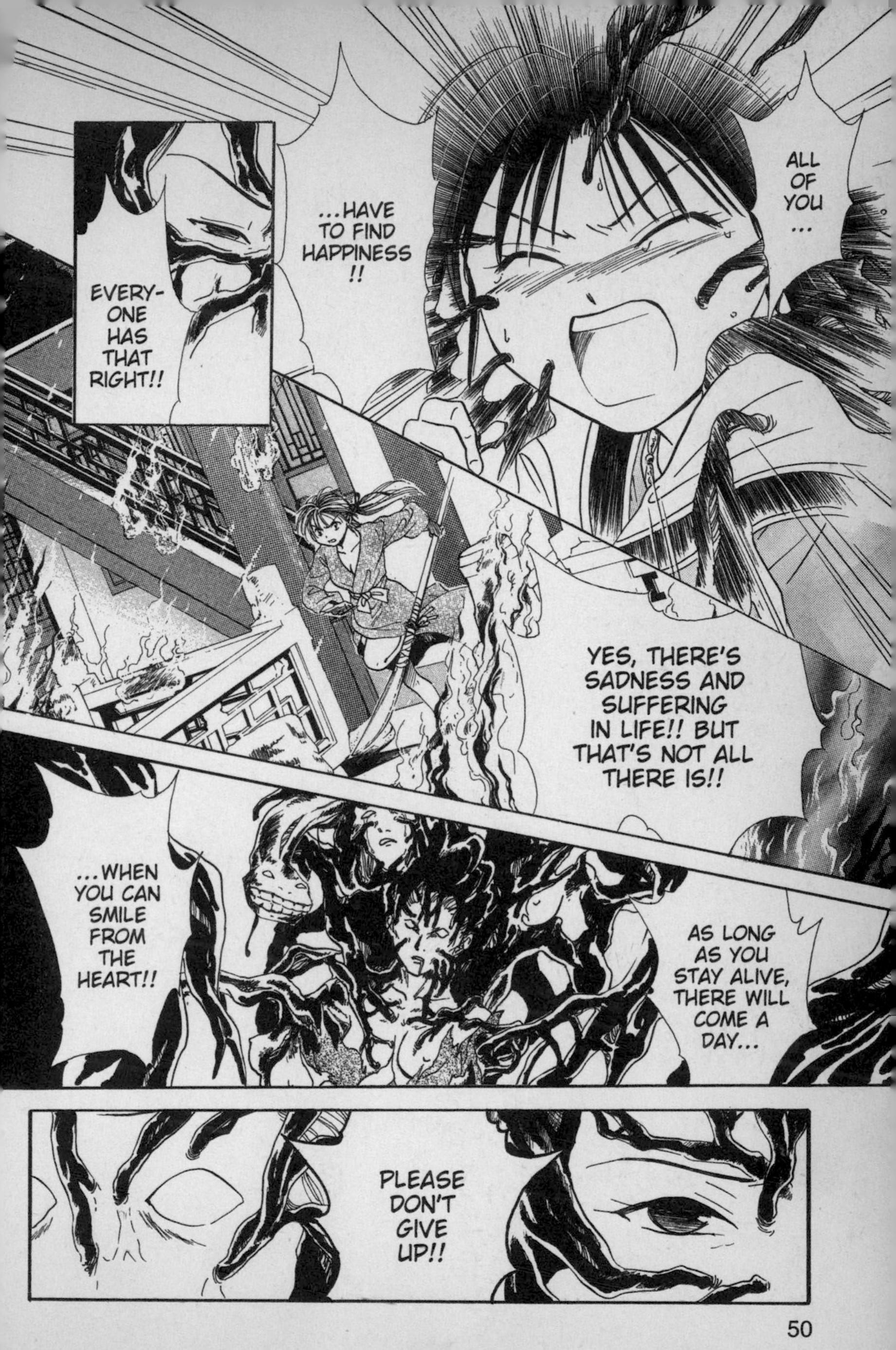
ALL OF YOU ...
...HAVE TO FIND HAPPINESS !!
EVERY-ONE HAS THAT RIGHT!!
YES, THERE'S SADNESS AND SUFFERING IN LIFE!! BUT THAT'S NOT ALL THERE IS!!
AS LONG AS YOU STAY ALIVE, THERE WILL COME A DAY...
...WHEN YOU CAN SMILE FROM THE HEART!!
PLEASE DON'T GIVE UP!!

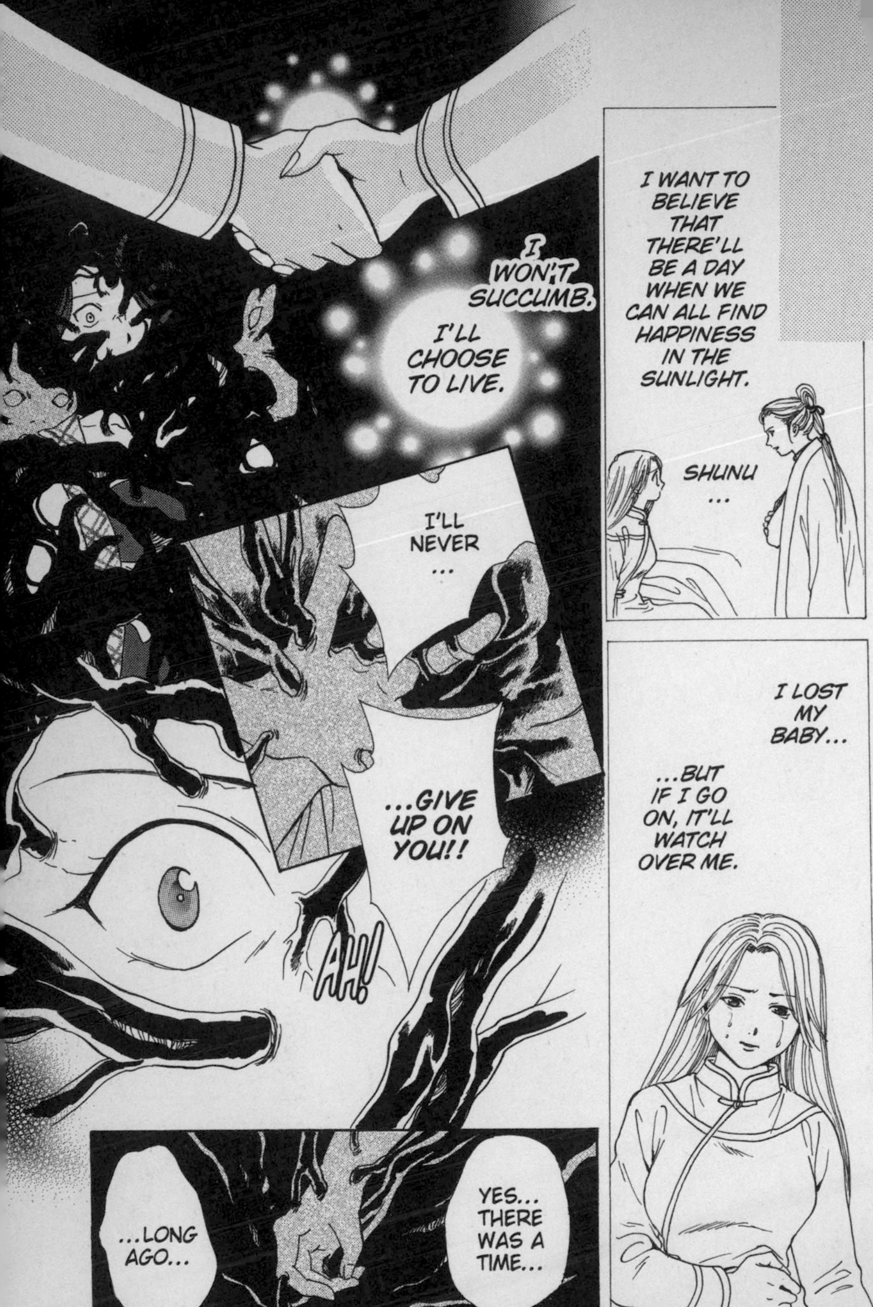
I WANT TO BELIEVE THAT THERE'LL BE A DAY WHEN WE CAN ALL FIND HAPPINESS IN THE SUNLIGHT.
SHUNU ...
I LOST MY BABY...
...BUT IF I GO ON, IT'LL WATCH OVER ME.
I WON'T SUCCUMB.
I'LL CHOOSE TO LIVE.
I'LL NEVER ...
...GIVE UP ON YOU!!
AH!
YES... THERE WAS A TIME...
...LONG AGO...

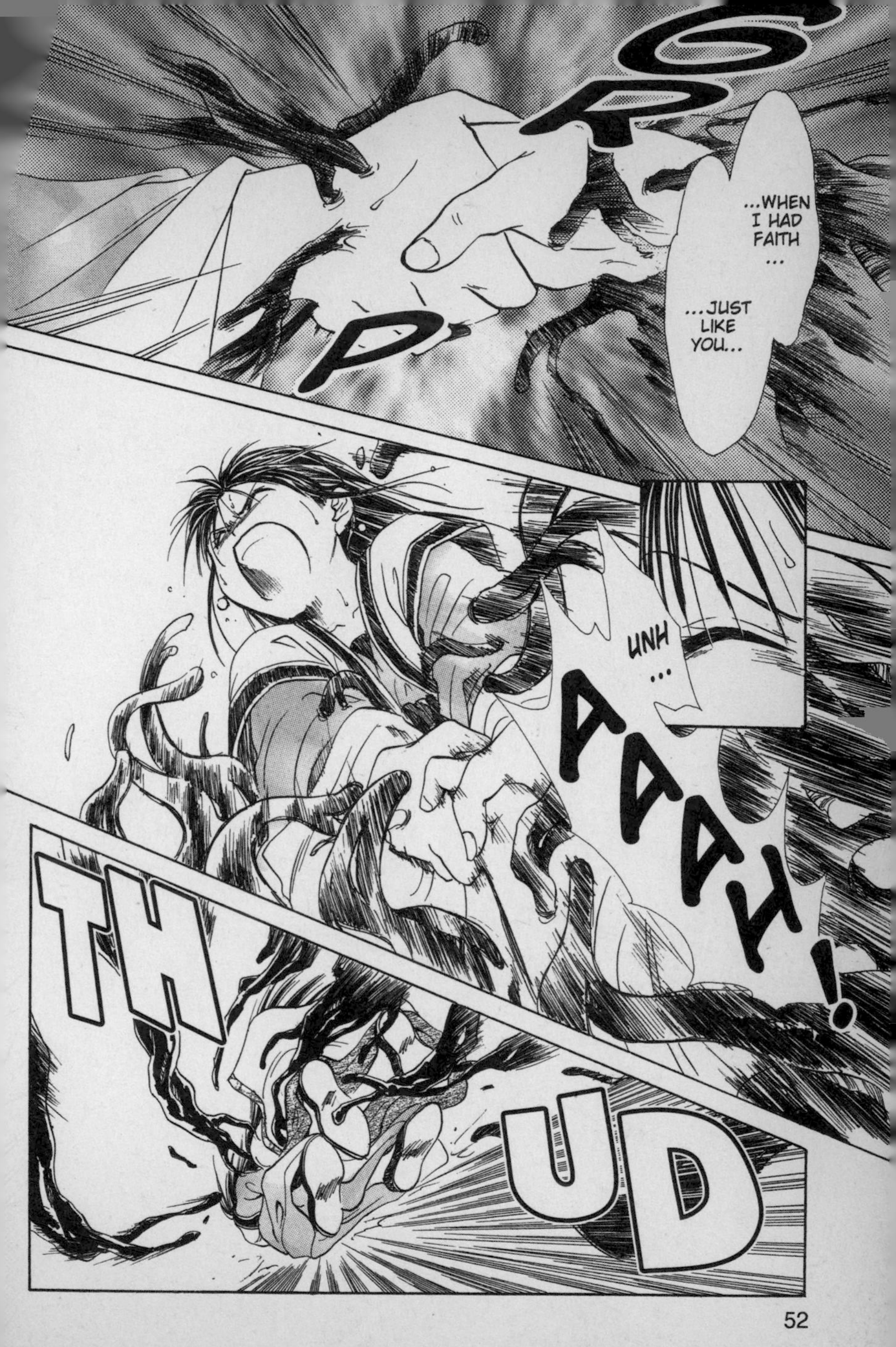
...WHEN I HAD FAITH ...
...JUST LIKE YOU...
GRIP
UNH ...
AAAH!
THUD

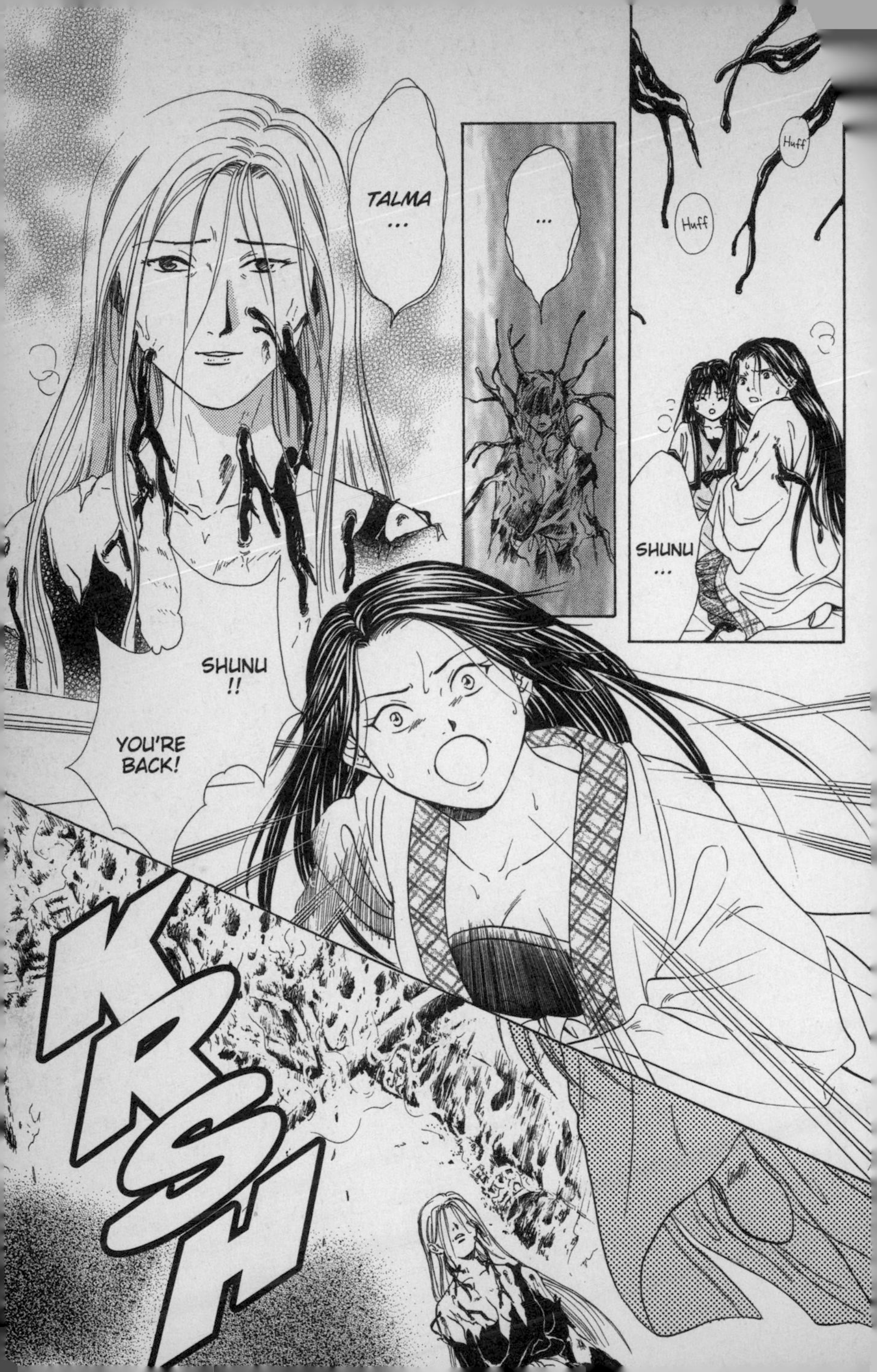
Huff
Huff
SHUNU ...
...
TALMA ...
SHUNU !!
YOU'RE BACK!
KRSH

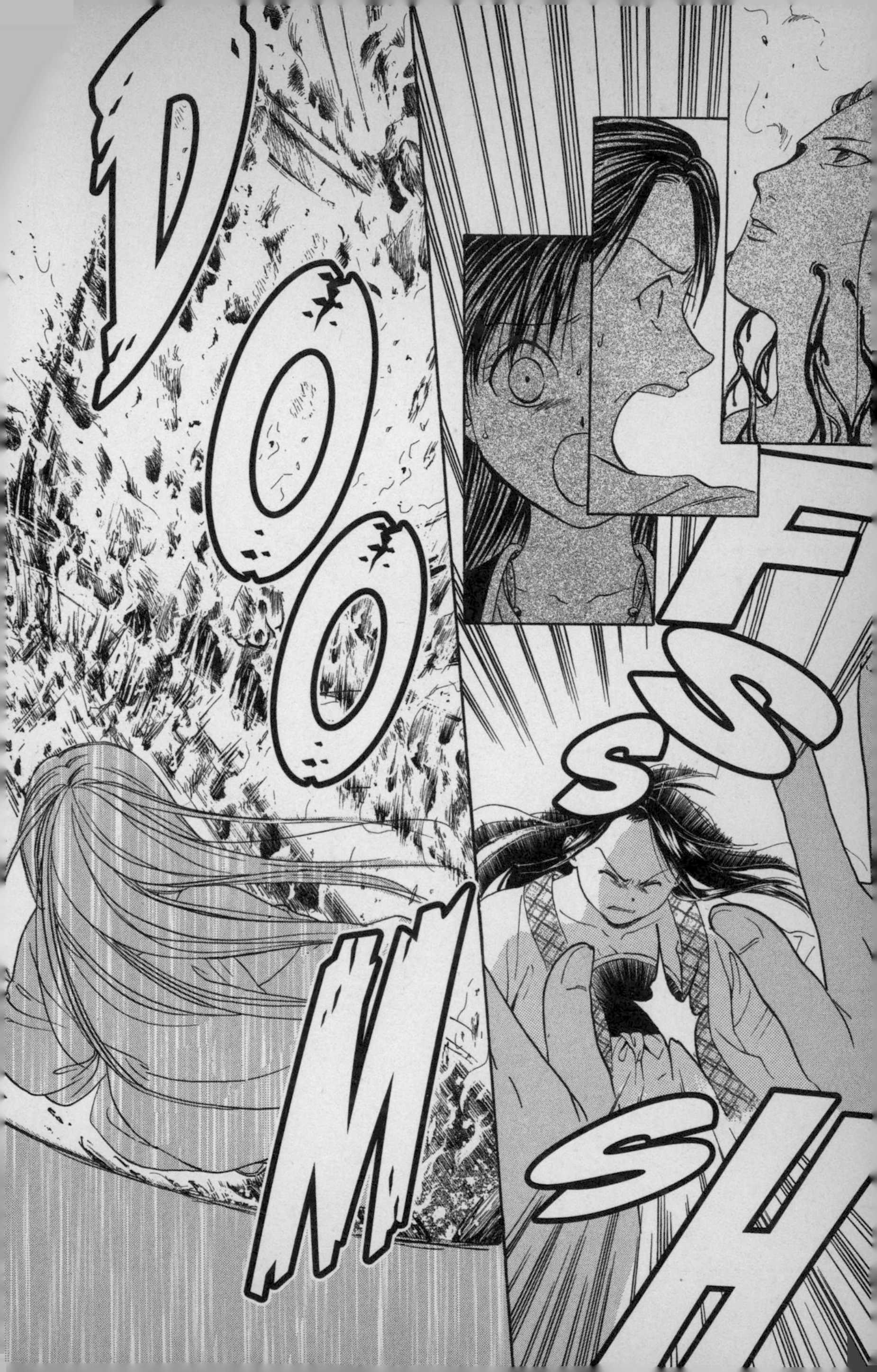
FSSSH
DOOOM

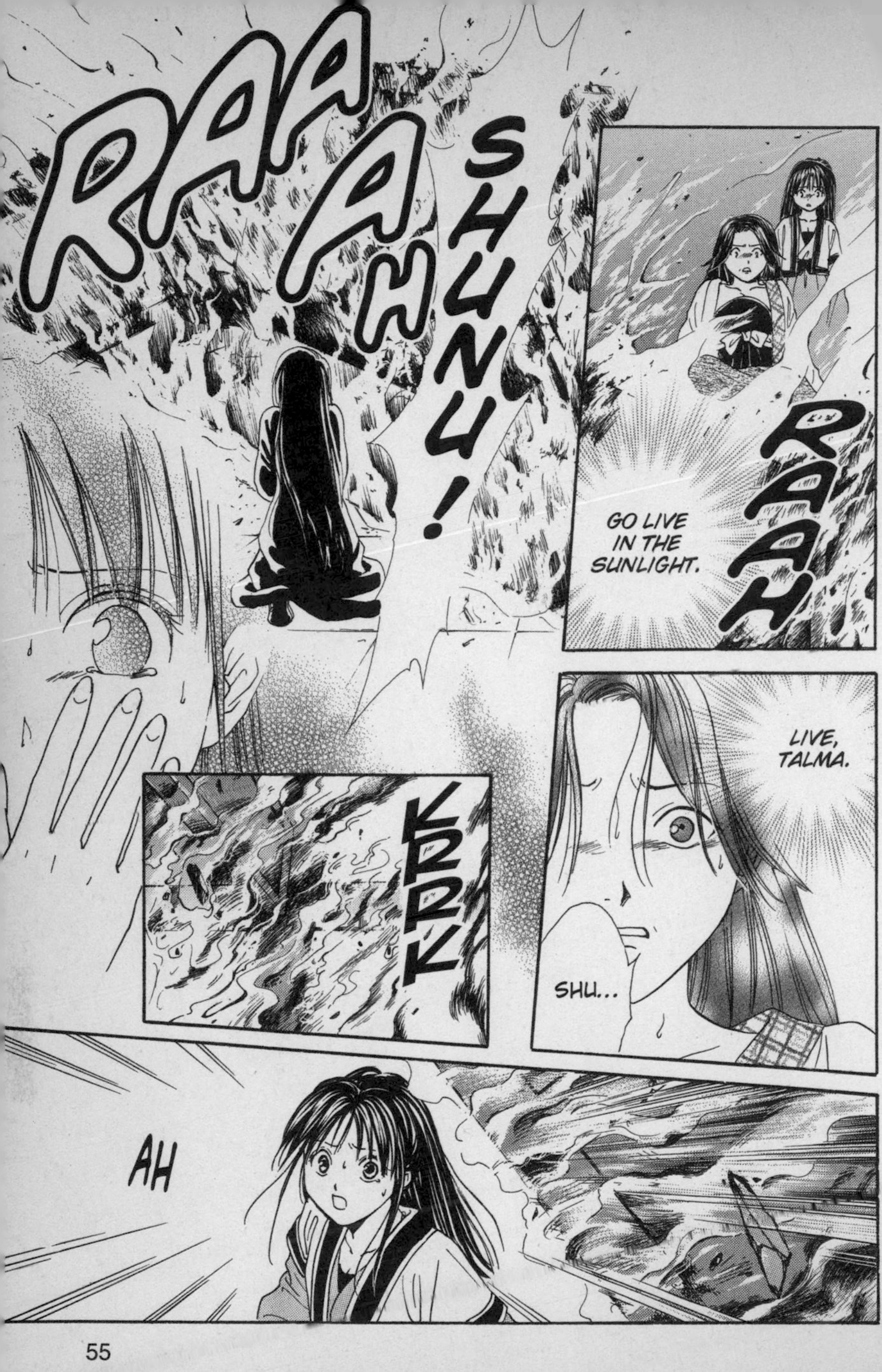
GO LIVE IN THE SUNLIGHT.
RAAH
RAAAH
SHUNU!
LIVE, TALMA.
SHU...
KRRK
AH

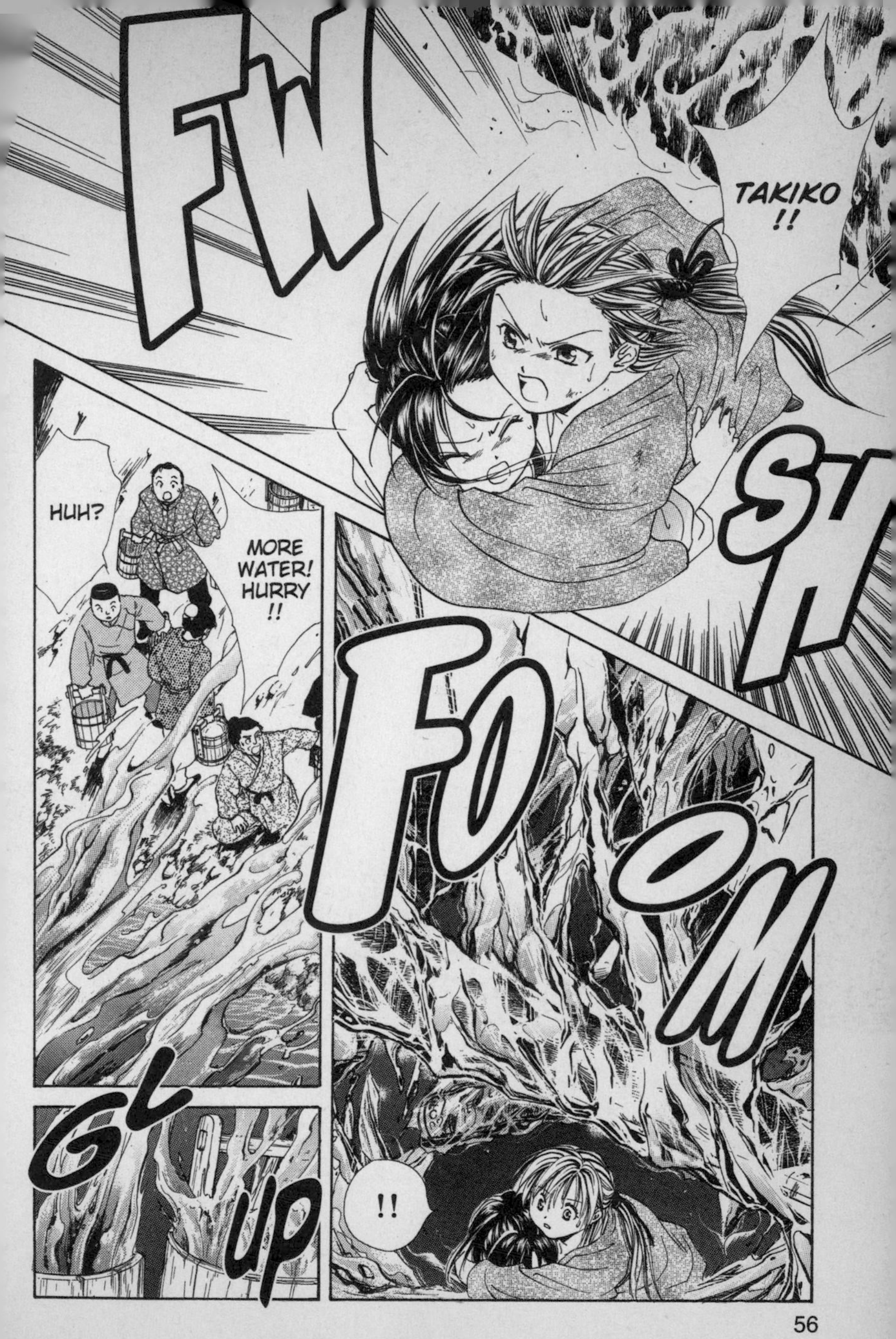
TAKIKO !!
FWSH
FOOM
!!
MORE WATER! HURRY !!
HUH?
GLUP

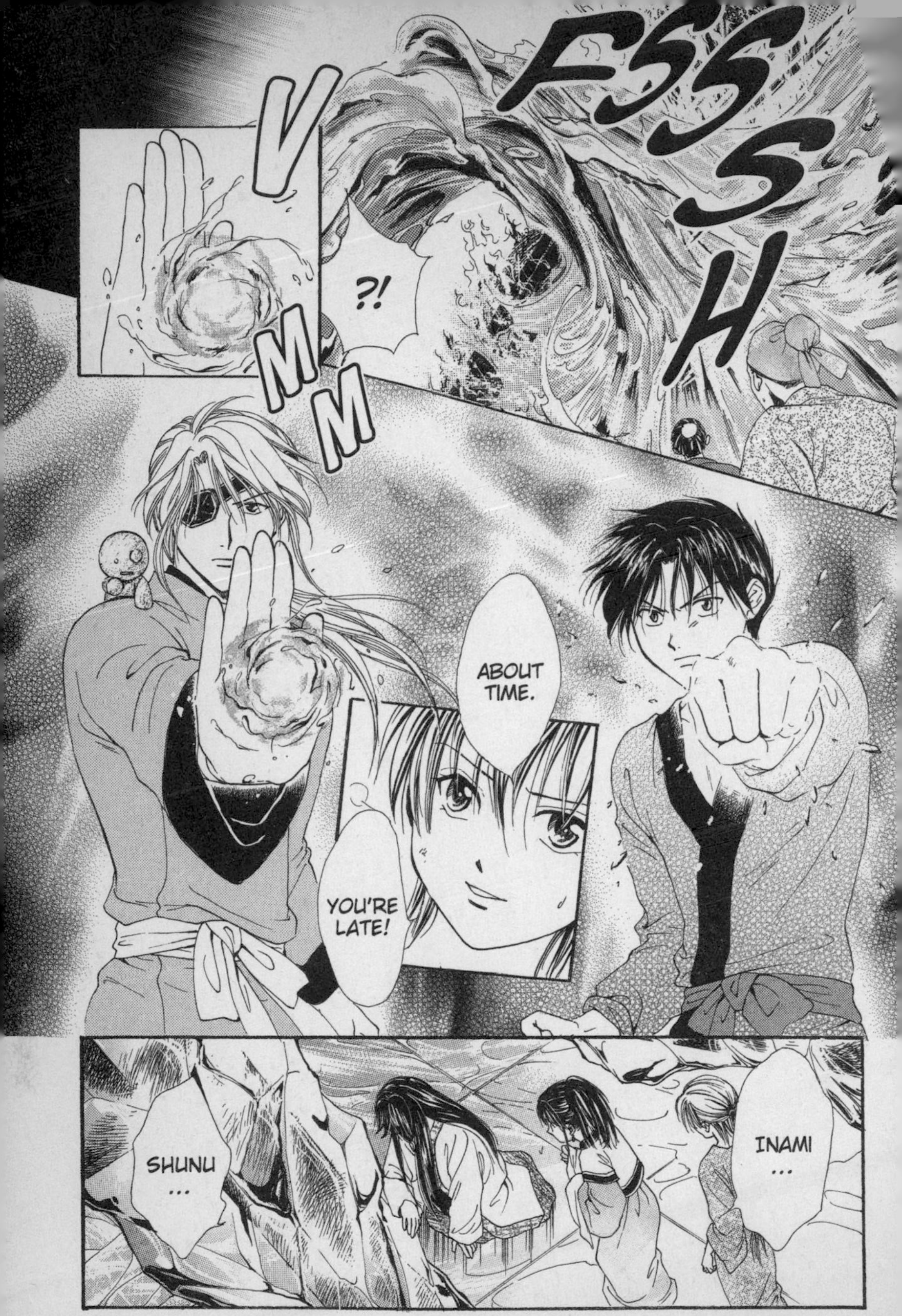
FSSSH
?!
VMMM
ABOUT TIME.
YOU'RE LATE!
INAMI ...
SHUNU ...

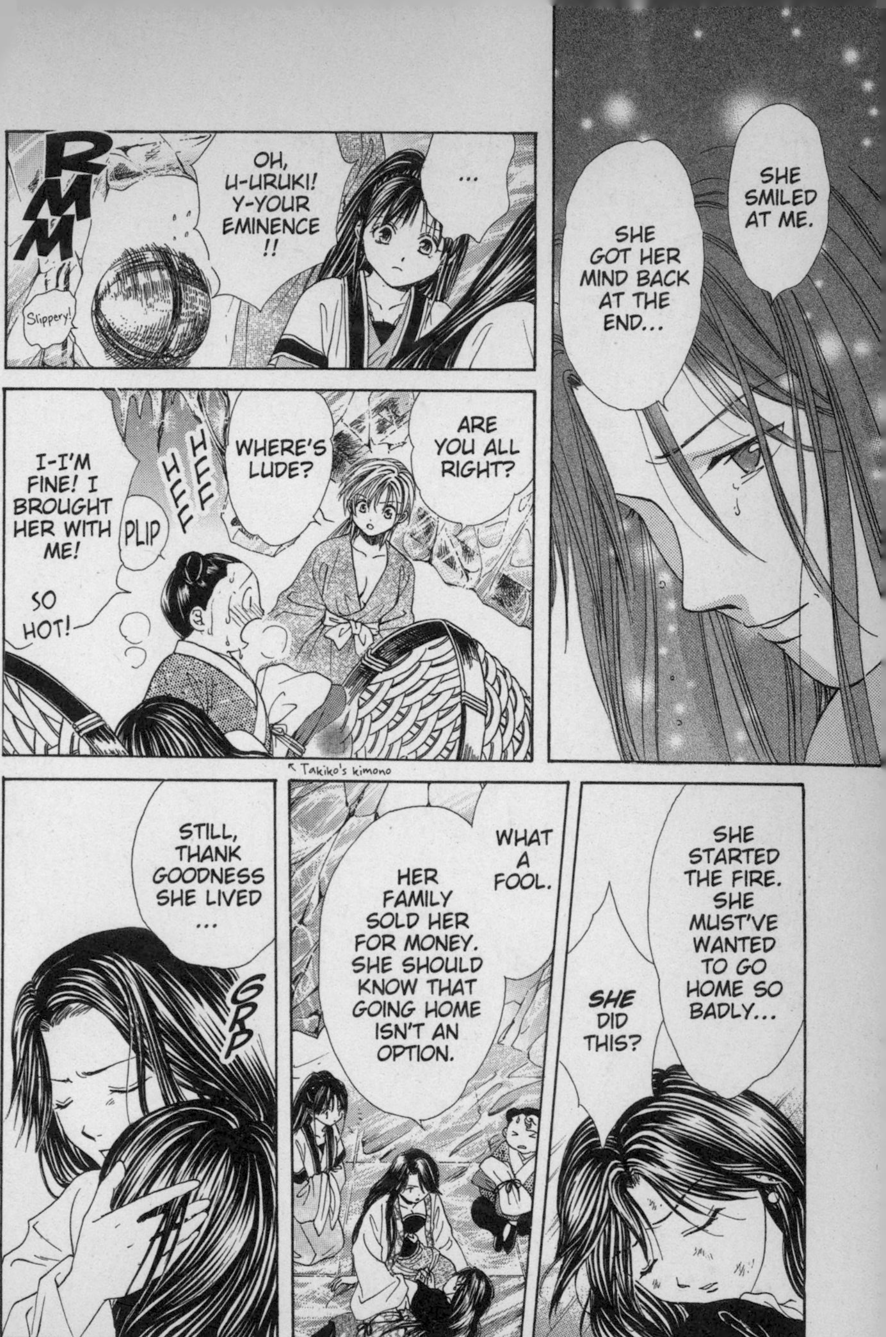
SHE SMILED AT ME.
SHE GOT HER MIND BACK AT THE END...
RMM
OH, U-URUKI! Y-YOUR EMINENCE !!
...
Slippery!
ARE YOU ALL RIGHT?
WHERE'S LUDE?
HEFF HEFF
I-I'M FINE! I BROUGHT HER WITH ME!
PLIP
SO HOT!
Takiko's kimono
SHE STARTED THE FIRE. SHE MUST'VE WANTED TO GO HOME SO BADLY...
SHE DID THIS?
WHAT A FOOL.
HER FAMILY SOLD HER FOR MONEY. SHE SHOULD KNOW THAT GOING HOME ISN'T AN OPTION.
STILL, THANK GOODNESS SHE LIVED ...
GRP

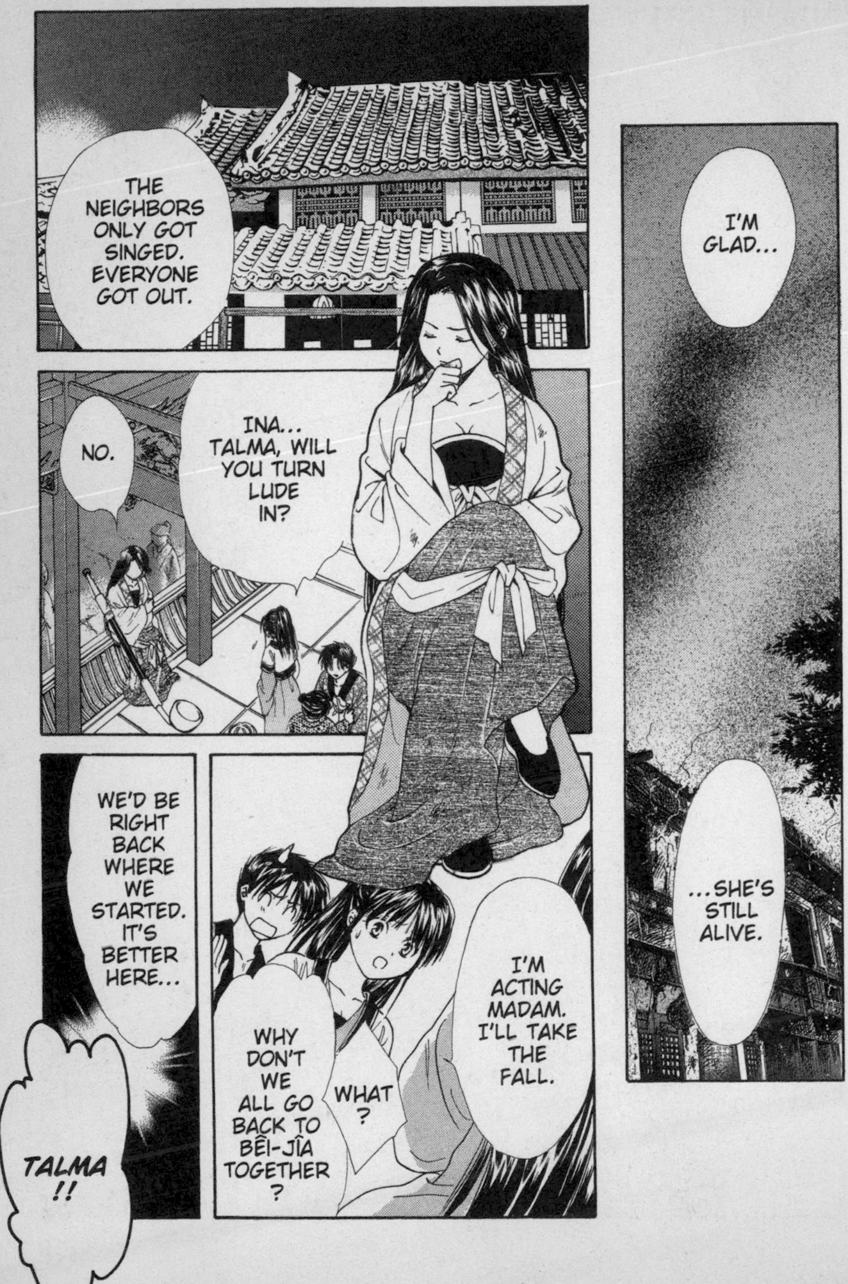
I'M GLAD...
...SHE'S STILL ALIVE.
THE NEIGHBORS ONLY GOT SINGED. EVERYONE GOT OUT.
INA... TALMA, WILL YOU TURN LUDE IN?
NO.
I'M ACTING MADAM. I'LL TAKE THE FALL.
WHAT?
WHY DON'T WE ALL GO BACK TO BÊI-JĪA TOGETHER?
WE'D BE RIGHT BACK WHERE WE STARTED. IT'S BETTER HERE...
TALMA!!

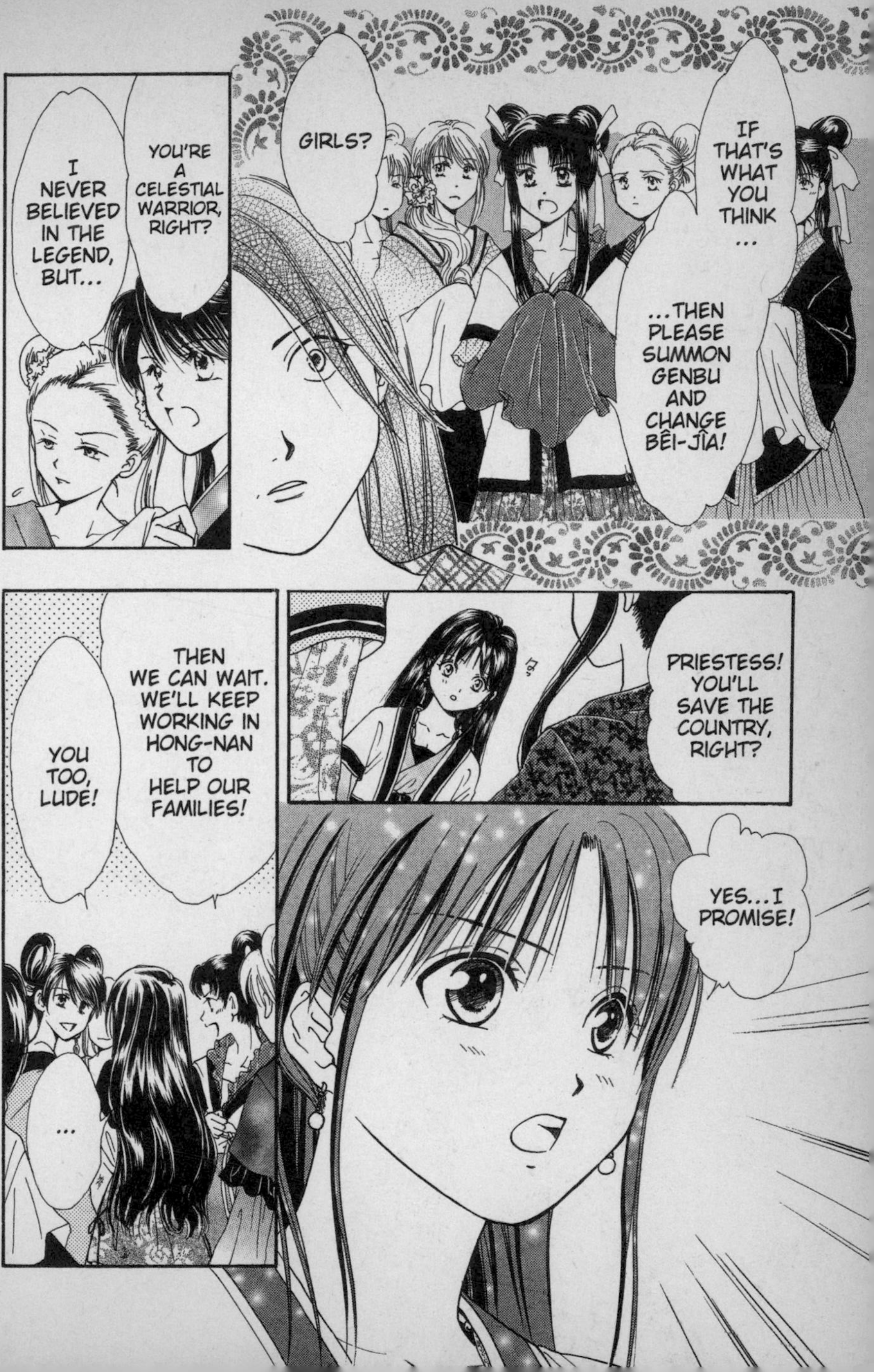
IF THAT'S WHAT YOU THINK...
...THEN PLEASE SUMMON GENBU AND CHANGE BÊI-JÎA!
GIRLS?
YOU'RE A CELESTIAL WARRIOR, RIGHT?
I NEVER BELIEVED IN THE LEGEND, BUT...
PRIESTESS! YOU'LL SAVE THE COUNTRY, RIGHT?
YES...I PROMISE!
THEN WE CAN WAIT. WE'LL KEEP WORKING IN HONG-NAN TO HELP OUR FAMILIES!
YOU TOO, LUDE!
...

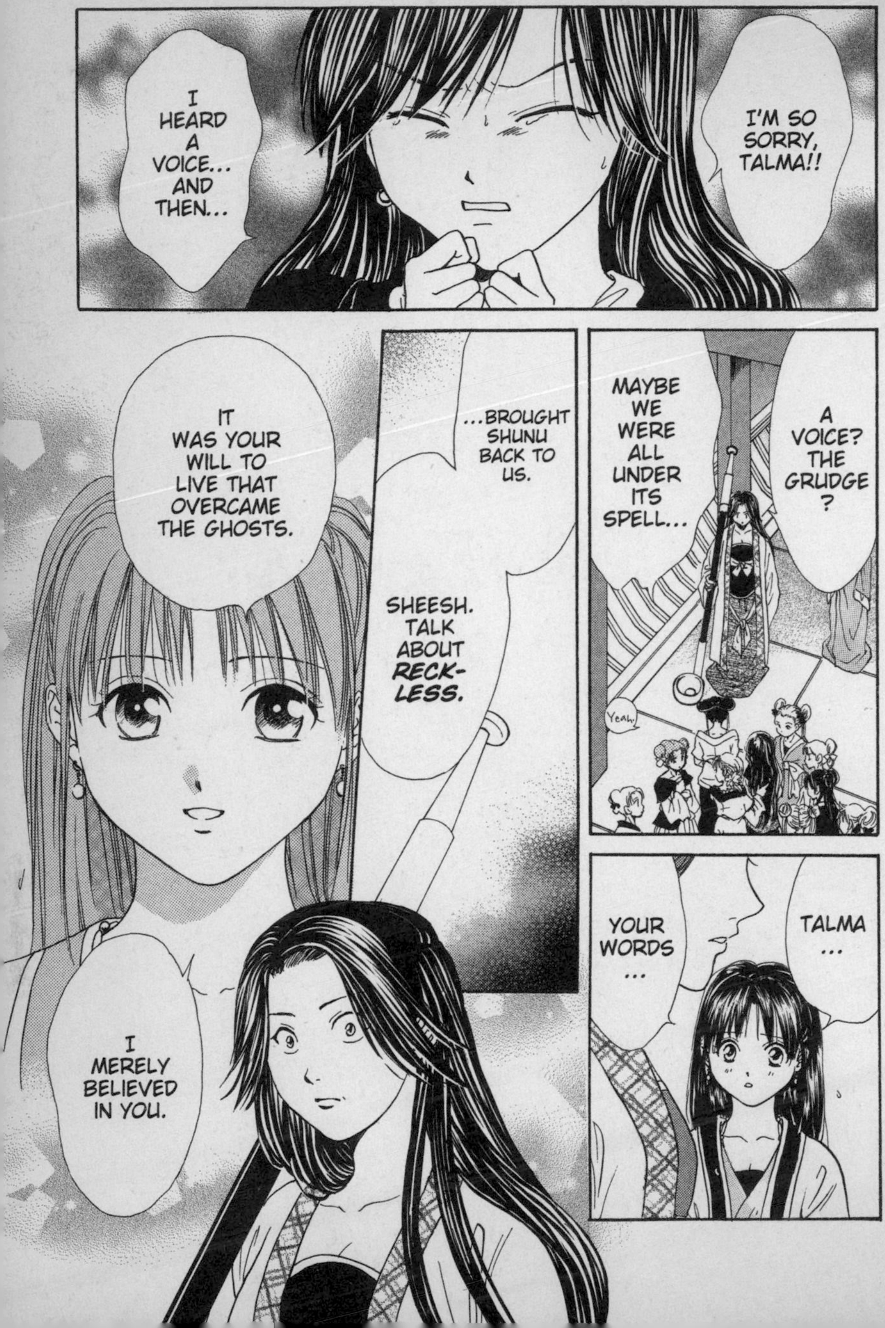
I'M SO SORRY, TALMA!!
I HEARD A VOICE... AND THEN...
A VOICE? THE GRUDGE ?
MAYBE WE WERE ALL UNDER ITS SPELL...
Yeah
TALMA ...
YOUR WORDS ...
...BROUGHT SHUNU BACK TO US.
SHEESH. TALK ABOUT *RECK-LESS.*
IT WAS YOUR WILL TO LIVE THAT OVERCAME THE GHOSTS.
I MERELY BELIEVED IN YOU.

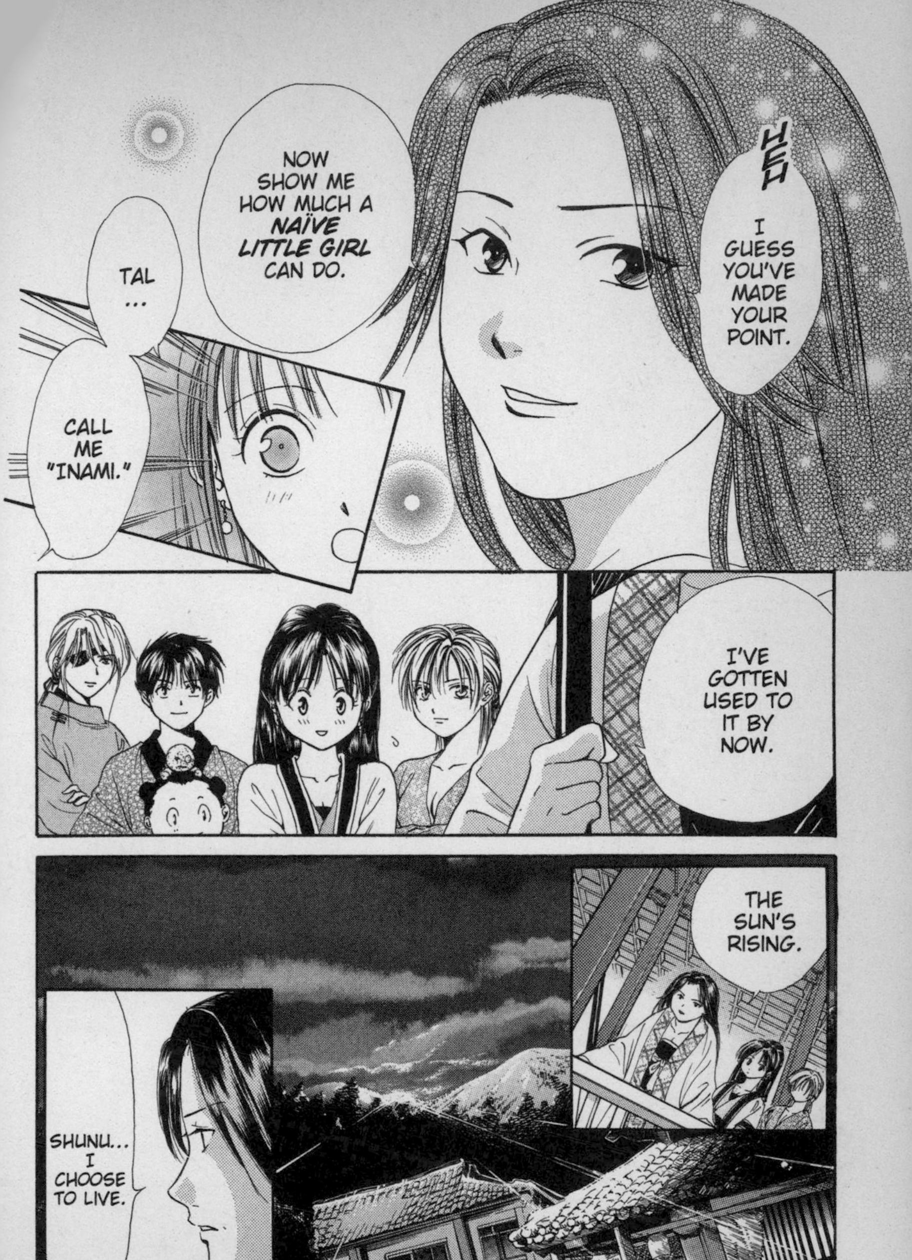
HEH
I GUESS YOU'VE MADE YOUR POINT.
NOW SHOW ME HOW MUCH A *NAÏVE LITTLE GIRL* CAN DO.
TAL...
CALL ME "INAMI."
I'VE GOTTEN USED TO IT BY NOW.
THE SUN'S RISING.
SHUNU... I CHOOSE TO LIVE.

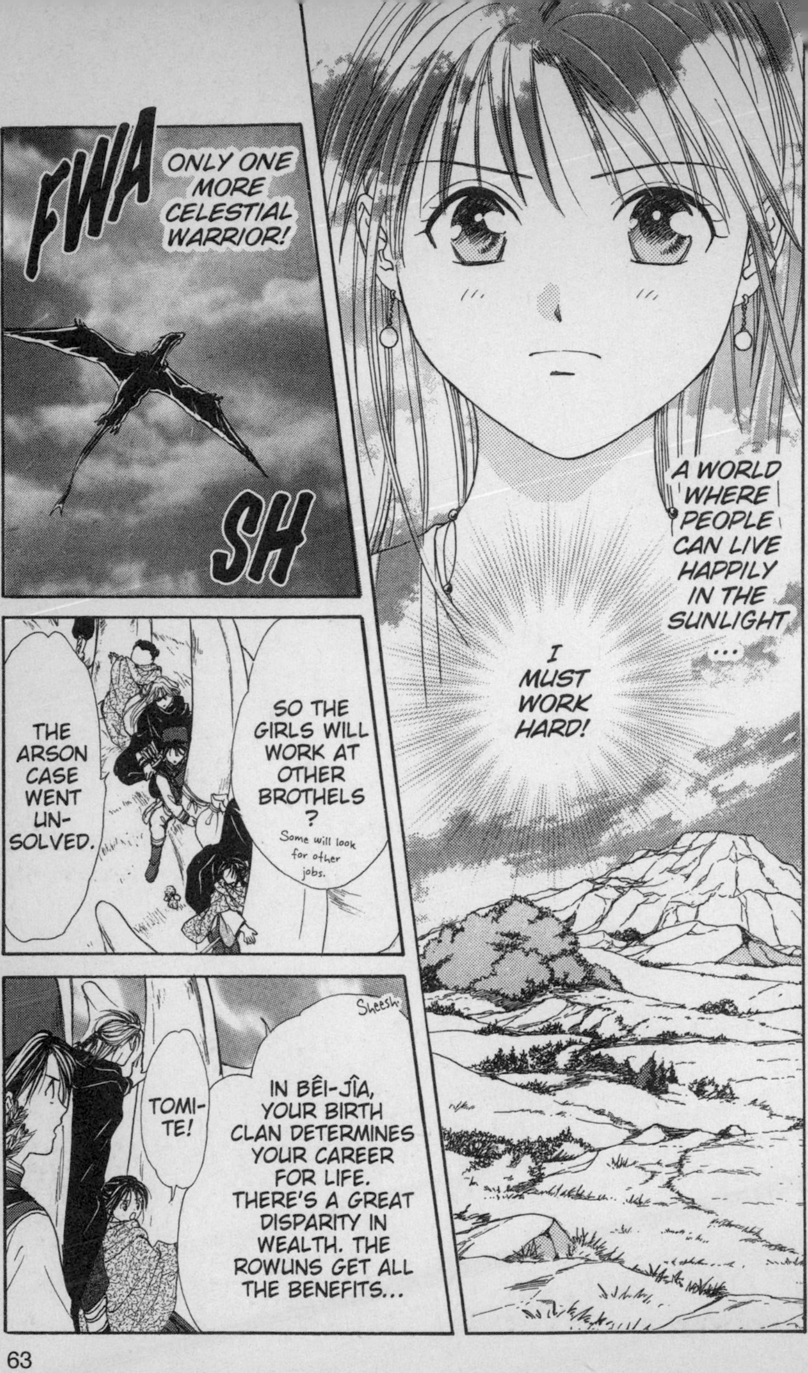
A WORLD WHERE PEOPLE CAN LIVE HAPPILY IN THE SUNLIGHT...
I MUST WORK HARD!
FWA
ONLY ONE MORE CELESTIAL WARRIOR!
SH
SO THE GIRLS WILL WORK AT OTHER BROTHELS?
Some will look for other jobs.
THE ARSON CASE WENT UN-SOLVED.
Sheesh.
IN BÊI-JÎA, YOUR BIRTH CLAN DETERMINES YOUR CAREER FOR LIFE. THERE'S A GREAT DISPARITY IN WEALTH. THE ROWUNS GET ALL THE BENEFITS...
TOMI-TE!

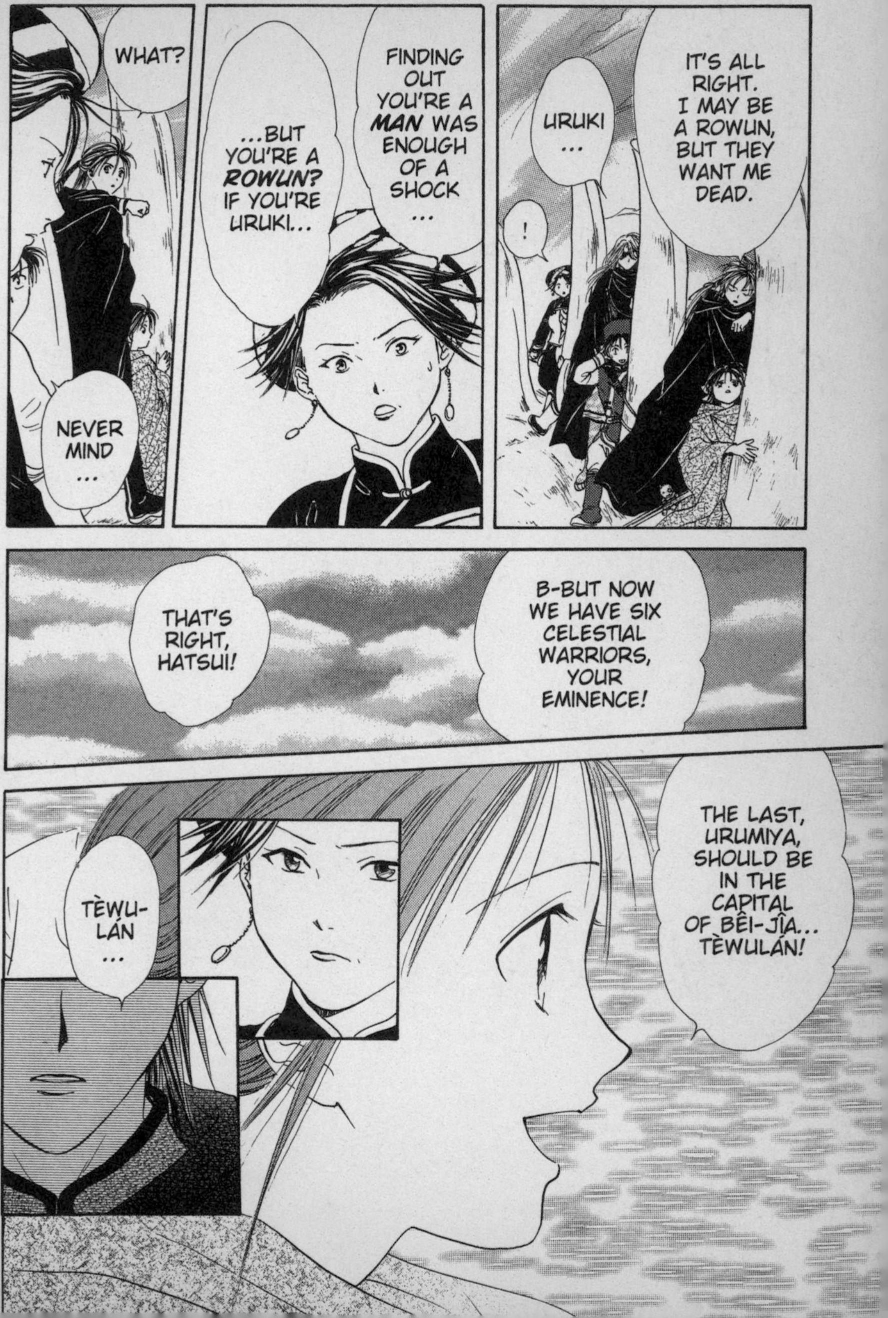
IT'S ALL RIGHT. I MAY BE A ROWUN, BUT THEY WANT ME DEAD.
URUKI ...
!
FINDING OUT YOU'RE A **MAN** WAS ENOUGH OF A SHOCK ...
...BUT YOU'RE A **ROWUN?** IF YOU'RE URUKI...
WHAT?
NEVER MIND ...
B-BUT NOW WE HAVE SIX CELESTIAL WARRIORS, YOUR EMINENCE!
THAT'S RIGHT, HATSUI!
THE LAST, URUMIYA, SHOULD BE IN THE CAPITAL OF BÊI-JÎA... TÈWULÁN!
TÈWU-LÁN ...

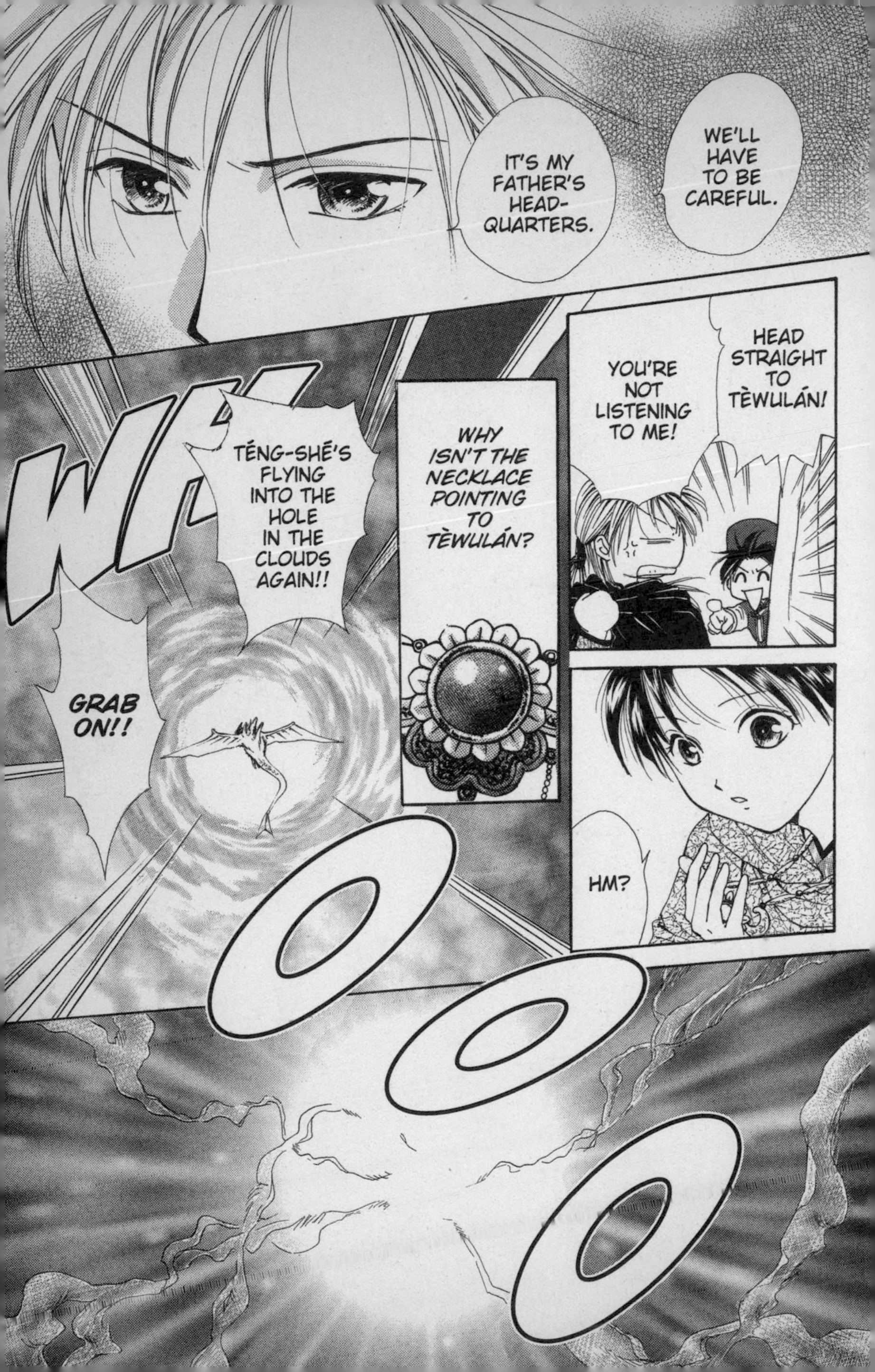
WE'LL HAVE TO BE CAREFUL.
IT'S MY FATHER'S HEAD-QUARTERS.
HEAD STRAIGHT TO TÈWULÁN!
YOU'RE NOT LISTENING TO ME!
HM?
WHY ISN'T THE NECKLACE POINTING TO TÈWULÁN?
TÉNG-SHÉ'S FLYING INTO THE HOLE IN THE CLOUDS AGAIN!!
GRAB ON!!
WHOOOO

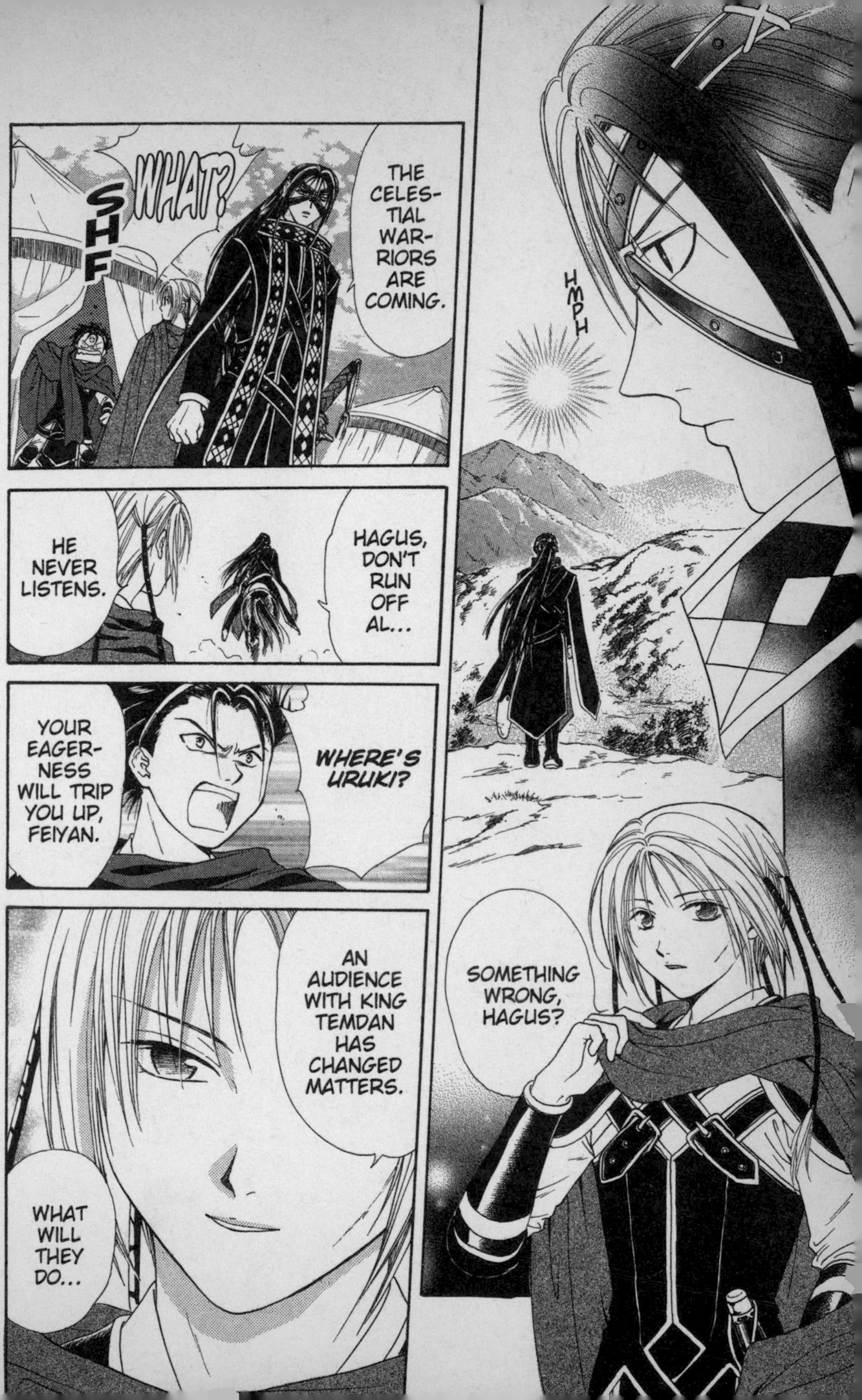
HMPH
SOMETHING WRONG, HAGUS?
THE CELESTIAL WARRIORS ARE COMING.
WHAT?
SHF
HAGUS, DON'T RUN OFF AL...
HE NEVER LISTENS.
WHERE'S URUKI?
YOUR EAGERNESS WILL TRIP YOU UP, FEIYAN.
AN AUDIENCE WITH KING TEMDAN HAS CHANGED MATTERS.
WHAT WILL THEY DO...

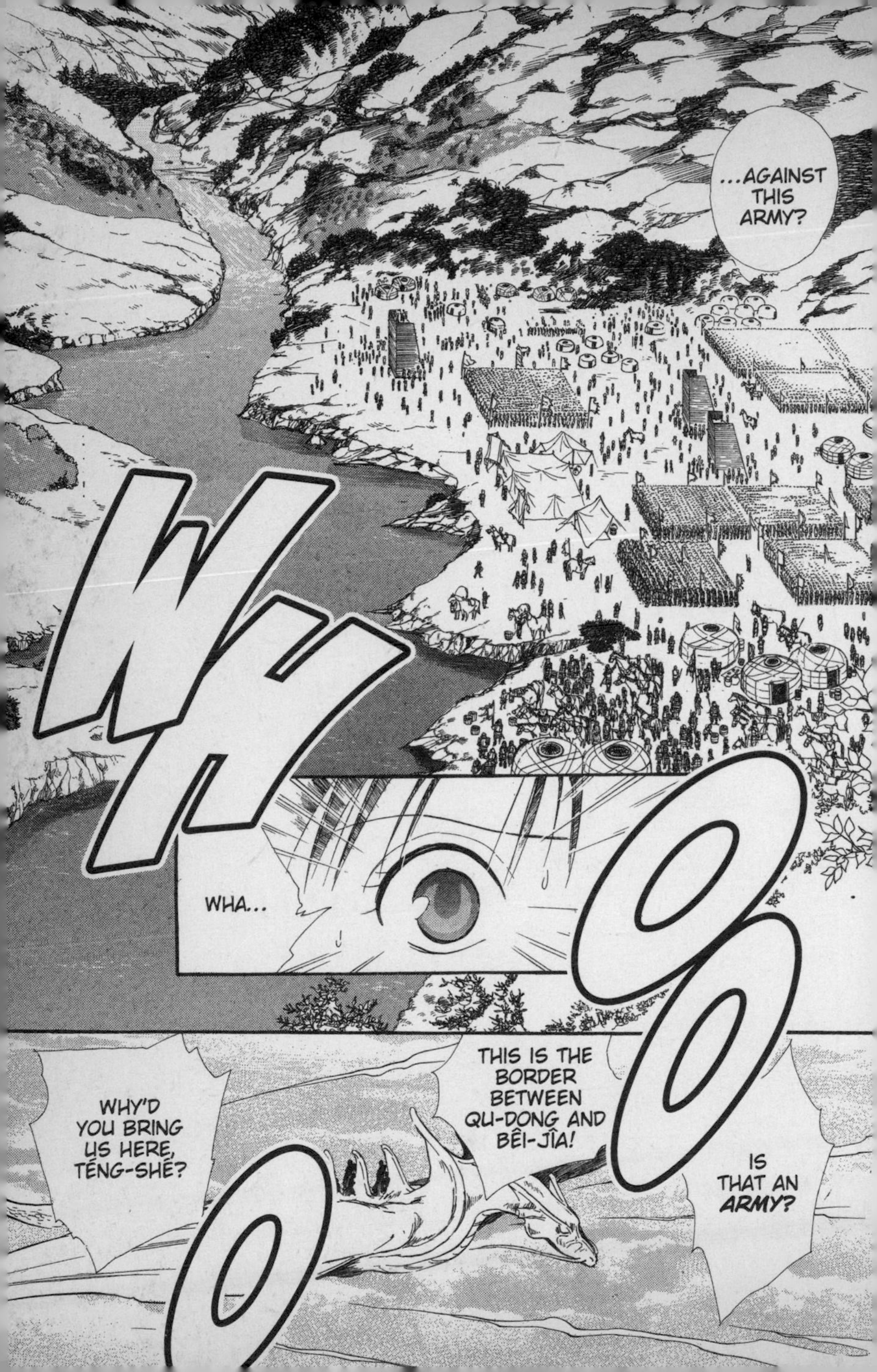
...AGAINST THIS ARMY?
WHA...
WHOOOO
IS THAT AN ARMY?
THIS IS THE BORDER BETWEEN QU-DONG AND BÊI-JÎA!
WHY'D YOU BRING US HERE, TÉNG-SHÉ?

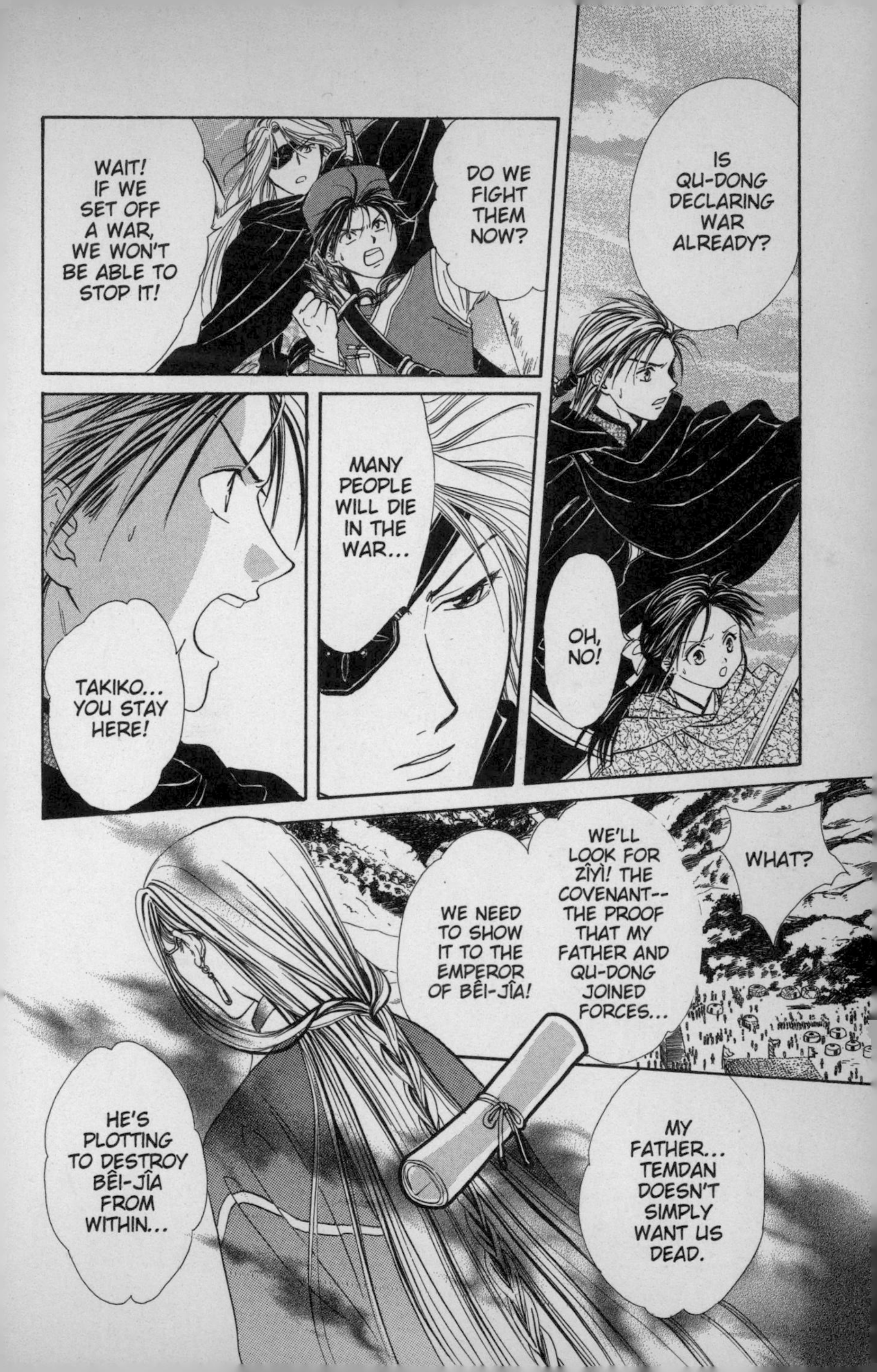
IS QU-DONG DECLARING WAR ALREADY?
OH, NO!
DO WE FIGHT THEM NOW?
WAIT! IF WE SET OFF A WAR, WE WON'T BE ABLE TO STOP IT!
MANY PEOPLE WILL DIE IN THE WAR...
TAKIKO... YOU STAY HERE!
WHAT?
WE'LL LOOK FOR ZÎYÌ! THE COVENANT-- THE PROOF THAT MY FATHER AND QU-DONG JOINED FORCES...
WE NEED TO SHOW IT TO THE EMPEROR OF BÊI-JÎA!
MY FATHER... TEMDAN DOESN'T SIMPLY WANT US DEAD.
HE'S PLOTTING TO DESTROY BÊI-JÎA FROM WITHIN...

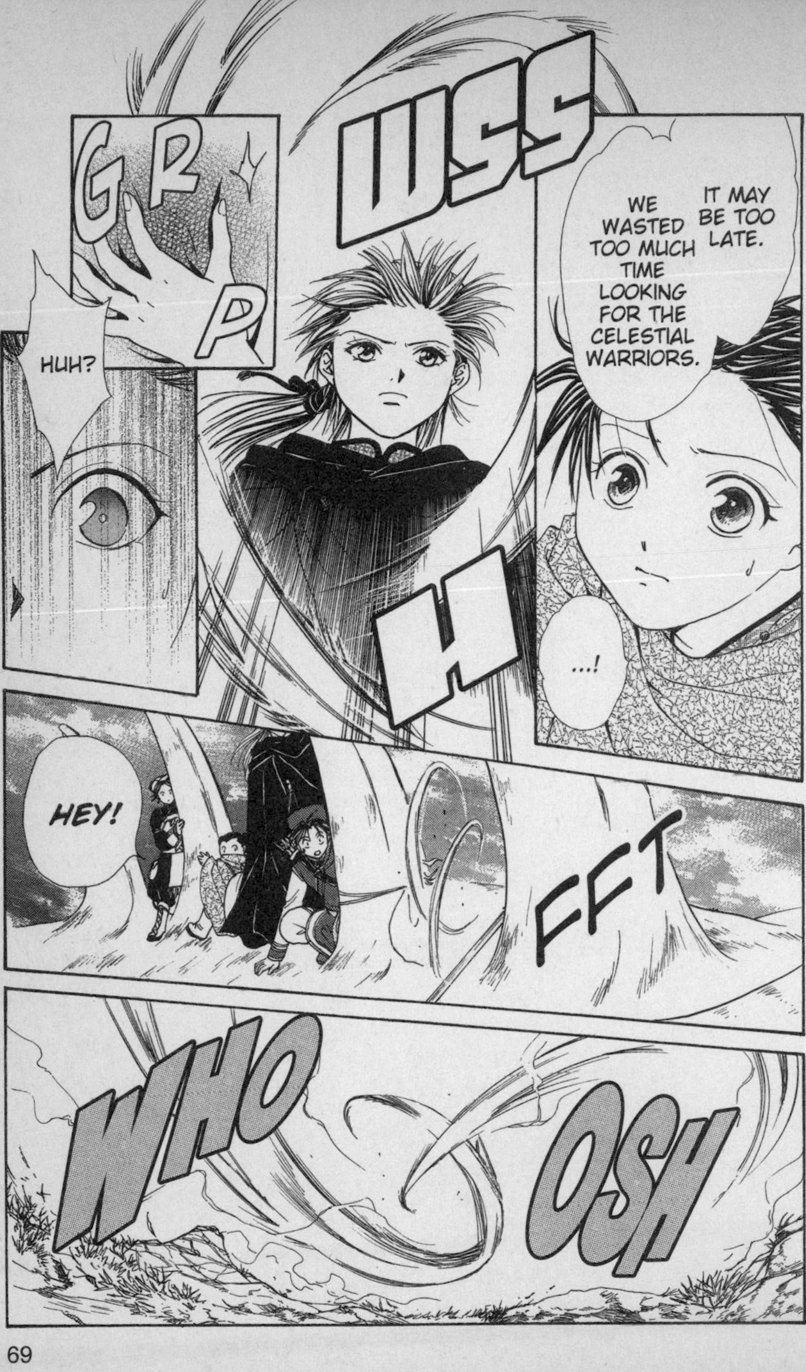
IT MAY BE TOO LATE.
WE WASTED TOO MUCH TIME LOOKING FOR THE CELESTIAL WARRIORS.
WSS
GRP
HUH?
H
...!
FFT
HEY!
WHOOSH

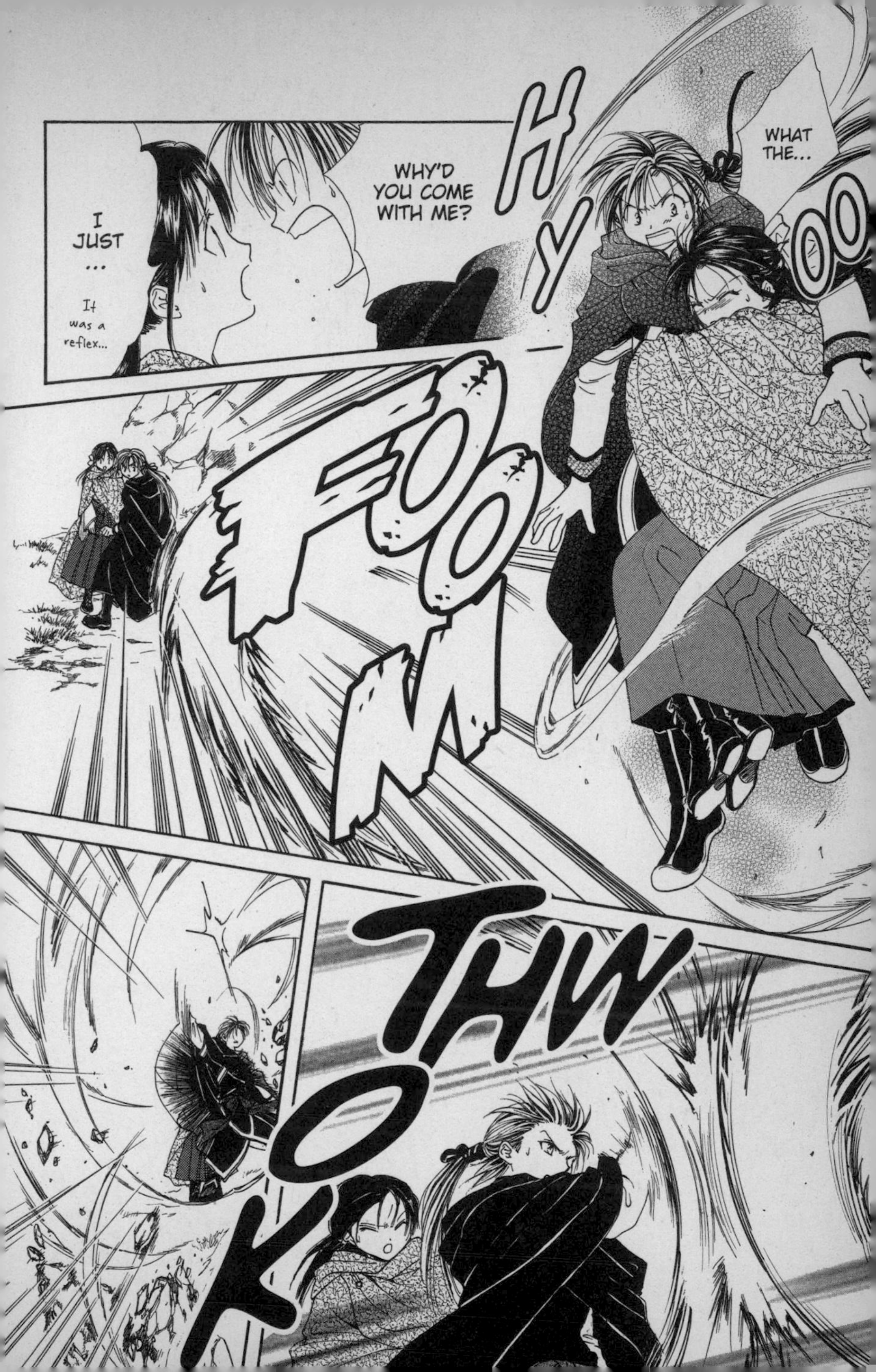
HYOO
WHAT THE...
WHY'D YOU COME WITH ME?
I JUST ...
It was a reflex...
FOOM
THWOK

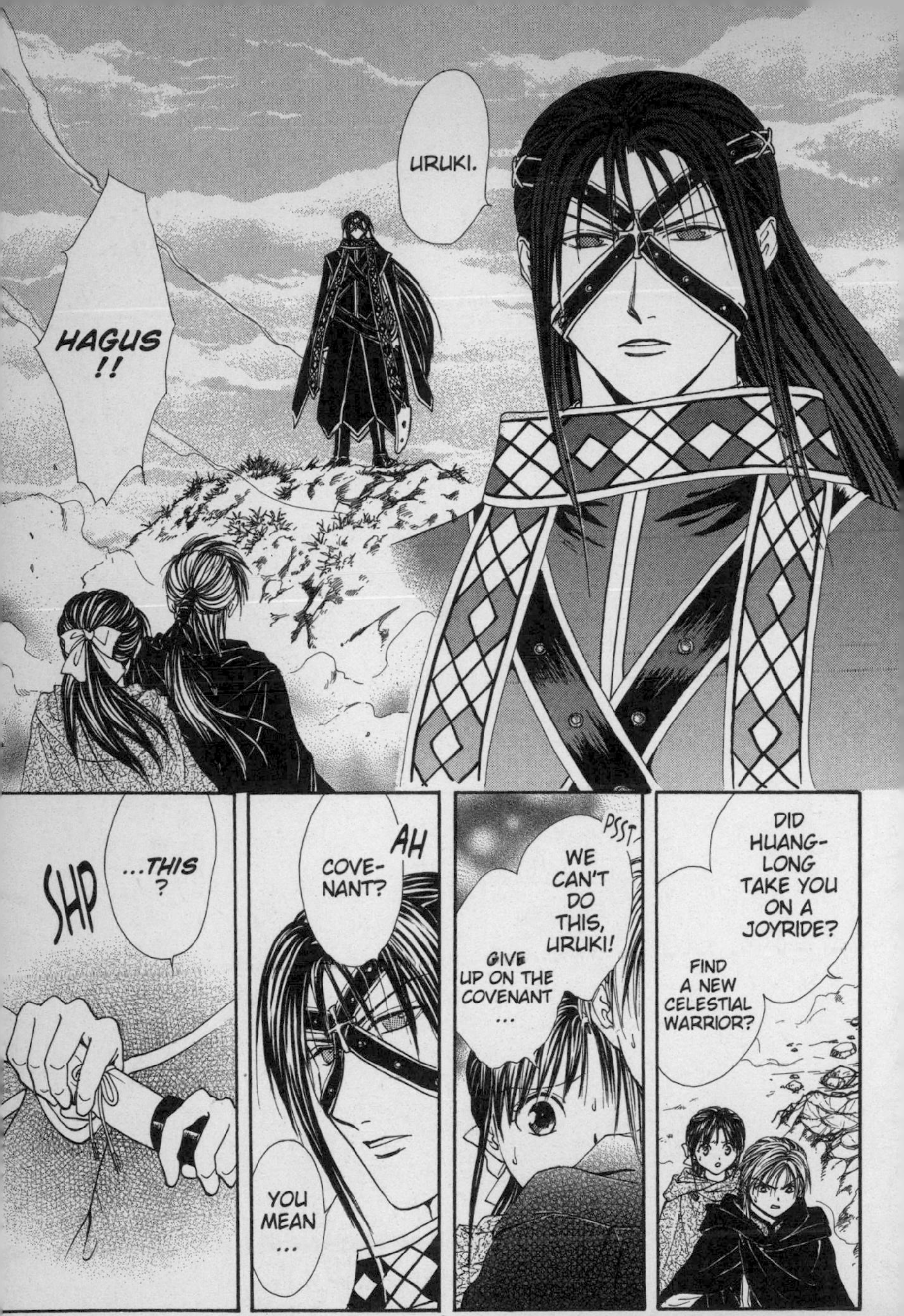
URUKI.
HAGUS !!
DID HUANG-LONG TAKE YOU ON A JOYRIDE?
FIND A NEW CELESTIAL WARRIOR?
PSST
WE CAN'T DO THIS, URUKI!
GIVE UP ON THE COVENANT ...
AH
COVE-NANT?
YOU MEAN ...
SHP
...THIS ?

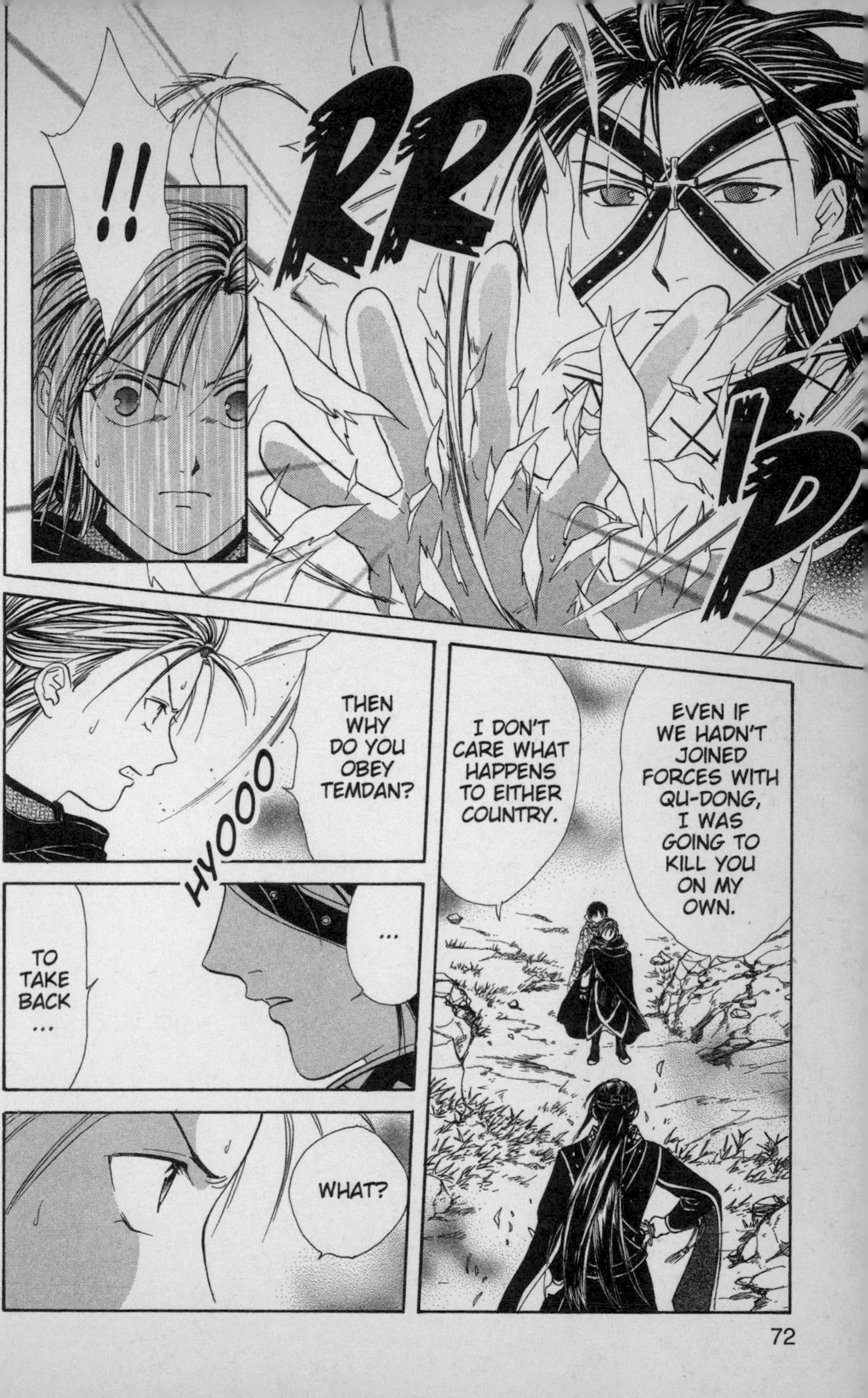
RRIP
!!
EVEN IF WE HADN'T JOINED FORCES WITH QU-DONG, I WAS GOING TO KILL YOU ON MY OWN.
I DON'T CARE WHAT HAPPENS TO EITHER COUNTRY.
THEN WHY DO YOU OBEY TEMDAN?
HYOOO
...
TO TAKE BACK ...
WHAT?

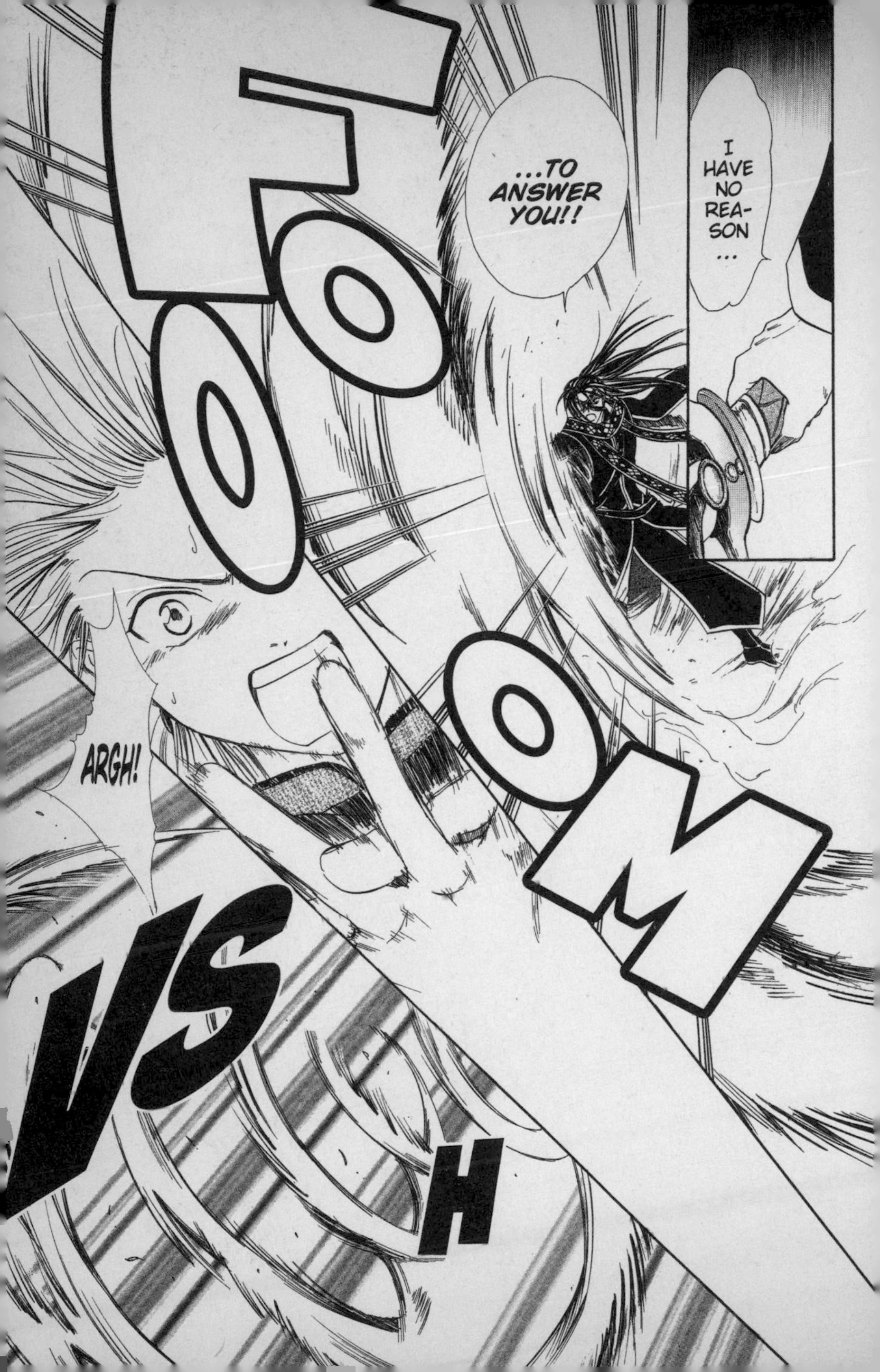
I HAVE NO REA-SON...
...TO ANSWER YOU!!
FOOOOM
ARGH!
VSH

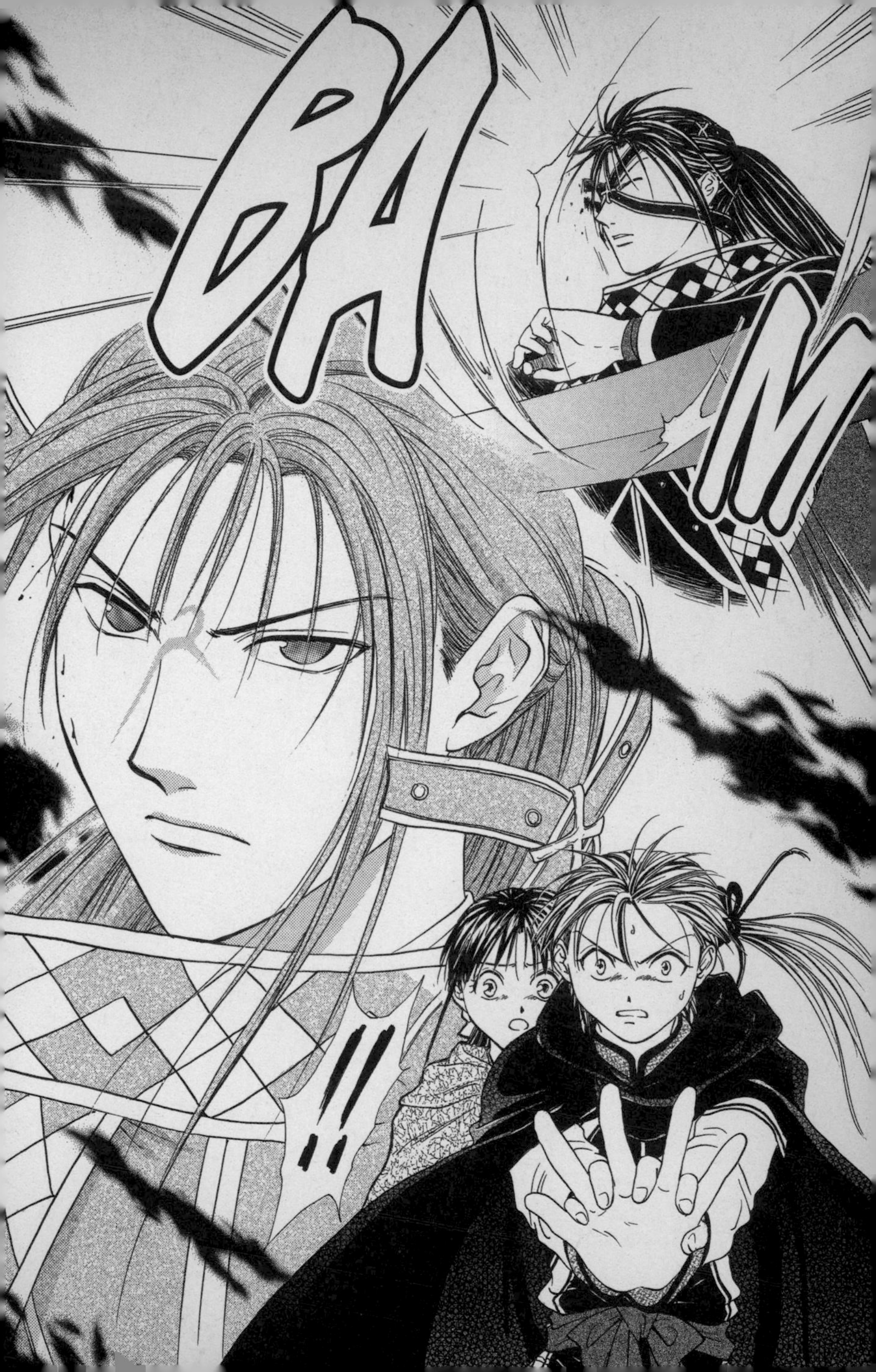
BAM
!!

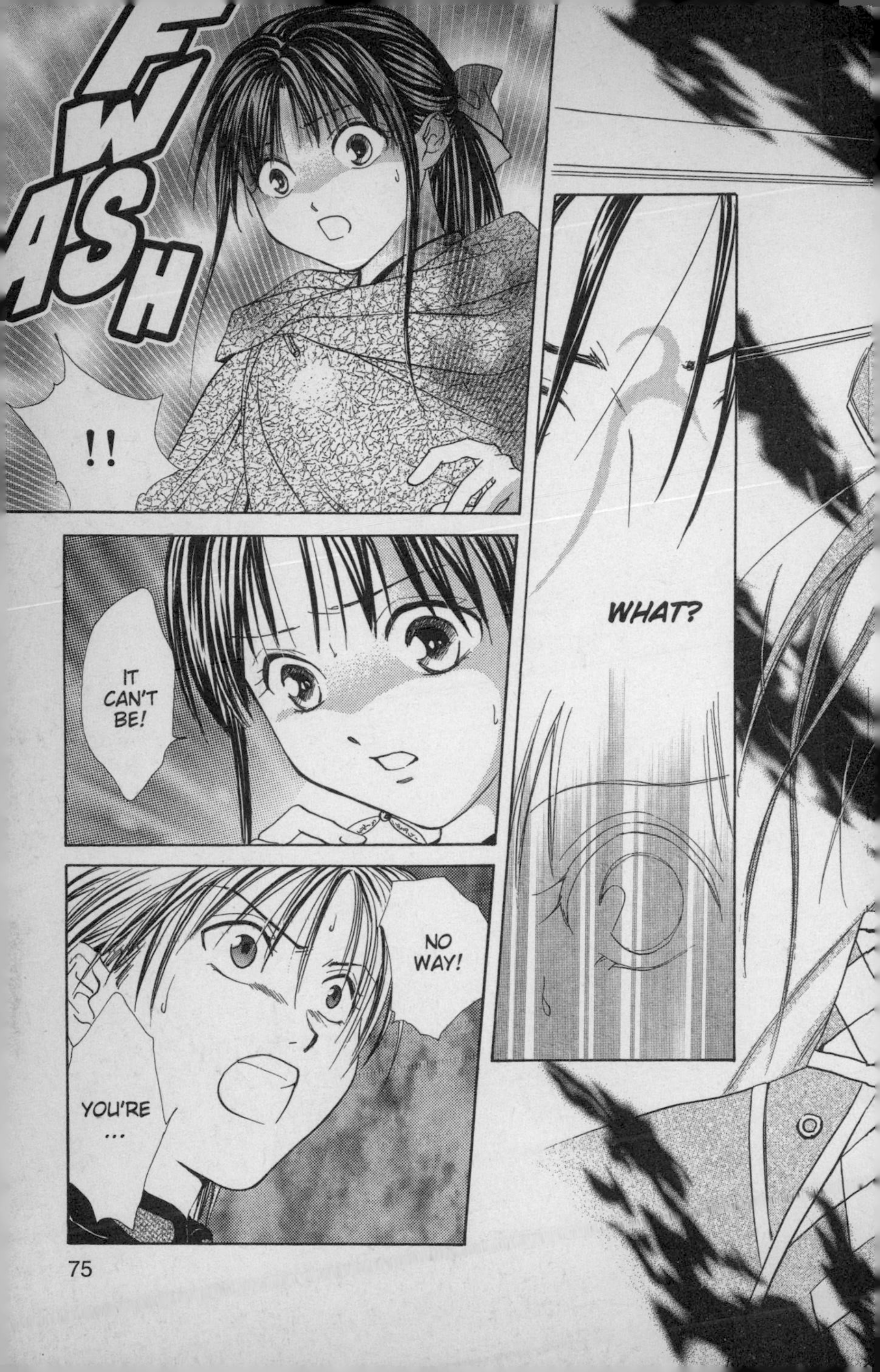
WHAT?
WASH
!!
IT CAN'T BE!
NO WAY!
YOU'RE ...

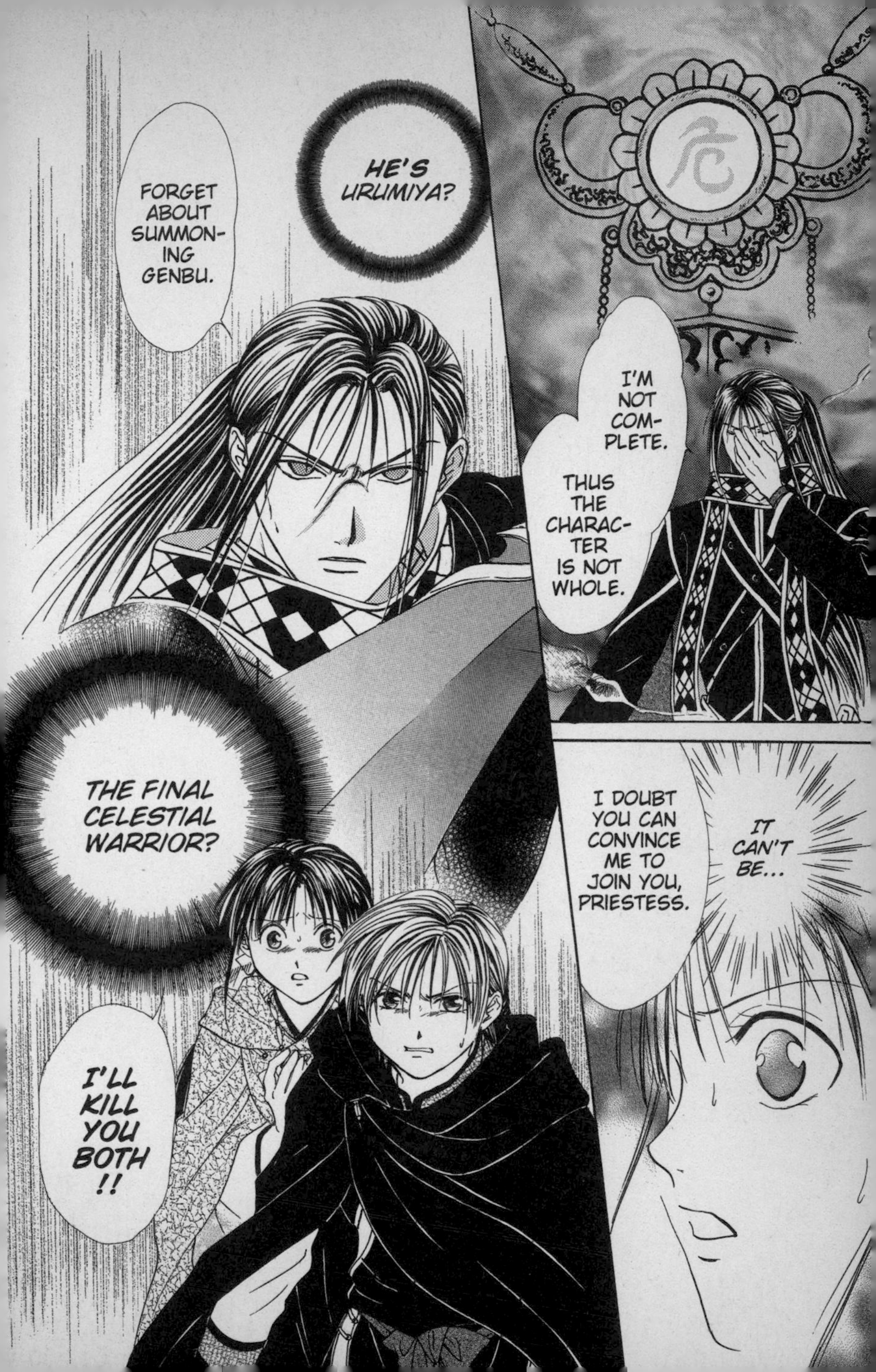
危
I'M NOT COMPLETE.
THUS THE CHARACTER IS NOT WHOLE.
I DOUBT YOU CAN CONVINCE ME TO JOIN YOU, PRIESTESS.
IT CAN'T BE...
HE'S URUMIYA?
FORGET ABOUT SUMMONING GENBU.
THE FINAL CELESTIAL WARRIOR?
I'LL KILL YOU BOTH!!

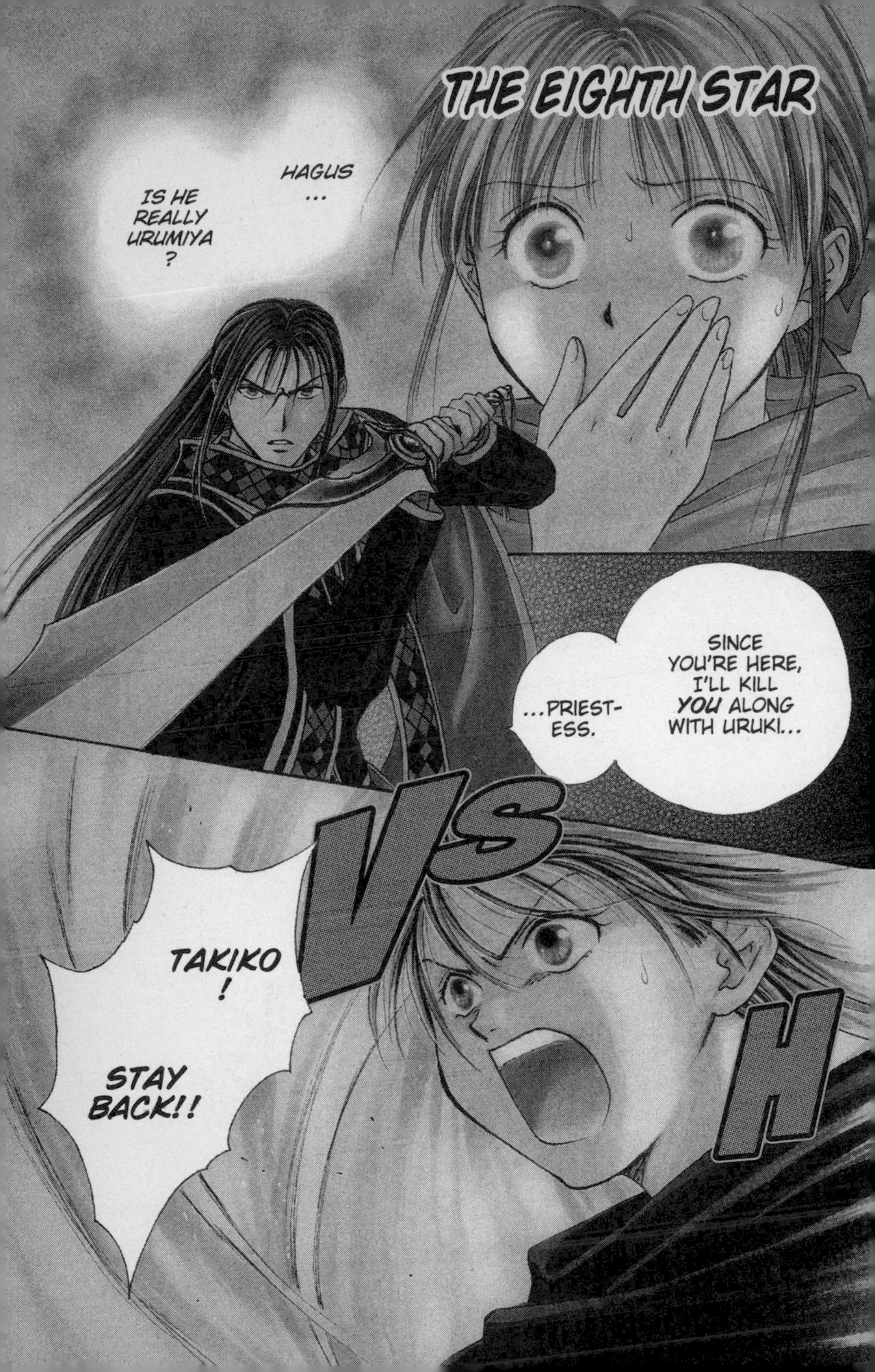
THE EIGHTH STAR
HAGUS...
IS HE REALLY URUMIYA?
SINCE YOU'RE HERE, I'LL KILL *YOU* ALONG WITH URUKI...
...PRIEST-ESS.
VS
TAKIKO!
STAY BACK!!
H

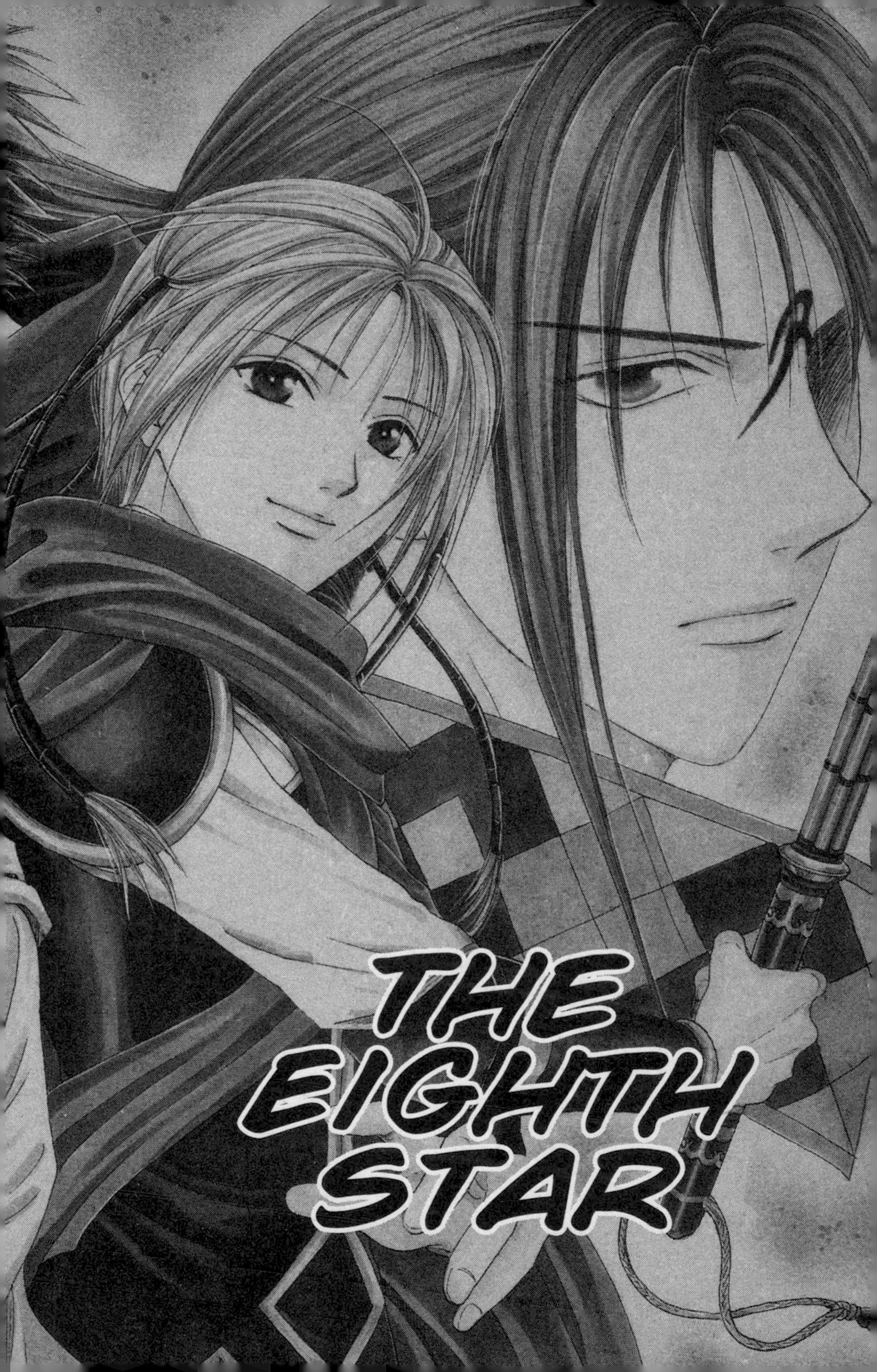
THE EIGHTH STAR

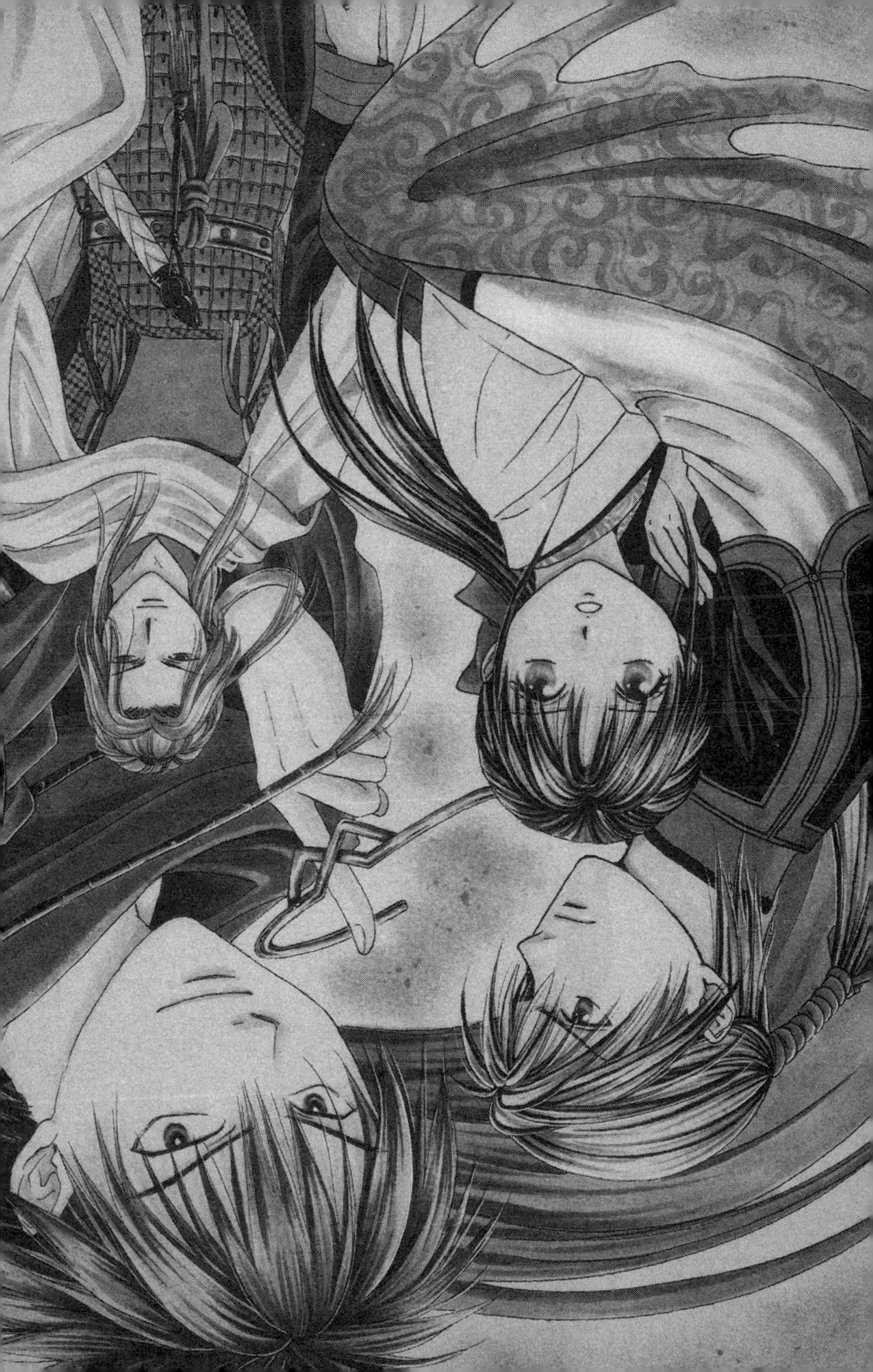

Come to think of it, there weren't any older people in the old FY either. We had to appeal to the readers of the magazine *Shojo Comic* (though I guess there were some weirdoes among the Seiryu... ○). The idea for the big pipe just came to me one day. ○ I had an image of her fighting Takiko with it. Inspiration is a major part of my storytelling process.

We already had a string of elemental abilities with wind, ice, water and rock, so I wanted a "material" ability to go with Hatsui. I considered smoke, since she had the pipe. I guess Hikitsu has the most abilities. He has water **and** ice. That's because I originally planned to make the ancestors of Hikitsu and Tomite into brothers, and I wanted them to have related abilities. He produced ice when he met Miaka in the first FY. He has that power in his eye, too!

I always wanted to do the scene where Takiko gets frozen! Because they'd seen this, Tomite and Hikitsu did the same thing when Miaka came along 200 years later, and told her to be a Priestess and tough it out. I was happy that some of my old readers realized my intent. ⌒⌒

So...I was working on Inami's storyline when I started to get ill, ○ so I wasn't thinking very well. It turned out kind of goofy...And the art was awful (in my opinion ○).
Volume 6 is back to normal (but hopefully this kind of thing isn't noticeable to the readers ○).
I was seeing quintuple while I worked.

↰ From fatigue. ○

The rough sketches were all blurry, and I was inking them mostly by instinct. It was such a mess. ○

The seventh Celestial Warrior, Urumiya, finally shows up in the second half of this volume! Well, I'm sure some people had figured it out already. ⌒⌒○
I mean, he has powers...
He's totally hostile, so we'll see what happens. Takiko, you have a long way to go before you get to summon Genbu...(And I've got a long way to go before my work ends!) I considered dragging out Hagus's story and the mystery of the eight Celestial Warriors a bit longer, but in the end I brought it forward as a challenge for Takiko. It was fun drawing the twins. :) So this is the turning point for *Genbu*-- the real crux of the story. I've really got my work cut out for me (already⌒○). I'll put my heart and soul into bringing this story to my readers.

I'm sure the people who read the magazine know by now that my new work, *Sakura Gari*, will be serialized in a (new!) special edition of the magazine *Flowers*. (It's due out in May or June...But I haven't finished it yet... ○) I hope you'll check it out (though it's not recommended for kids under 15 ○). I'll be putting out titles besides FY this year, so I hope you can see many sides of me!! Thanks for your support! ♪ And I'll put news up on my official website! Thanks to my friends' help, I finally made one. (Actually, it's still under construction.○)
"Wa no Hana" [My Flower]
http://www.y-watase.com
My blog is updated semi-periodically... I promise to put up new art sometime! ○ ↑
See you in the next volume!
Around August...

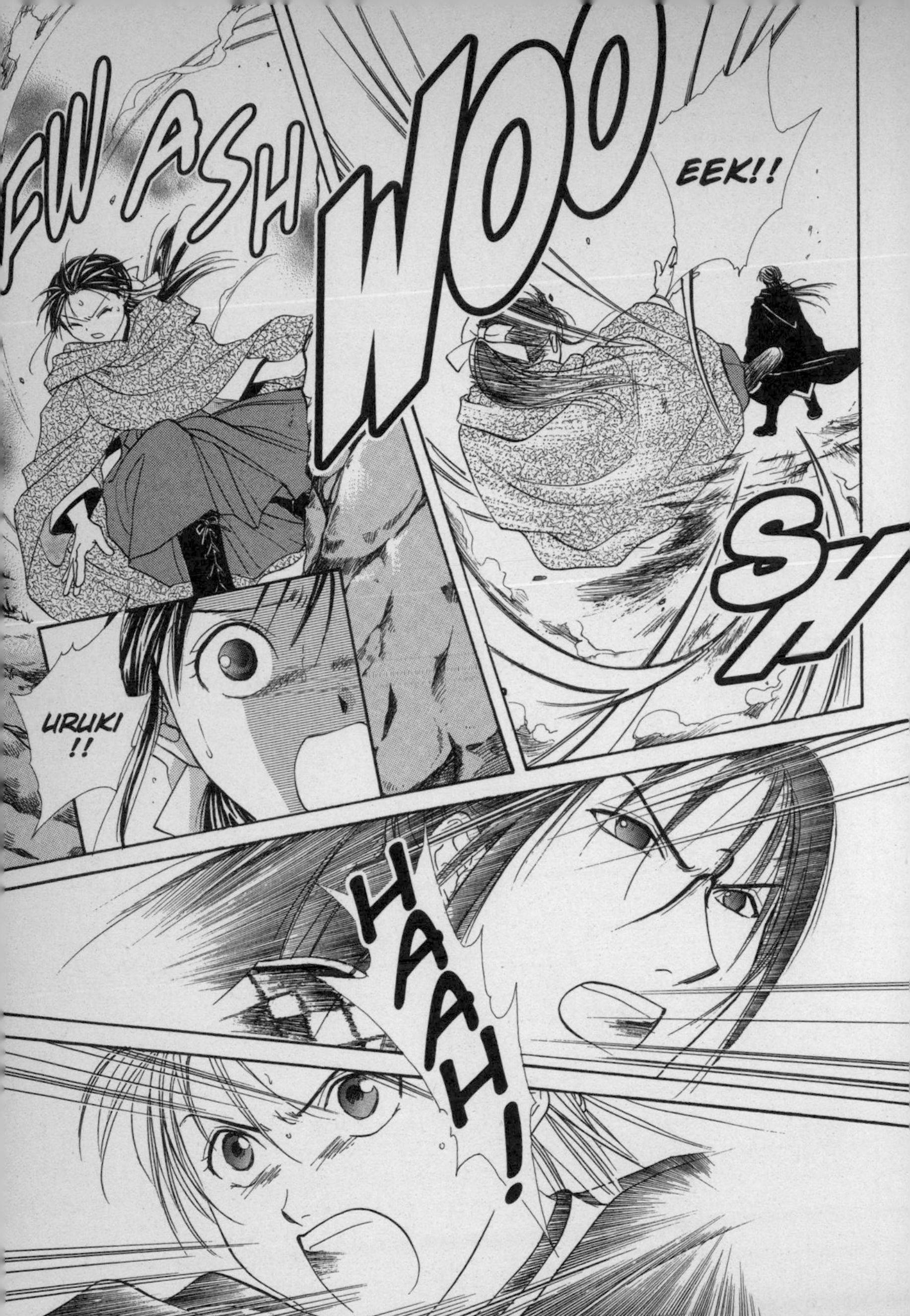
EEK!!
WOO
FWASH
SH
URUKI !!
HAAAH!

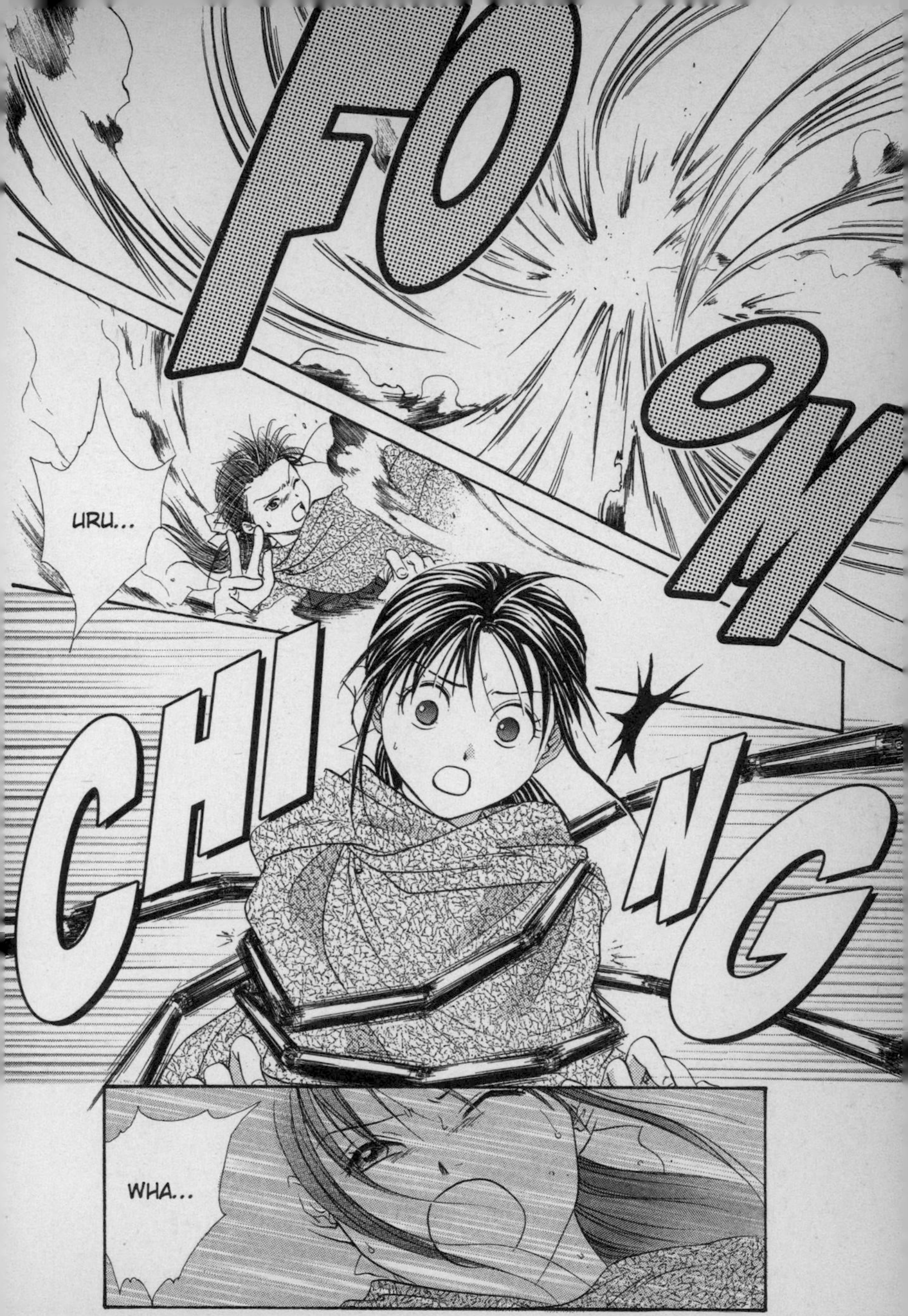
FOOM
URU...
CHING
WHA...

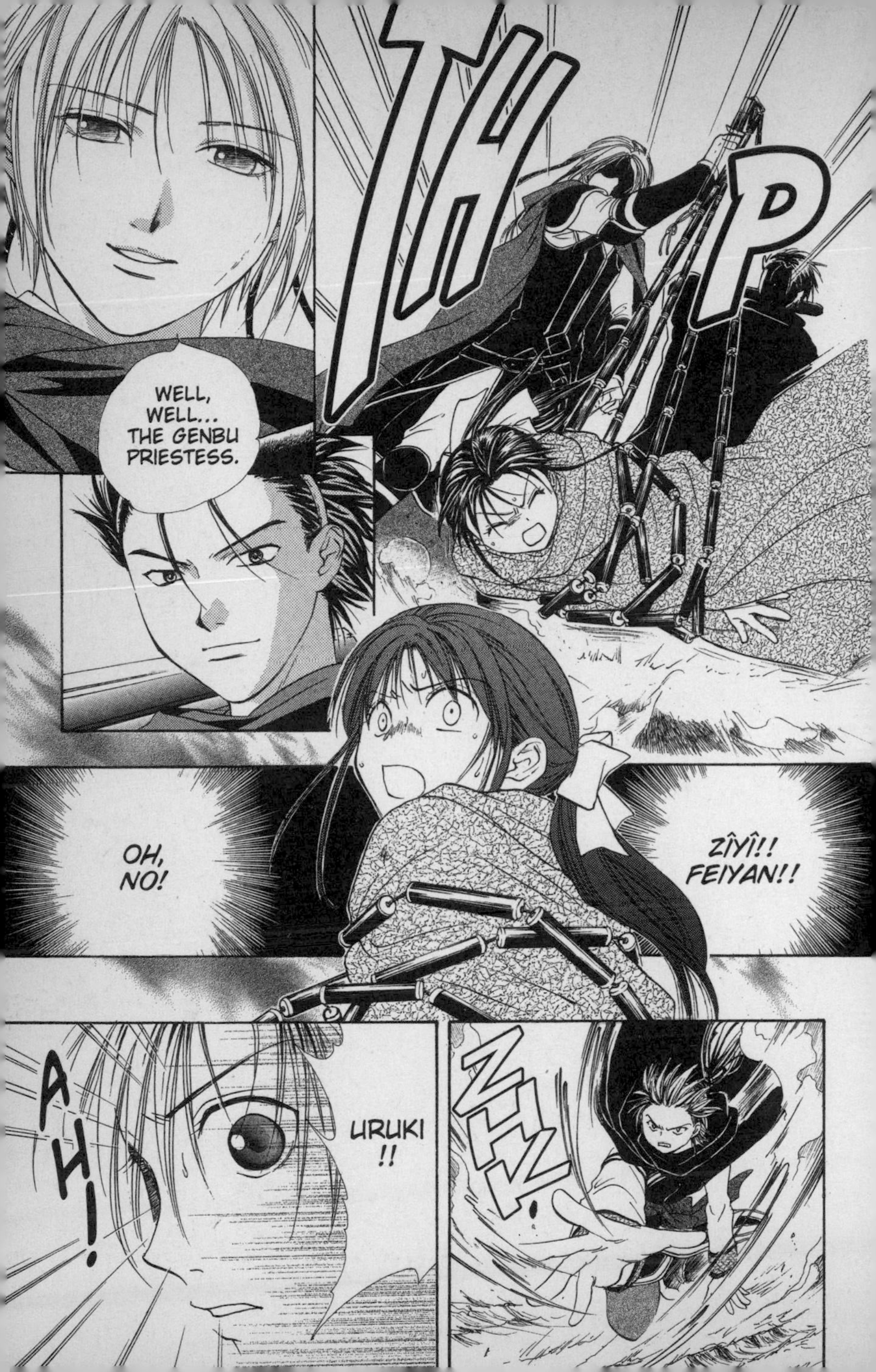
THP
WELL, WELL... THE GENBU PRIESTESS.
ZÎYÎ!! FEIYAN!!
OH, NO!
ZNNN!
URUKI !!
AH!

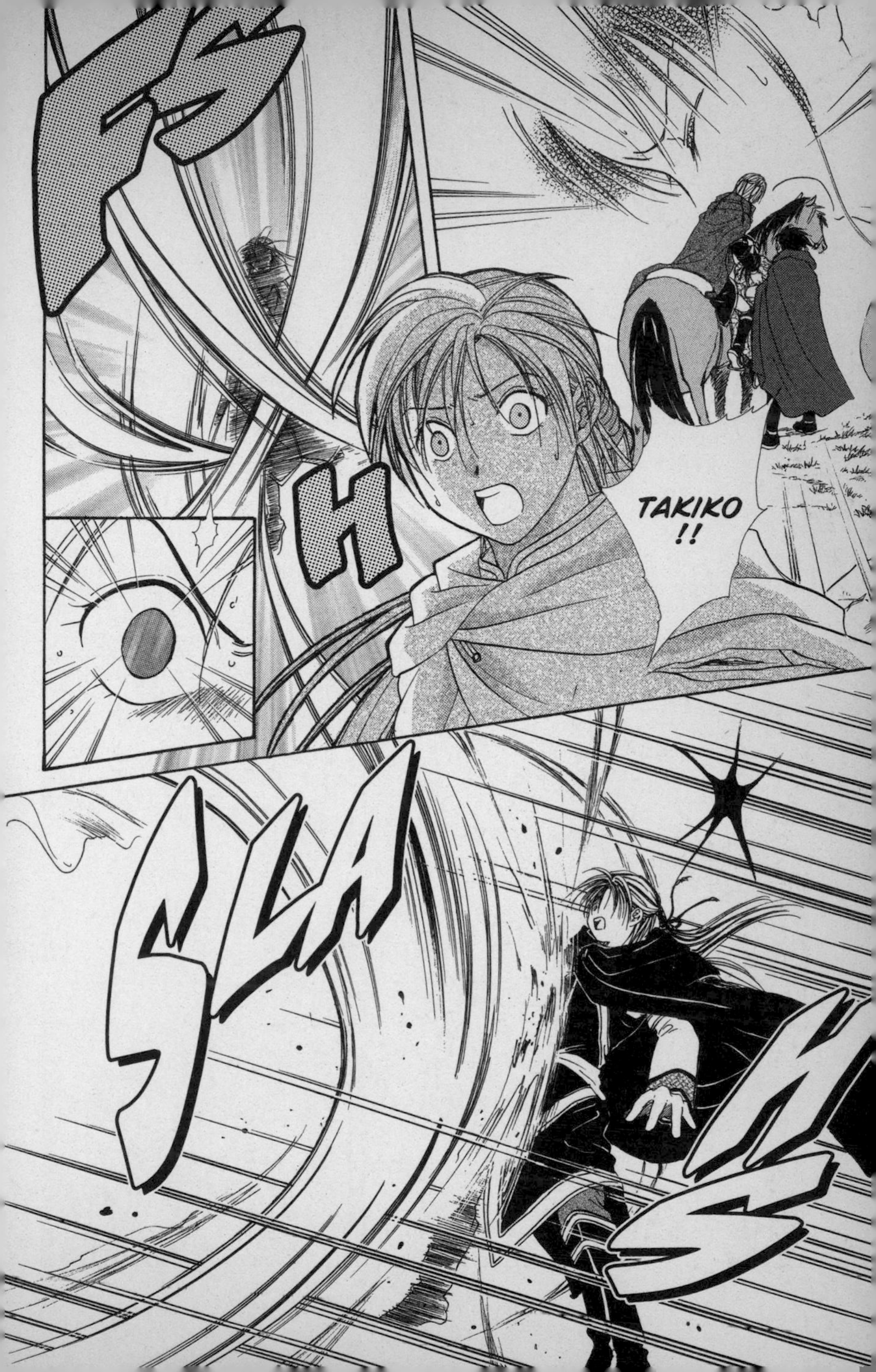
TAKIKO !!
H
SLA

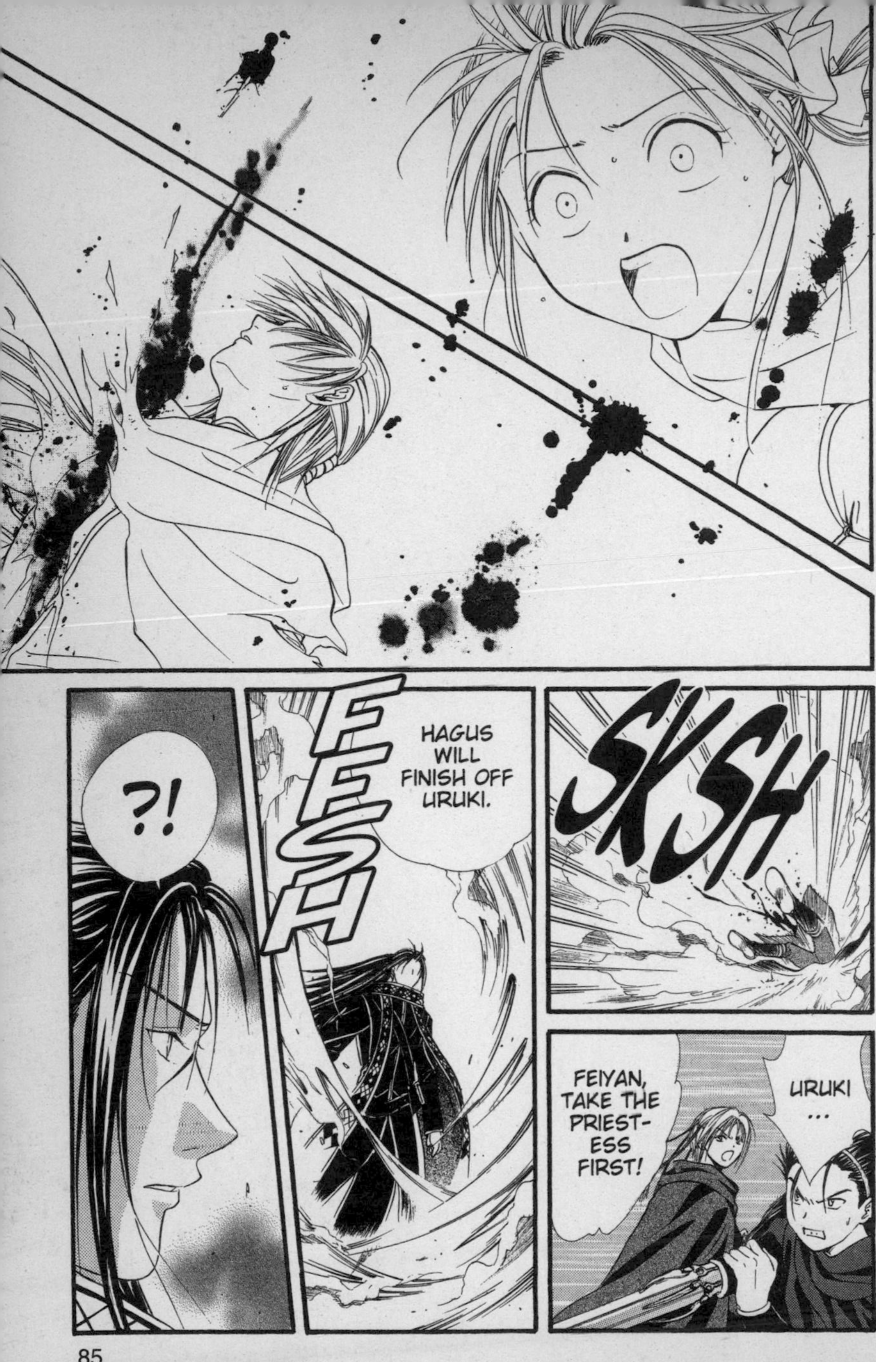
SKSH
URUKI
...
FEIYAN, TAKE THE PRIEST-ESS FIRST!
FESH
HAGUS WILL FINISH OFF URUKI.
?!

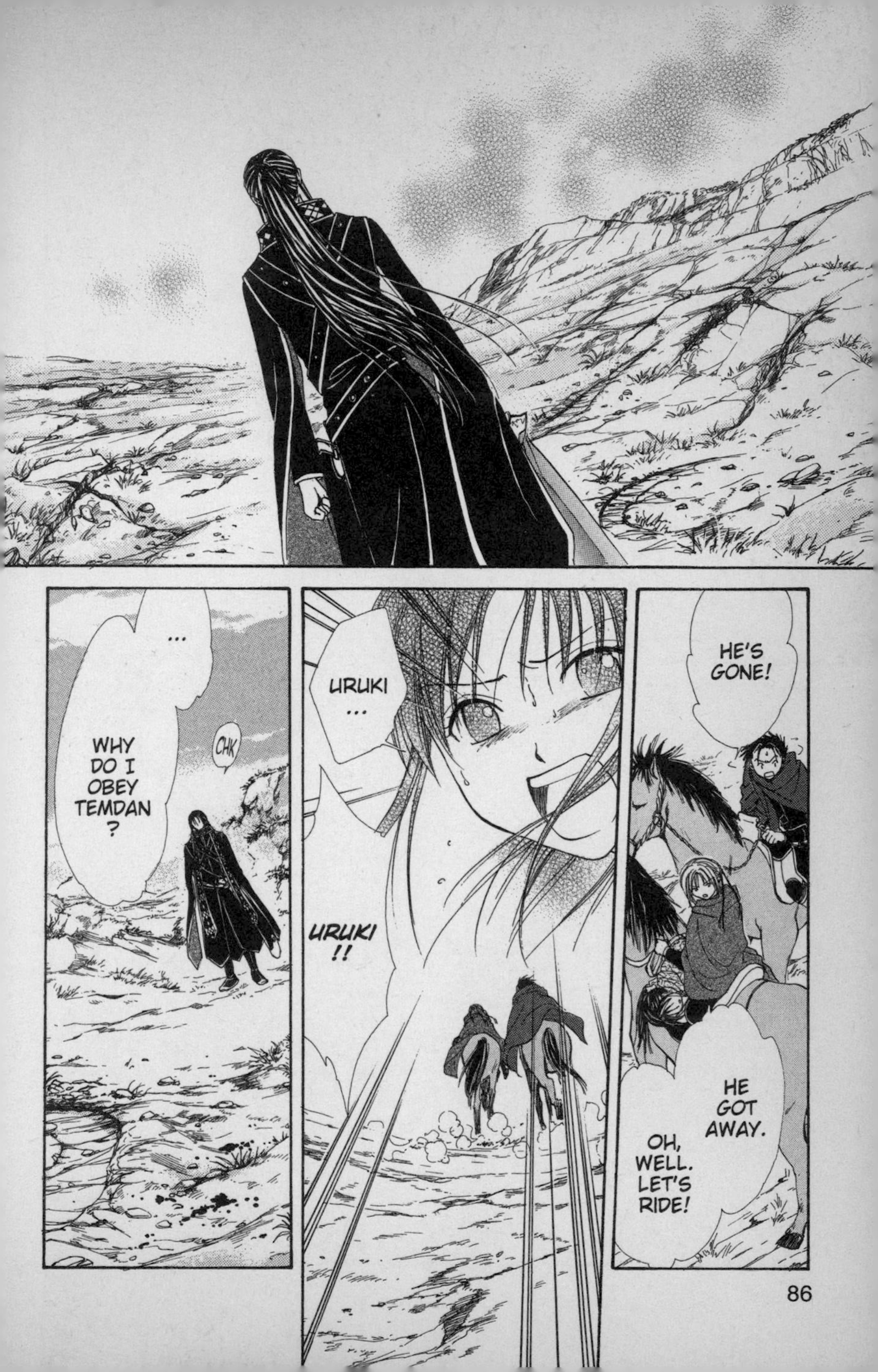
HE'S GONE!
HE GOT AWAY.
OH, WELL. LET'S RIDE!
URUKI...
URUKI!!
...
CHK
WHY DO I OBEY TEMDAN?

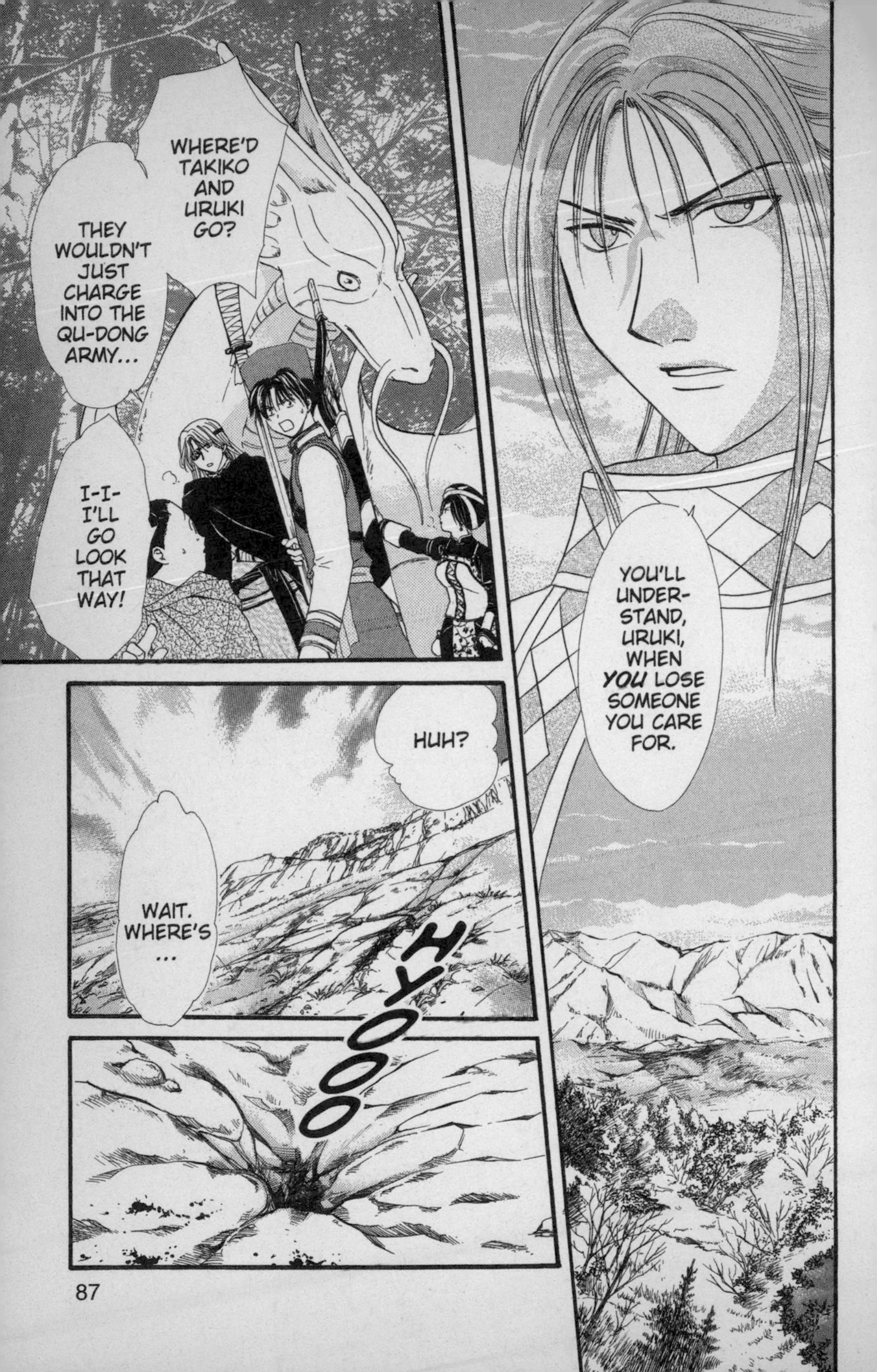
YOU'LL UNDER-STAND, URUKI, WHEN *YOU* LOSE SOMEONE YOU CARE FOR.
WHERE'D TAKIKO AND URUKI GO?
THEY WOULDN'T JUST CHARGE INTO THE QU-DONG ARMY...
I-I-I'LL GO LOOK THAT WAY!
HUH?
WAIT. WHERE'S ...
HYOOOO

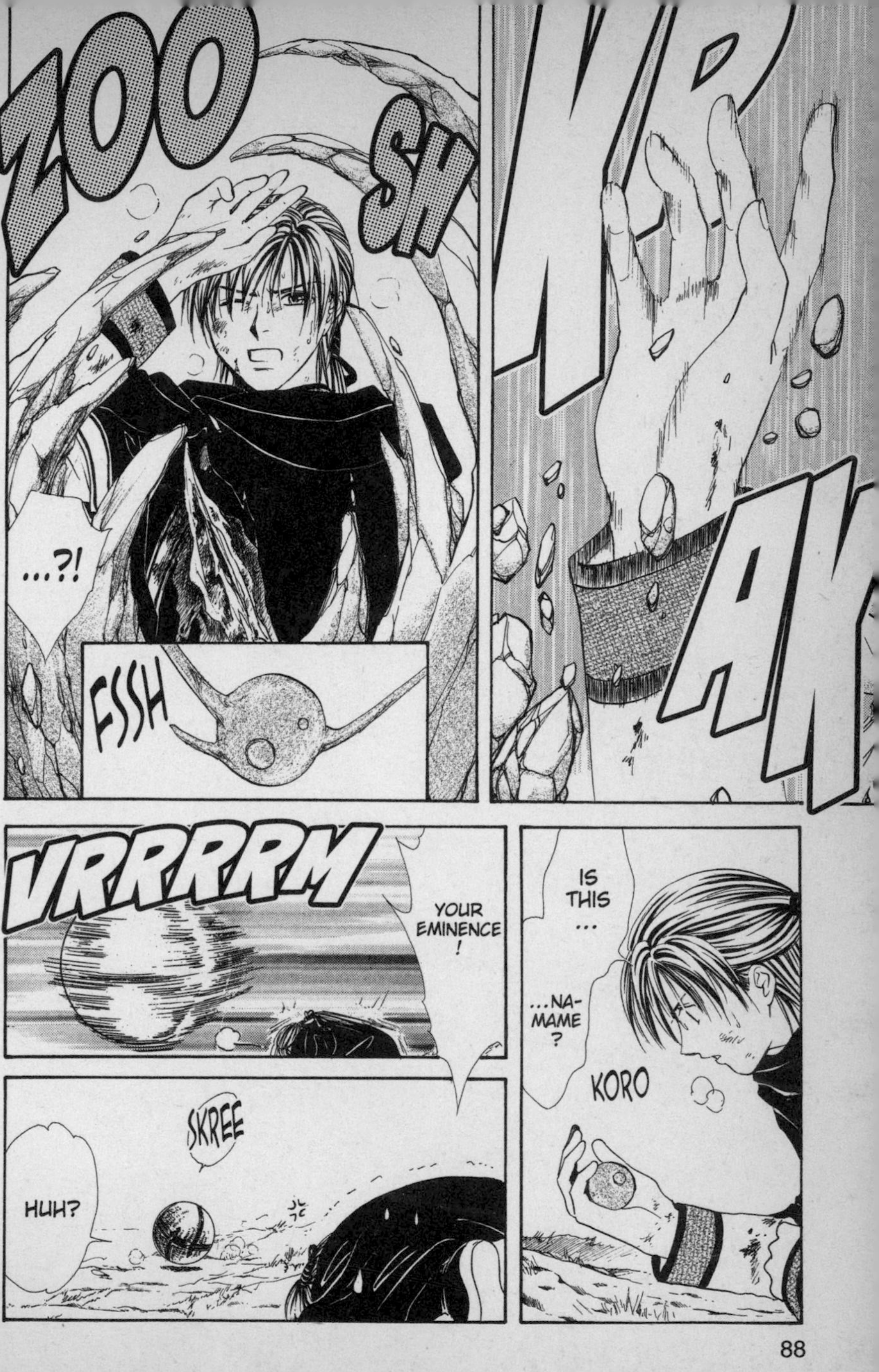
ZOOSH
...?!
FSSH
IS THIS ...
...NA-MAME ?
KORO
VRRRRM
YOUR EMINENCE !
SKREE
HUH?

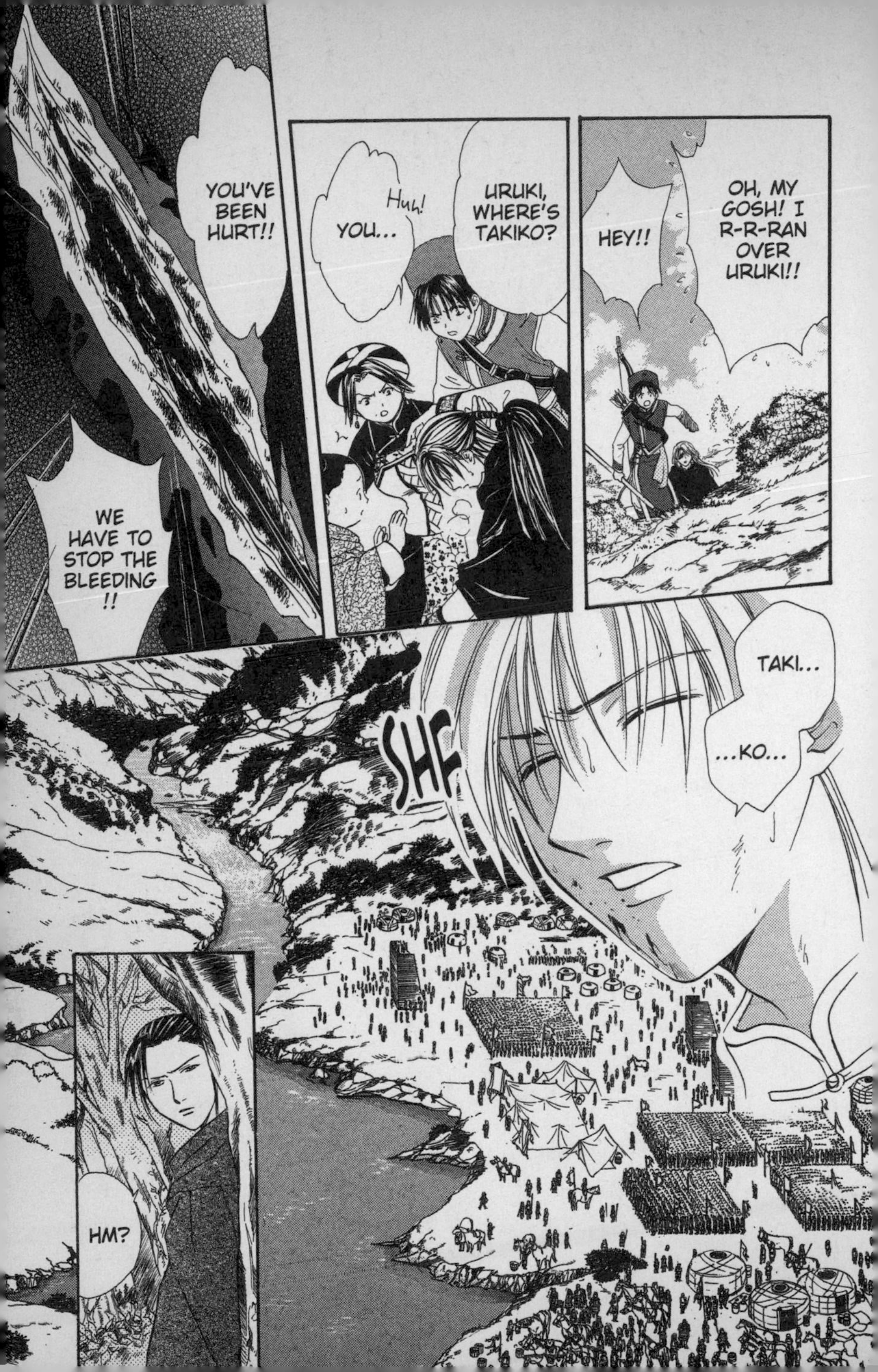
OH, MY GOSH! I R-R-RAN OVER URUKI!!
HEY!!
URUKI, WHERE'S TAKIKO?
Huh!
YOU...
YOU'VE BEEN HURT!!
WE HAVE TO STOP THE BLEEDING!!
TAKI...
...KO...
SHF
HM?

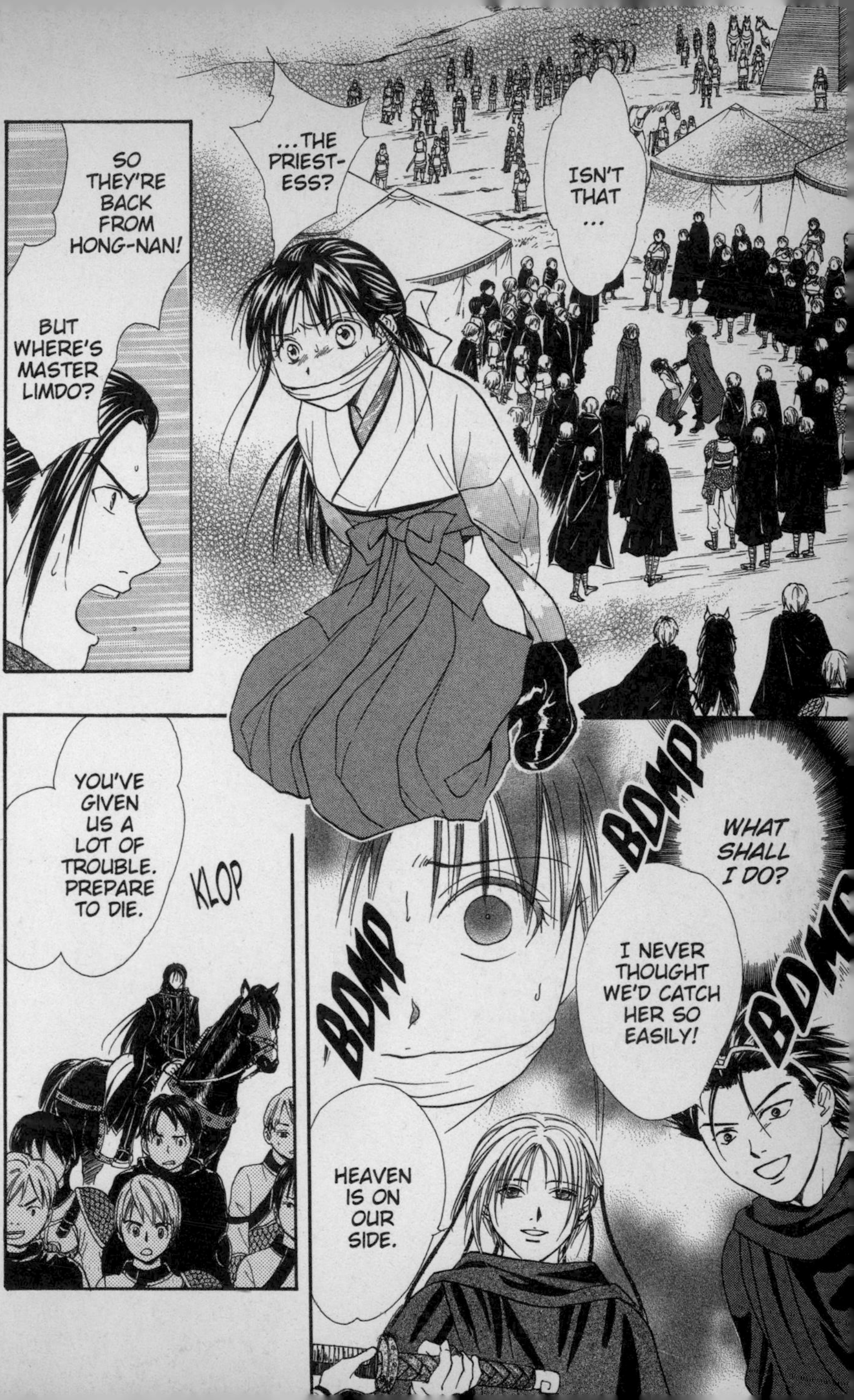
ISN'T THAT ...
...THE PRIEST-ESS?
SO THEY'RE BACK FROM HONG-NAN!
BUT WHERE'S MASTER LIMDO?
BDMP
BDMP
WHAT SHALL I DO?
BDMP
I NEVER THOUGHT WE'D CATCH HER SO EASILY!
HEAVEN IS ON OUR SIDE.
YOU'VE GIVEN US A LOT OF TROUBLE. PREPARE TO DIE.
KLOP

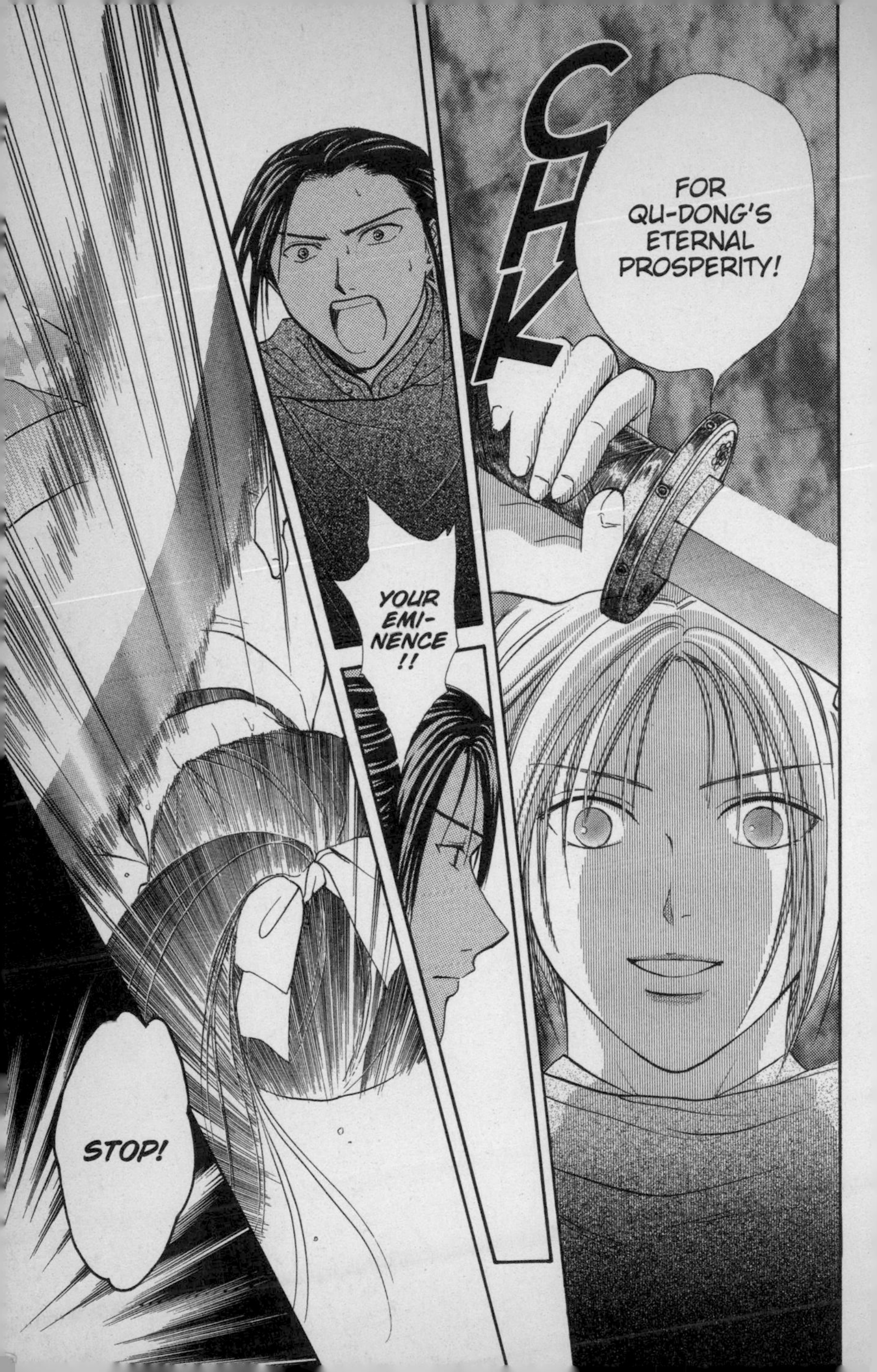
CHK
FOR QU-DONG'S ETERNAL PROSPERITY!
YOUR EMI-NENCE!!
STOP!

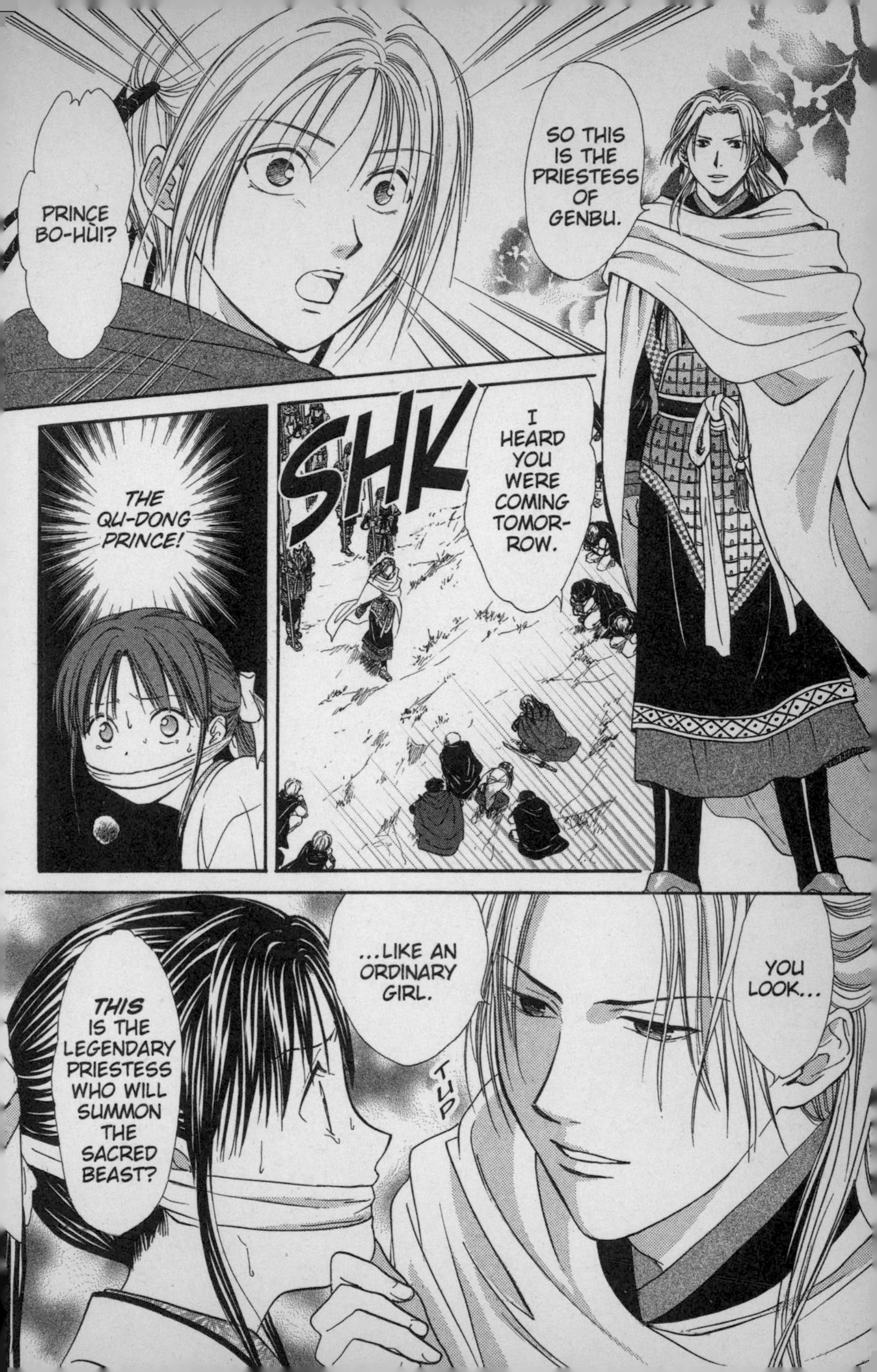
SO THIS IS THE PRIESTESS OF GENBU.
PRINCE BO-HUI?
I HEARD YOU WERE COMING TOMORROW.
SHK
THE QU-DONG PRINCE!
YOU LOOK...
...LIKE AN ORDINARY GIRL.
TUP
THIS IS THE LEGENDARY PRIESTESS WHO WILL SUMMON THE SACRED BEAST?

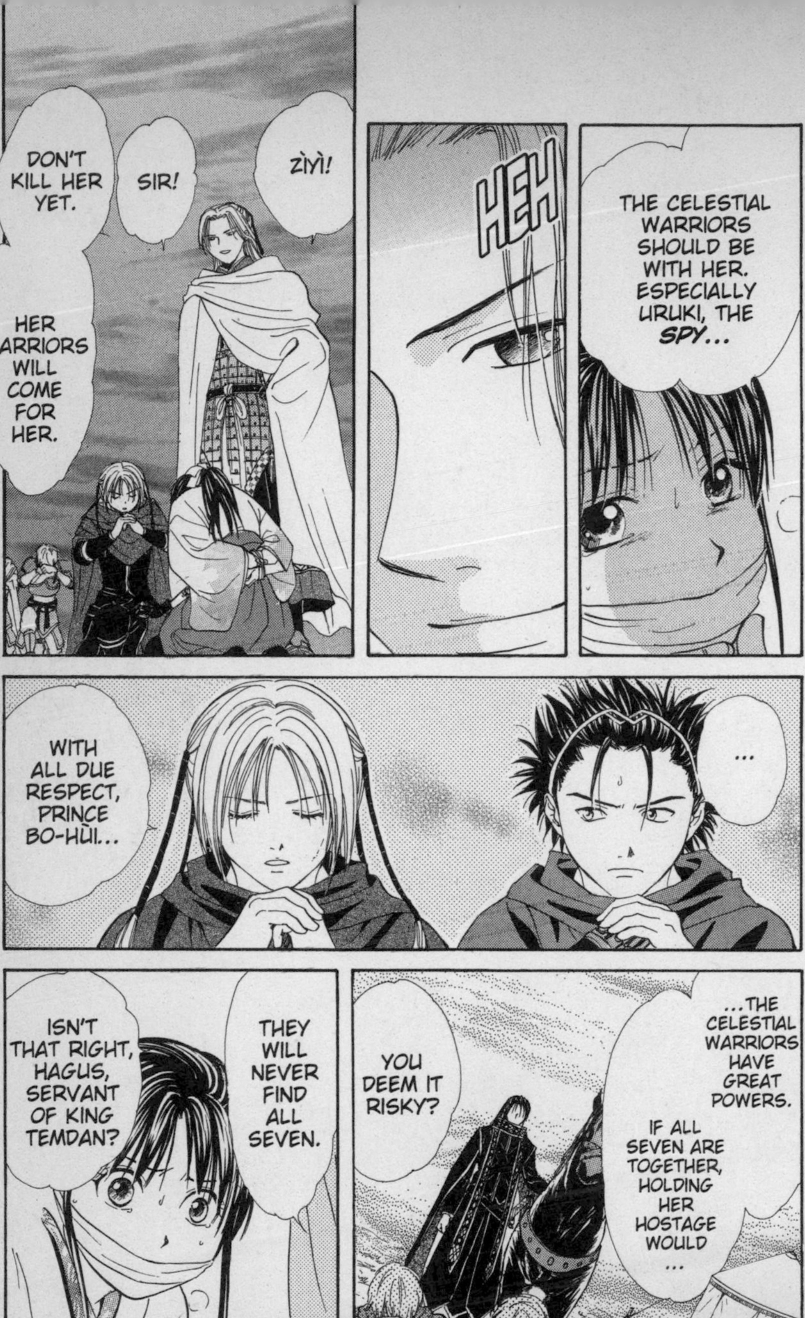
THE CELESTIAL WARRIORS SHOULD BE WITH HER. ESPECIALLY URUKI, THE SPY...
HEH
ZÌYÌ!
SIR!
DON'T KILL HER YET.
HER WARRIORS WILL COME FOR HER.
...
WITH ALL DUE RESPECT, PRINCE BO-HÙI...
...THE CELESTIAL WARRIORS HAVE GREAT POWERS.
IF ALL SEVEN ARE TOGETHER, HOLDING HER HOSTAGE WOULD ...
YOU DEEM IT RISKY?
THEY WILL NEVER FIND ALL SEVEN.
ISN'T THAT RIGHT, HAGUS, SERVANT OF KING TEMDAN?

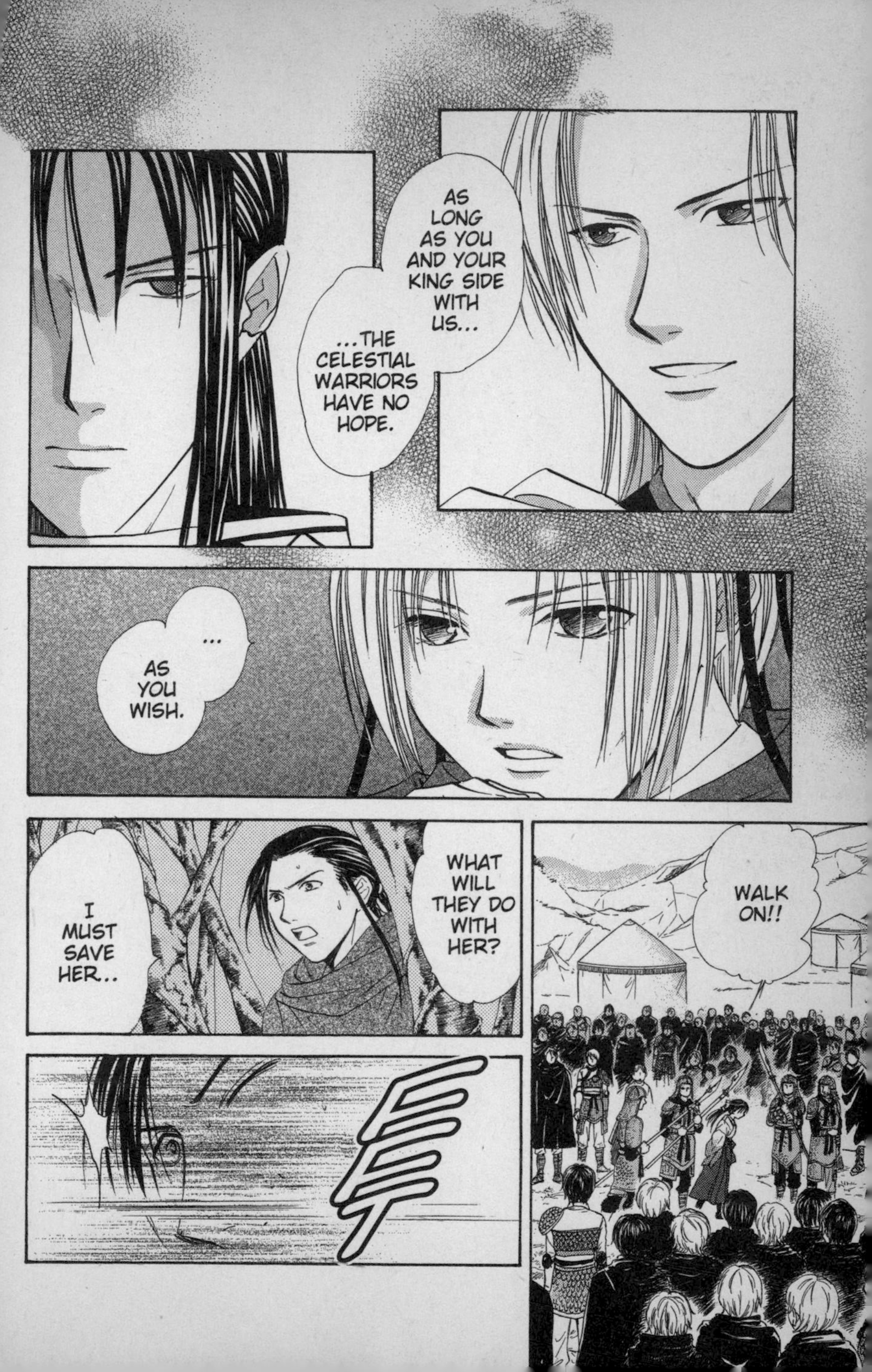
AS LONG AS YOU AND YOUR KING SIDE WITH US...
...THE CELESTIAL WARRIORS HAVE NO HOPE.
... AS YOU WISH.
WALK ON!!
WHAT WILL THEY DO WITH HER?
I MUST SAVE HER...

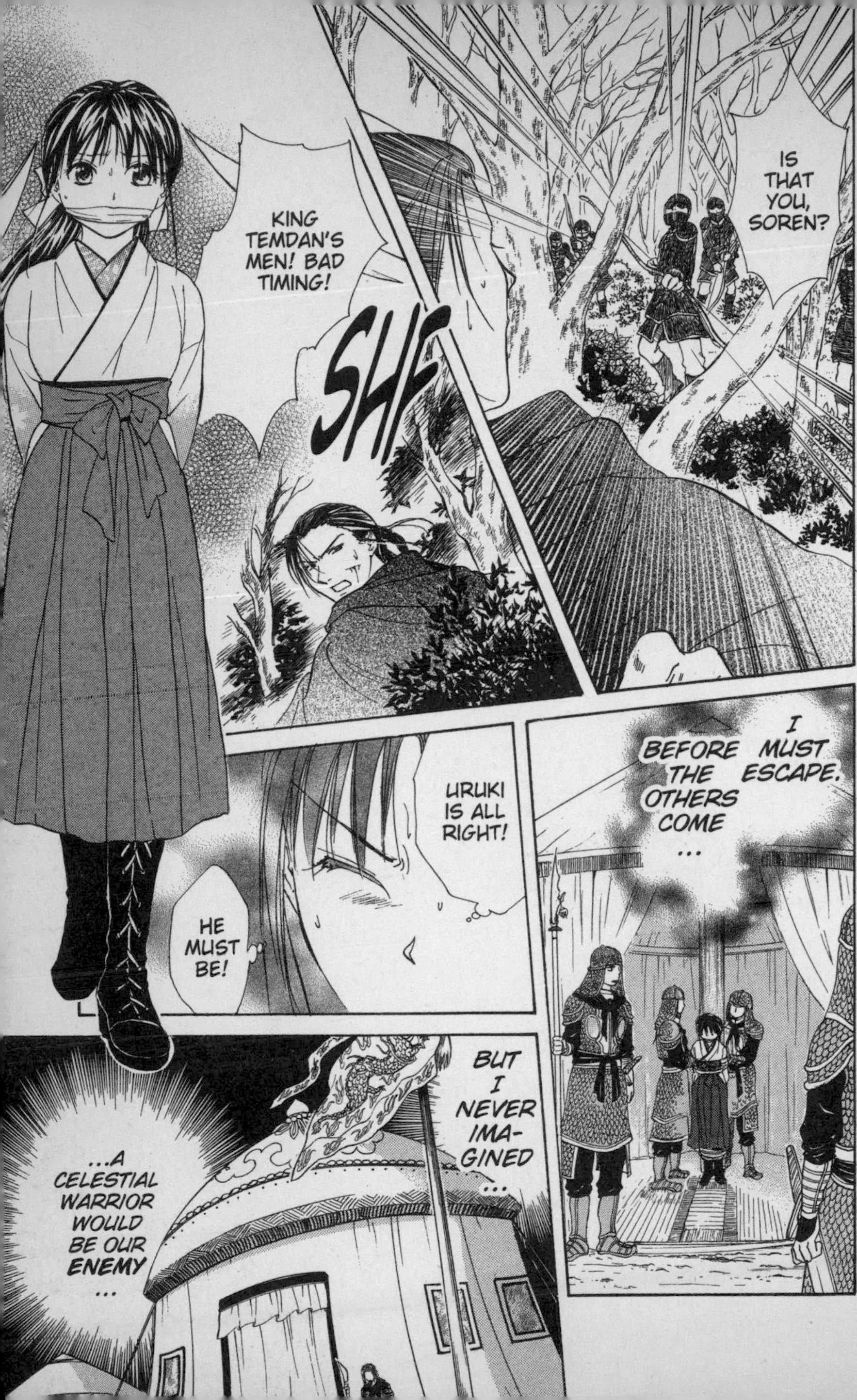
IS THAT YOU, SOREN?
SHF
KING TEMDAN'S MEN! BAD TIMING!
I MUST ESCAPE.
BEFORE THE OTHERS COME ...
URUKI IS ALL RIGHT!
HE MUST BE!
BUT I NEVER IMA-GINED ...
...A CELESTIAL WARRIOR WOULD BE OUR ENEMY ...

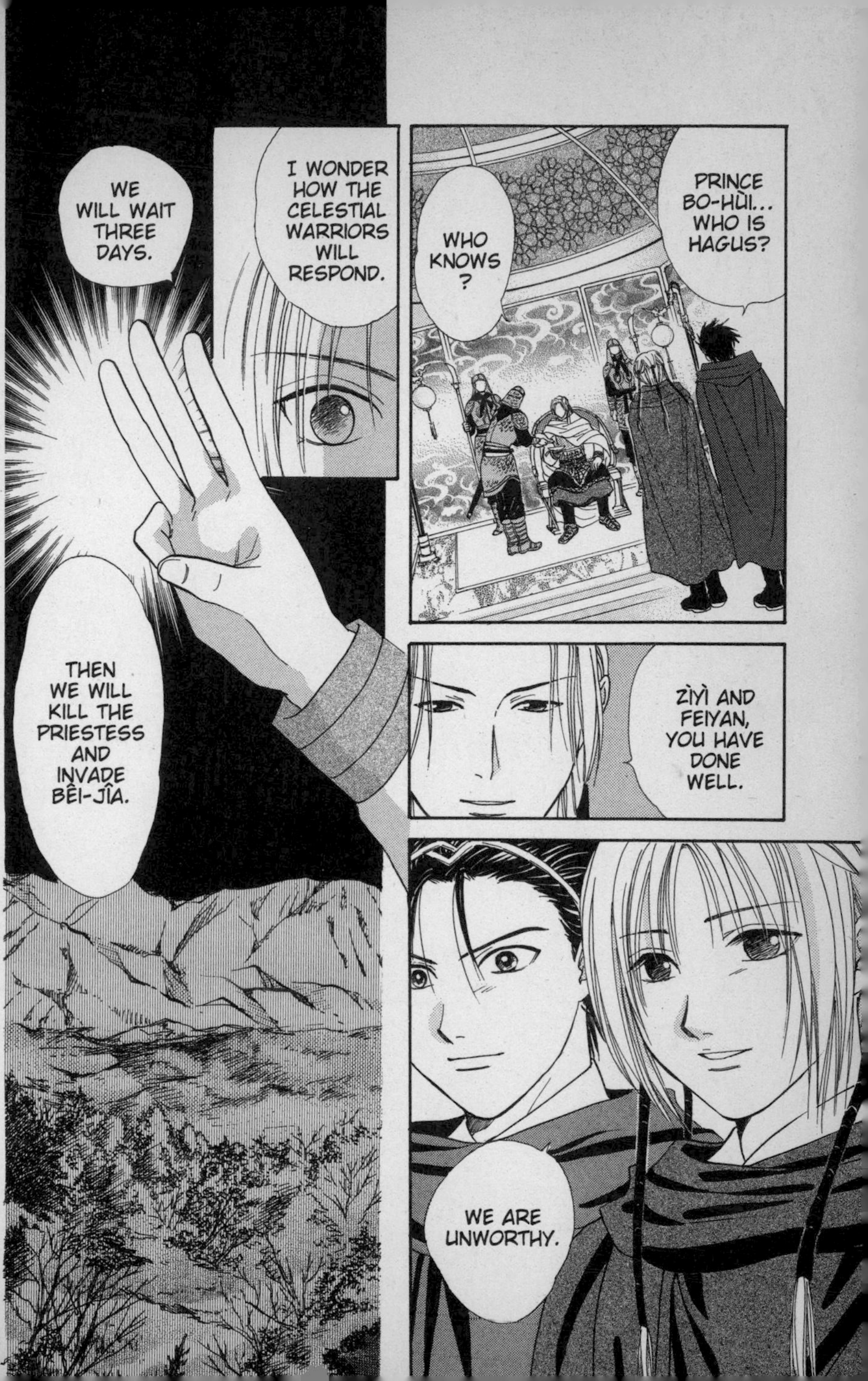
PRINCE BO-HÙI... WHO IS HAGUS?
WHO KNOWS?
I WONDER HOW THE CELESTIAL WARRIORS WILL RESPOND.
WE WILL WAIT THREE DAYS.
THEN WE WILL KILL THE PRIESTESS AND INVADE BÊI-JÎA.
ZÌYÌ AND FEIYAN, YOU HAVE DONE WELL.
WE ARE UNWORTHY.

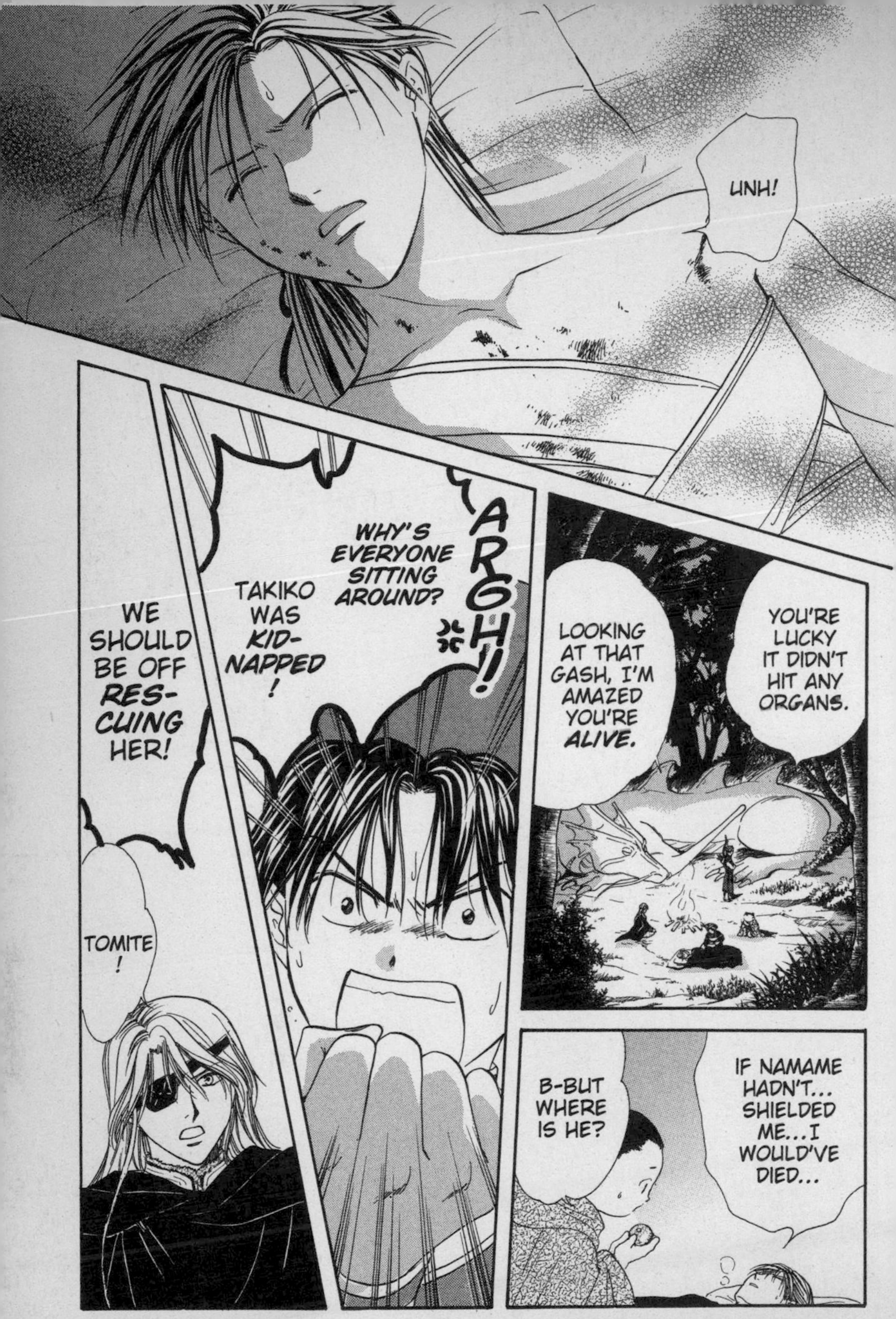
UNH!
YOU'RE LUCKY IT DIDN'T HIT ANY ORGANS.
LOOKING AT THAT GASH, I'M AMAZED YOU'RE ALIVE.
IF NAMAME HADN'T... SHIELDED ME...I WOULD'VE DIED...
B-BUT WHERE IS HE?
ARGH!
WHY'S EVERYONE SITTING AROUND?
TAKIKO WAS KIDNAPPED!
WE SHOULD BE OFF RESCUING HER!
TOMITE!

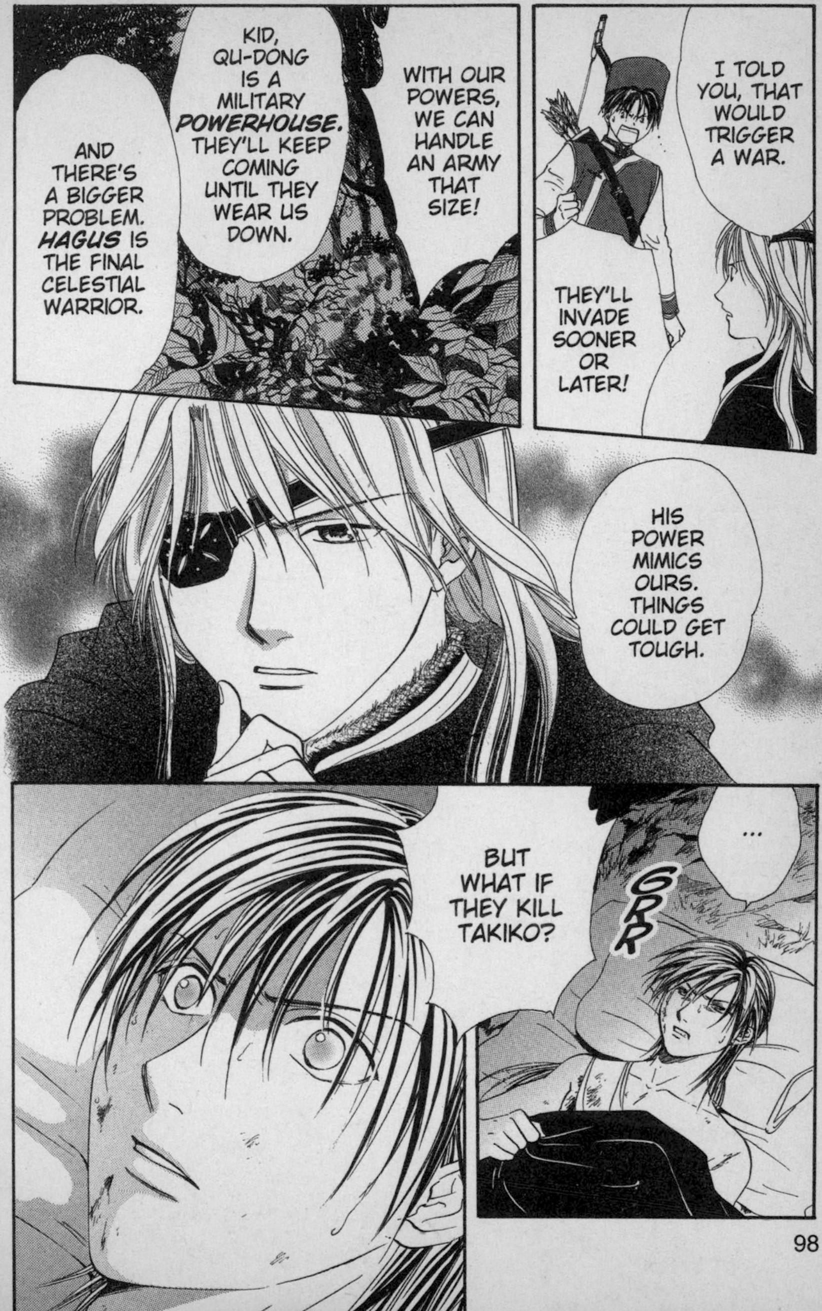
I TOLD YOU, THAT WOULD TRIGGER A WAR.
THEY'LL INVADE SOONER OR LATER!
WITH OUR POWERS, WE CAN HANDLE AN ARMY THAT SIZE!
KID, QU-DONG IS A MILITARY **POWERHOUSE.** THEY'LL KEEP COMING UNTIL THEY WEAR US DOWN.
AND THERE'S A BIGGER PROBLEM. ***HAGUS*** IS THE FINAL CELESTIAL WARRIOR.
HIS POWER MIMICS OURS. THINGS COULD GET TOUGH.
...
GRR
BUT WHAT IF THEY KILL TAKIKO?

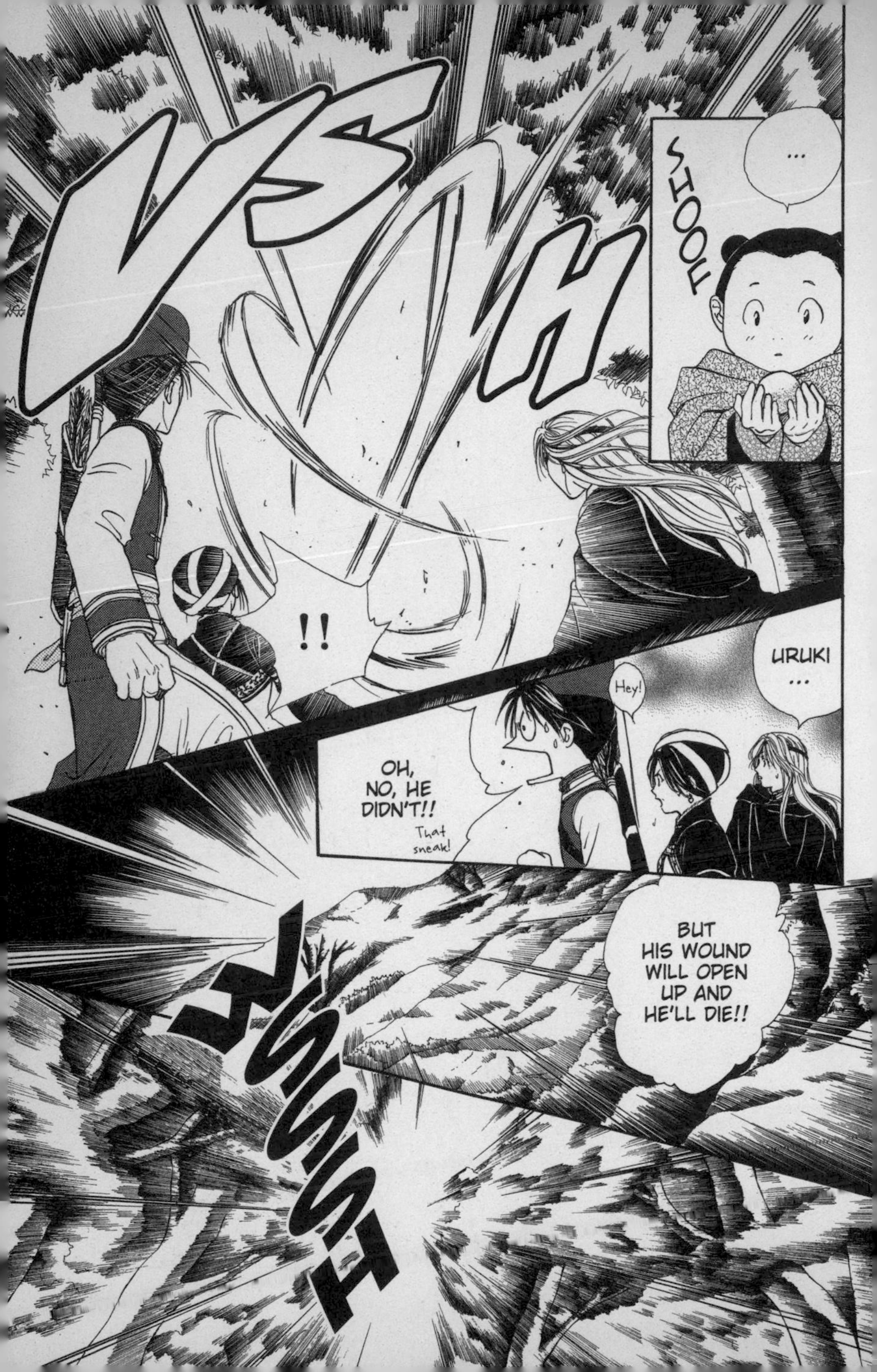
...
SHOOOT
VWAH
!!
URUKI ...
Hey!
OH, NO, HE DIDN'T!!
That sneak!
BUT HIS WOUND WILL OPEN UP AND HE'LL DIE!!
XSSSH

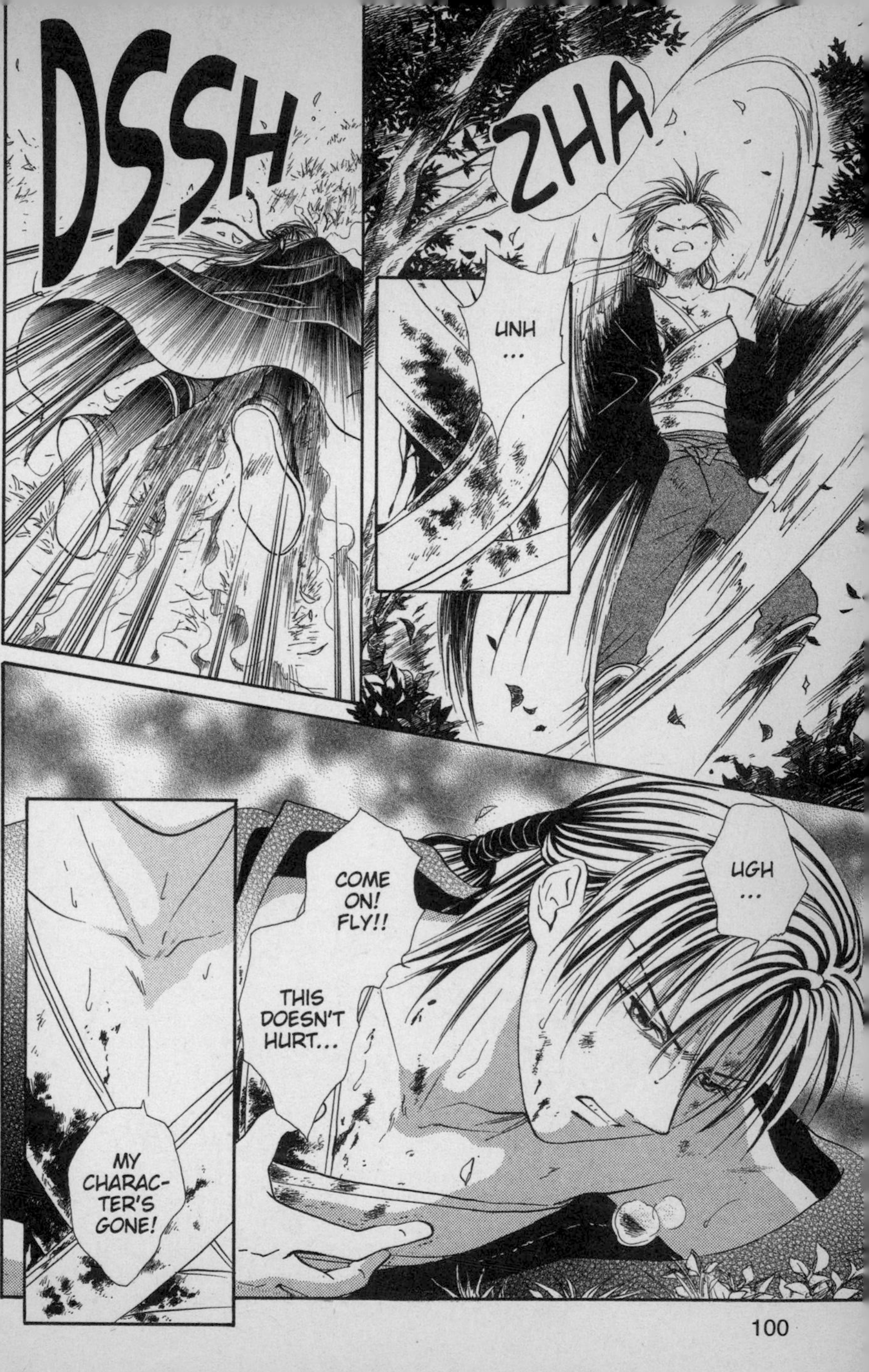
ZHA
UNH ...
DSSH
UGH ...
COME ON! FLY!!
THIS DOESN'T HURT...
MY CHARAC-TER'S GONE!

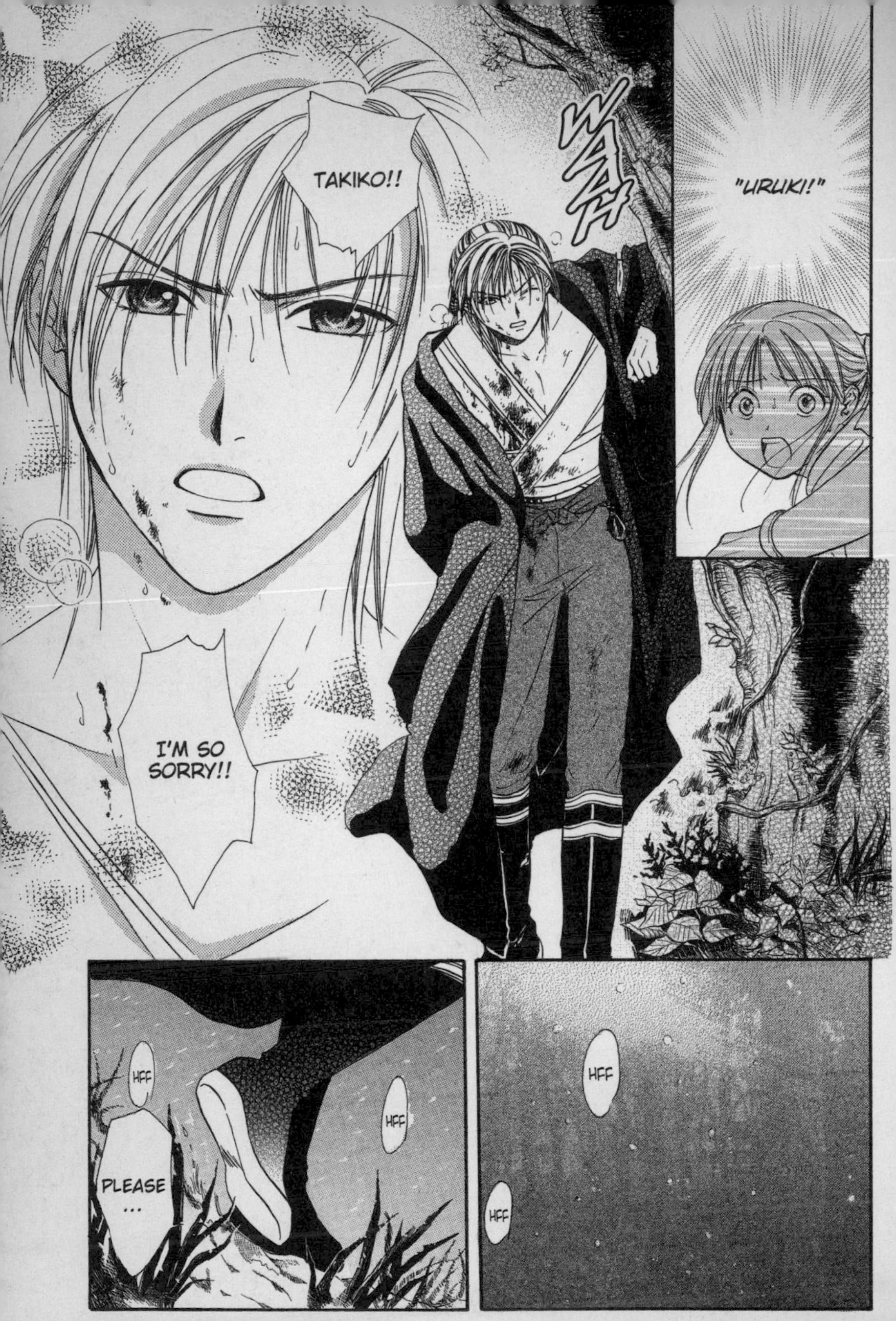
"URUKI!"
WAAH
TAKIKO!!
I'M SO SORRY!!
HFF
HFF
HFF
HFF
PLEASE ...

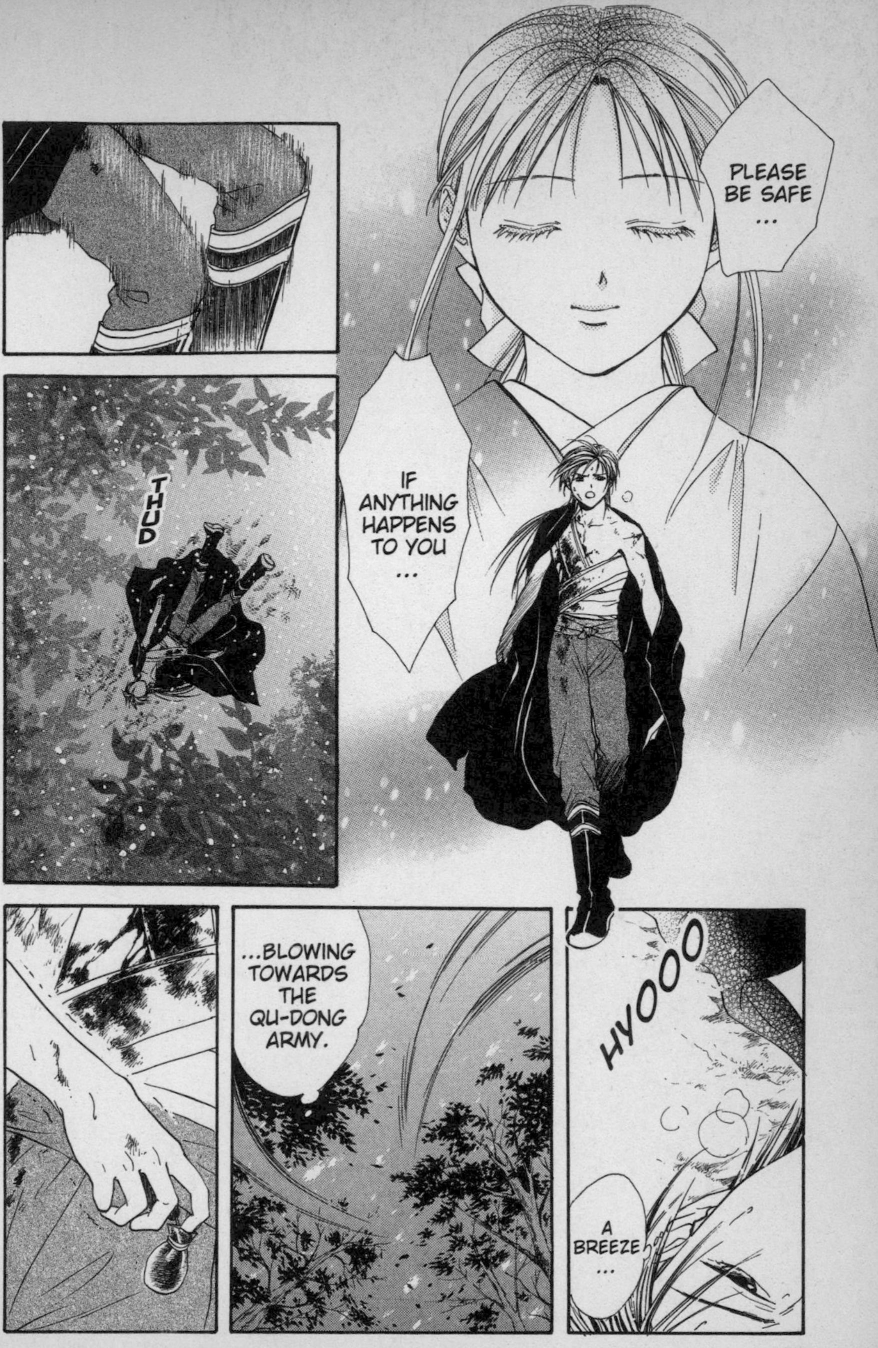
PLEASE BE SAFE ...
IF ANYTHING HAPPENS TO YOU ...
THUD
HYOOO
A BREEZE ...
...BLOWING TOWARDS THE QU-DONG ARMY.

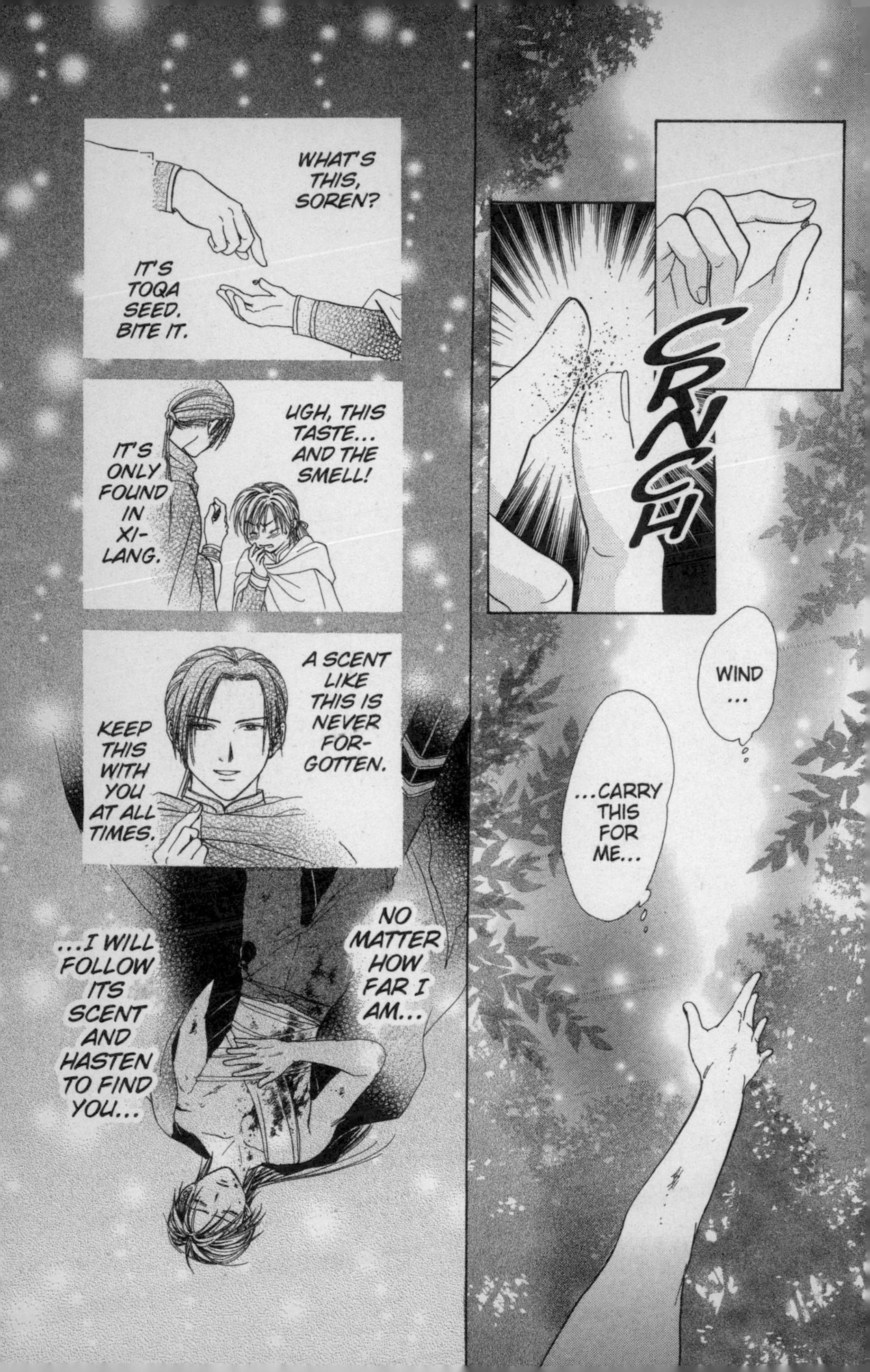
CRNCH
WIND...
...CARRY THIS FOR ME...
WHAT'S THIS, SOREN?
IT'S TOQA SEED. BITE IT.
UGH, THIS TASTE... AND THE SMELL!
IT'S ONLY FOUND IN XI-LANG.
A SCENT LIKE THIS IS NEVER FOR-GOTTEN.
KEEP THIS WITH YOU AT ALL TIMES.
NO MATTER HOW FAR I AM...
...I WILL FOLLOW ITS SCENT AND HASTEN TO FIND YOU...

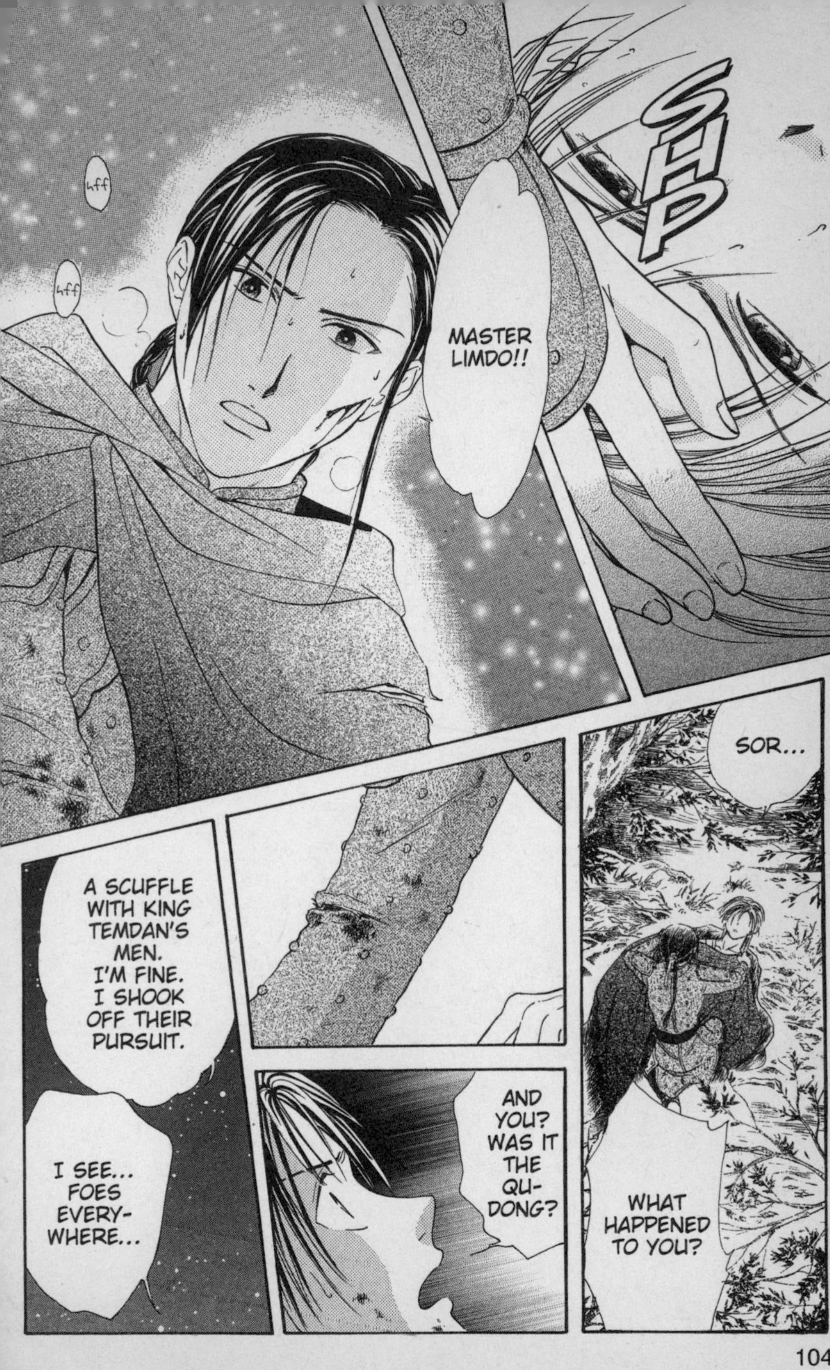
SHP
MASTER LIMDO!!
hff
hff
SOR...
WHAT HAPPENED TO YOU?
AND YOU? WAS IT THE QU-DONG?
A SCUFFLE WITH KING TEMDAN'S MEN. I'M FINE. I SHOOK OFF THEIR PURSUIT.
I SEE... FOES EVERY-WHERE...

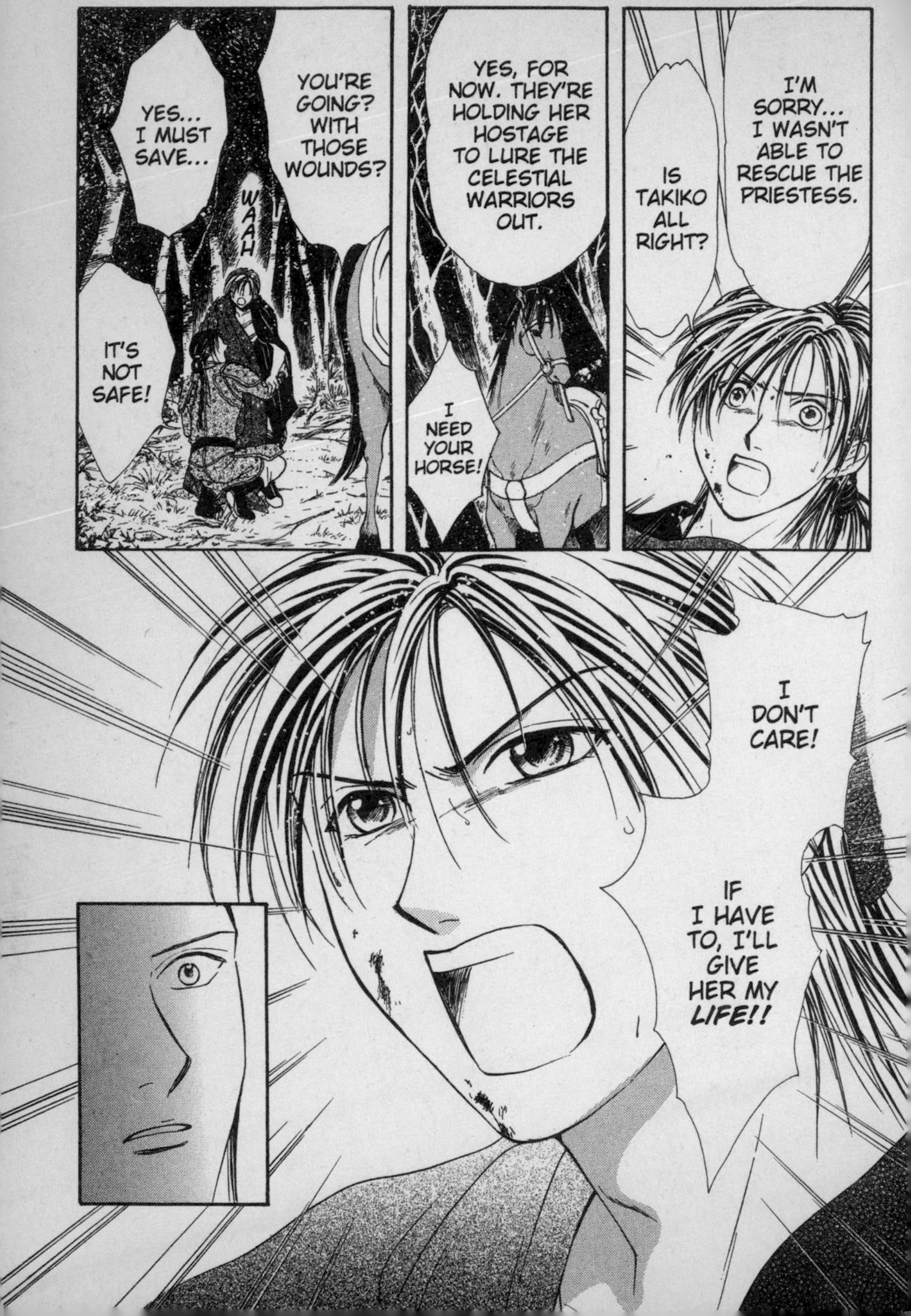
I'M SORRY... I WASN'T ABLE TO RESCUE THE PRIESTESS.
IS TAKIKO ALL RIGHT?
YES, FOR NOW. THEY'RE HOLDING HER HOSTAGE TO LURE THE CELESTIAL WARRIORS OUT.
I NEED YOUR HORSE!
YOU'RE GOING? WITH THOSE WOUNDS?
YES... I MUST SAVE...
WAAH
IT'S NOT SAFE!
I DON'T CARE!
IF I HAVE TO, I'LL GIVE HER MY *LIFE!!*

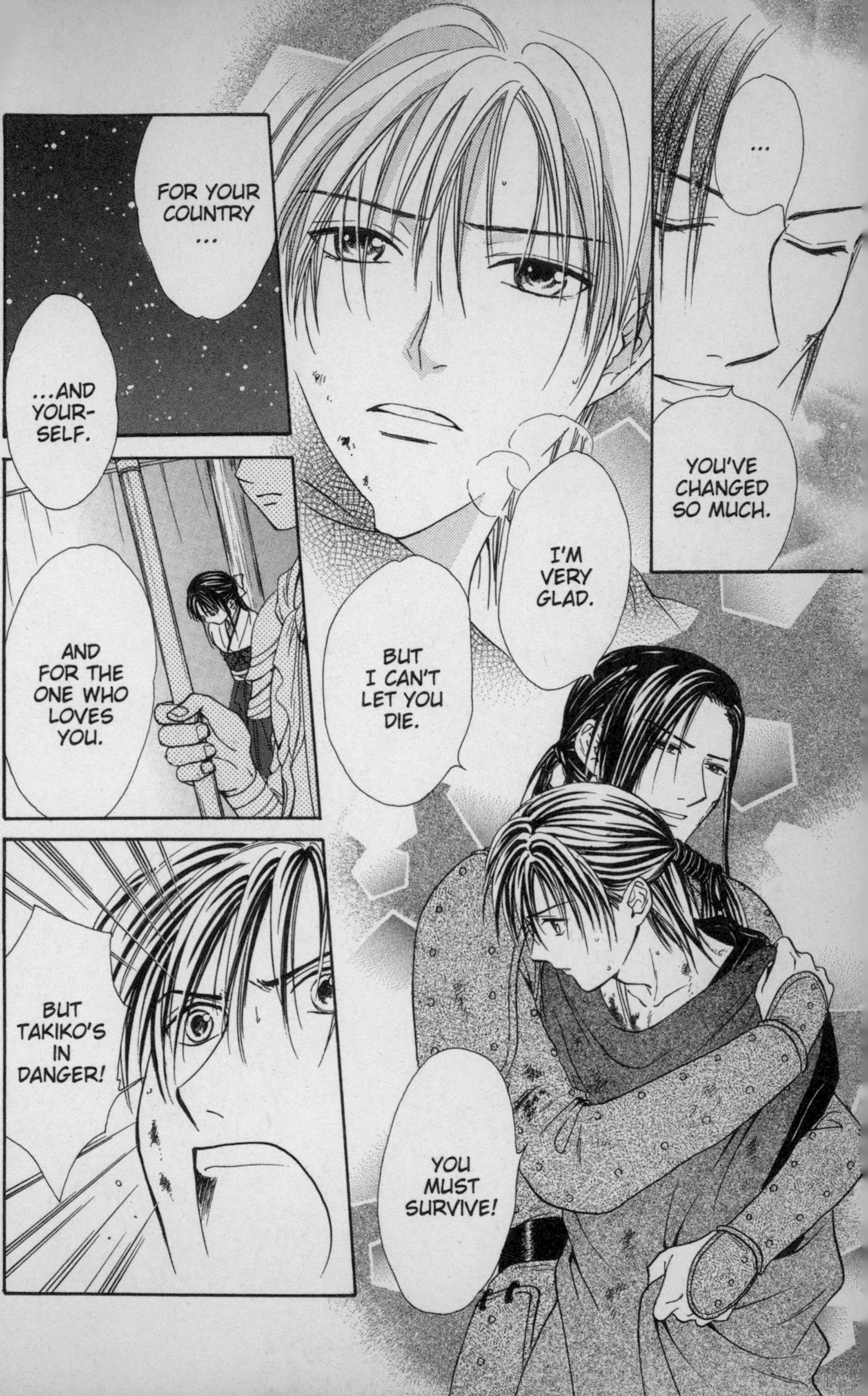
...
YOU'VE CHANGED SO MUCH.
I'M VERY GLAD.
BUT I CAN'T LET YOU DIE.
FOR YOUR COUNTRY ...
...AND YOURSELF.
AND FOR THE ONE WHO LOVES YOU.
YOU MUST SURVIVE!
BUT TAKIKO'S IN DANGER!

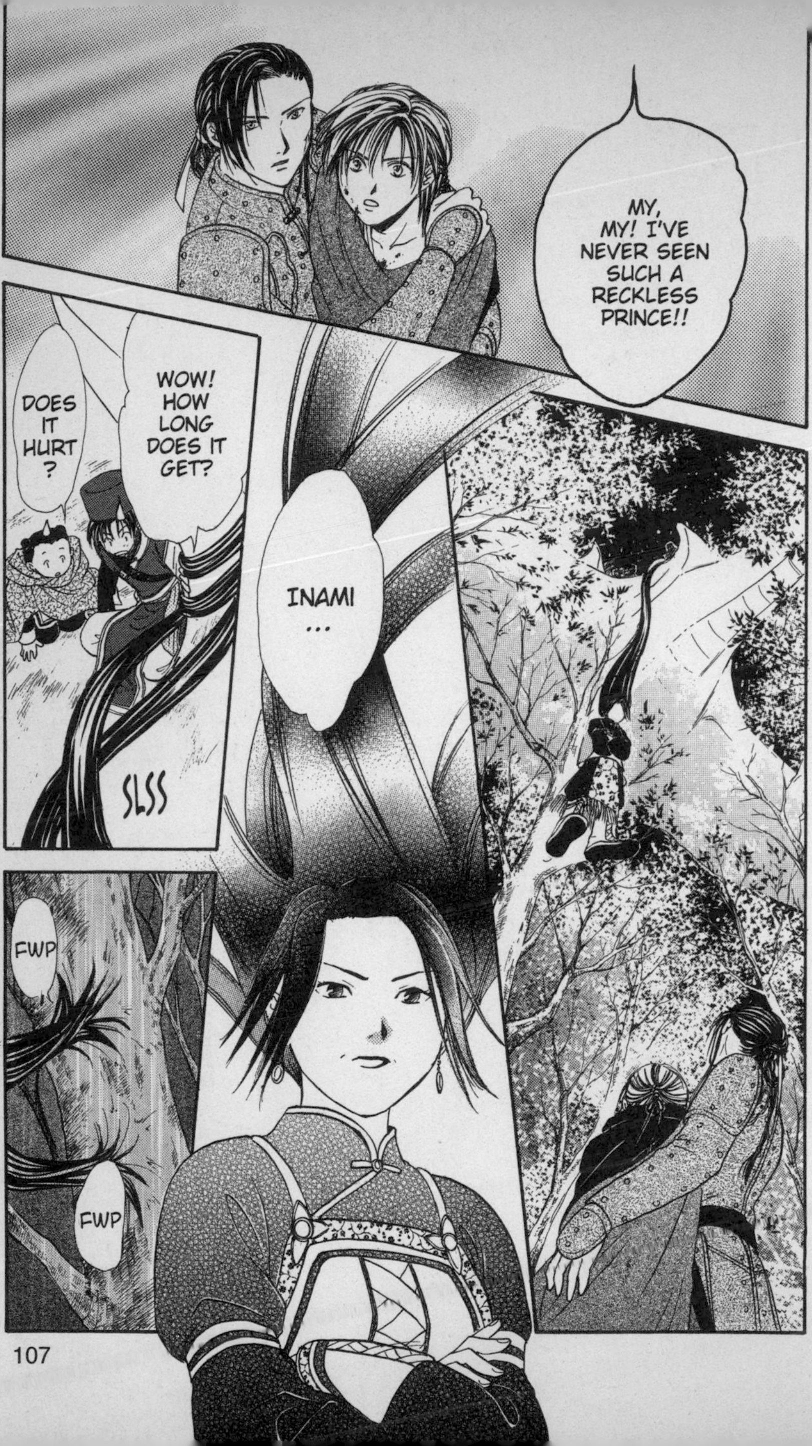
MY, MY! I'VE NEVER SEEN SUCH A RECKLESS PRINCE!!
WOW! HOW LONG DOES IT GET?
DOES IT HURT?
SLSS
INAMI...
FWP
FWP

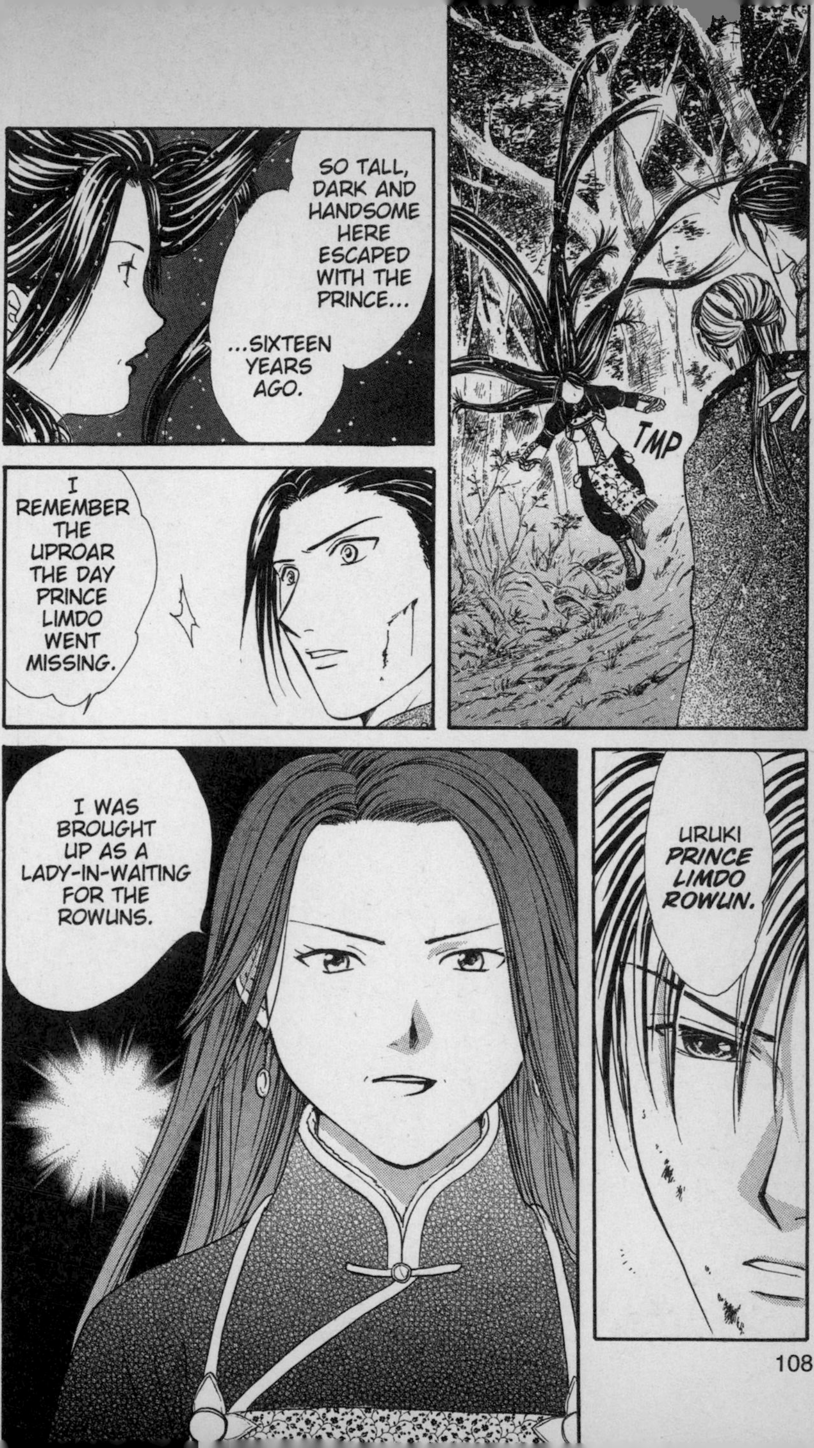
TMP
SO TALL, DARK AND HANDSOME HERE ESCAPED WITH THE PRINCE...
...SIXTEEN YEARS AGO.
I REMEMBER THE UPROAR THE DAY PRINCE LIMDO WENT MISSING.
URUKI PRINCE LIMDO ROWUN.
I WAS BROUGHT UP AS A LADY-IN-WAITING FOR THE ROWUNS.

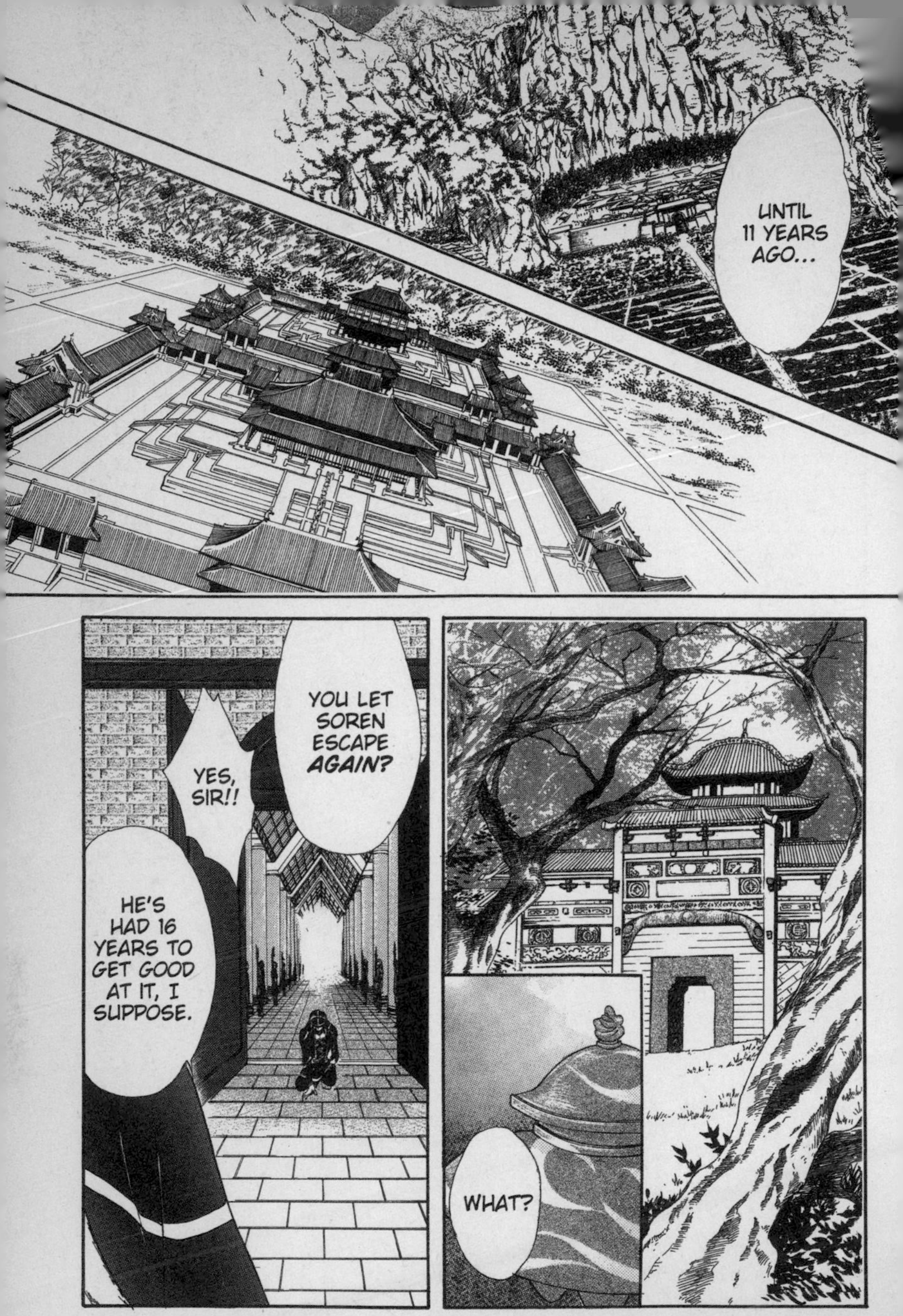
UNTIL 11 YEARS AGO...
WHAT?
YOU LET SOREN ESCAPE AGAIN?
YES, SIR!!
HE'S HAD 16 YEARS TO GET GOOD AT IT, I SUPPOSE.

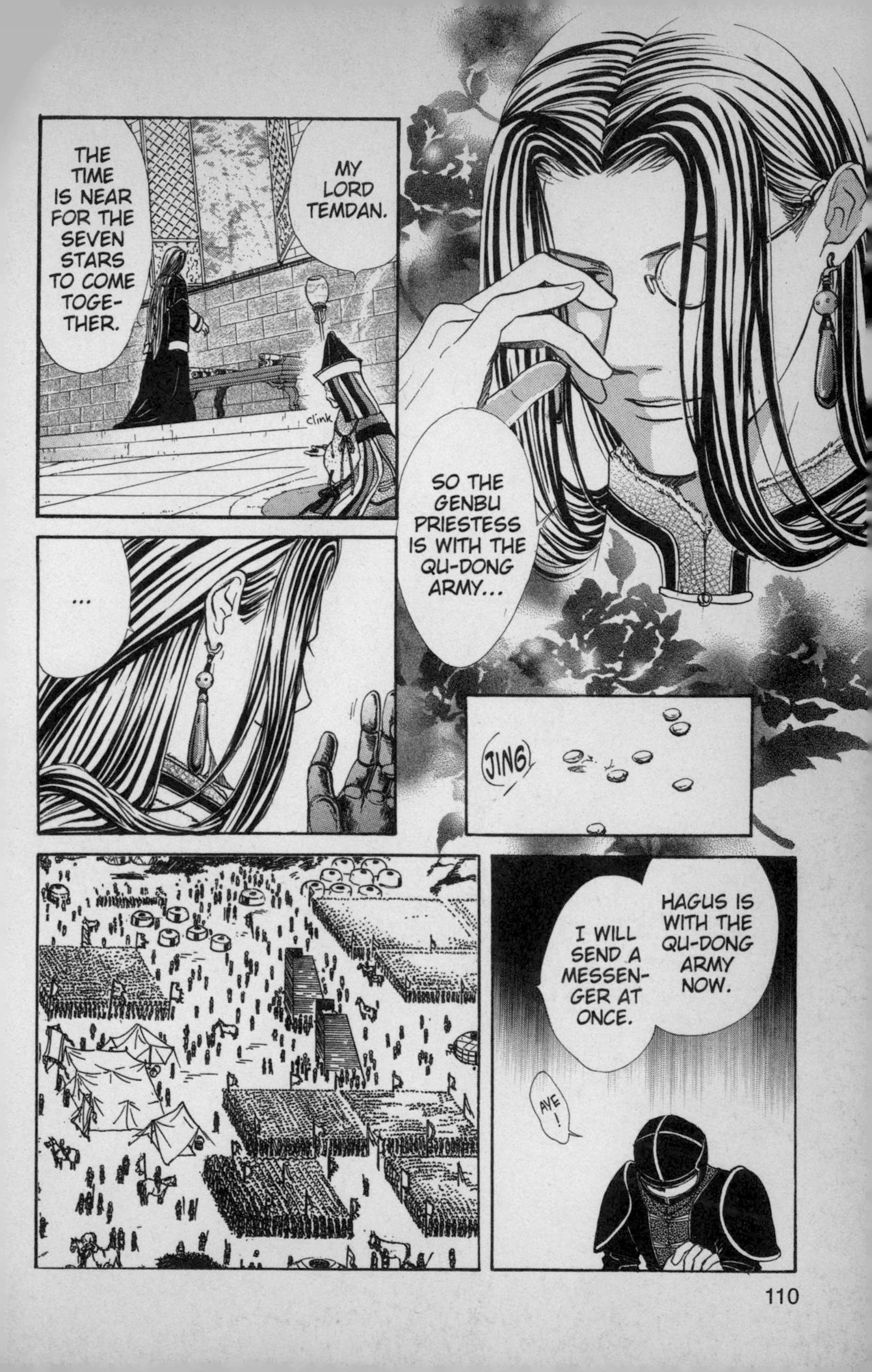
SO THE GENBU PRIESTESS IS WITH THE QU-DONG ARMY...
MY LORD TEMDAN.
THE TIME IS NEAR FOR THE SEVEN STARS TO COME TOGE-THER.
clink
JING
...
HAGUS IS WITH THE QU-DONG ARMY NOW.
I WILL SEND A MESSEN-GER AT ONCE.
AYE!

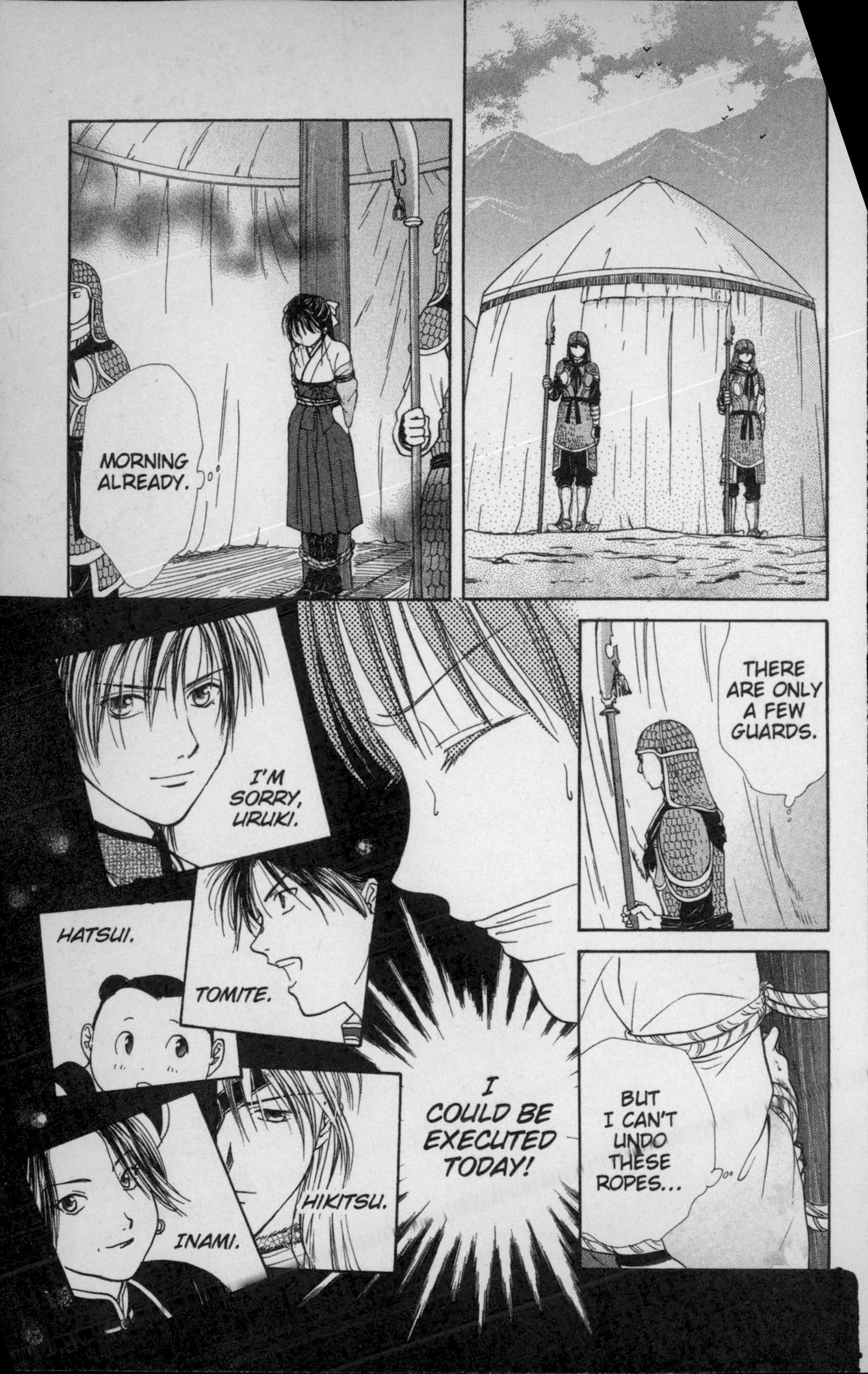
MORNING ALREADY.
THERE ARE ONLY A FEW GUARDS.
BUT I CAN'T UNDO THESE ROPES...
I COULD BE EXECUTED TODAY!
I'M SORRY, URUKI.
TOMITE.
HATSUI.
HIKITSU.
INAMI.

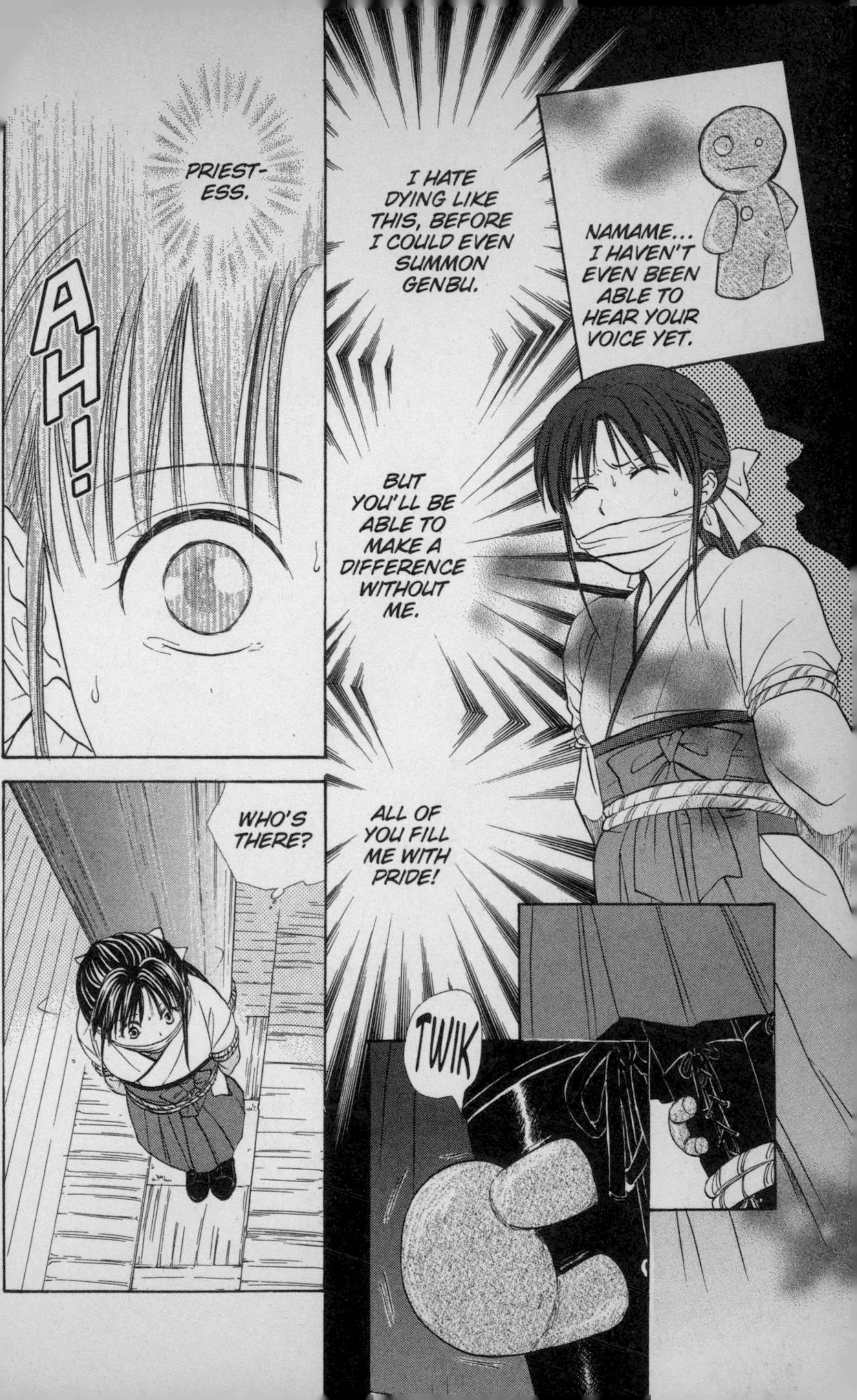
NAMAME... I HAVEN'T EVEN BEEN ABLE TO HEAR YOUR VOICE YET.
I HATE DYING LIKE THIS, BEFORE I COULD EVEN SUMMON GENBU.
BUT YOU'LL BE ABLE TO MAKE A DIFFERENCE WITHOUT ME.
ALL OF YOU FILL ME WITH PRIDE!
TWIK
PRIEST-ESS.
AH!
WHO'S THERE?

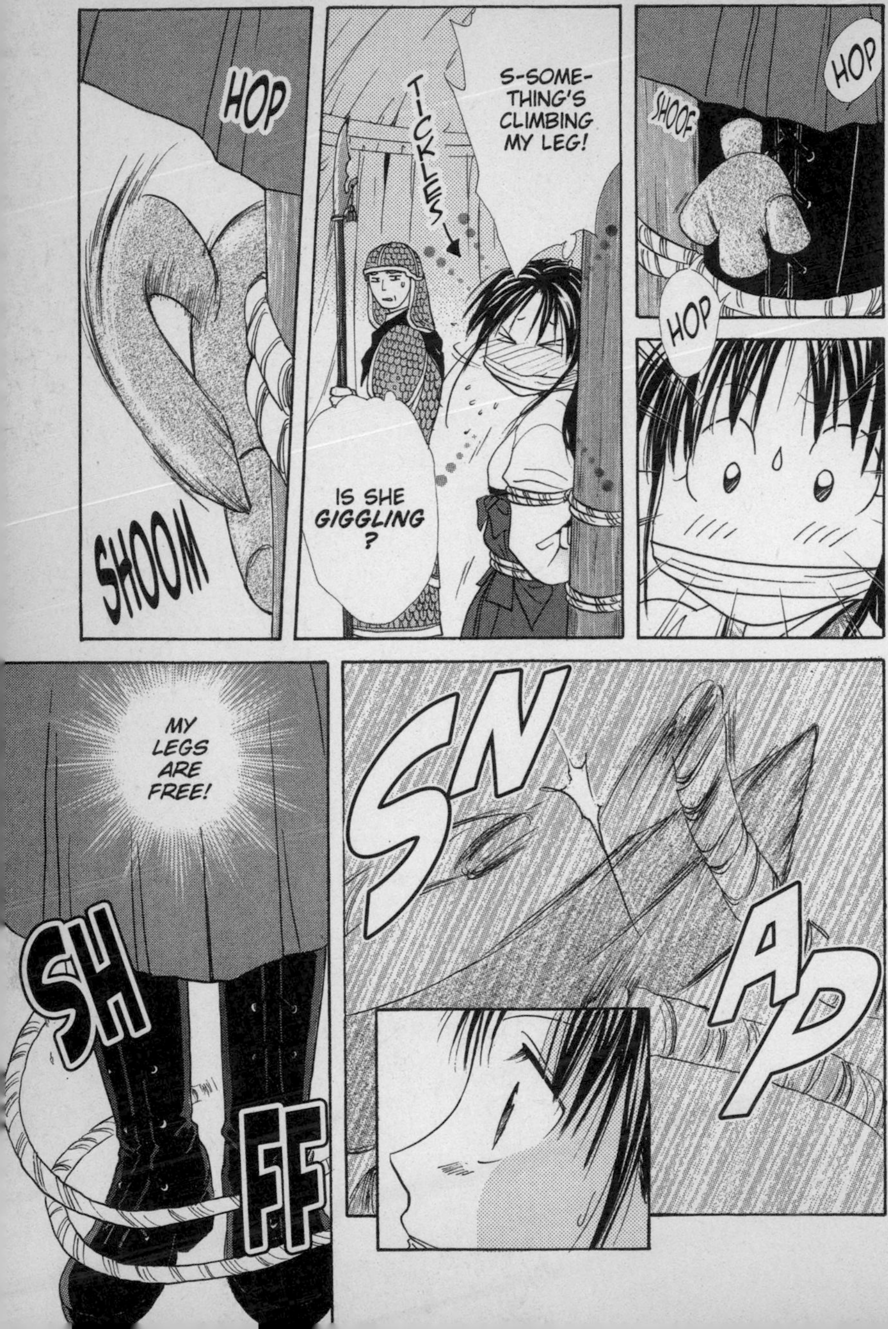
HOP
SHOOF
HOP
S-SOMETHING'S CLIMBING MY LEG!
TICKLES
IS SHE GIGGLING?
HOP
SHOOM
SNAP
MY LEGS ARE FREE!
SHFF

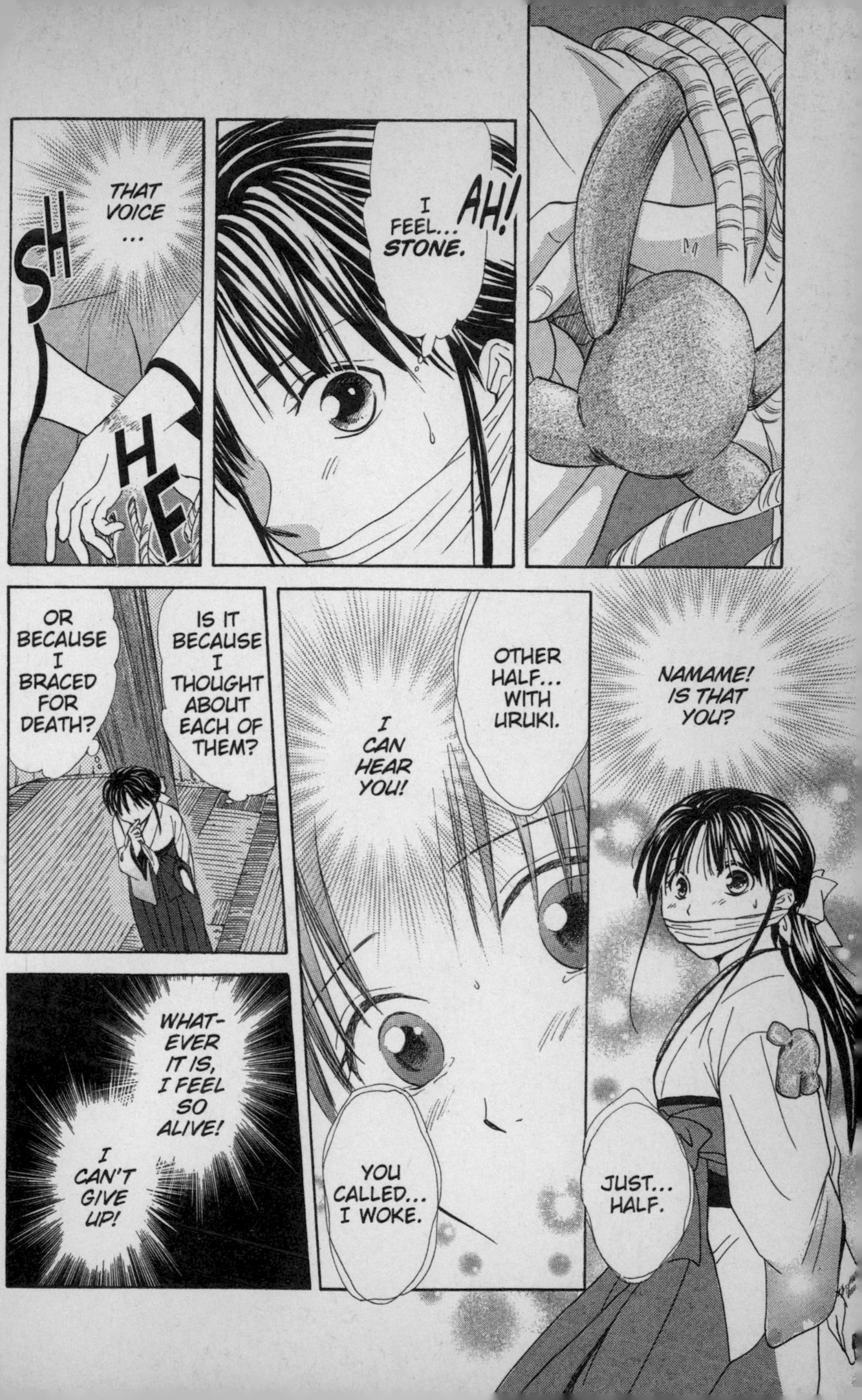
AH!
I FEEL... STONE.
THAT VOICE...
SH
HF
NAMAME! IS THAT YOU?
JUST... HALF.
OTHER HALF... WITH URUKI.
I CAN HEAR YOU!
YOU CALLED... I WOKE.
IS IT BECAUSE I THOUGHT ABOUT EACH OF THEM?
OR BECAUSE I BRACED FOR DEATH?
WHATEVER IT IS, I FEEL SO ALIVE!
I CAN'T GIVE UP!

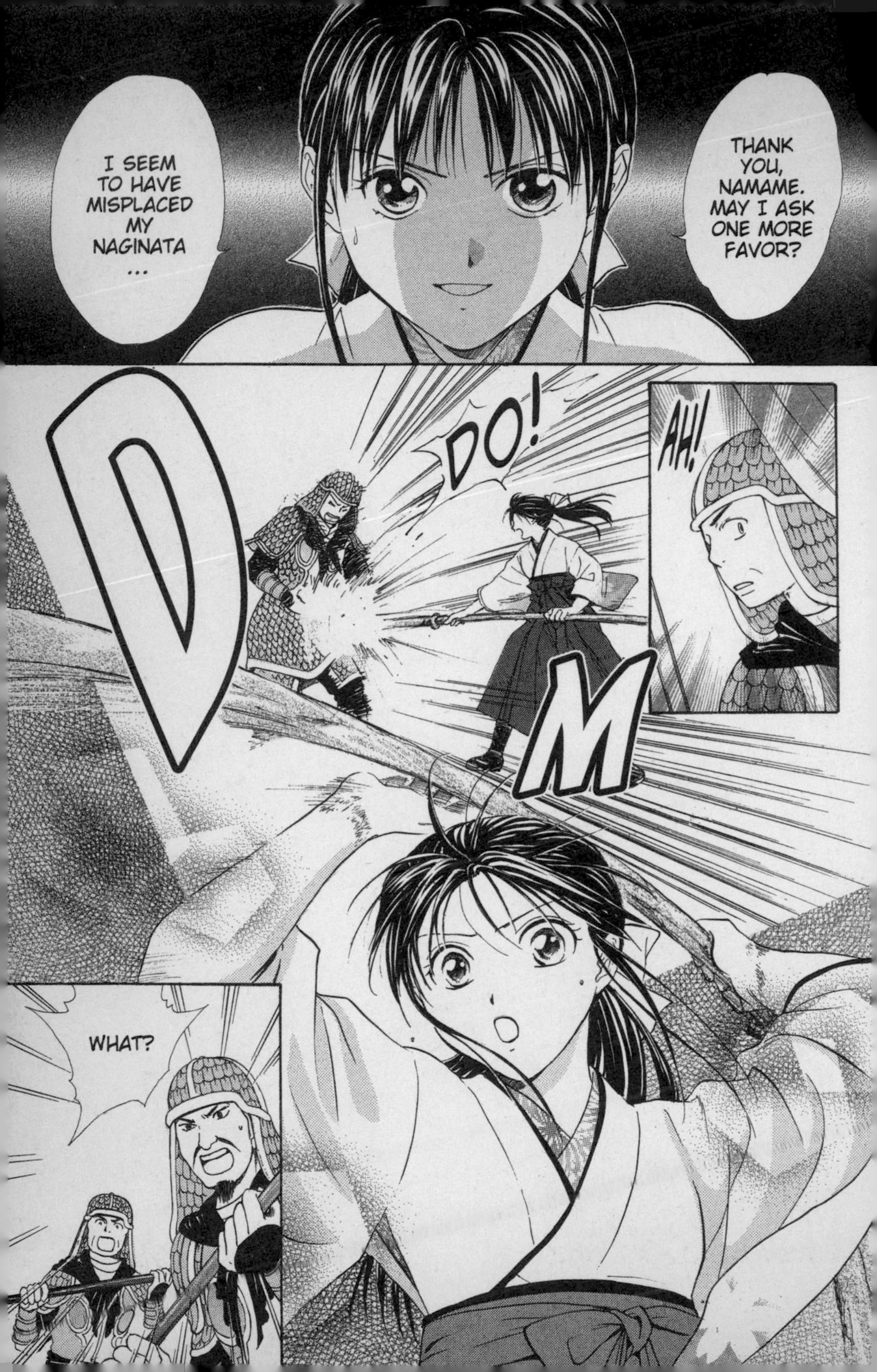
THANK YOU, NAMAME. MAY I ASK ONE MORE FAVOR?
I SEEM TO HAVE MISPLACED MY NAGINATA ...
AH!
DO!
M
D
WHAT?

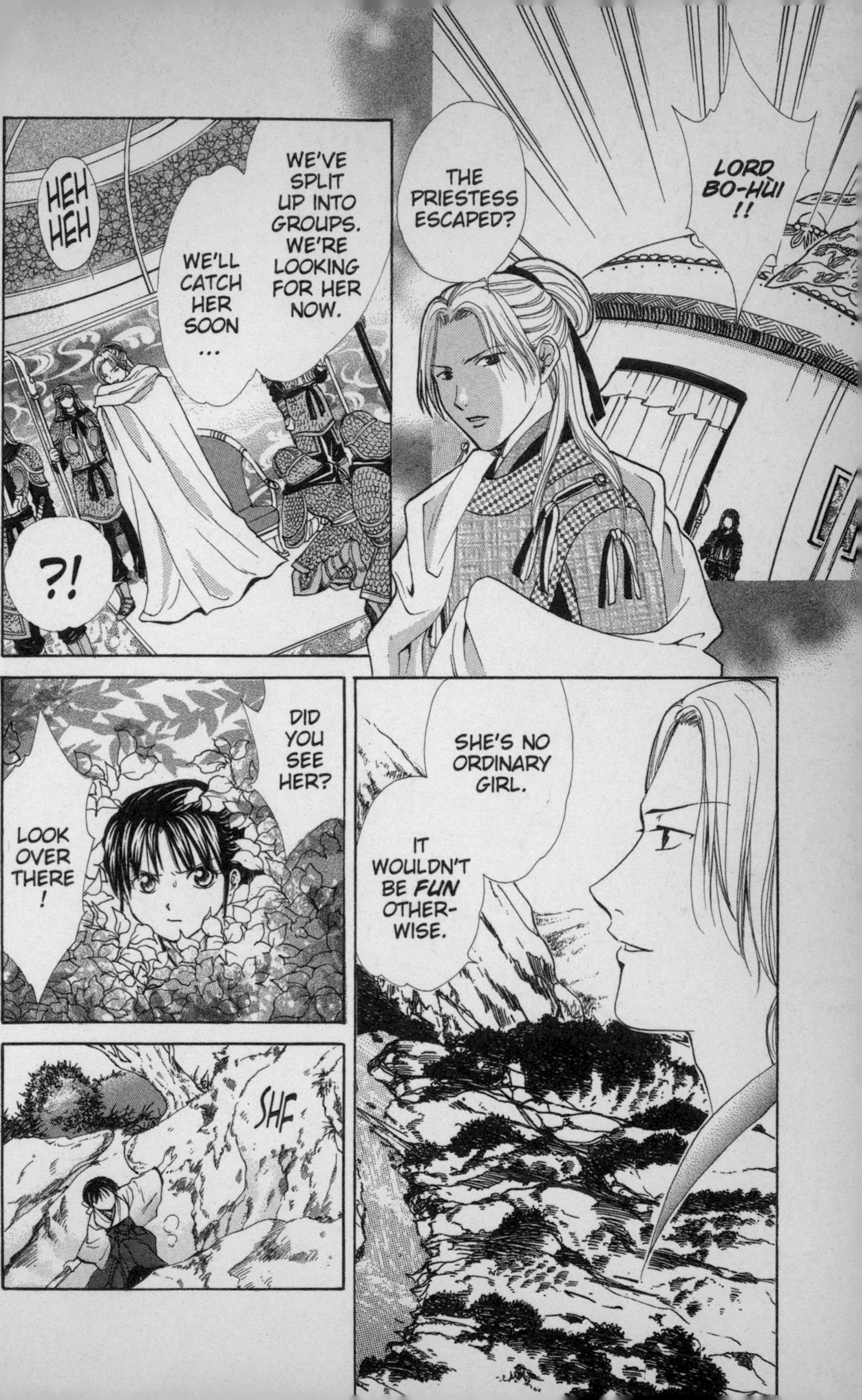
LORD BO-HŬI !!
THE PRIESTESS ESCAPED?
WE'VE SPLIT UP INTO GROUPS. WE'RE LOOKING FOR HER NOW.
WE'LL CATCH HER SOON ...
HEH HEH
?!
SHE'S NO ORDINARY GIRL.
IT WOULDN'T BE *FUN* OTHER-WISE.
DID YOU SEE HER?
LOOK OVER THERE !
SHF

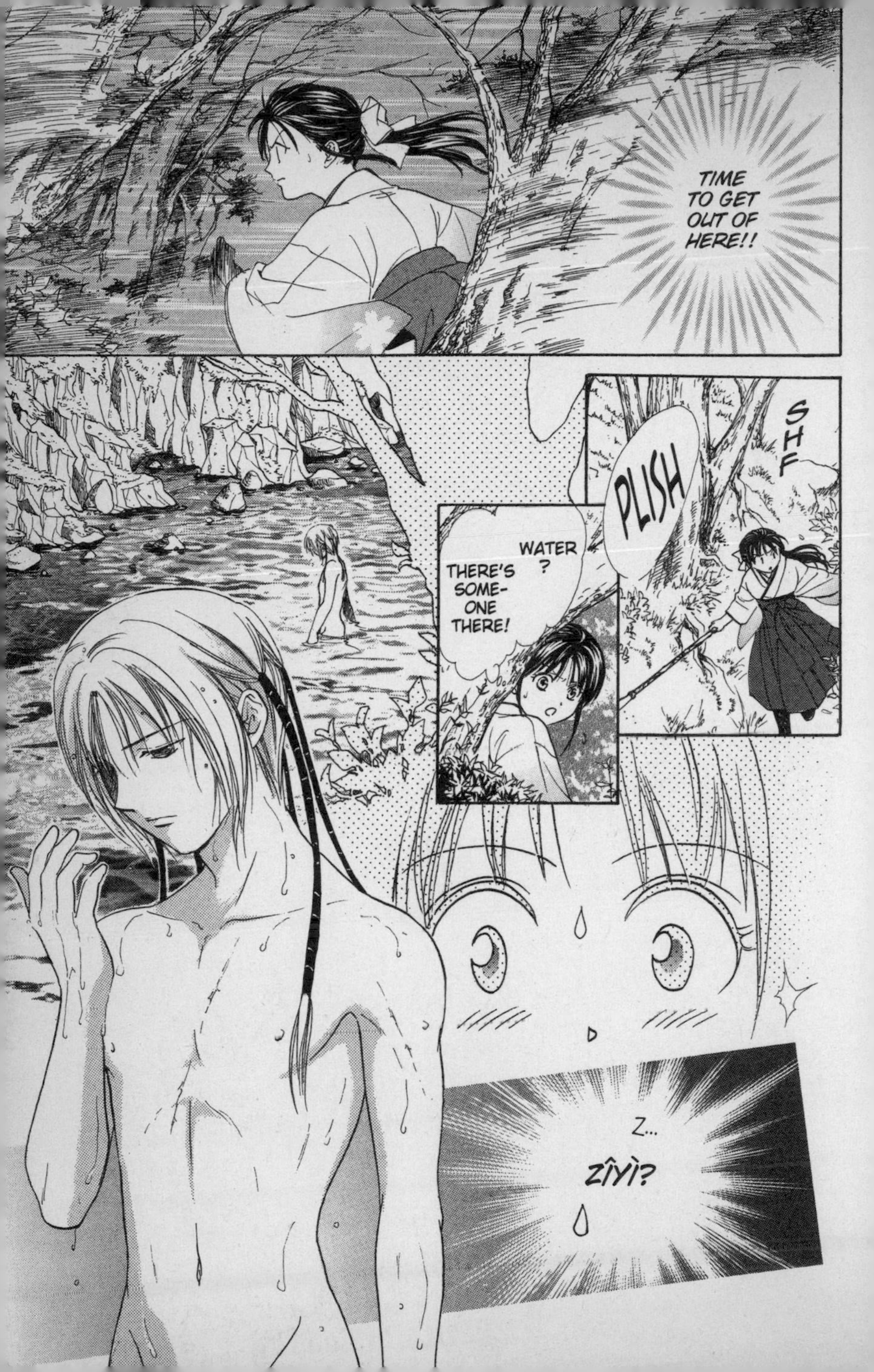
TIME TO GET OUT OF HERE!!
SHF
PLISH
WATER ?
THERE'S SOME-ONE THERE!
Z...
ZÎYÌ?

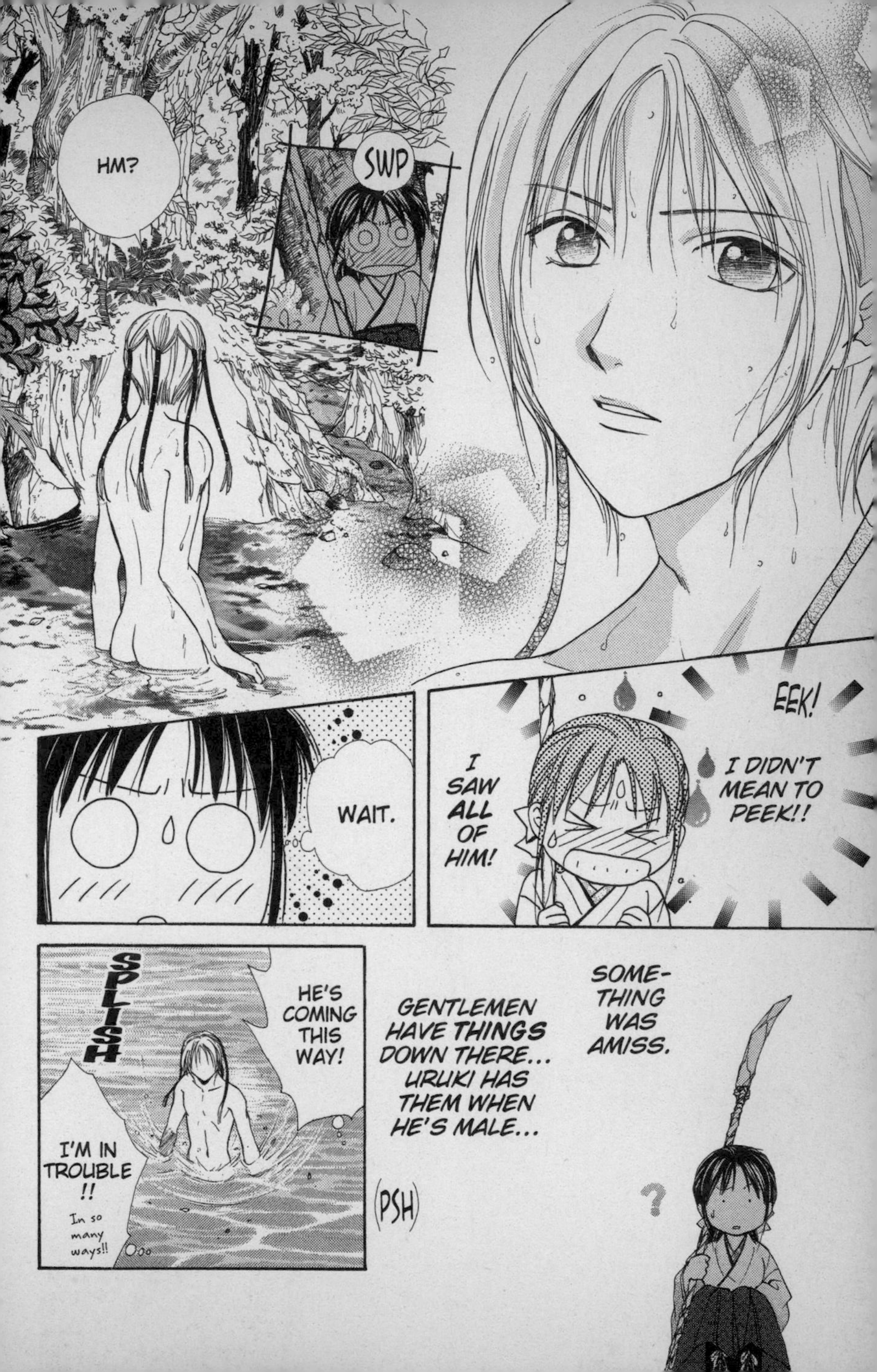
HM?
SWP
EEK!
I DIDN'T MEAN TO PEEK!!
I SAW ALL OF HIM!
WAIT.
SOME-THING WAS AMISS.
GENTLEMEN HAVE THINGS DOWN THERE... URUKI HAS THEM WHEN HE'S MALE...
(PSH)
HE'S COMING THIS WAY!
SPLISH
I'M IN TROUBLE!!
In so many ways!!

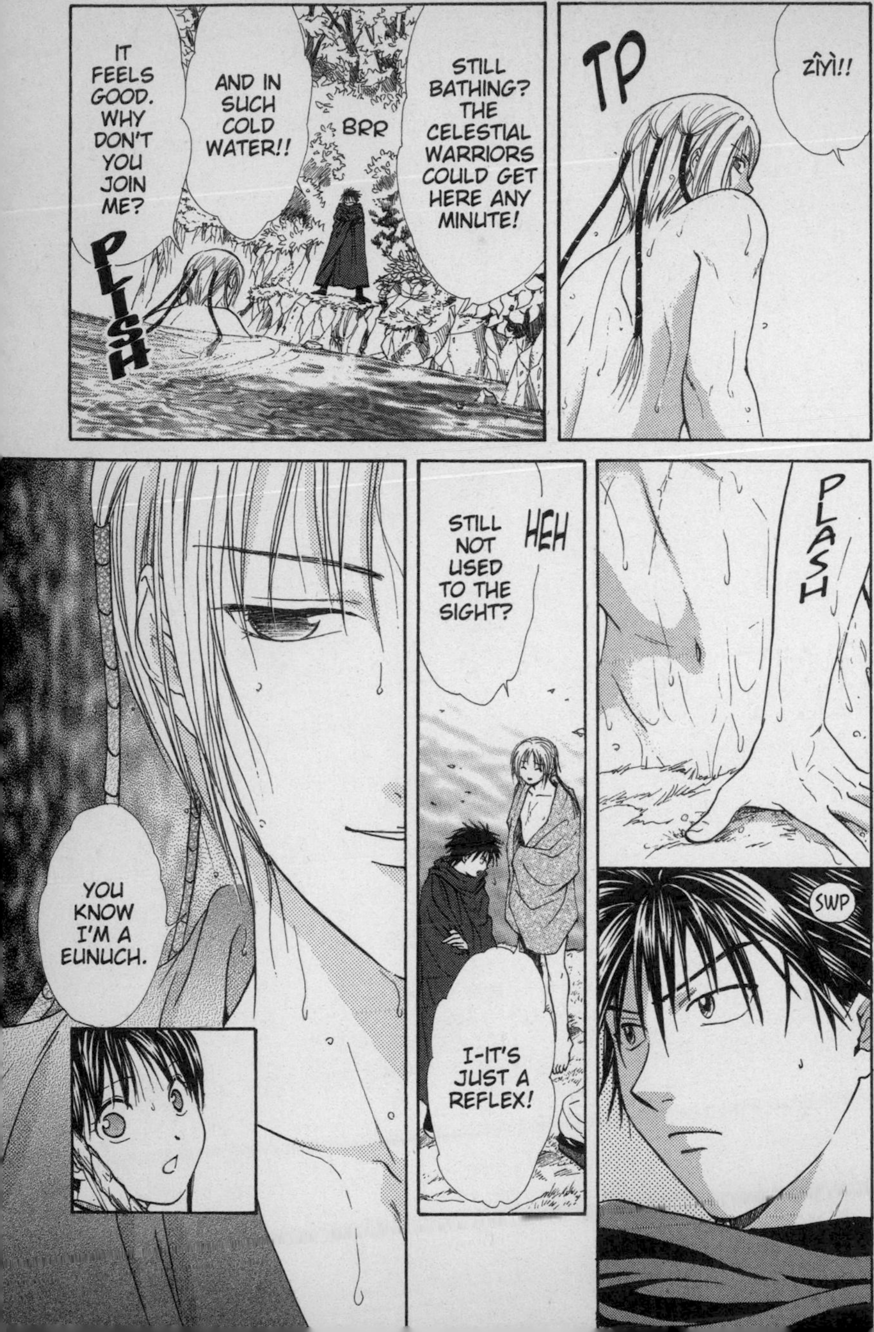
TP
ZÎYÌ!!
STILL BATHING? THE CELESTIAL WARRIORS COULD GET HERE ANY MINUTE!
BRR
AND IN SUCH COLD WATER!!
IT FEELS GOOD. WHY DON'T YOU JOIN ME?
PLISH
PLASH
SWP
HEH
STILL NOT USED TO THE SIGHT?
I-IT'S JUST A REFLEX!
YOU KNOW I'M A EUNUCH.

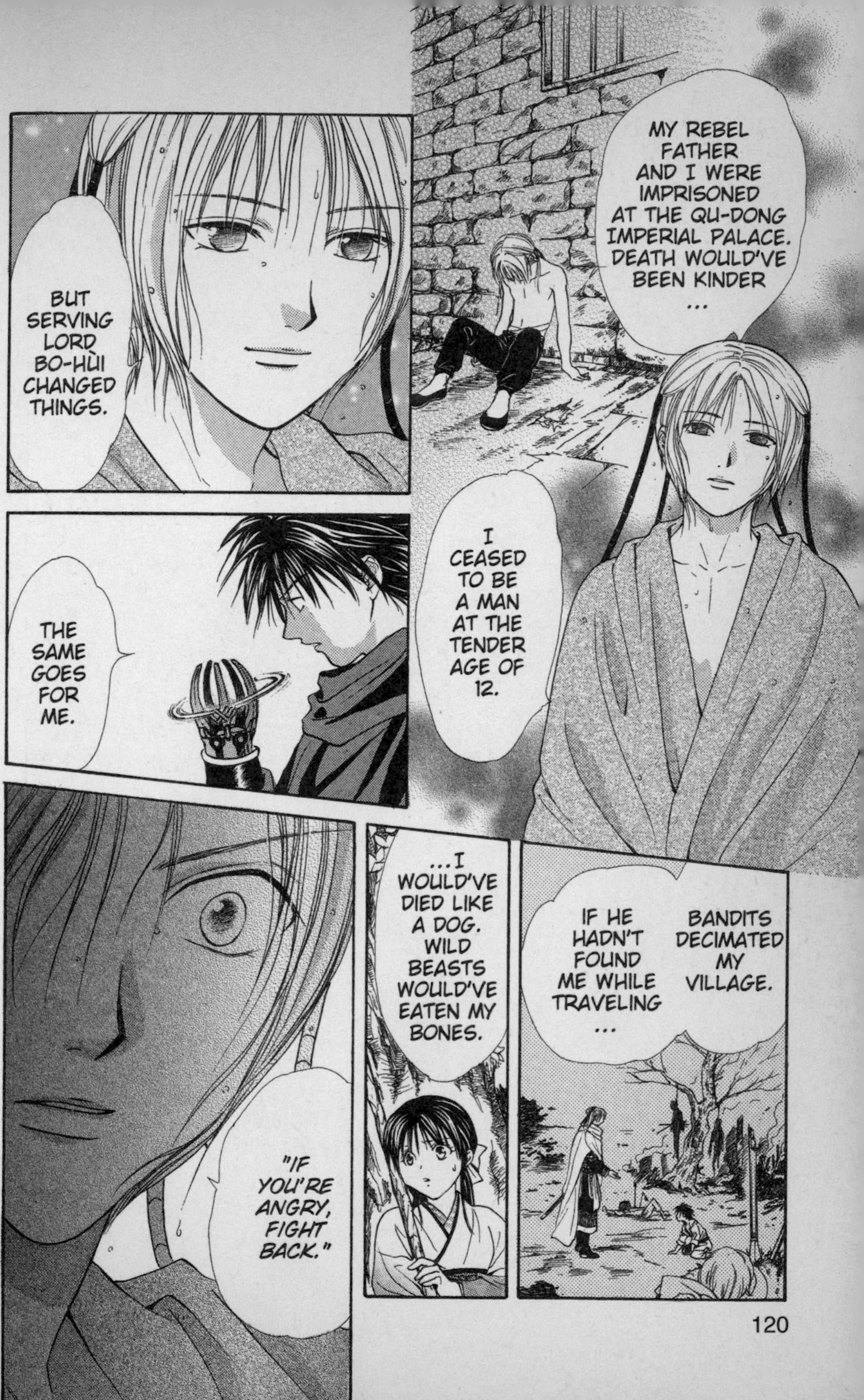
MY REBEL FATHER AND I WERE IMPRISONED AT THE QU-DONG IMPERIAL PALACE. DEATH WOULD'VE BEEN KINDER ...
I CEASED TO BE A MAN AT THE TENDER AGE OF 12.
BUT SERVING LORD BO-HUI CHANGED THINGS.
THE SAME GOES FOR ME.
BANDITS DECIMATED MY VILLAGE.
IF HE HADN'T FOUND ME WHILE TRAVELING ...
...I WOULD'VE DIED LIKE A DOG. WILD BEASTS WOULD'VE EATEN MY BONES.
"IF YOU'RE ANGRY, FIGHT BACK."

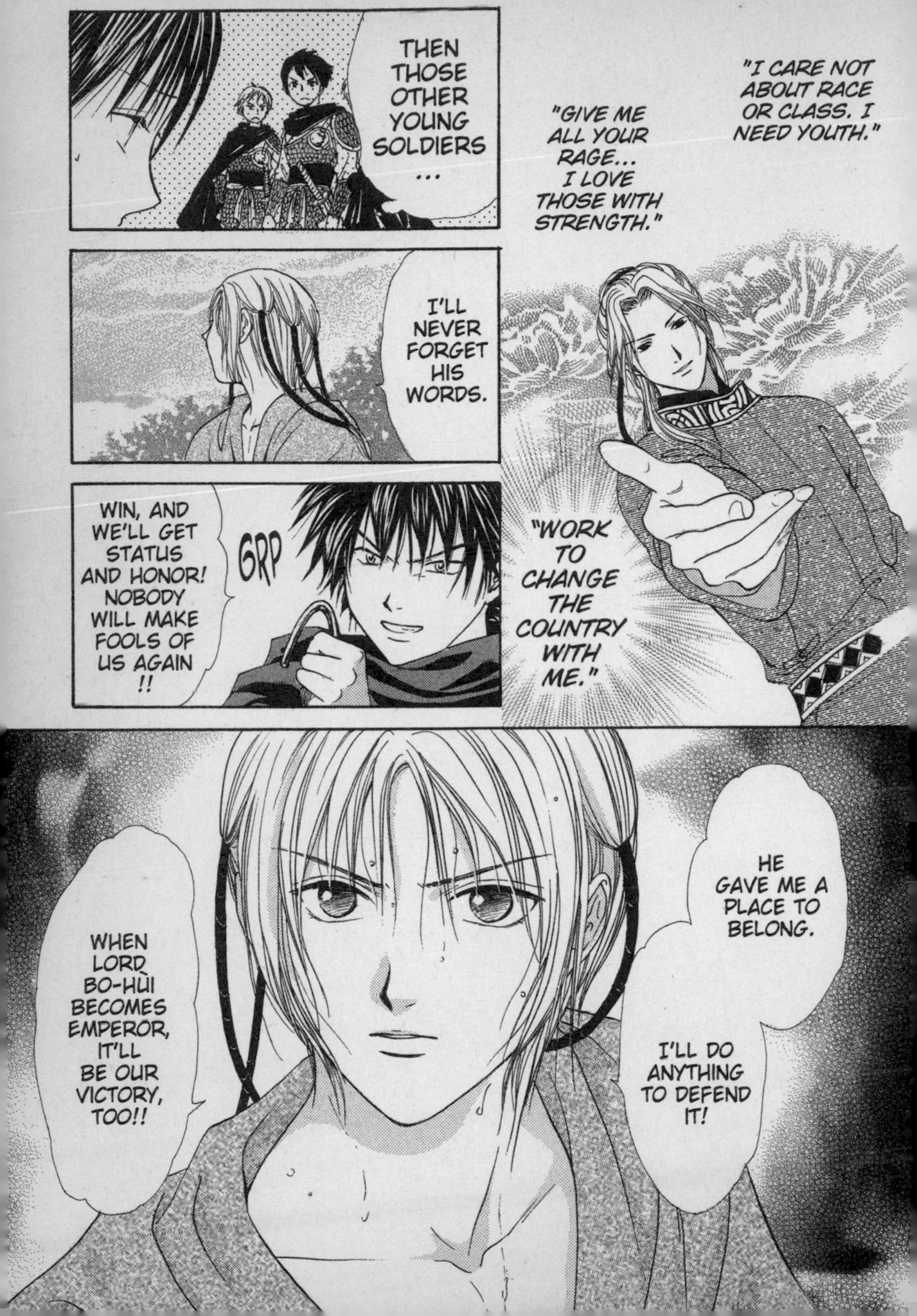
"I CARE NOT ABOUT RACE OR CLASS. I NEED YOUTH."
"GIVE ME ALL YOUR RAGE... I LOVE THOSE WITH STRENGTH."
"WORK TO CHANGE THE COUNTRY WITH ME."
THEN THOSE OTHER YOUNG SOLDIERS ...
I'LL NEVER FORGET HIS WORDS.
WIN, AND WE'LL GET STATUS AND HONOR! NOBODY WILL MAKE FOOLS OF US AGAIN !!
GRP
HE GAVE ME A PLACE TO BELONG.
I'LL DO ANYTHING TO DEFEND IT!
WHEN LORD BO-HŬI BECOMES EMPEROR, IT'LL BE OUR VICTORY, TOO!!

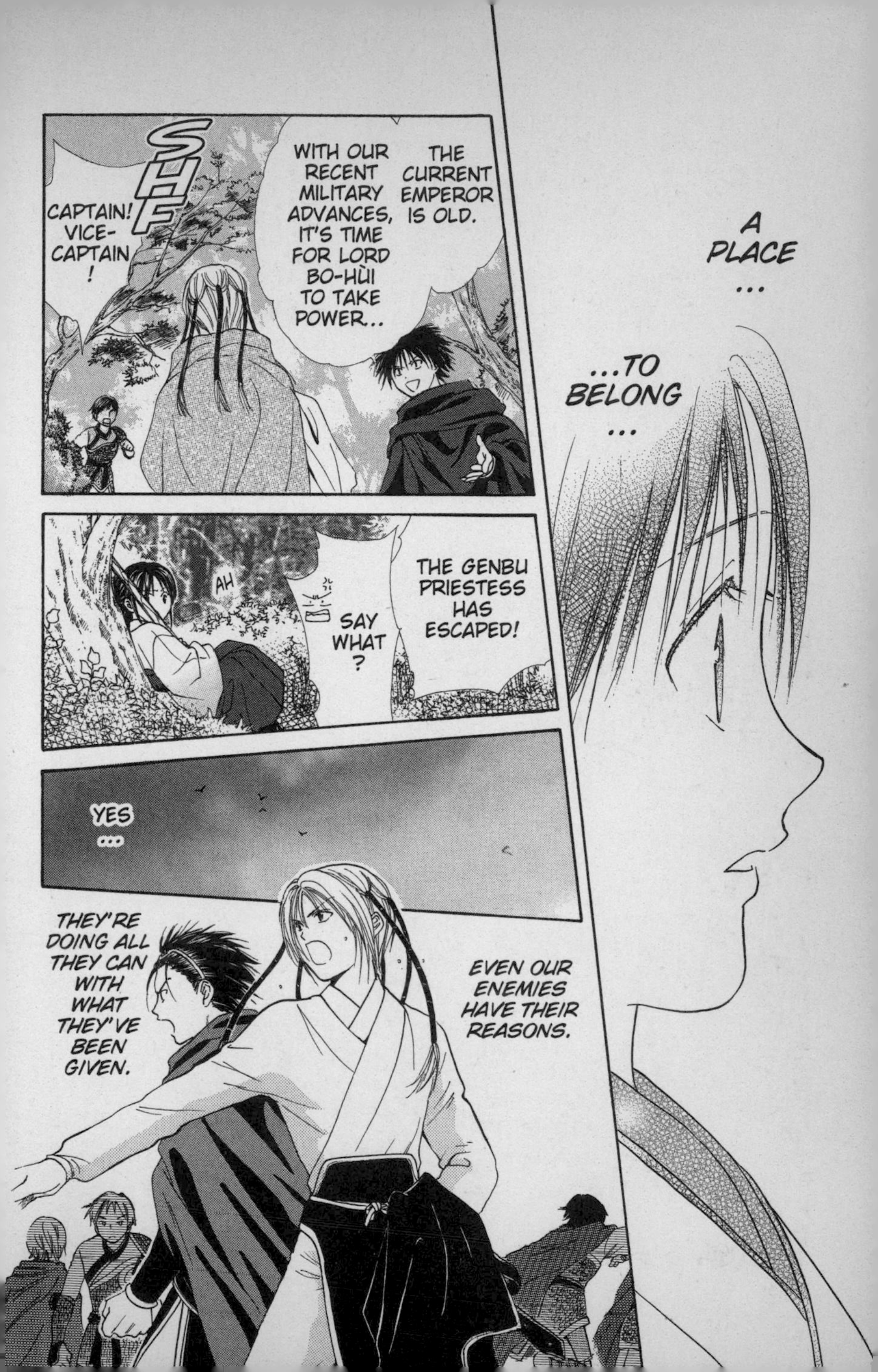
A PLACE ...
...TO BELONG ...
THE CURRENT EMPEROR IS OLD.
WITH OUR RECENT MILITARY ADVANCES, IT'S TIME FOR LORD BO-HÙI TO TAKE POWER...
SHF
CAPTAIN! VICE-CAPTAIN!
THE GENBU PRIESTESS HAS ESCAPED!
SAY WHAT?
AH
YES...
EVEN OUR ENEMIES HAVE THEIR REASONS.
THEY'RE DOING ALL THEY CAN WITH WHAT THEY'VE BEEN GIVEN.

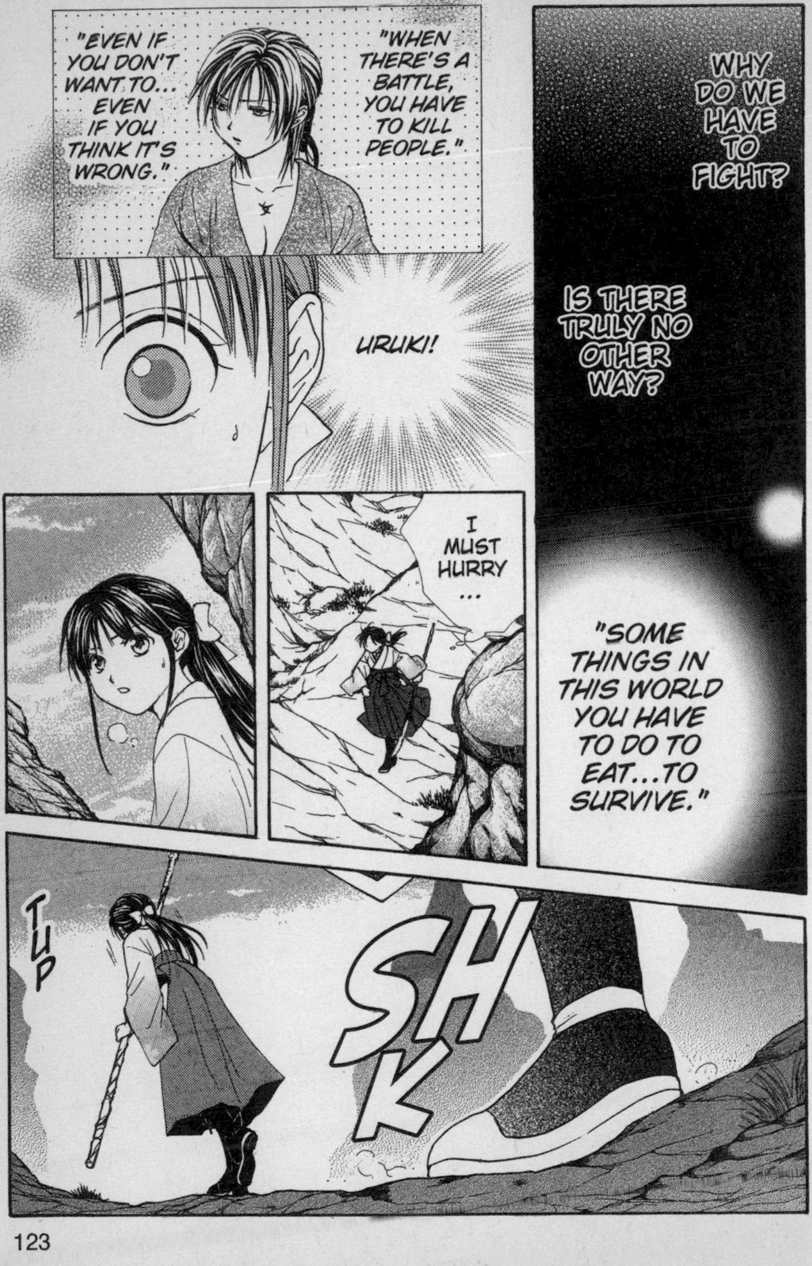
WHY DO WE HAVE TO FIGHT?
IS THERE TRULY NO OTHER WAY?
"SOME THINGS IN THIS WORLD YOU HAVE TO DO TO EAT...TO SURVIVE."
"WHEN THERE'S A BATTLE, YOU HAVE TO KILL PEOPLE."
"EVEN IF YOU DON'T WANT TO... EVEN IF YOU THINK IT'S WRONG."
URUKI!
I MUST HURRY ...
SHK
TUP

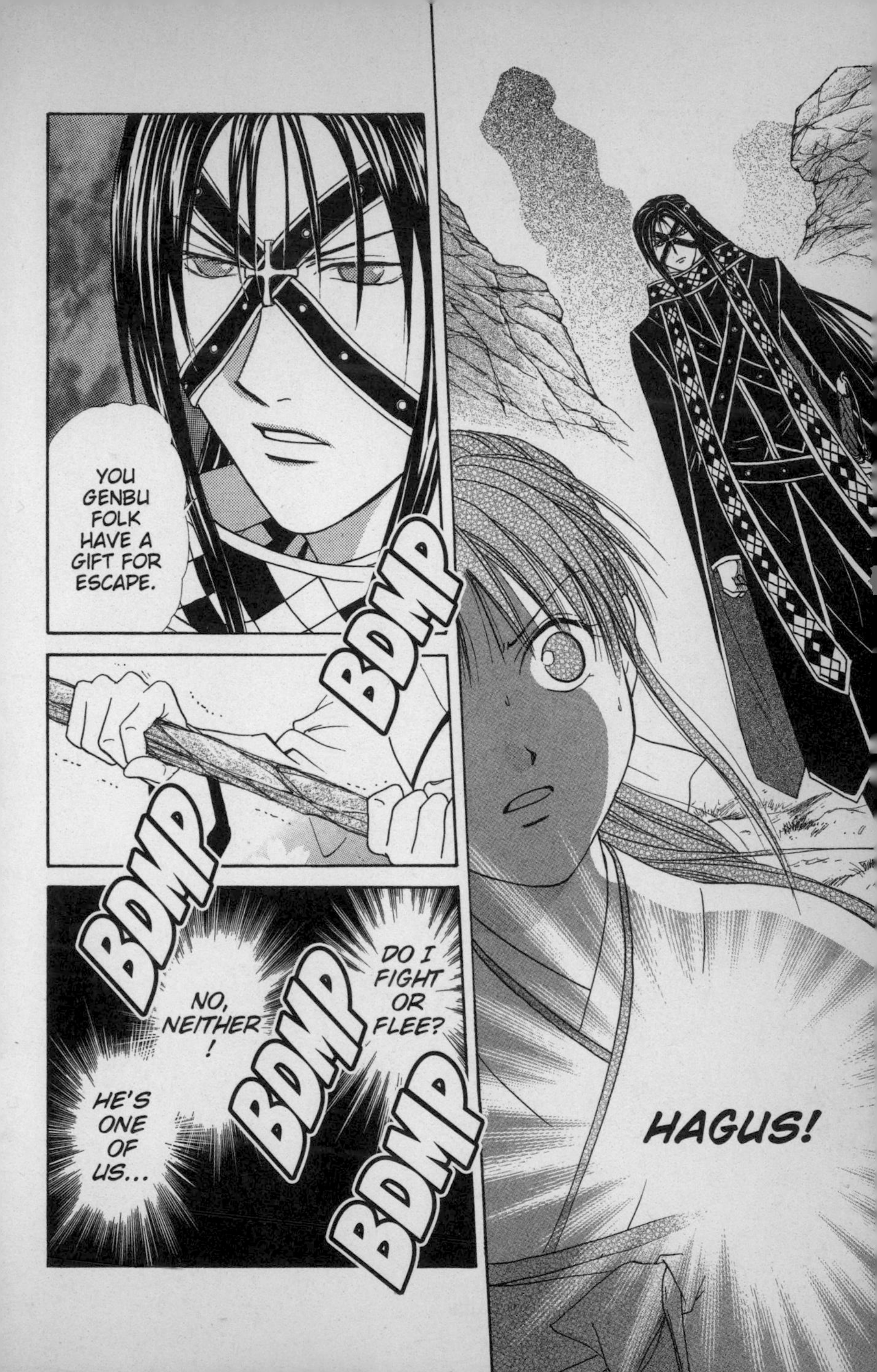
HAGUS!
YOU GENBU FOLK HAVE A GIFT FOR ESCAPE.
BDMP
BDMP
DO I FIGHT OR FLEE?
BDMP
NO, NEITHER!
BDMP
HE'S ONE OF US...
BDMP

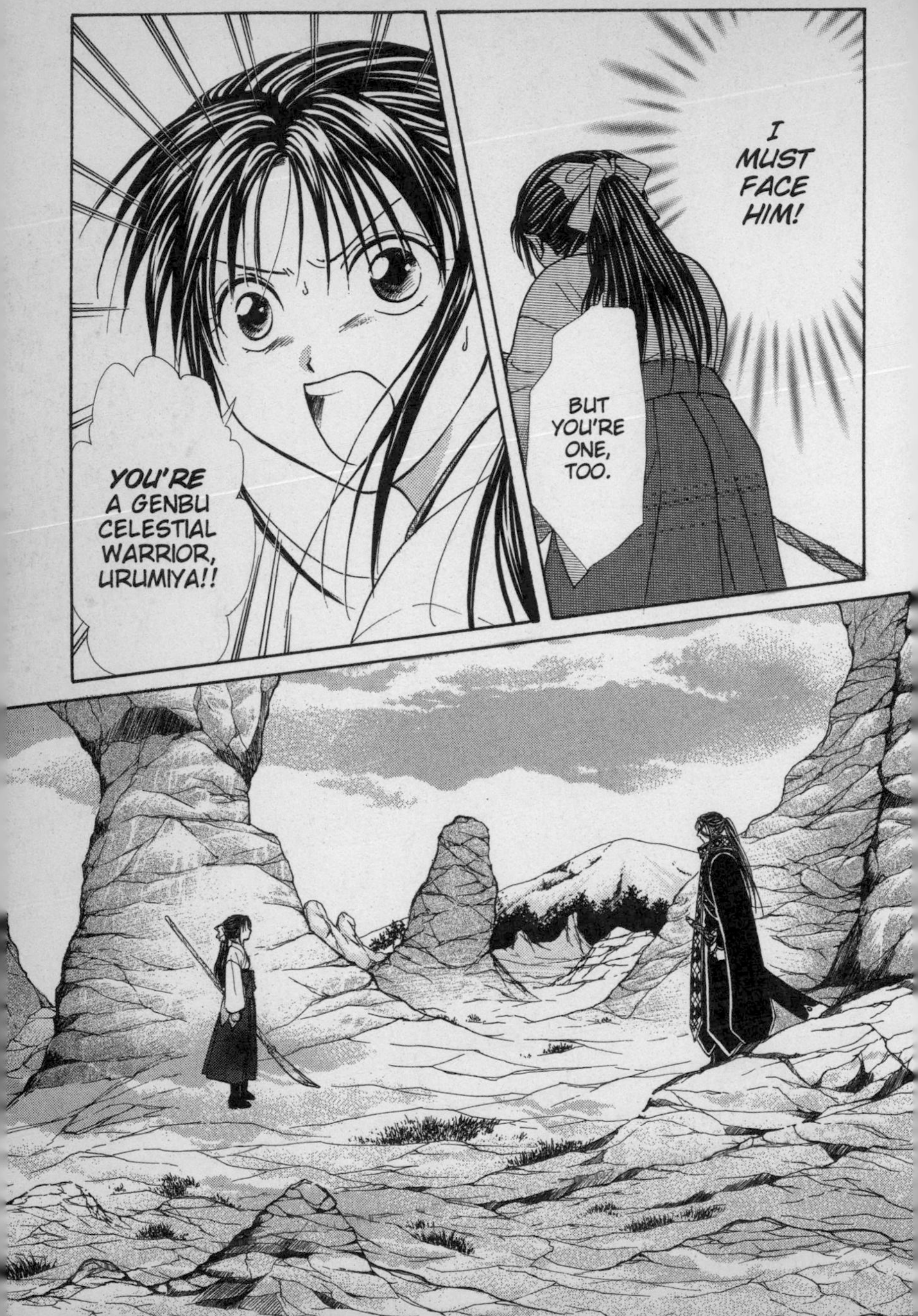
I MUST FACE HIM!
BUT YOU'RE ONE, TOO.
YOU'RE A GENBU CELESTIAL WARRIOR, URUMIYA!!

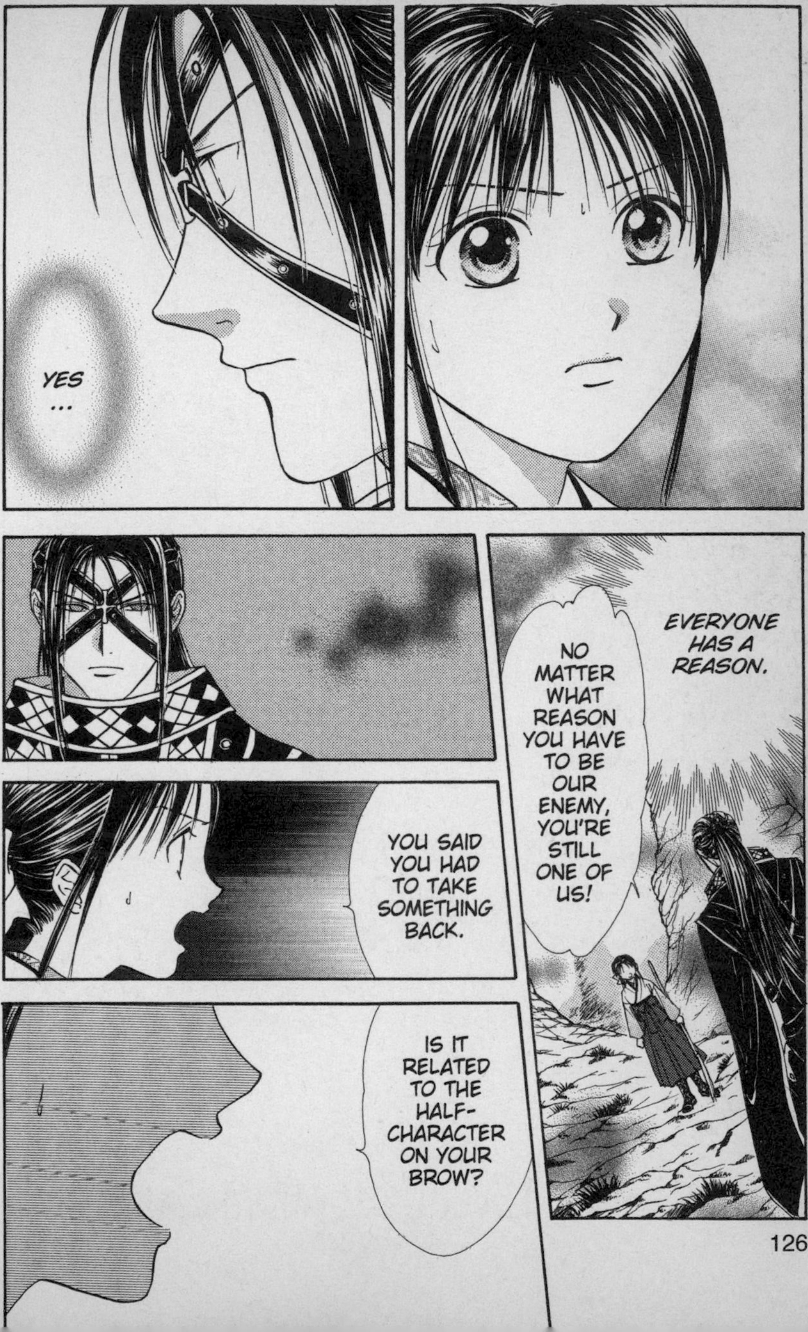
YES ...
EVERYONE HAS A REASON.
NO MATTER WHAT REASON YOU HAVE TO BE OUR ENEMY, YOU'RE STILL ONE OF US!
YOU SAID YOU HAD TO TAKE SOMETHING BACK.
IS IT RELATED TO THE HALF-CHARACTER ON YOUR BROW?

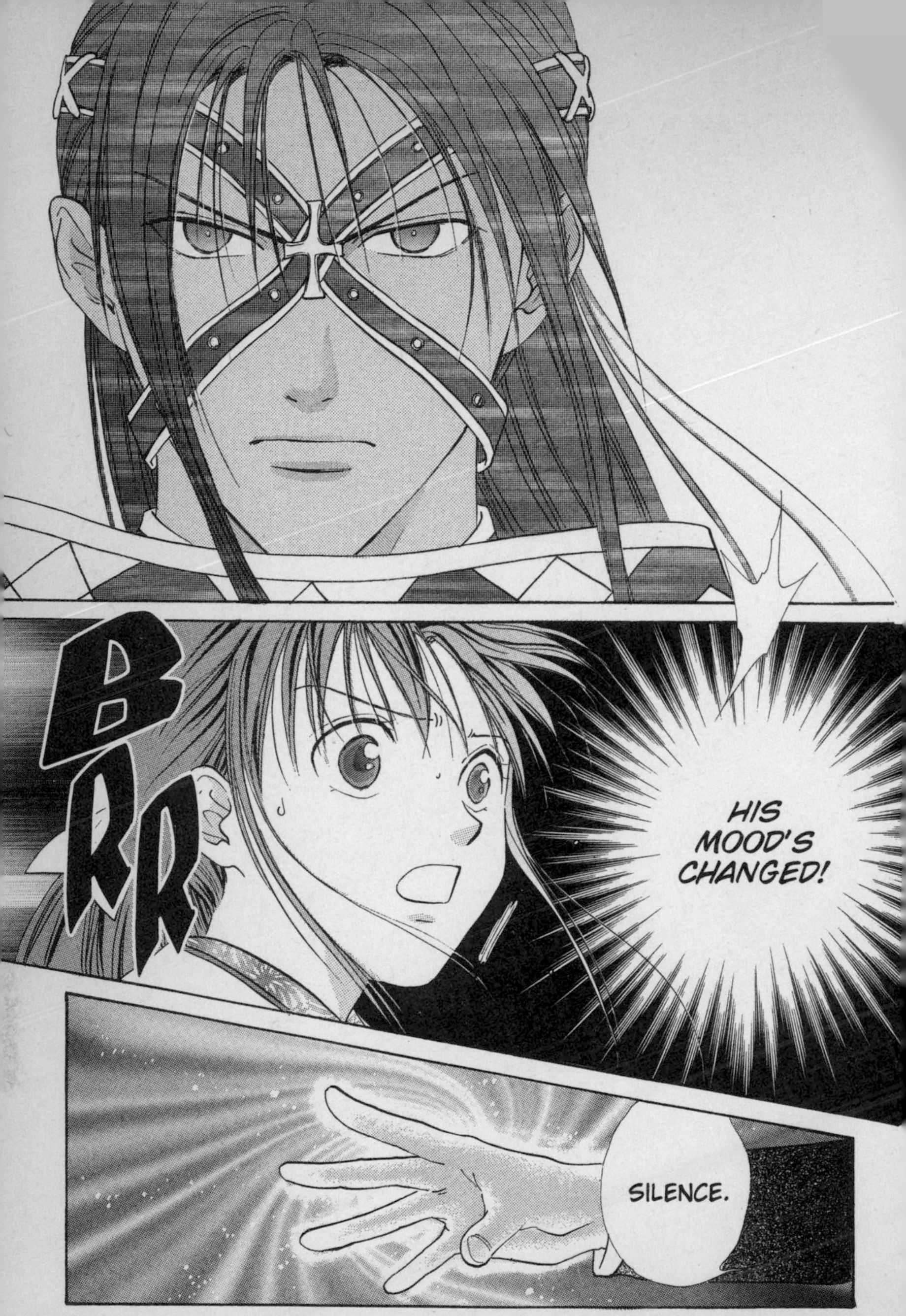
HIS MOOD'S CHANGED!
BRR
SILENCE.

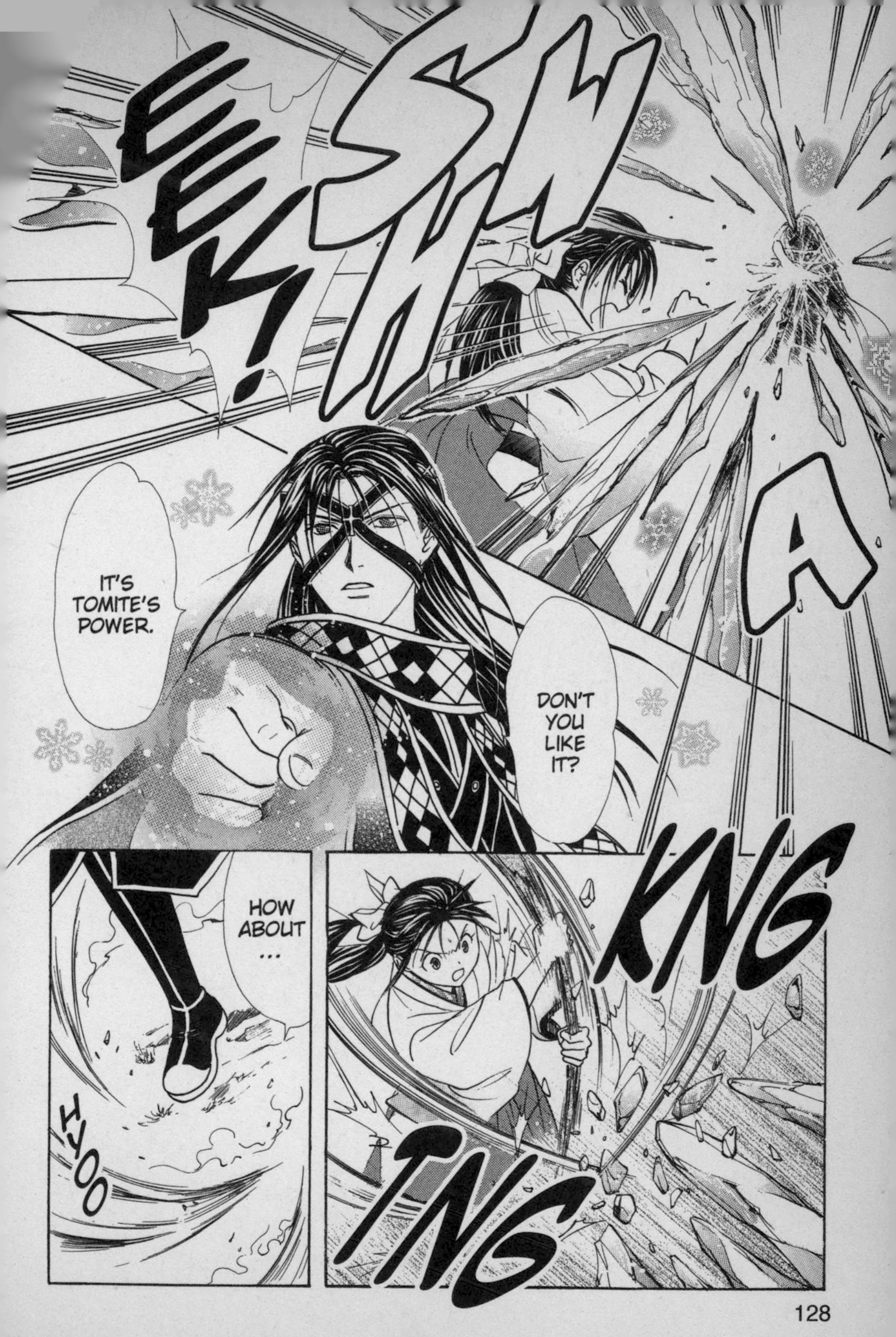
A
SHH
EEK!
DON'T YOU LIKE IT?
IT'S TOMITE'S POWER.
KNG
TNG
HOW ABOUT ...
HYOO

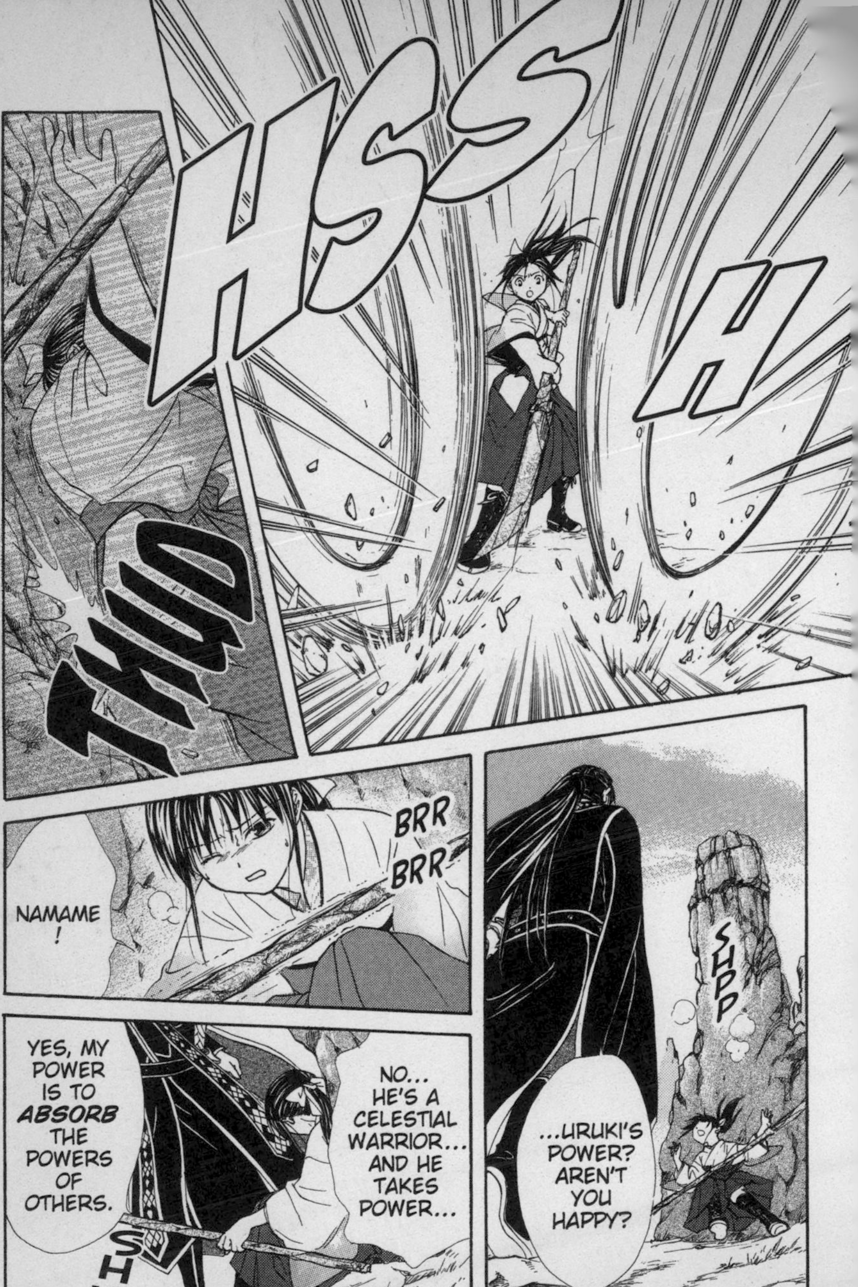
HSSH
THUD
SHPP
...URUKI'S POWER? AREN'T YOU HAPPY?
BRR BRR
NAMAME!
SHK
YES, MY POWER IS TO ***ABSORB*** THE POWERS OF OTHERS.
NO... HE'S A CELESTIAL WARRIOR... AND HE TAKES POWER...

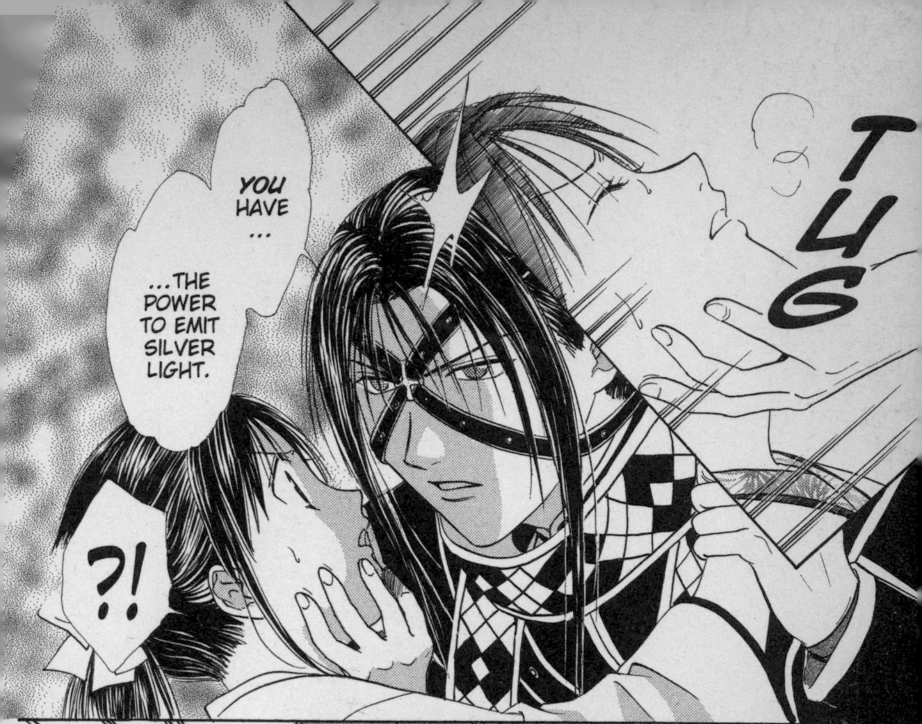
TUG
YOU HAVE ...
...THE POWER TO EMIT SILVER LIGHT.
?!
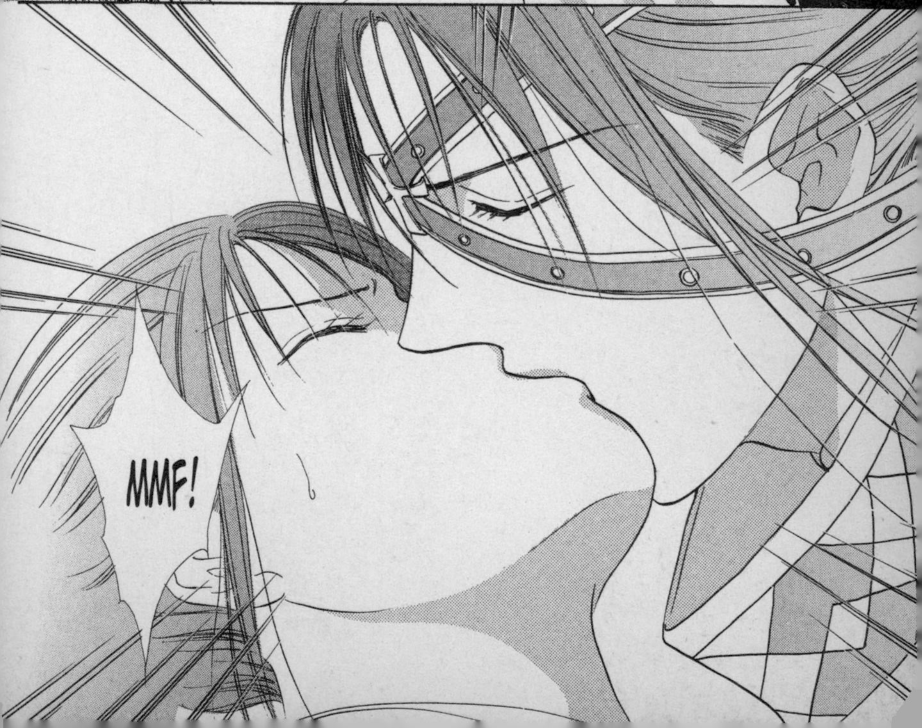
MMF!

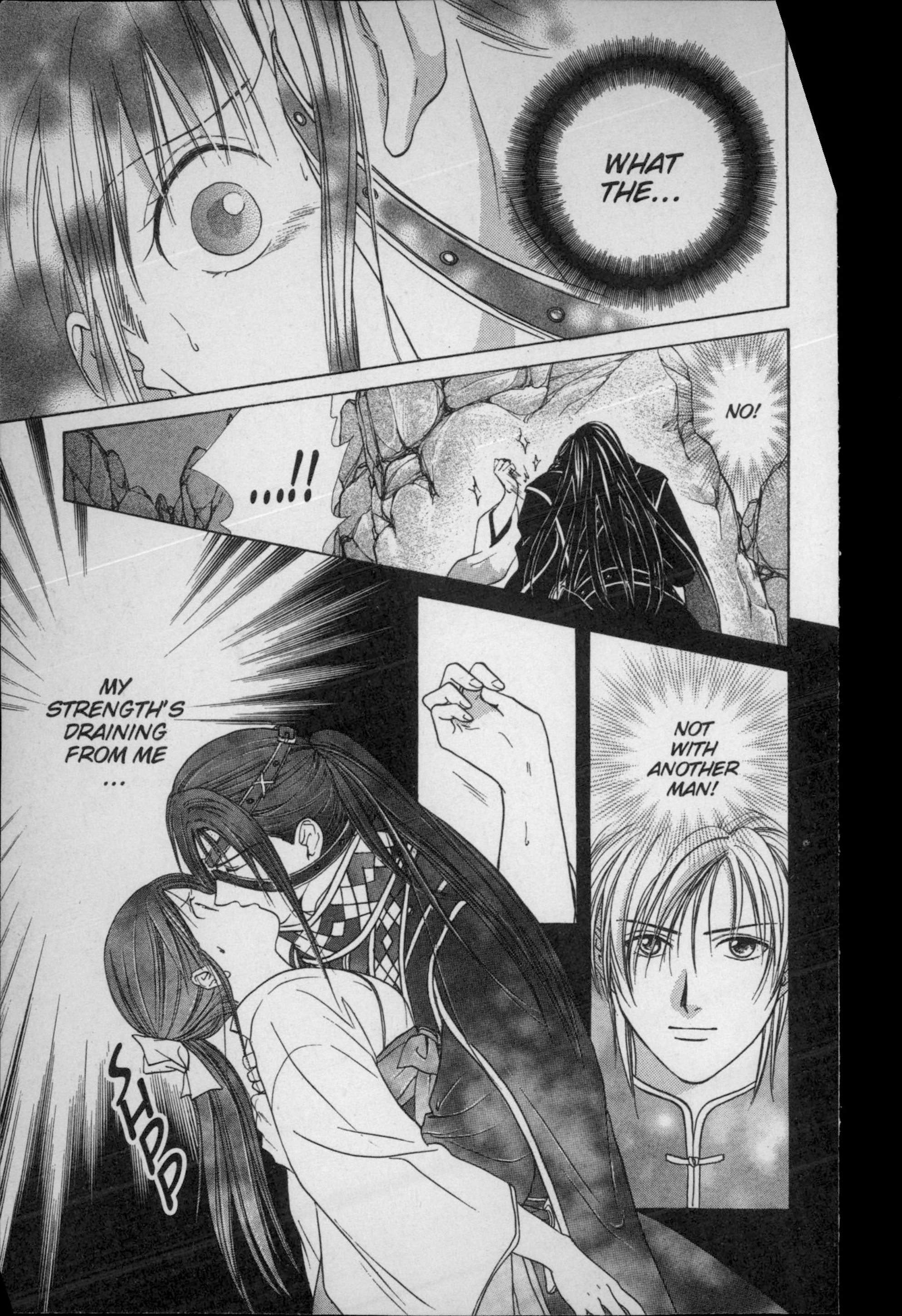
WHAT THE...
NO!
...!!
NOT WITH ANOTHER MAN!
MY STRENGTH'S DRAINING FROM ME ...
SHPP

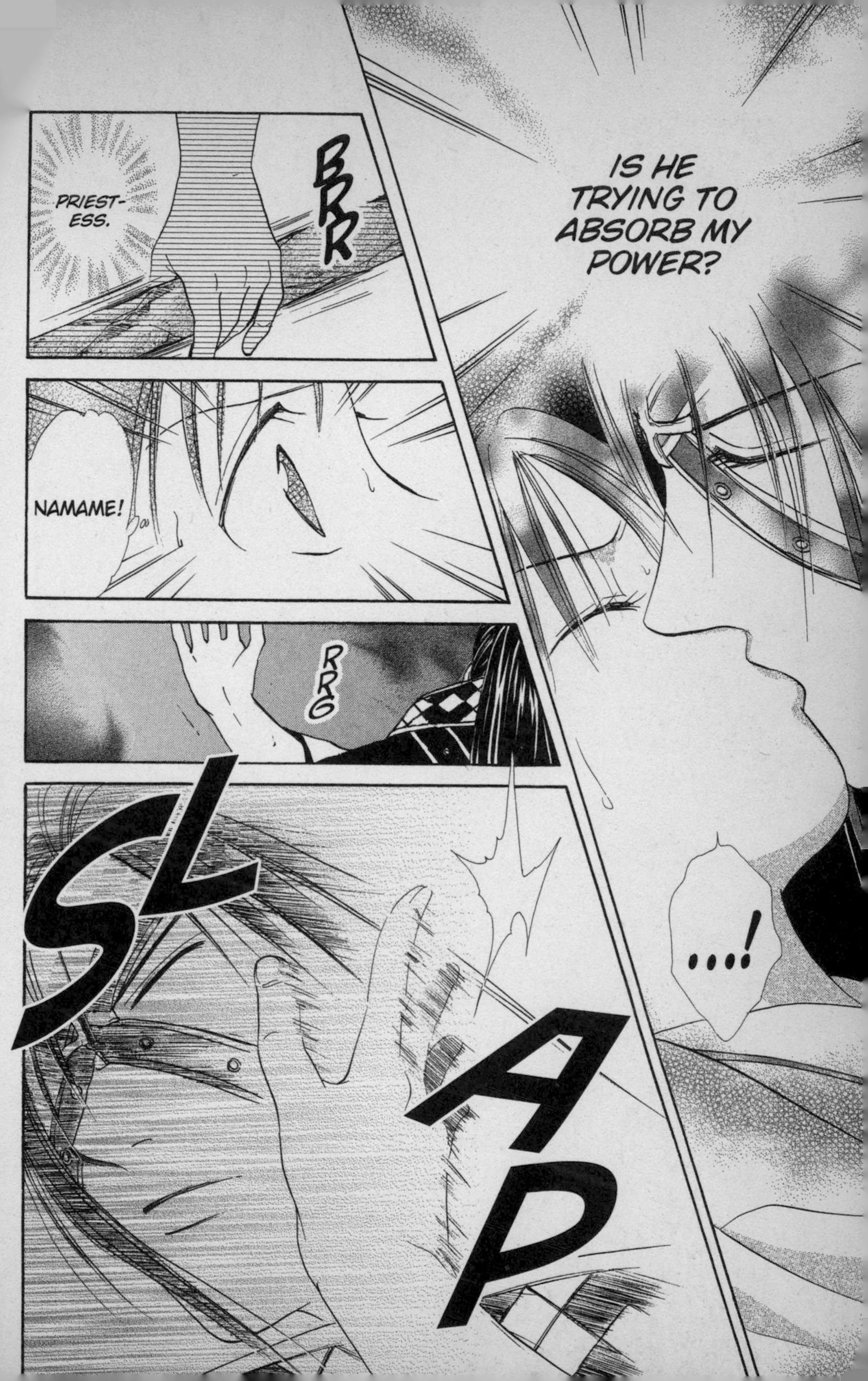
IS HE TRYING TO ABSORB MY POWER?
...!
BRRR
PRIEST-ESS.
NAMAME!
RRG
SLAP

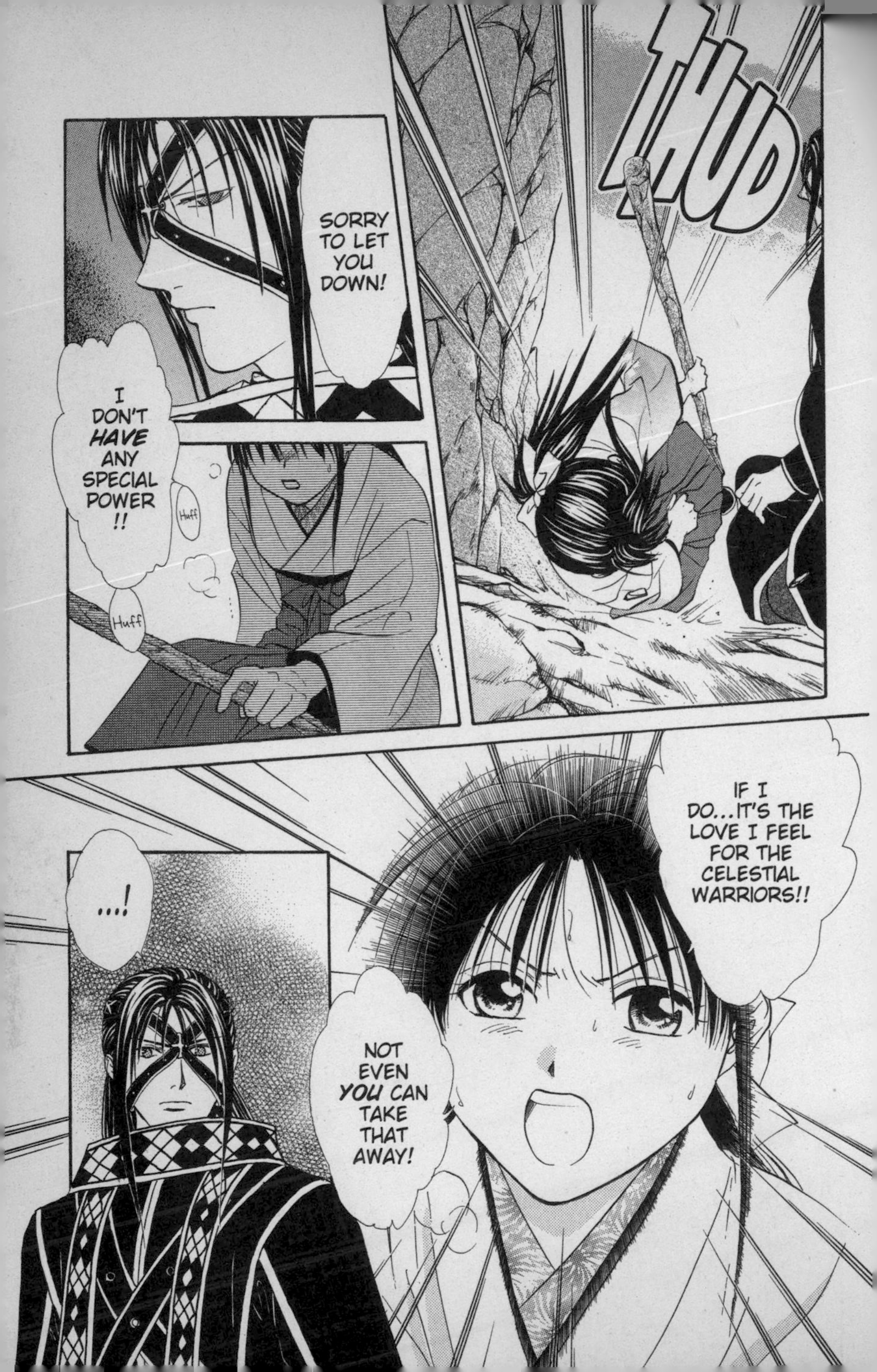
THUD
SORRY TO LET YOU DOWN!
I DON'T *HAVE* ANY SPECIAL POWER!!
Huff
Huff
IF I DO...IT'S THE LOVE I FEEL FOR THE CELESTIAL WARRIORS!!
NOT EVEN *YOU* CAN TAKE THAT AWAY!
...!

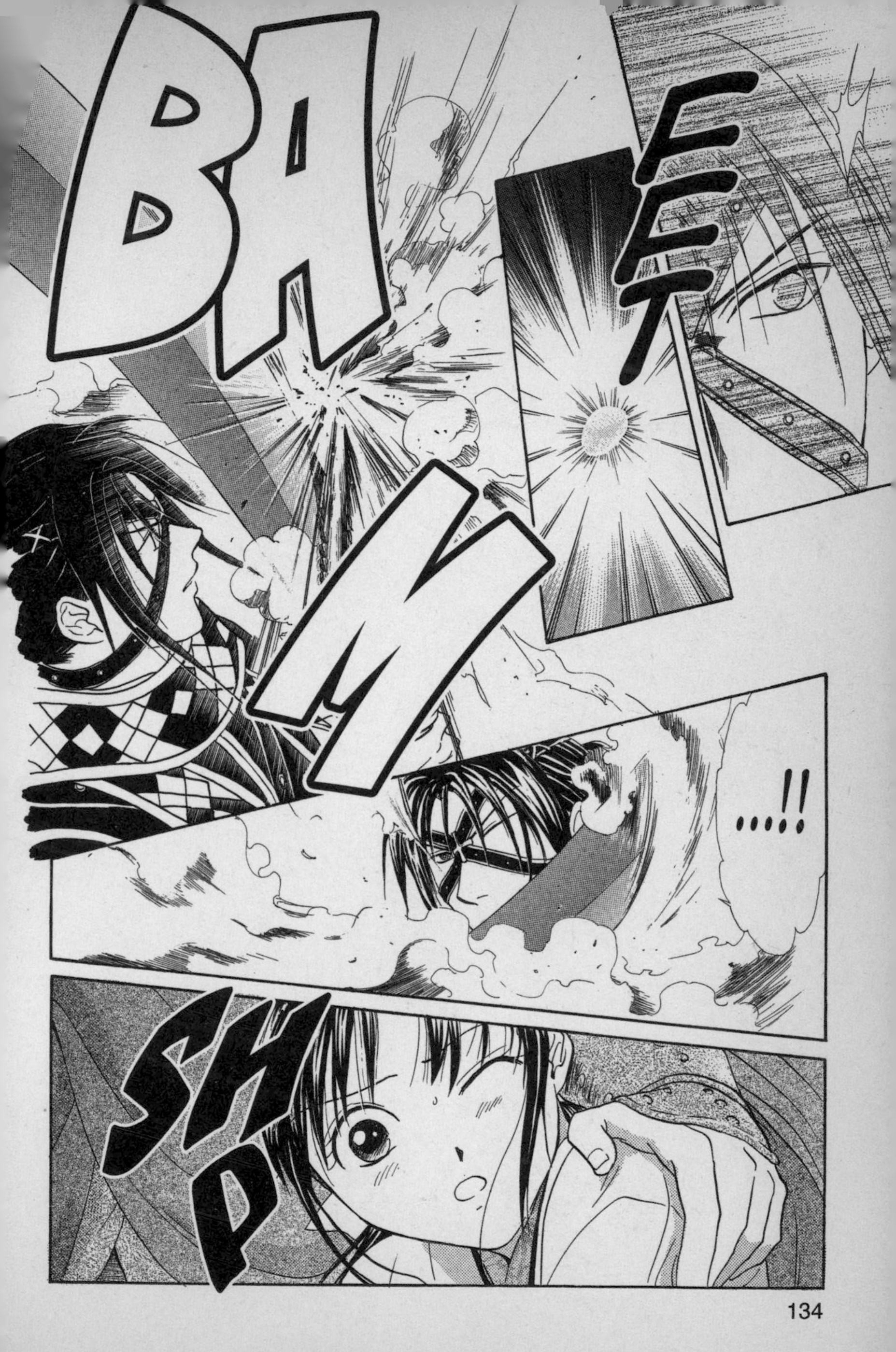
FFT
BAM
...!!
SHP

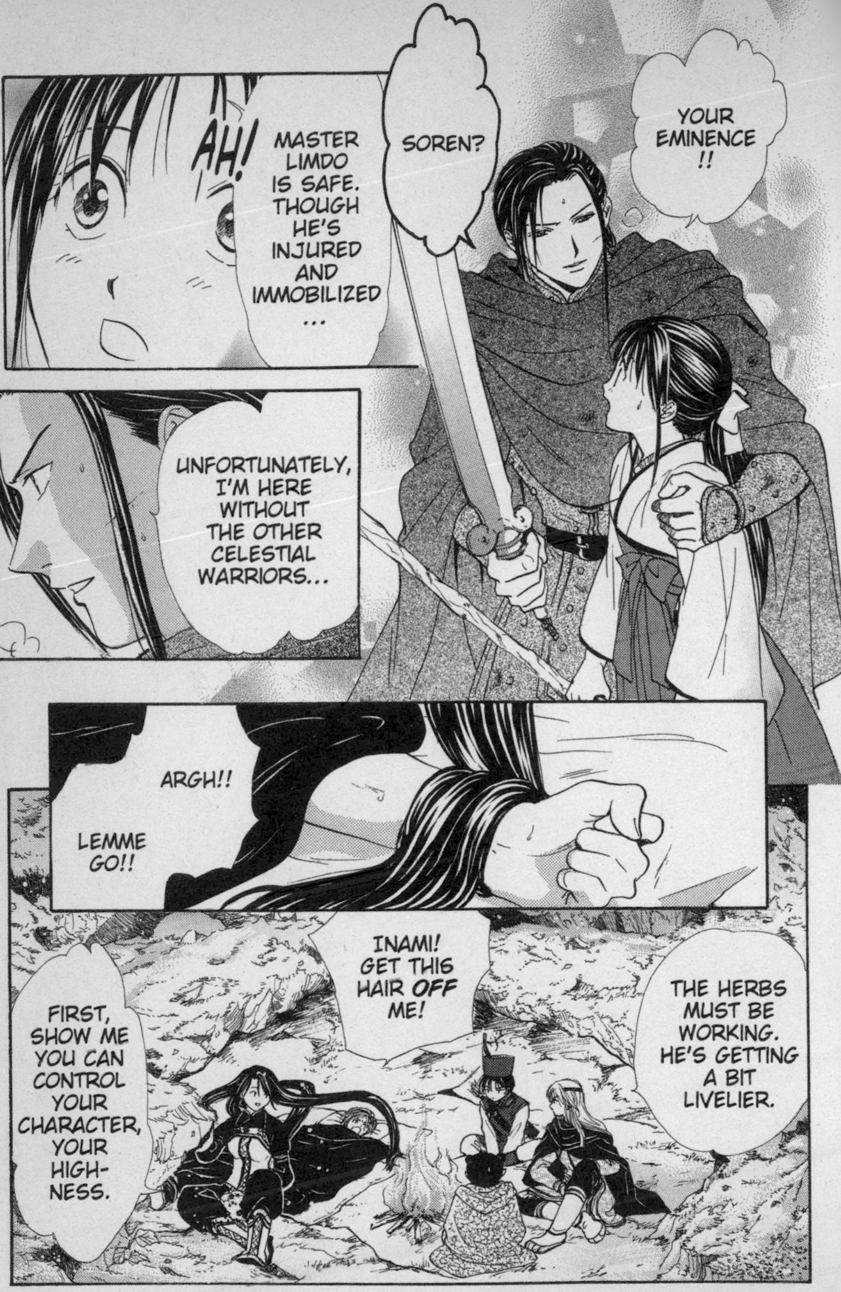
YOUR EMINENCE !!
SOREN?
AH!
MASTER LIMDO IS SAFE. THOUGH HE'S INJURED AND IMMOBILIZED ...
UNFORTUNATELY, I'M HERE WITHOUT THE OTHER CELESTIAL WARRIORS...
ARGH!!
LEMME GO!!
THE HERBS MUST BE WORKING. HE'S GETTING A BIT LIVELIER.
INAMI! GET THIS HAIR OFF ME!
FIRST, SHOW ME YOU CAN CONTROL YOUR CHARACTER, YOUR HIGH-NESS.

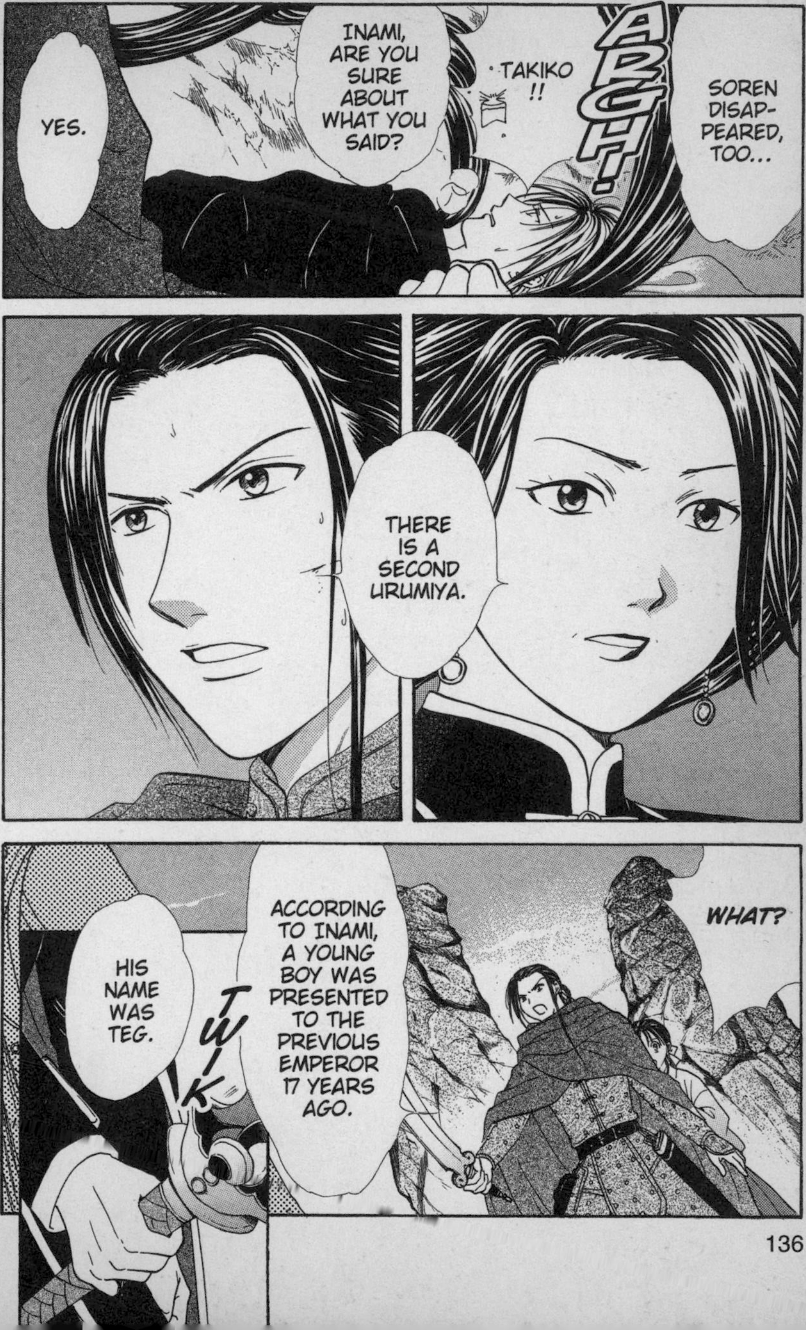
SOREN DISAPPEARED, TOO...
ARGH!
·TAKIKO !!
INAMI, ARE YOU SURE ABOUT WHAT YOU SAID?
YES.
THERE IS A SECOND URUMIYA.
WHAT?
ACCORDING TO INAMI, A YOUNG BOY WAS PRESENTED TO THE PREVIOUS EMPEROR 17 YEARS AGO.
TWIK
HIS NAME WAS TEG.

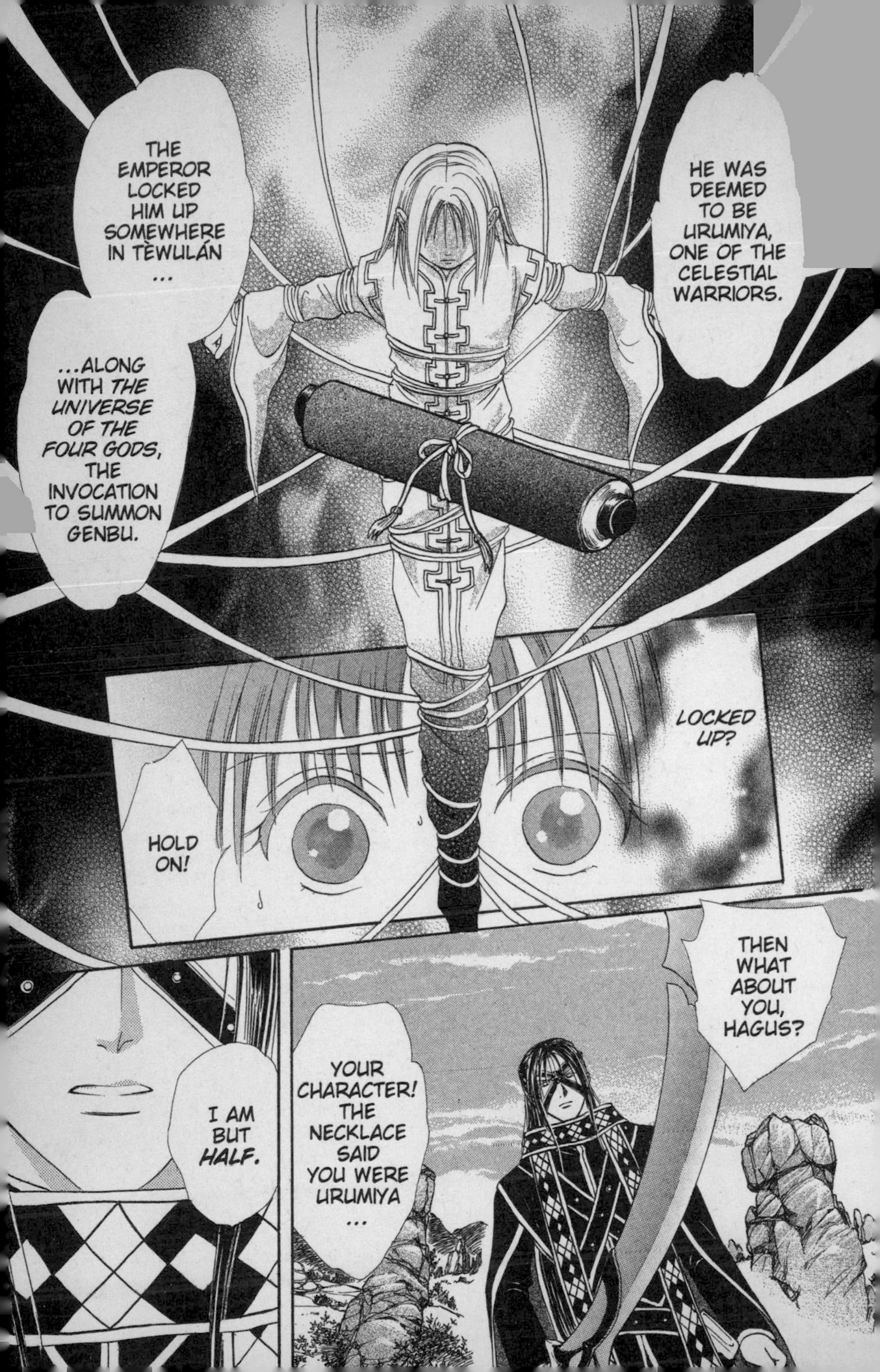
HE WAS DEEMED TO BE URUMIYA, ONE OF THE CELESTIAL WARRIORS.
THE EMPEROR LOCKED HIM UP SOMEWHERE IN TÈWULÁN ...
...ALONG WITH *THE UNIVERSE OF THE FOUR GODS*, THE INVOCATION TO SUMMON GENBU.
LOCKED UP?
HOLD ON!
THEN WHAT ABOUT YOU, HAGUS?
YOUR CHARACTER! THE NECKLACE SAID YOU WERE URUMIYA ...
I AM BUT *HALF*.

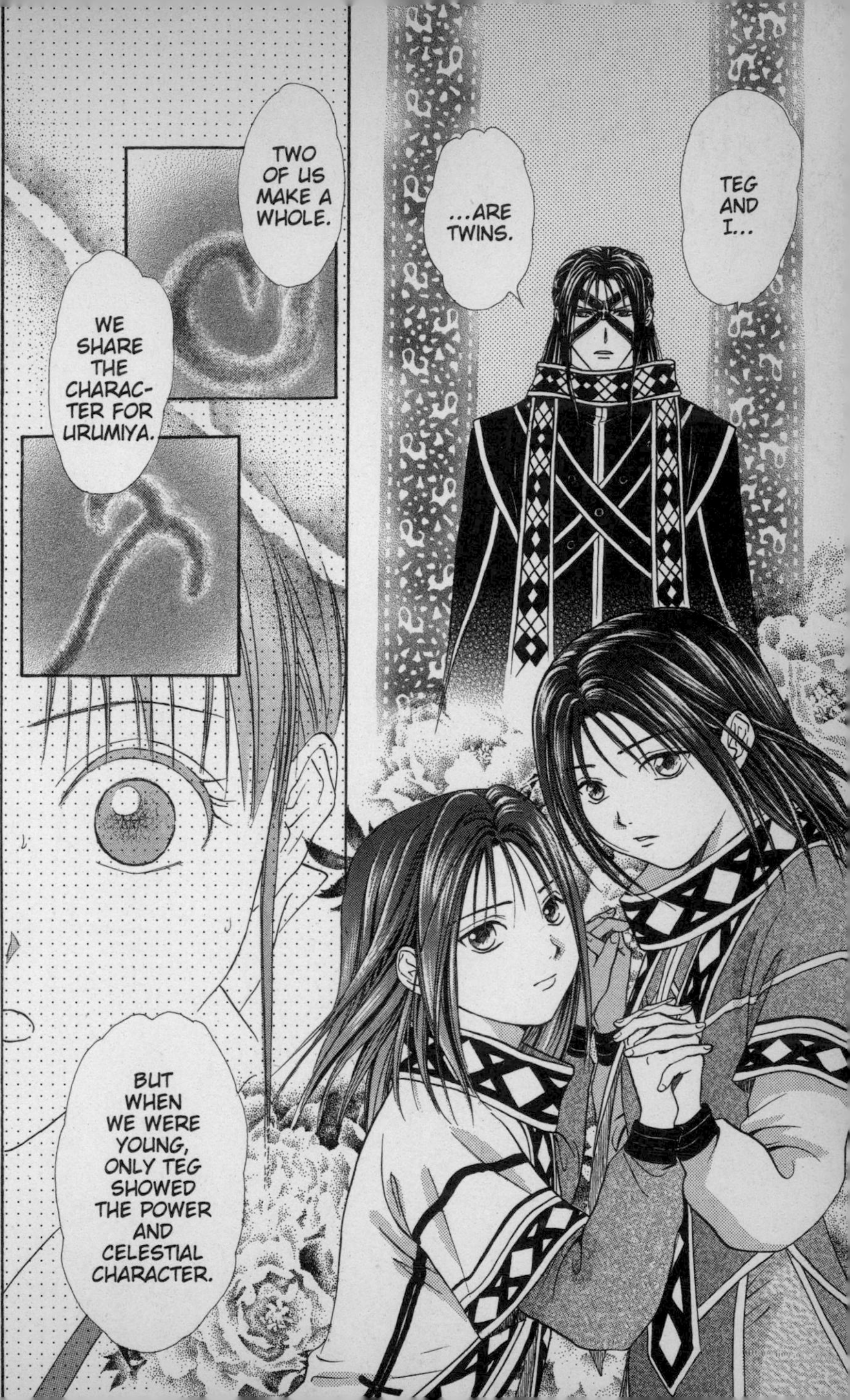
TEG AND I...
...ARE TWINS.
TWO OF US MAKE A WHOLE.
WE SHARE THE CHARAC-TER FOR URUMIYA.
BUT WHEN WE WERE YOUNG, ONLY TEG SHOWED THE POWER AND CELESTIAL CHARACTER.

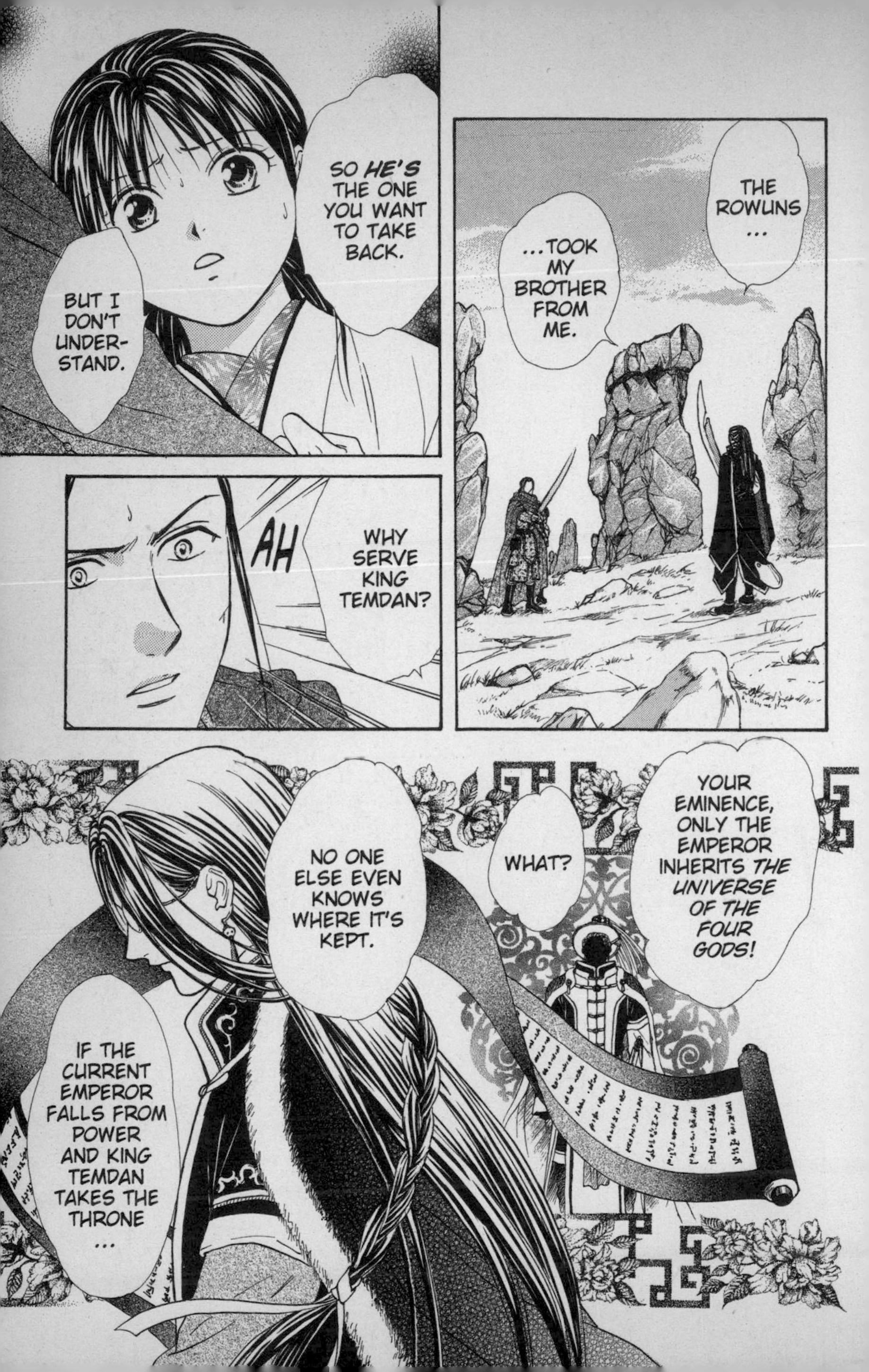
THE ROWUNS ...
...TOOK MY BROTHER FROM ME.
SO *HE'S* THE ONE YOU WANT TO TAKE BACK.
BUT I DON'T UNDER-STAND.
AH
WHY SERVE KING TEMDAN?
YOUR EMINENCE, ONLY THE EMPEROR INHERITS *THE UNIVERSE OF THE FOUR GODS!*
WHAT?
NO ONE ELSE EVEN KNOWS WHERE IT'S KEPT.
IF THE CURRENT EMPEROR FALLS FROM POWER AND KING TEMDAN TAKES THE THRONE ...

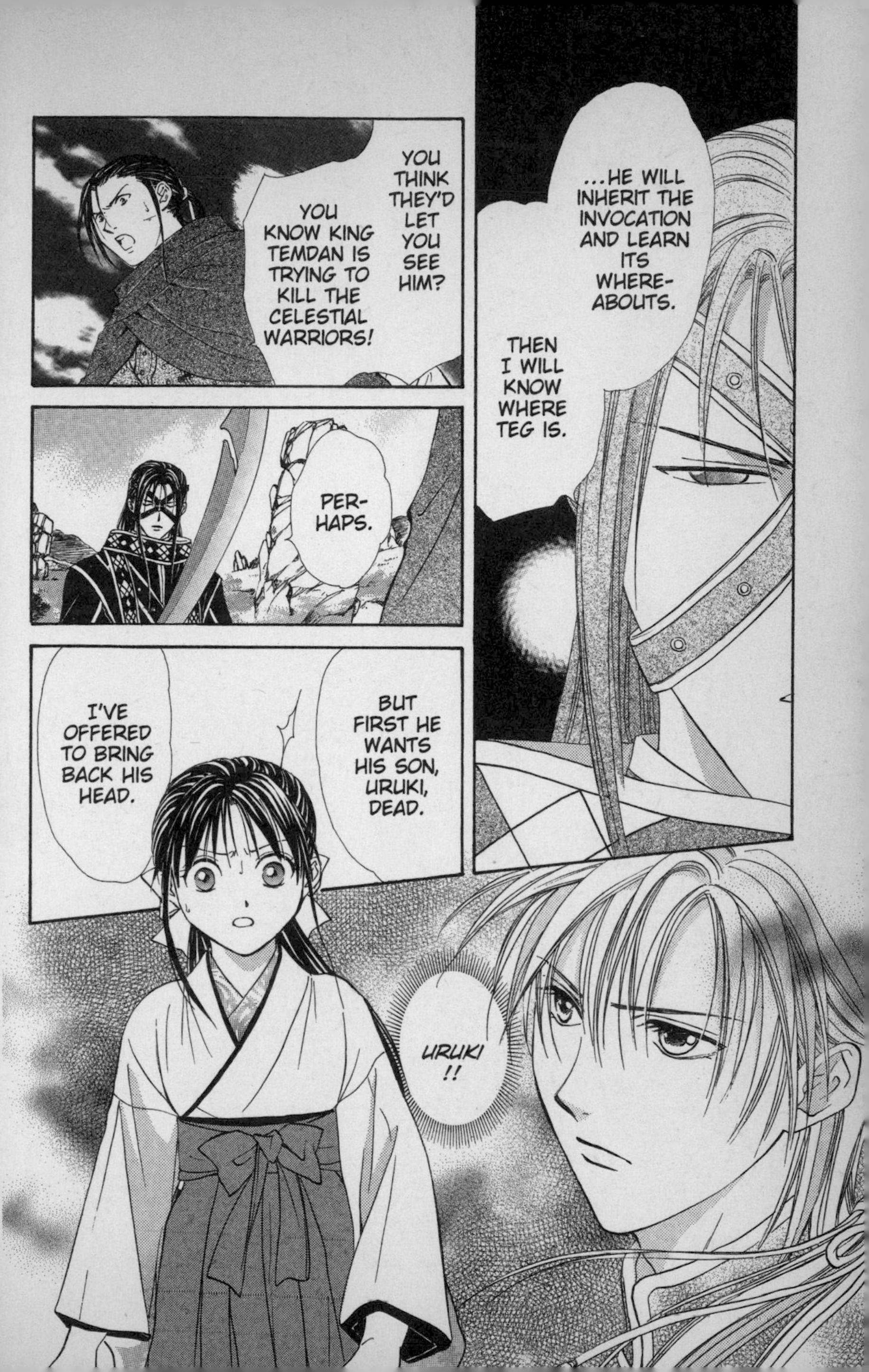
...HE WILL INHERIT THE INVOCATION AND LEARN ITS WHERE-ABOUTS.
THEN I WILL KNOW WHERE TEG IS.
YOU THINK THEY'D LET YOU SEE HIM?
YOU KNOW KING TEMDAN IS TRYING TO KILL THE CELESTIAL WARRIORS!
PER-HAPS.
I'VE OFFERED TO BRING BACK HIS HEAD.
BUT FIRST HE WANTS HIS SON, URUKI, DEAD.
URUKI !!

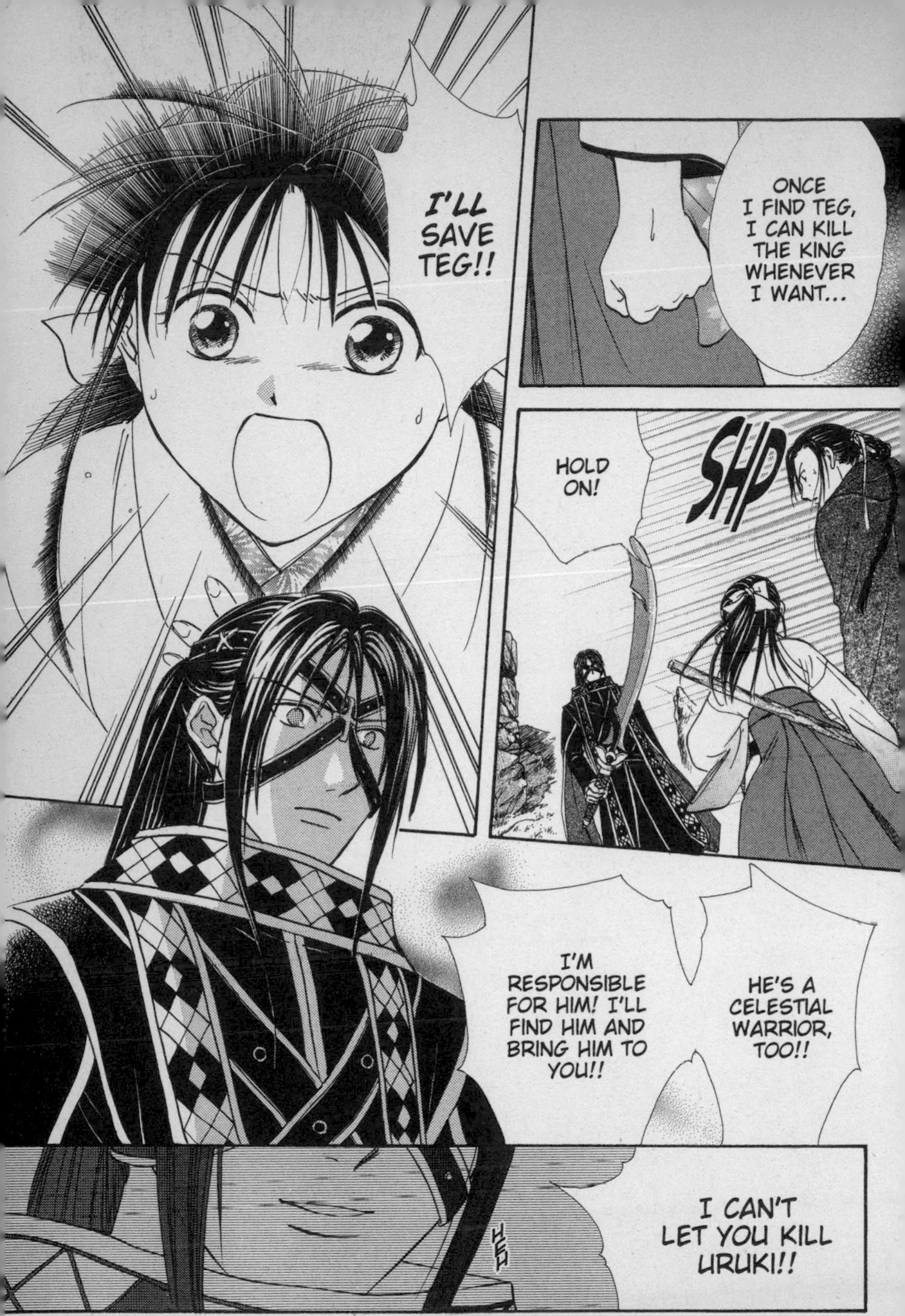
ONCE I FIND TEG, I CAN KILL THE KING WHENEVER I WANT...
I'LL SAVE TEG!!
SHP
HOLD ON!
HE'S A CELESTIAL WARRIOR, TOO!!
I'M RESPONSIBLE FOR HIM! I'LL FIND HIM AND BRING HIM TO YOU!!
I CAN'T LET YOU KILL URUKI!!
HEH

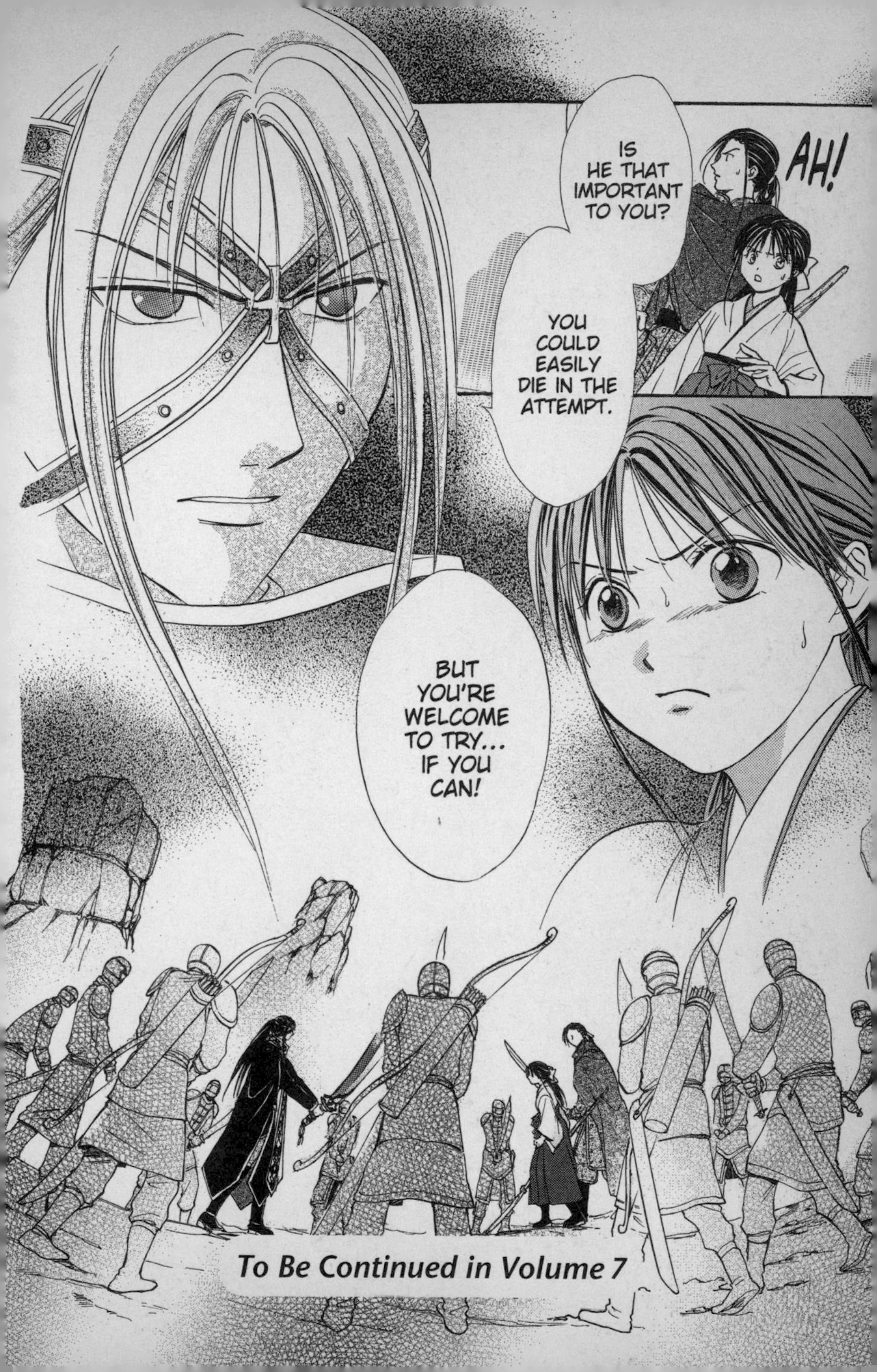
AH!
IS HE THAT IMPORTANT TO YOU?
YOU COULD EASILY DIE IN THE ATTEMPT.
BUT YOU'RE WELCOME TO TRY... IF YOU CAN!
To Be Continued in Volume 7

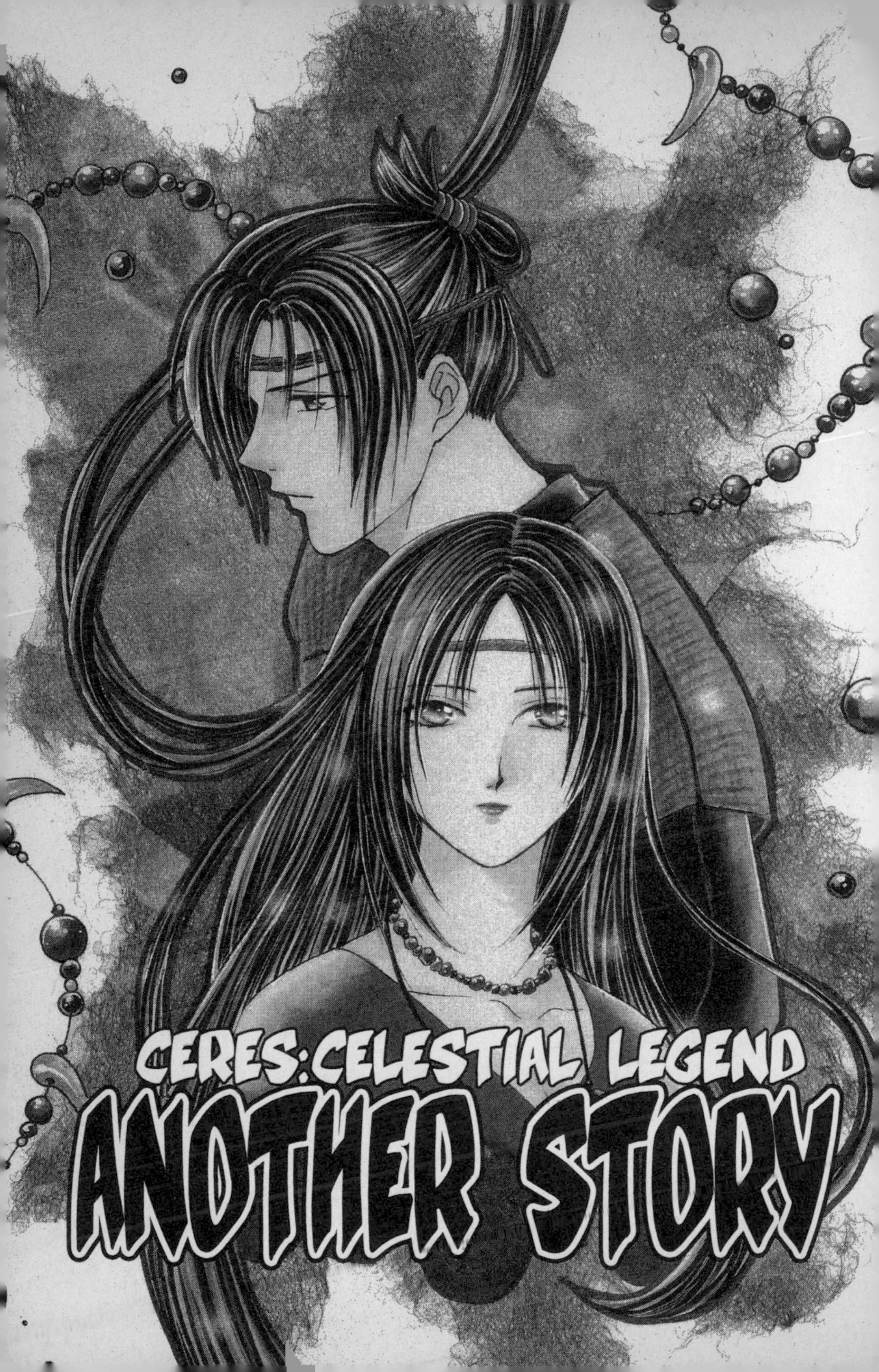
CERES: CELESTIAL LEGEND
ANOTHER STORY

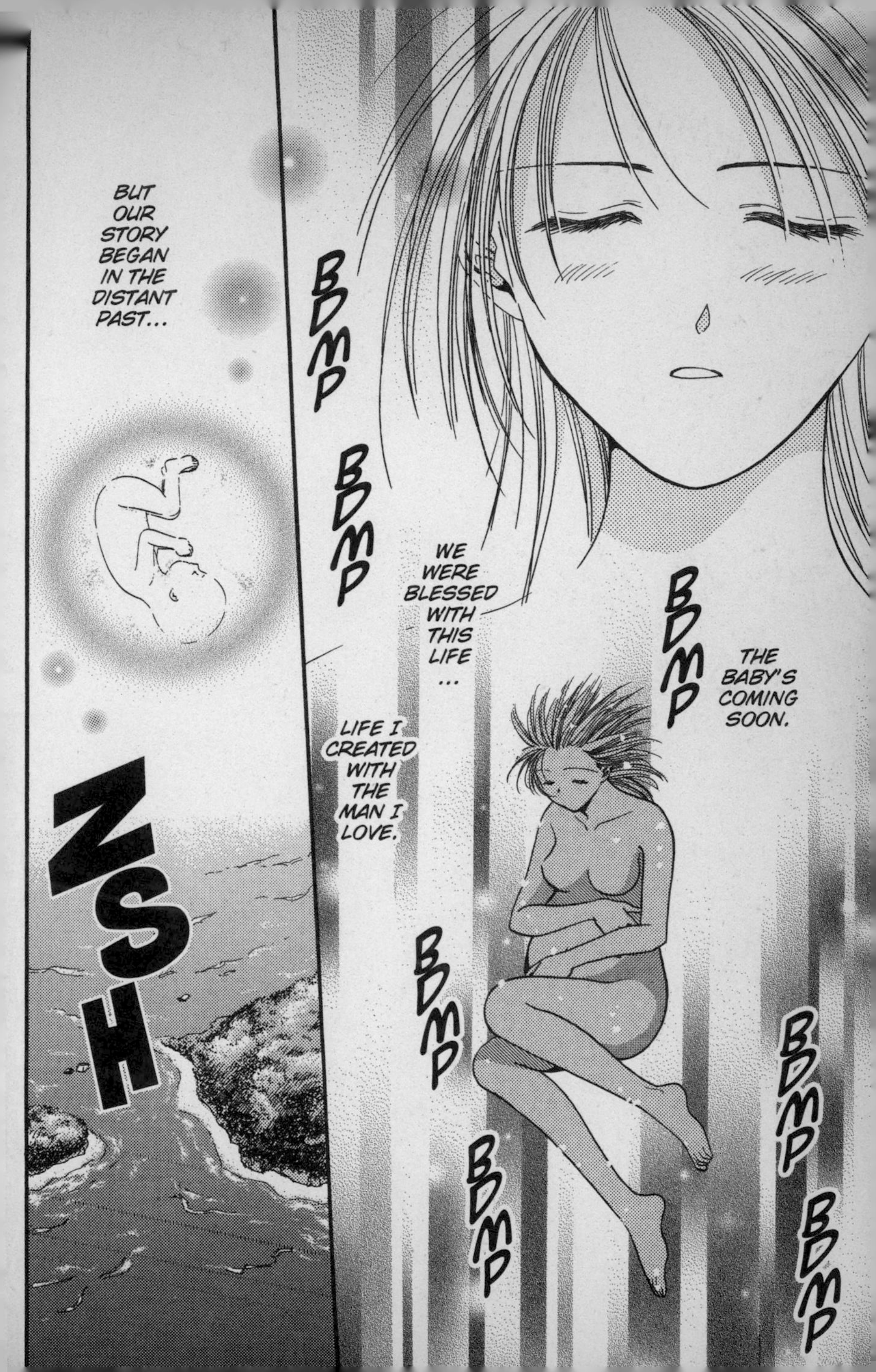
BDMP
THE BABY'S COMING SOON.
BDMP
BDMP
WE WERE BLESSED WITH THIS LIFE...
LIFE I CREATED WITH THE MAN I LOVE.
BDMP
BDMP
BDMP
BDMP
BDMP
BUT OUR STORY BEGAN IN THE DISTANT PAST...
NSH

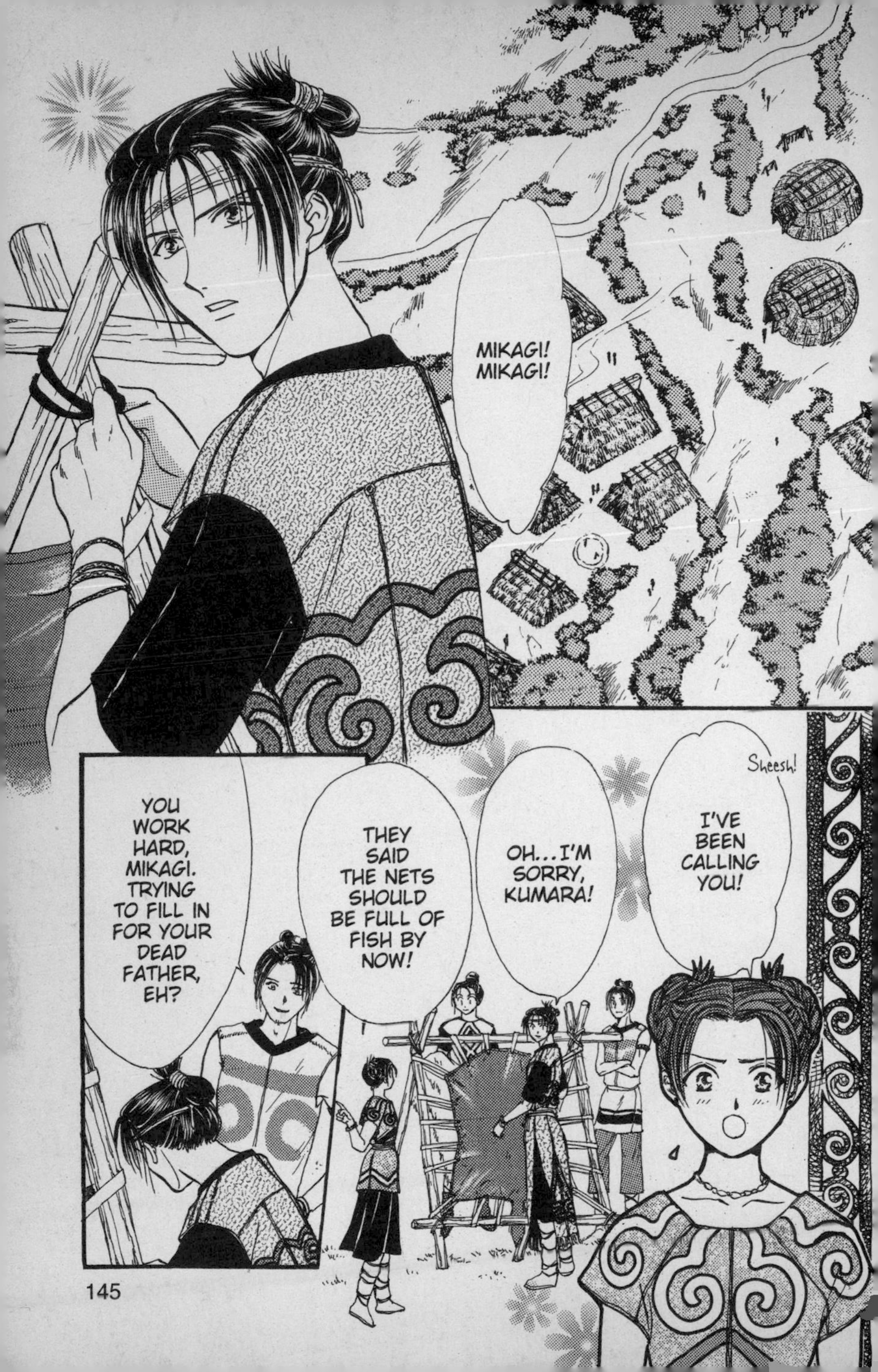
MIKAGI! MIKAGI!
Sheesh!
I'VE BEEN CALLING YOU!
OH...I'M SORRY, KUMARA!
THEY SAID THE NETS SHOULD BE FULL OF FISH BY NOW!
YOU WORK HARD, MIKAGI. TRYING TO FILL IN FOR YOUR DEAD FATHER, EH?

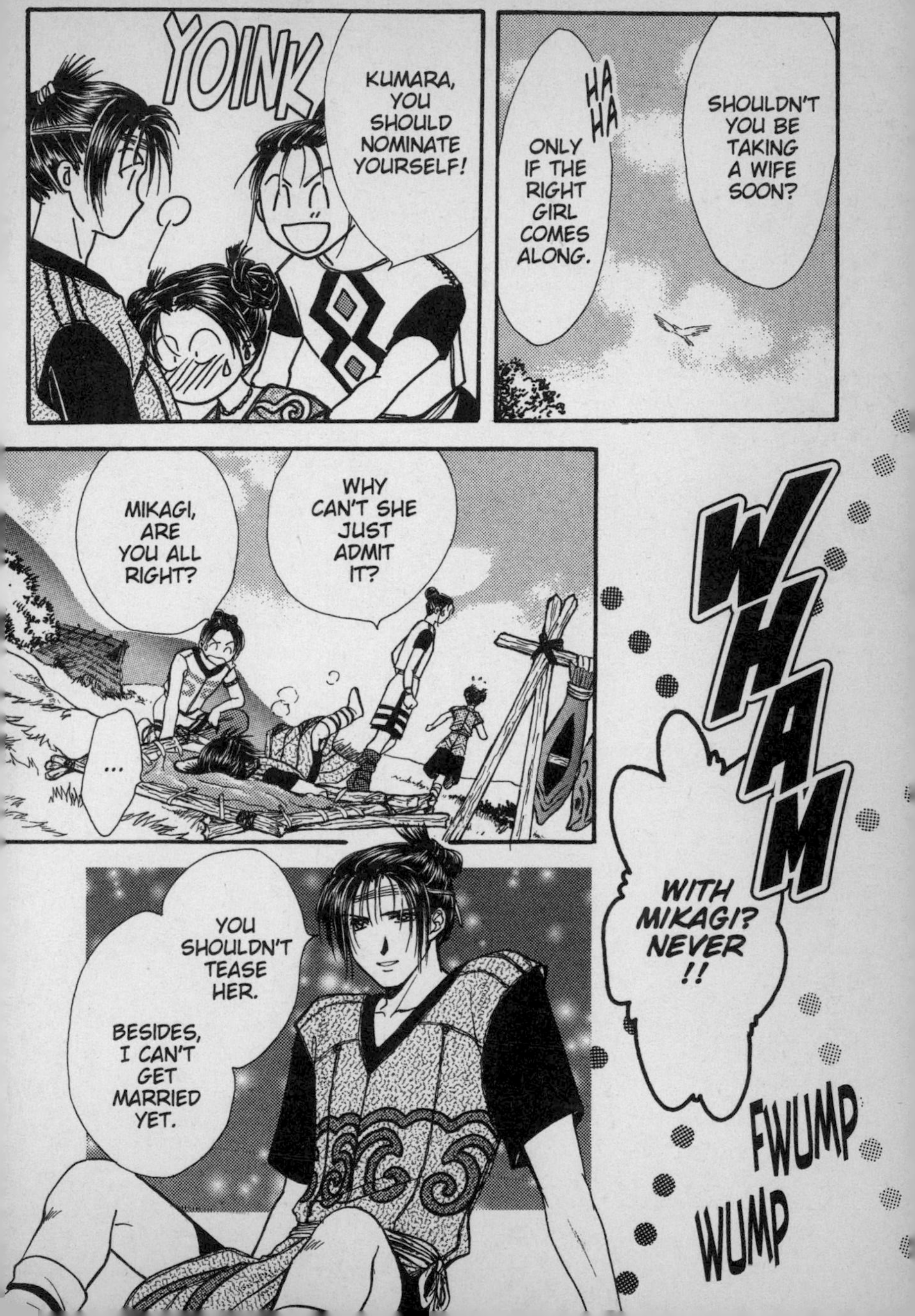
SHOULDN'T YOU BE TAKING A WIFE SOON?
HA HA
ONLY IF THE RIGHT GIRL COMES ALONG.
YOINK
KUMARA, YOU SHOULD NOMINATE YOURSELF!
WITH MIKAGI? NEVER !!
WHAM
FWUMP
WUMP
MIKAGI, ARE YOU ALL RIGHT?
WHY CAN'T SHE JUST ADMIT IT?
...
YOU SHOULDN'T TEASE HER.
BESIDES, I CAN'T GET MARRIED YET.

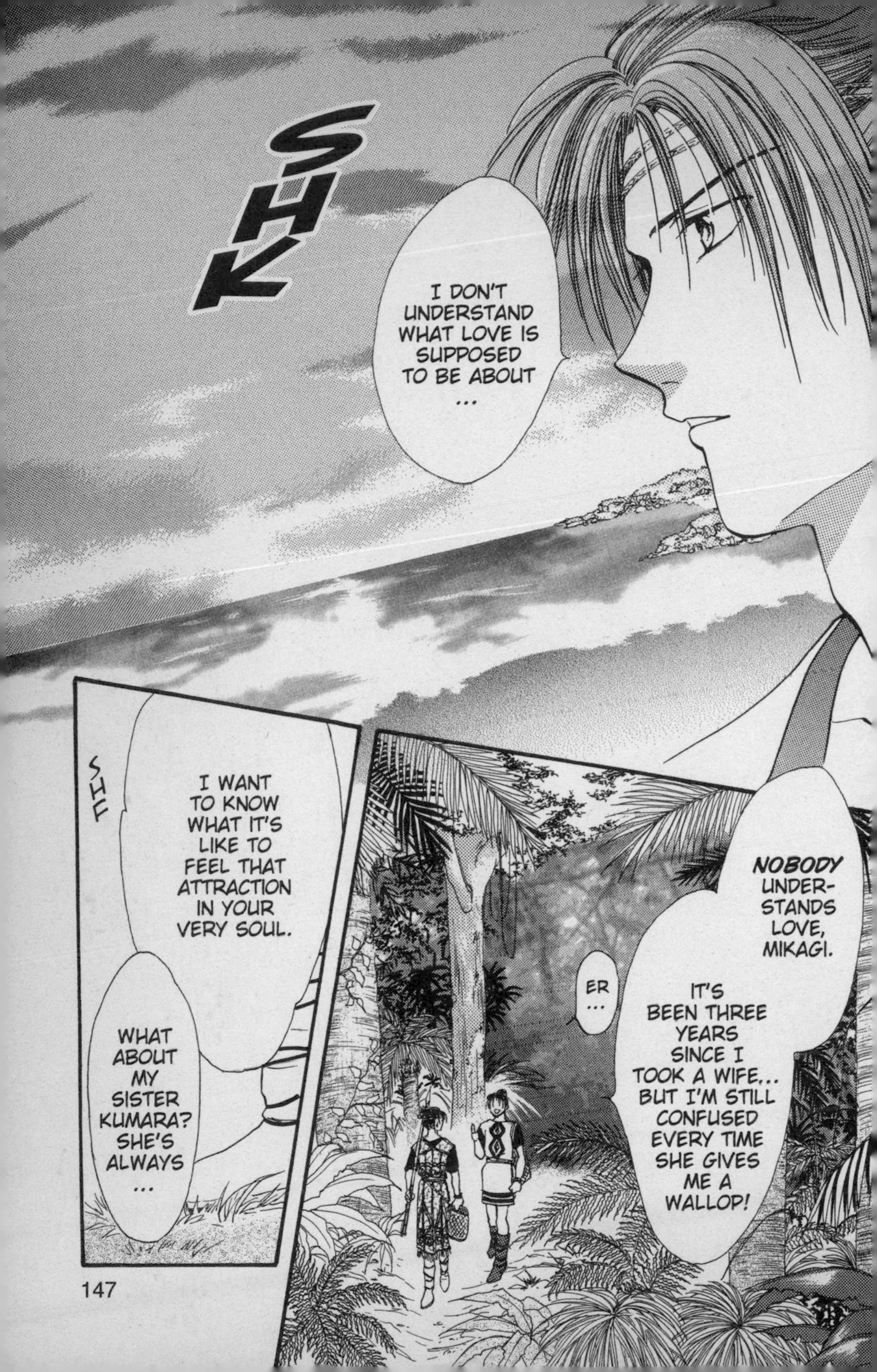
I DON'T UNDERSTAND WHAT LOVE IS SUPPOSED TO BE ABOUT ...
SHK
NOBODY UNDER-STANDS LOVE, MIKAGI.
IT'S BEEN THREE YEARS SINCE I TOOK A WIFE... BUT I'M STILL CONFUSED EVERY TIME SHE GIVES ME A WALLOP!
ER ...
I WANT TO KNOW WHAT IT'S LIKE TO FEEL THAT ATTRACTION IN YOUR VERY SOUL.
SHF
WHAT ABOUT MY SISTER KUMARA? SHE'S ALWAYS ...

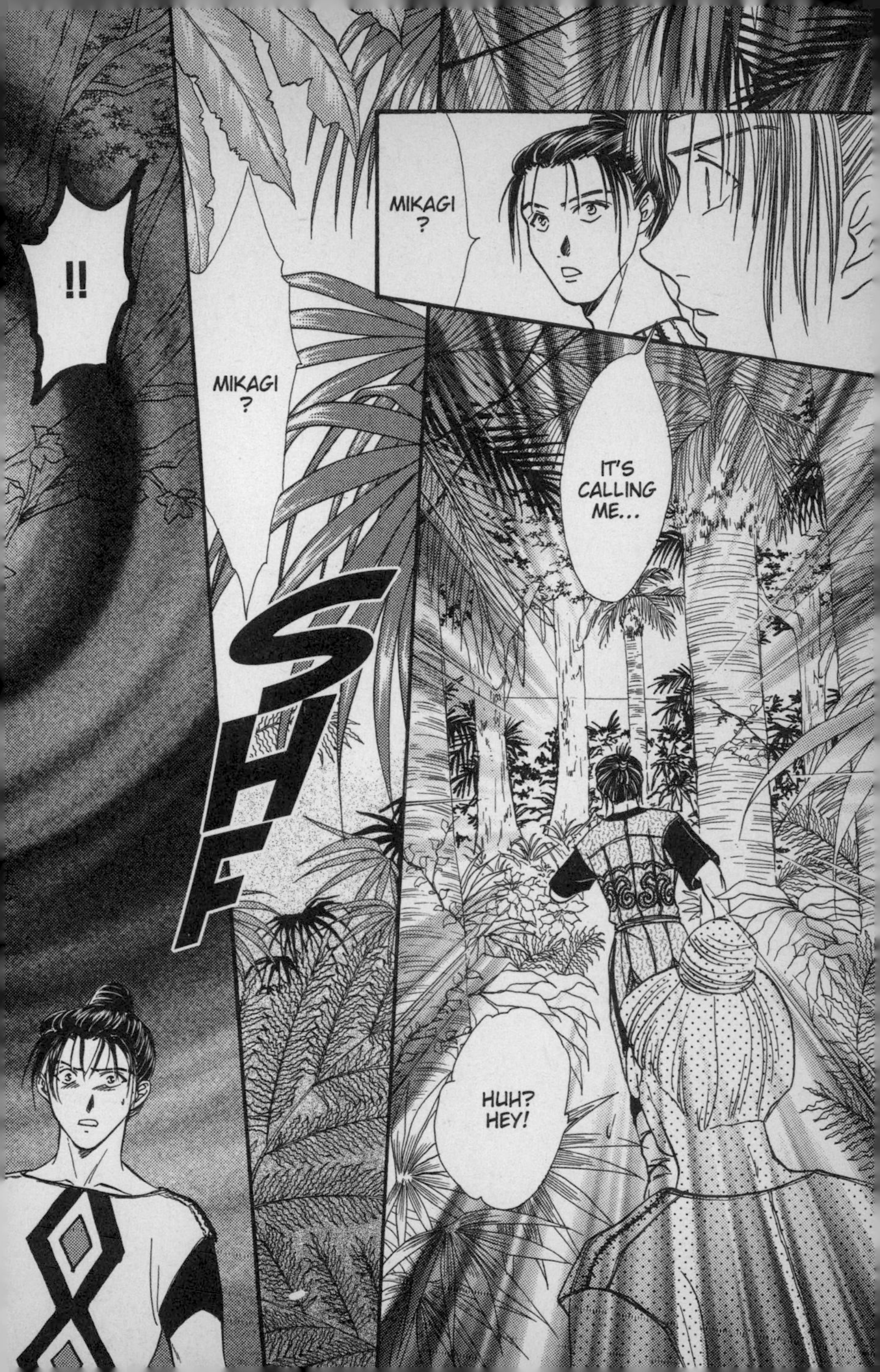
MIKAGI ?
IT'S CALLING ME...
HUH? HEY!
MIKAGI ?
SHFF
!!

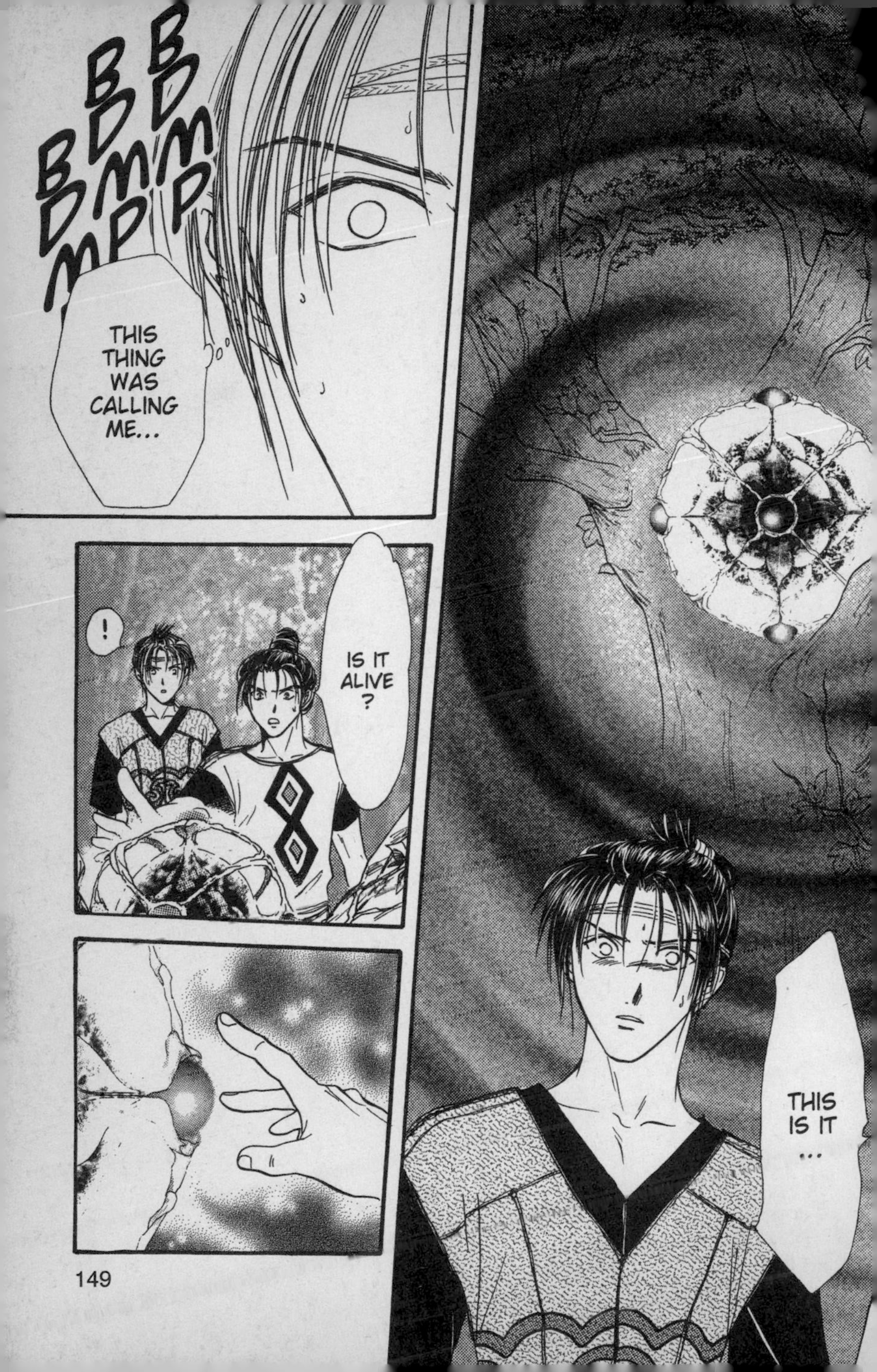
THIS IS IT...
BBDMMP BDMMP
THIS THING WAS CALLING ME...
IS IT ALIVE?
!

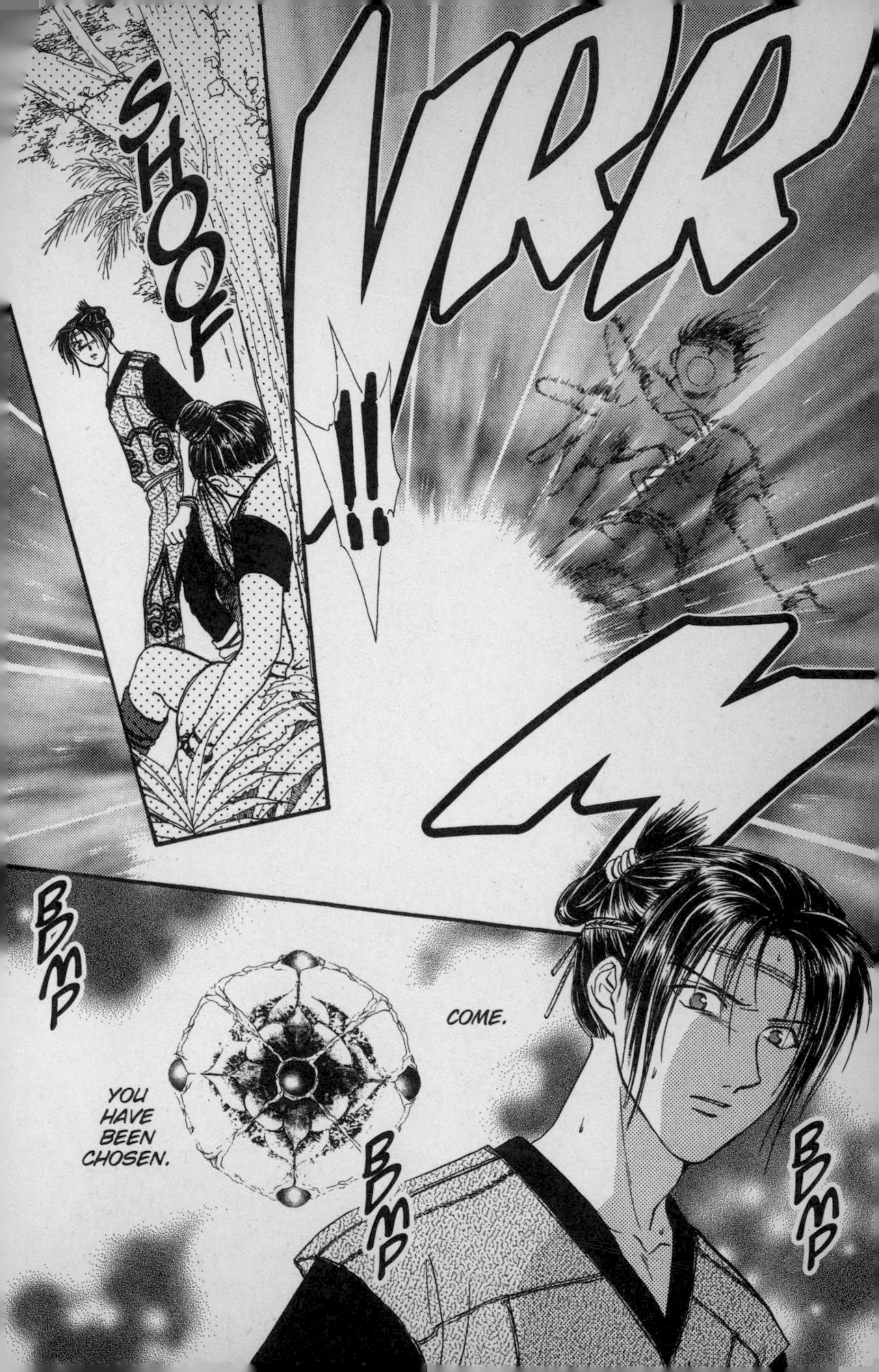
VRRR
!!
SHOOF
BDMP
COME.
YOU HAVE BEEN CHOSEN.
BDMP
BDMP

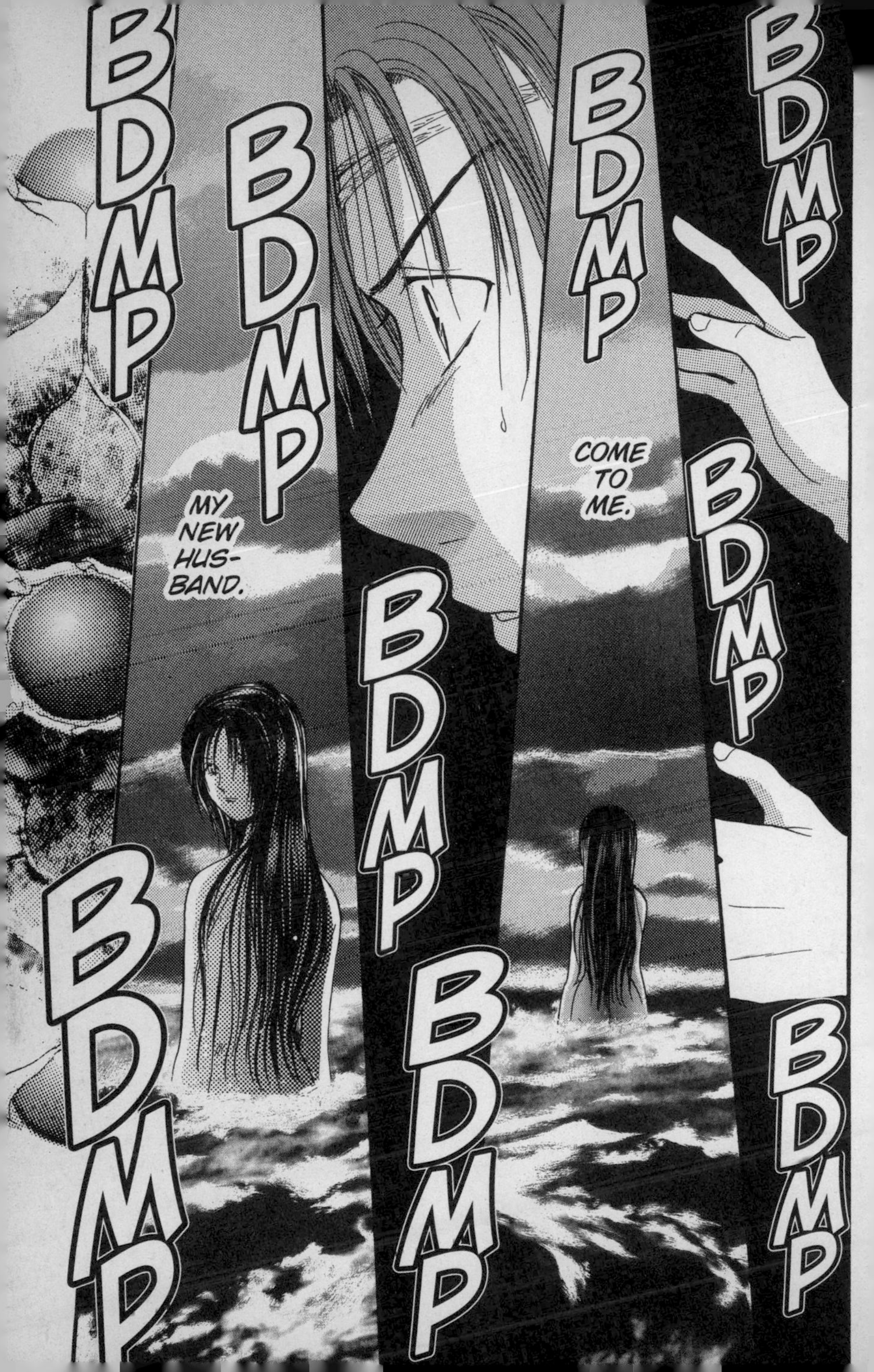
BDMP
BDMP
BDMP
BDMP
COME TO ME.
BDMP
BDMP
BDMP
MY NEW HUS-BAND.
BDMP
BDMP

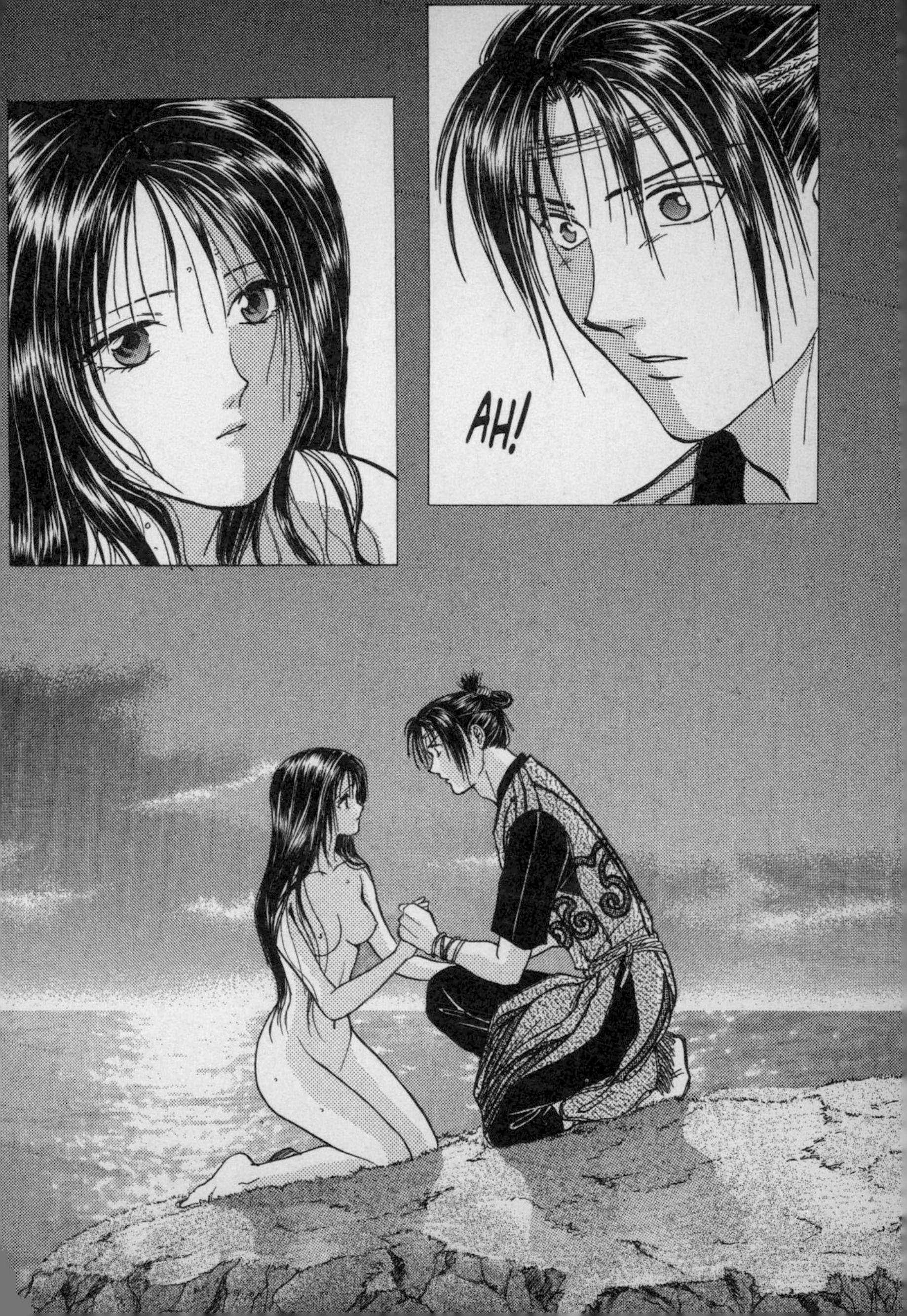
AH!

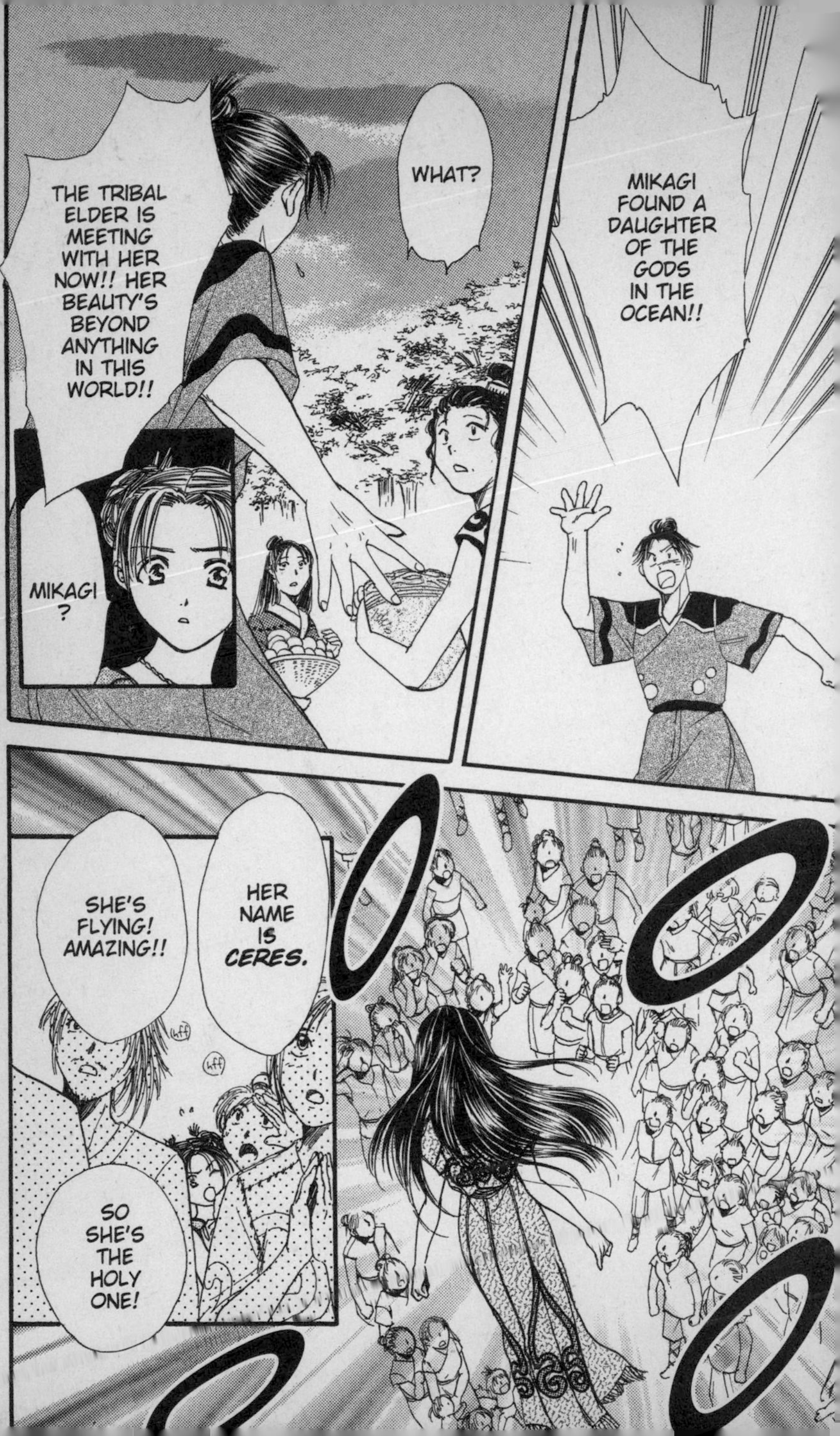
MIKAGI FOUND A DAUGHTER OF THE GODS IN THE OCEAN!!
WHAT?
THE TRIBAL ELDER IS MEETING WITH HER NOW!! HER BEAUTY'S BEYOND ANYTHING IN THIS WORLD!!
MIKAGI ?
HER NAME IS CERES.
SHE'S FLYING! AMAZING!!
hff
hff
SO SHE'S THE HOLY ONE!

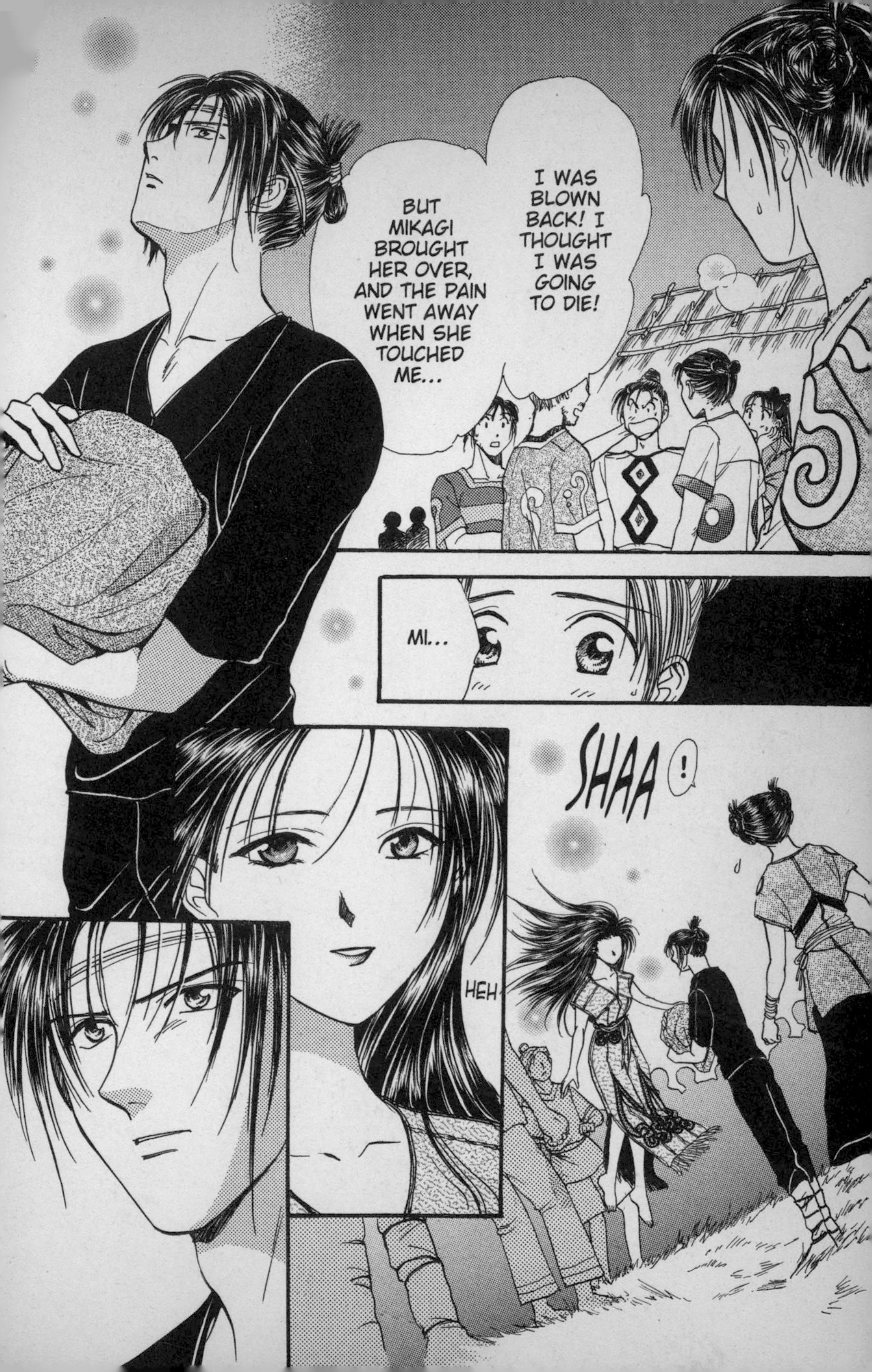
I WAS BLOWN BACK! I THOUGHT I WAS GOING TO DIE!
BUT MIKAGI BROUGHT HER OVER, AND THE PAIN WENT AWAY WHEN SHE TOUCHED ME...
MI...
SHAA
!
HEH

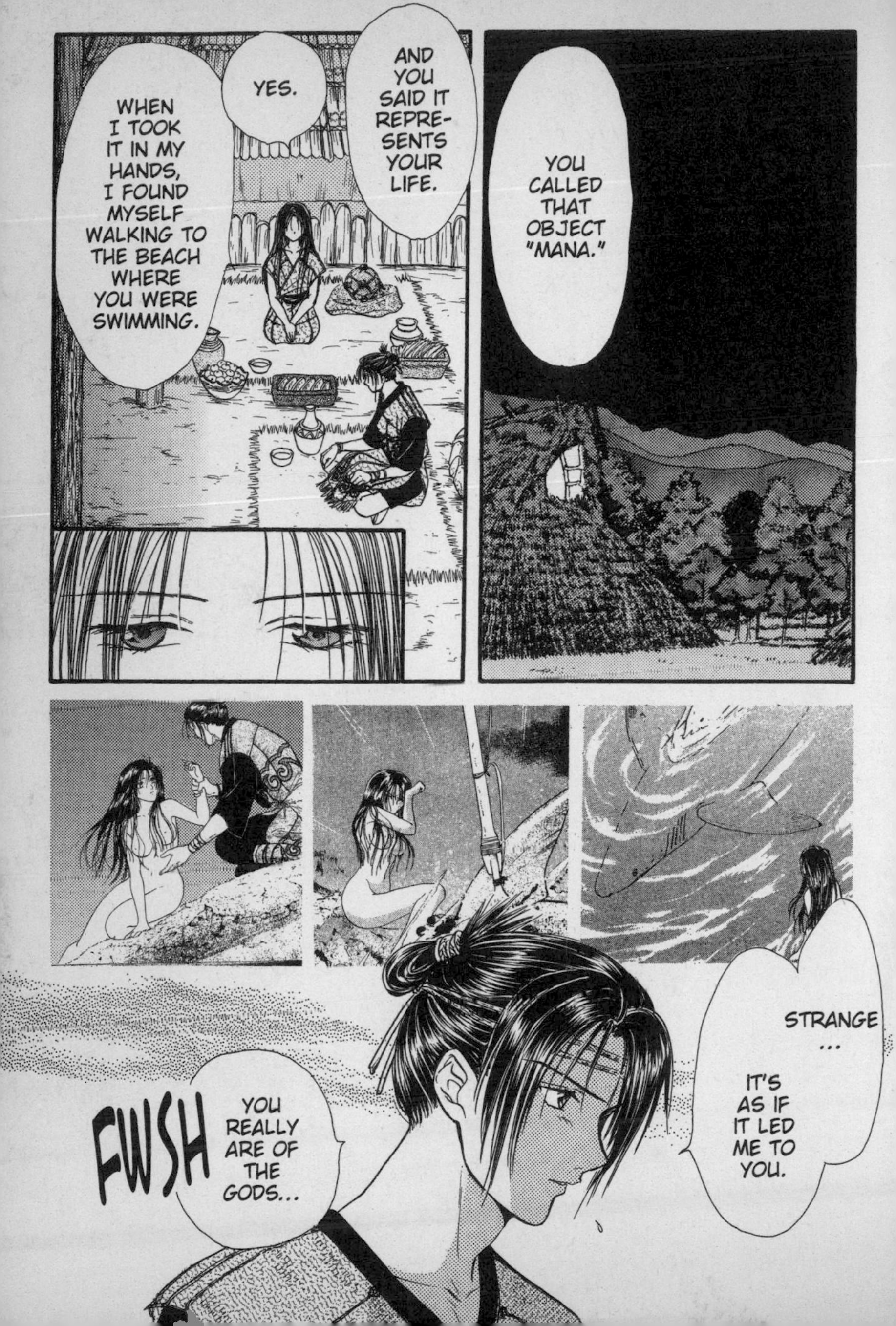
YOU CALLED THAT OBJECT "MANA."
AND YOU SAID IT REPRESENTS YOUR LIFE.
YES.
WHEN I TOOK IT IN MY HANDS, I FOUND MYSELF WALKING TO THE BEACH WHERE YOU WERE SWIMMING.
STRANGE ...
IT'S AS IF IT LED ME TO YOU.
YOU REALLY ARE OF THE GODS...
FWSH

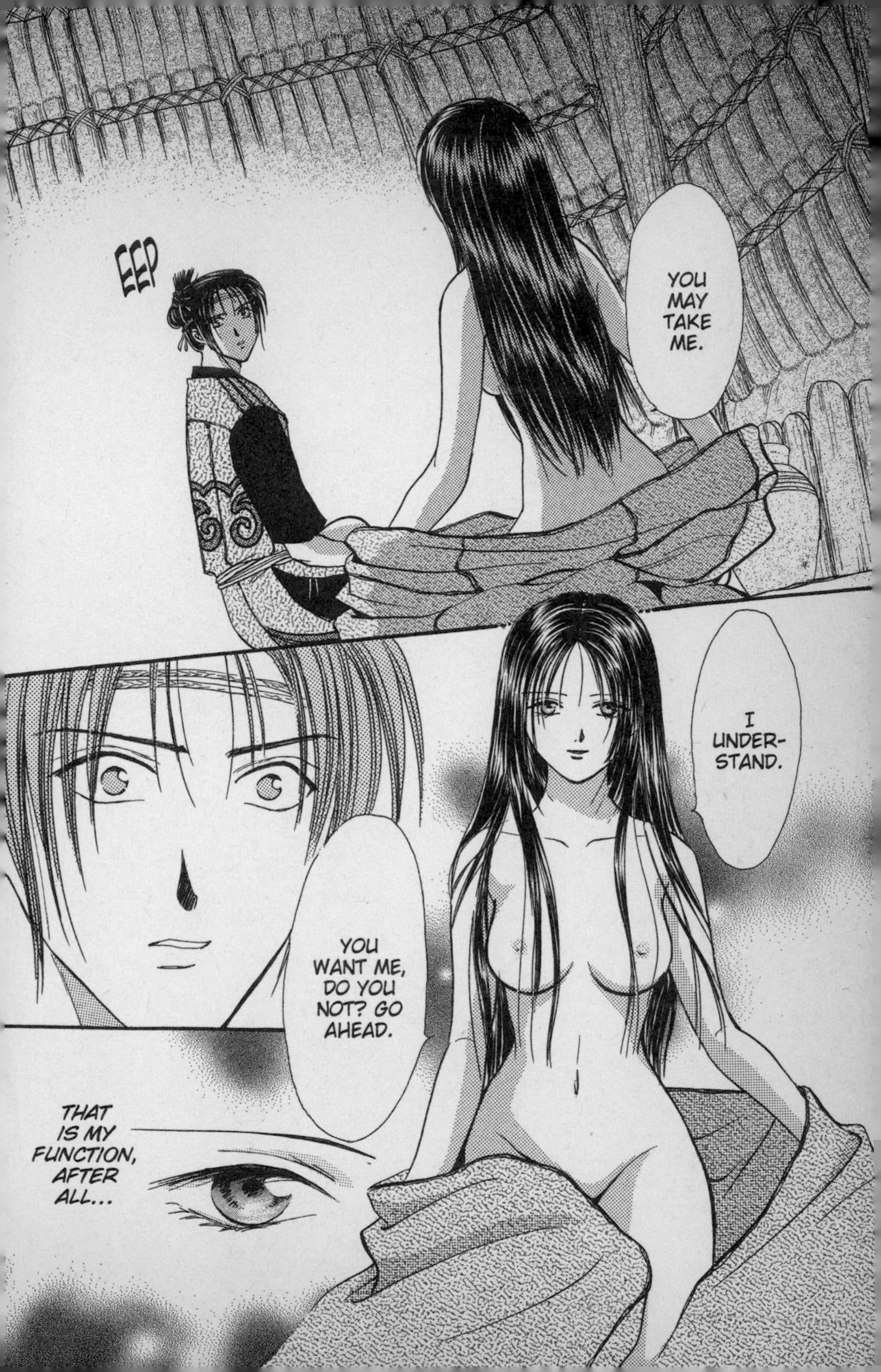
YOU MAY TAKE ME.
EEP
I UNDER-STAND.
YOU WANT ME, DO YOU NOT? GO AHEAD.
THAT IS MY FUNCTION, AFTER ALL...

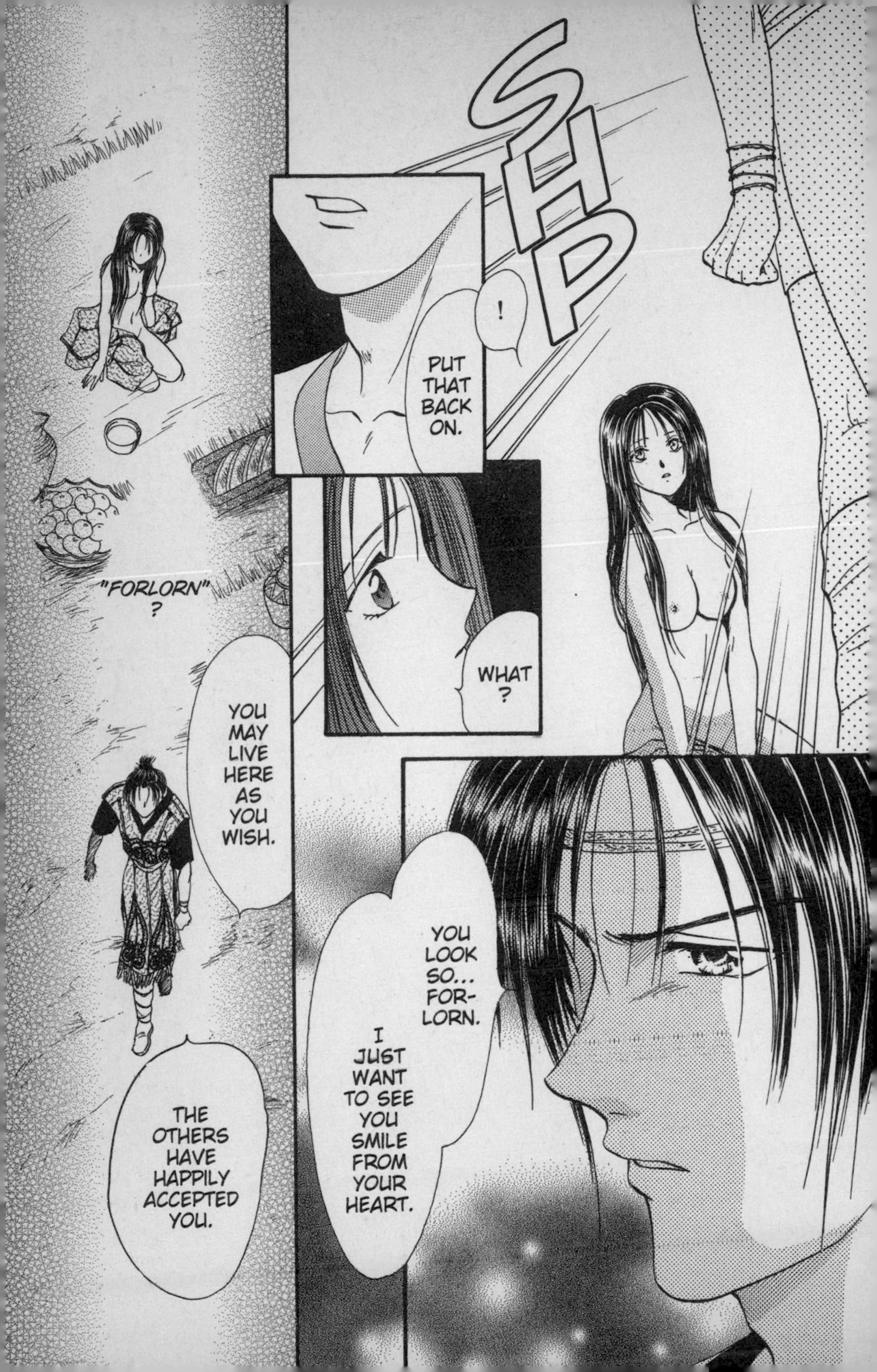
SHP
!
PUT THAT BACK ON.
WHAT?
YOU LOOK SO... FOR-LORN.
I JUST WANT TO SEE YOU SMILE FROM YOUR HEART.
"FORLORN"?
YOU MAY LIVE HERE AS YOU WISH.
THE OTHERS HAVE HAPPILY ACCEPTED YOU.

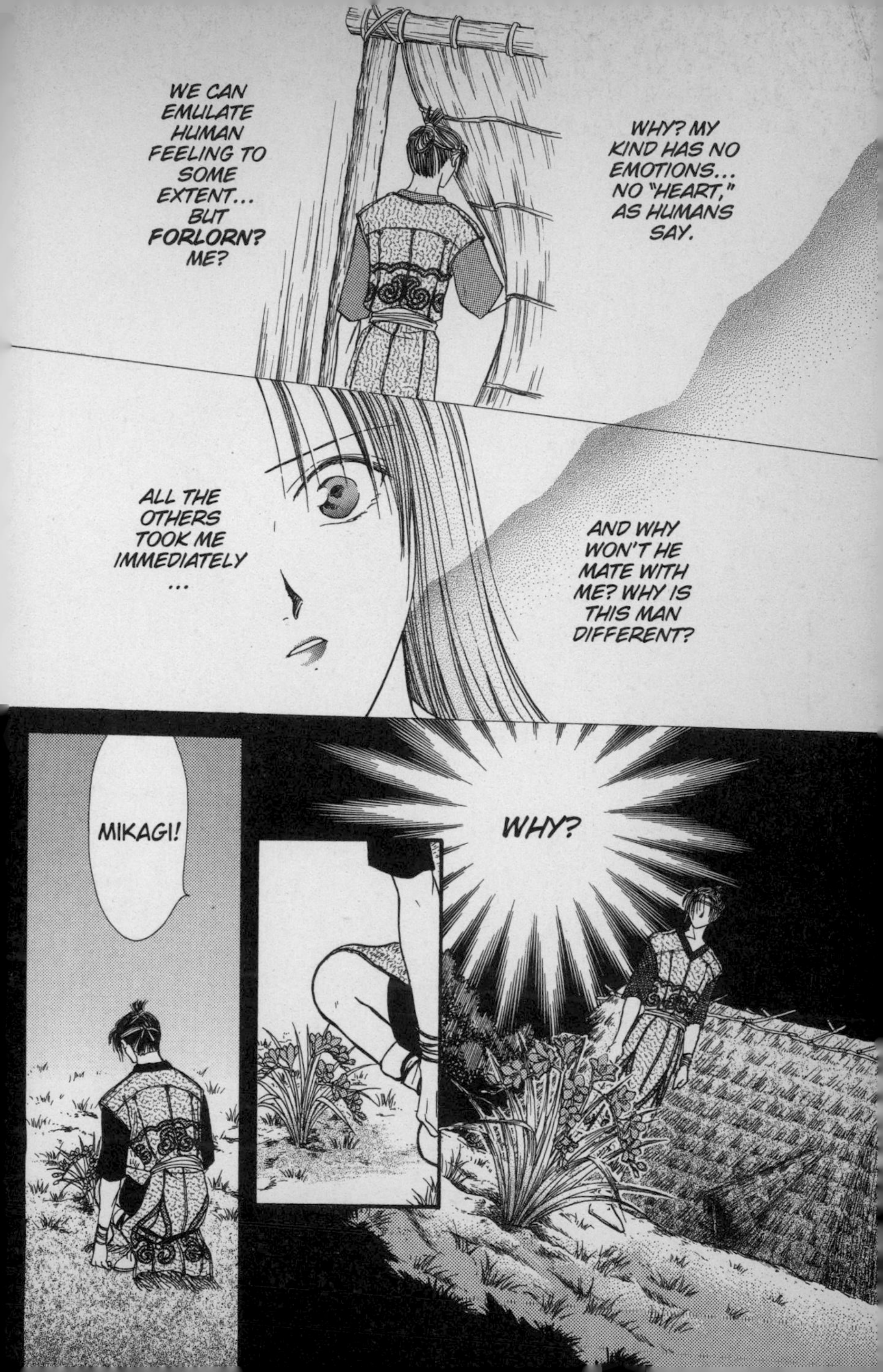
WHY? MY KIND HAS NO EMOTIONS... NO "HEART," AS HUMANS SAY.
WE CAN EMULATE HUMAN FEELING TO SOME EXTENT... BUT FORLORN? ME?
AND WHY WON'T HE MATE WITH ME? WHY IS THIS MAN DIFFERENT?
ALL THE OTHERS TOOK ME IMMEDIATELY ...
WHY?
MIKAGI!

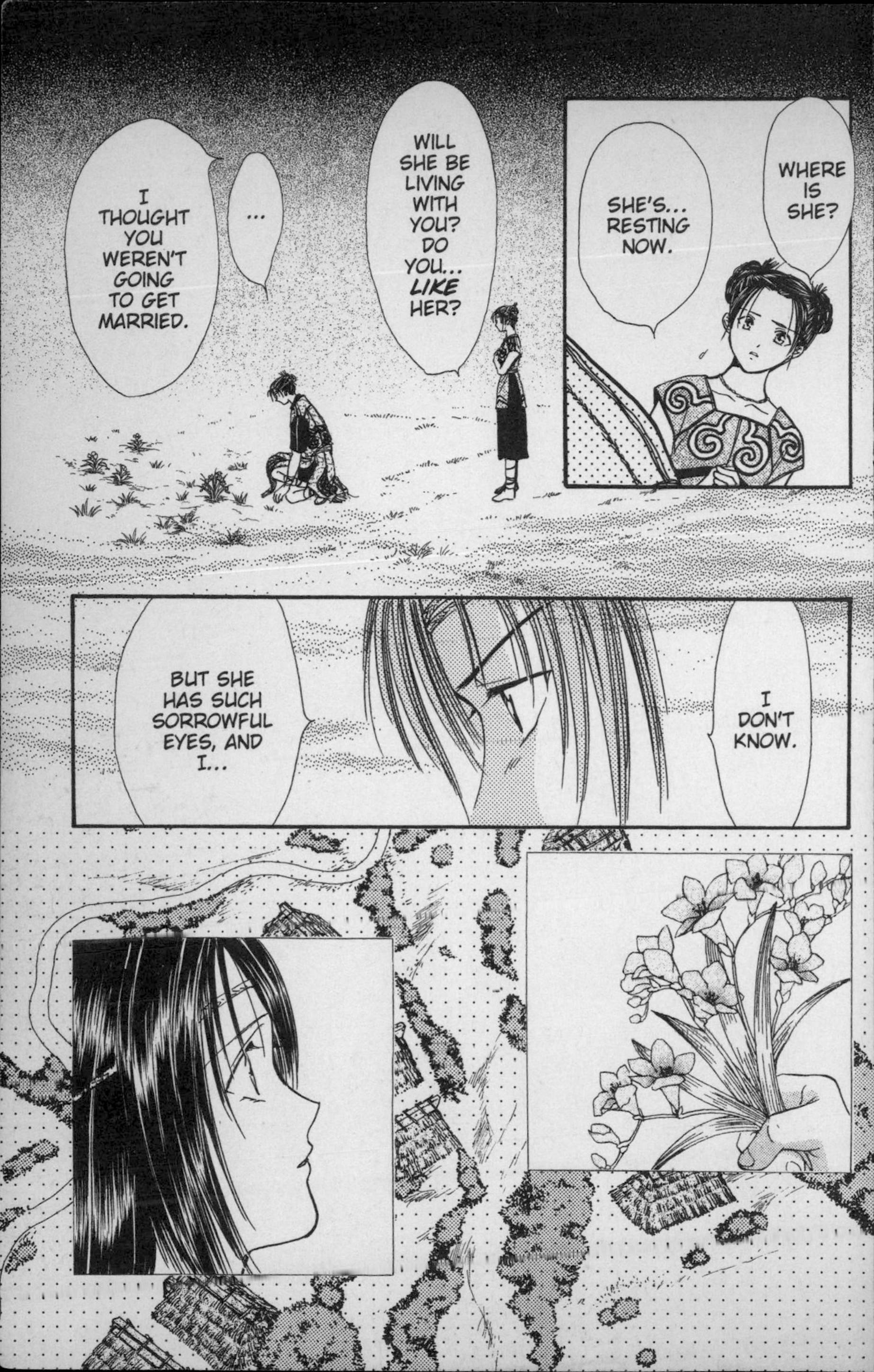
WHERE IS SHE?
SHE'S... RESTING NOW.
WILL SHE BE LIVING WITH YOU? DO YOU... *LIKE* HER?
...
I THOUGHT YOU WEREN'T GOING TO GET MARRIED.
I DON'T KNOW.
BUT SHE HAS SUCH SORROWFUL EYES, AND I...

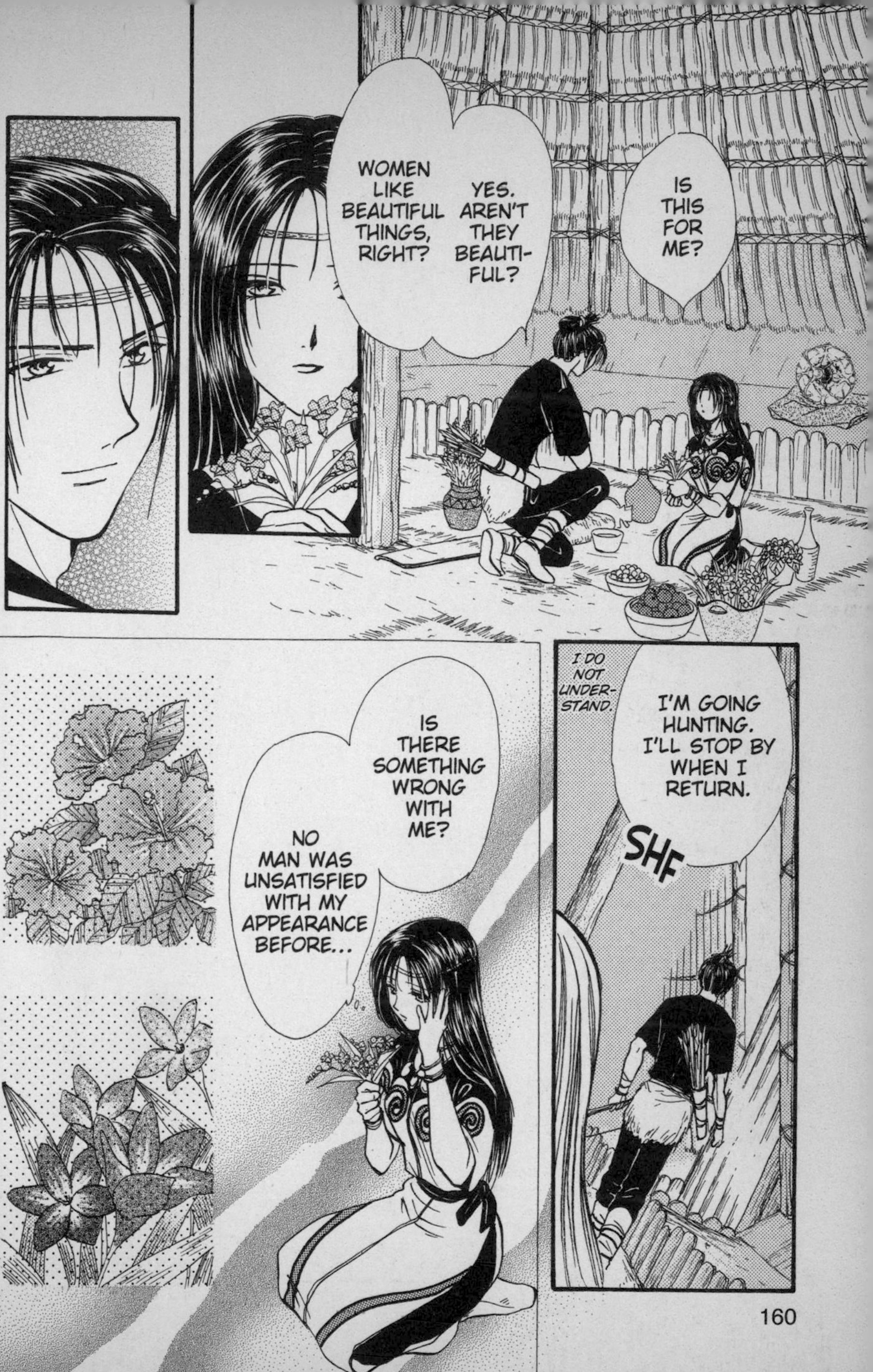
IS THIS FOR ME?
YES. AREN'T THEY BEAUTIFUL?
WOMEN LIKE BEAUTIFUL THINGS, RIGHT?
I'M GOING HUNTING. I'LL STOP BY WHEN I RETURN.
SHF
I DO NOT UNDERSTAND.
IS THERE SOMETHING WRONG WITH ME?
NO MAN WAS UNSATISFIED WITH MY APPEARANCE BEFORE...

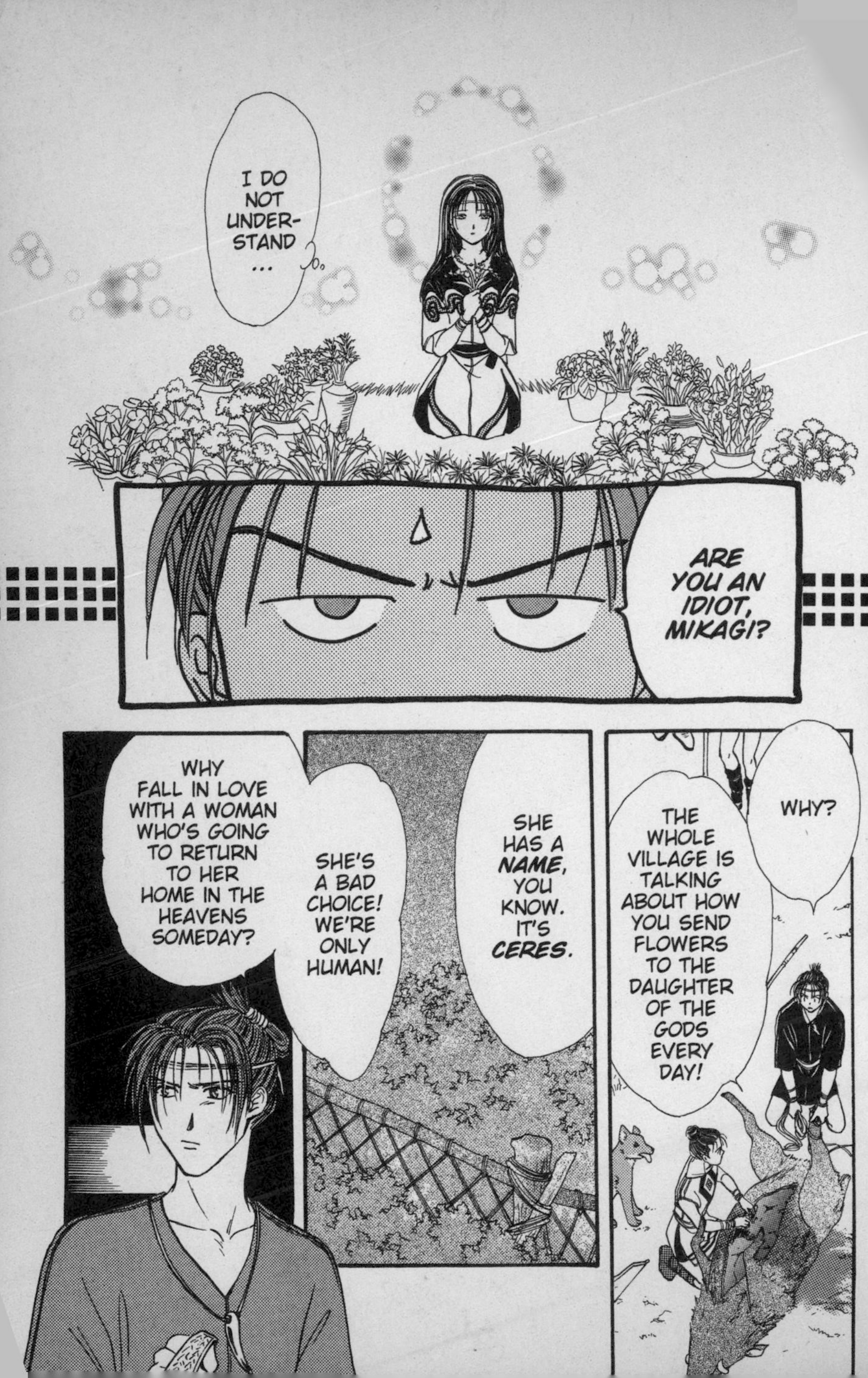
I DO NOT UNDER-STAND...
ARE YOU AN IDIOT, MIKAGI?
WHY?
THE WHOLE VILLAGE IS TALKING ABOUT HOW YOU SEND FLOWERS TO THE DAUGHTER OF THE GODS EVERY DAY!
SHE HAS A NAME, YOU KNOW. IT'S CERES.
SHE'S A BAD CHOICE! WE'RE ONLY HUMAN!
WHY FALL IN LOVE WITH A WOMAN WHO'S GOING TO RETURN TO HER HOME IN THE HEAVENS SOMEDAY?

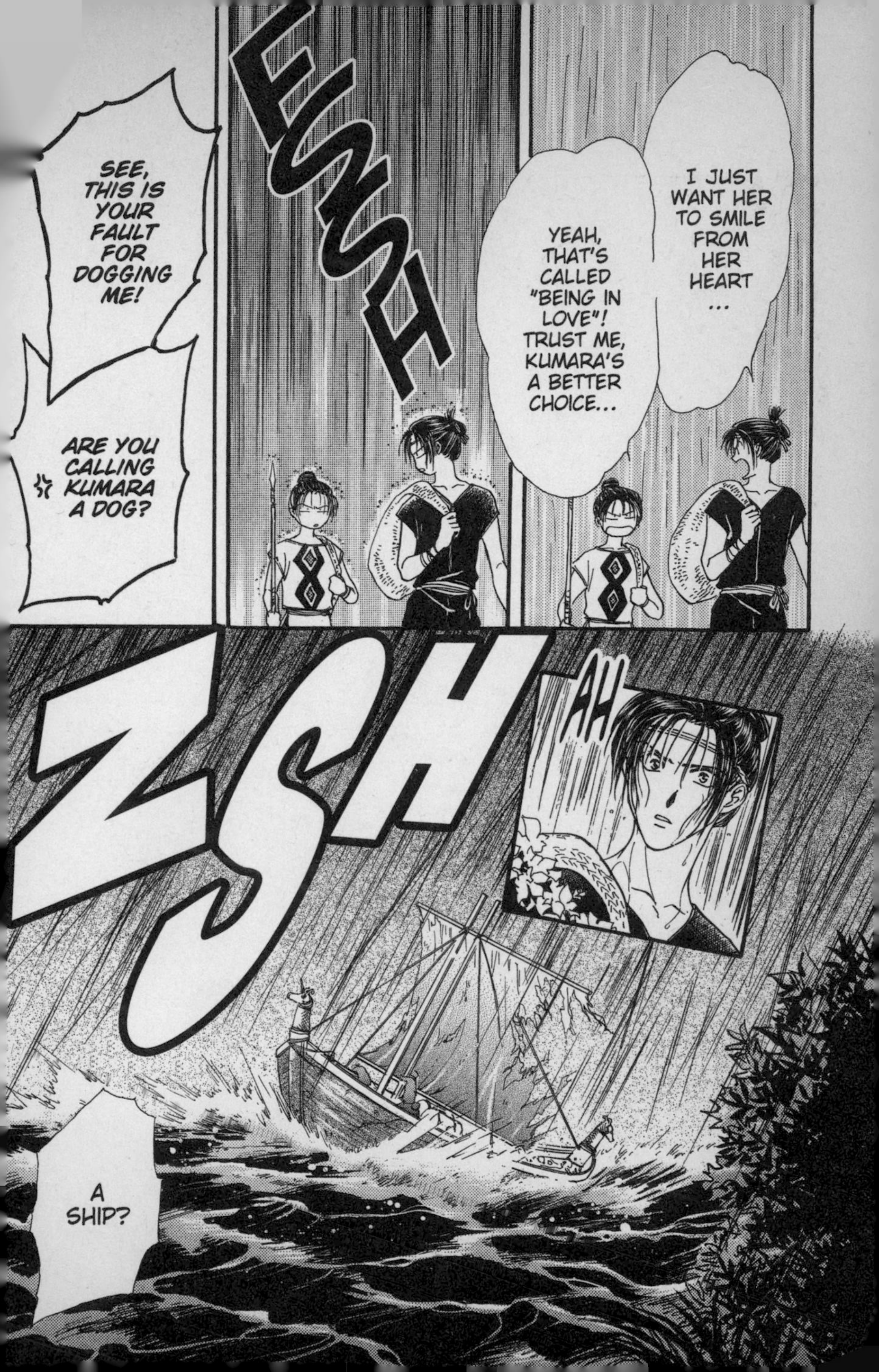
I JUST WANT HER TO SMILE FROM HER HEART ...
YEAH, THAT'S CALLED "BEING IN LOVE"! TRUST ME, KUMARA'S A BETTER CHOICE...
SEE, THIS IS YOUR FAULT FOR DOGGING ME!
ARE YOU CALLING KUMARA A DOG?
AH
ZSH
A SHIP?

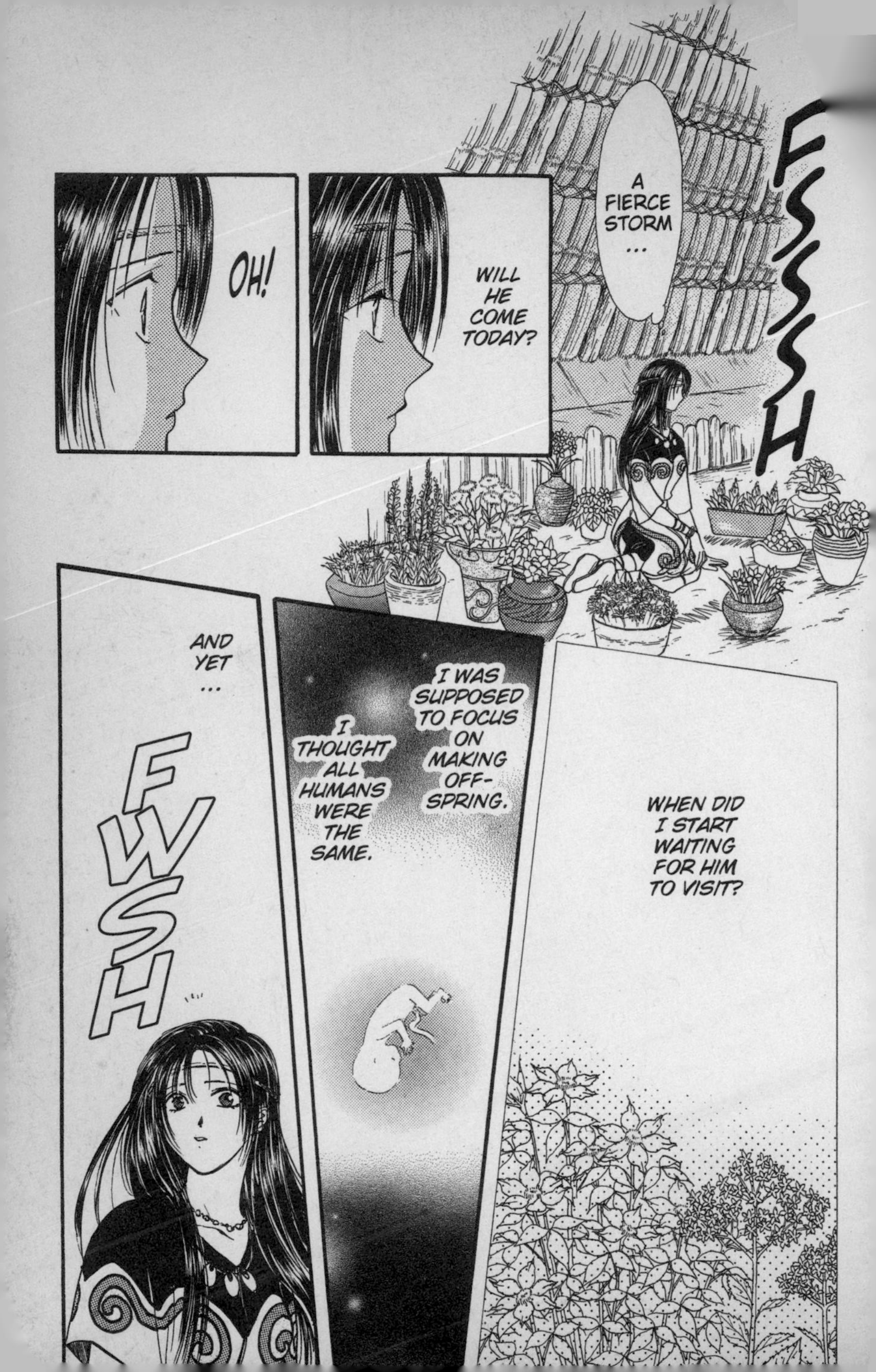
FSSSH
A FIERCE STORM ...
WILL HE COME TODAY?
OH!
WHEN DID I START WAITING FOR HIM TO VISIT?
I WAS SUPPOSED TO FOCUS ON MAKING OFF-SPRING.
I THOUGHT ALL HUMANS WERE THE SAME.
AND YET ...
FWSH

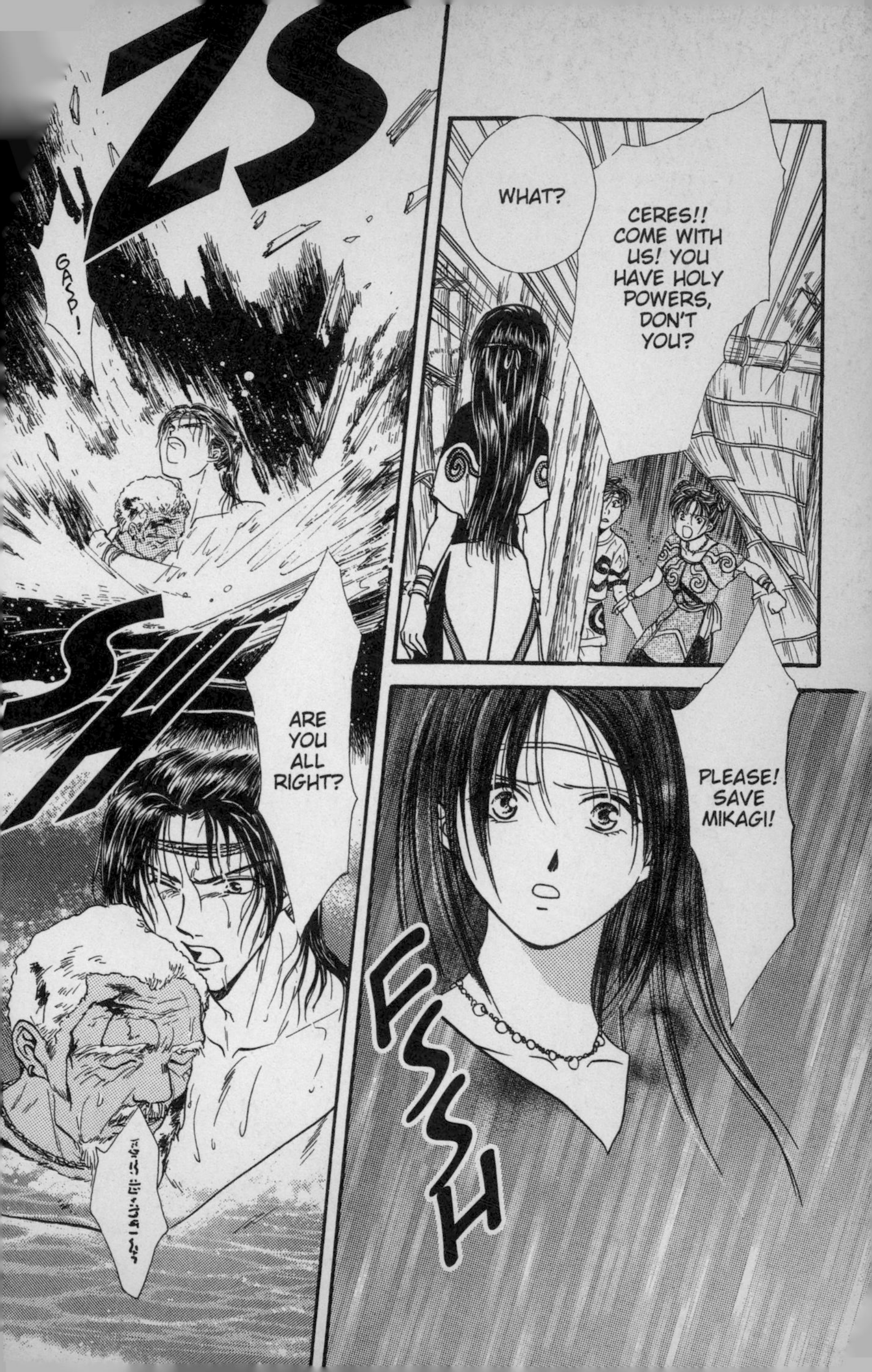
WHAT?
CERES!! COME WITH US! YOU HAVE HOLY POWERS, DON'T YOU?
PLEASE! SAVE MIKAGI!
FSSH
ZS
GASP!
SH
ARE YOU ALL RIGHT?

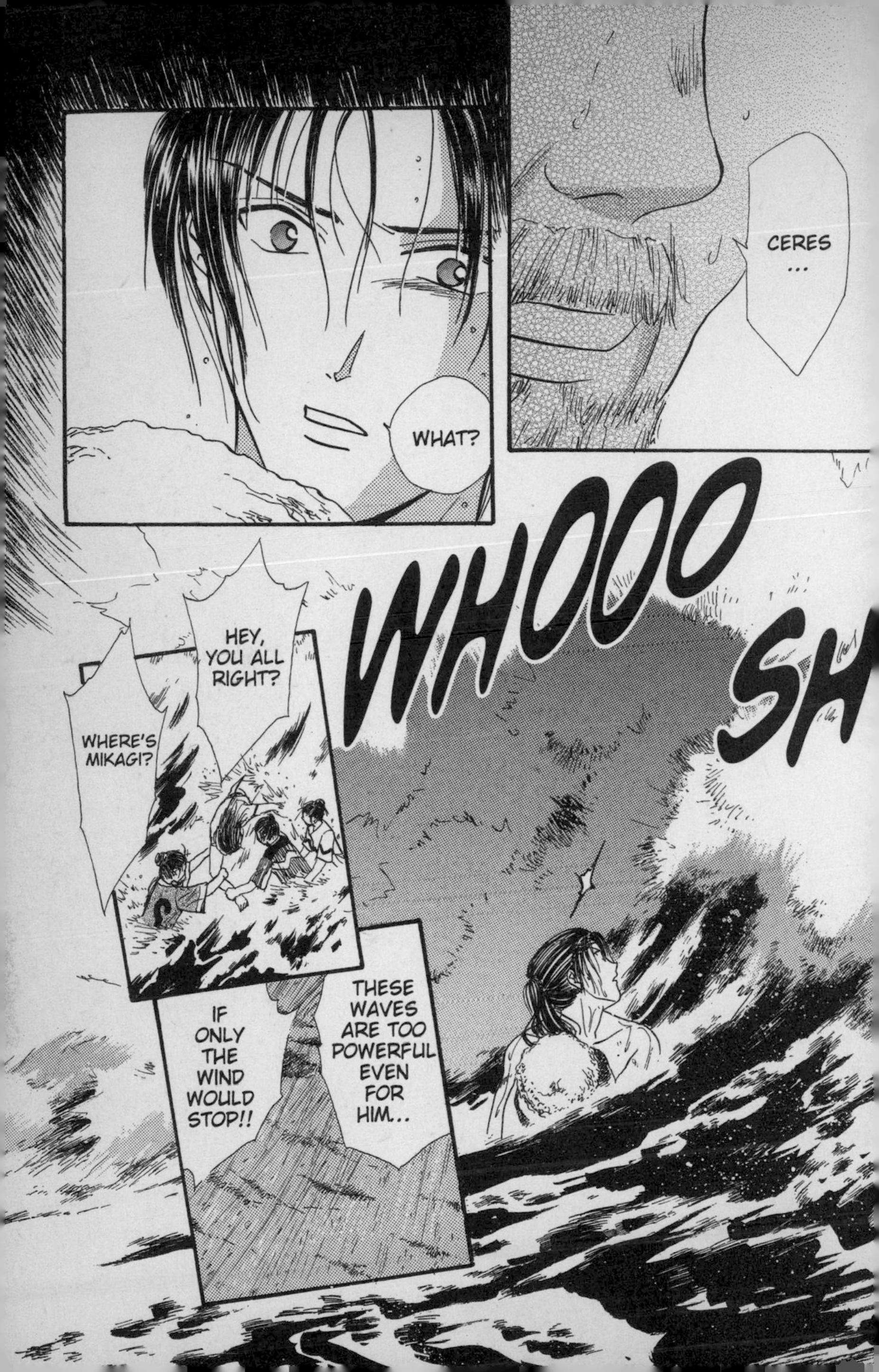
CERES ...
WHAT?
WHOOOSH
HEY, YOU ALL RIGHT?
WHERE'S MIKAGI?
THESE WAVES ARE TOO POWERFUL EVEN FOR HIM...
IF ONLY THE WIND WOULD STOP!!

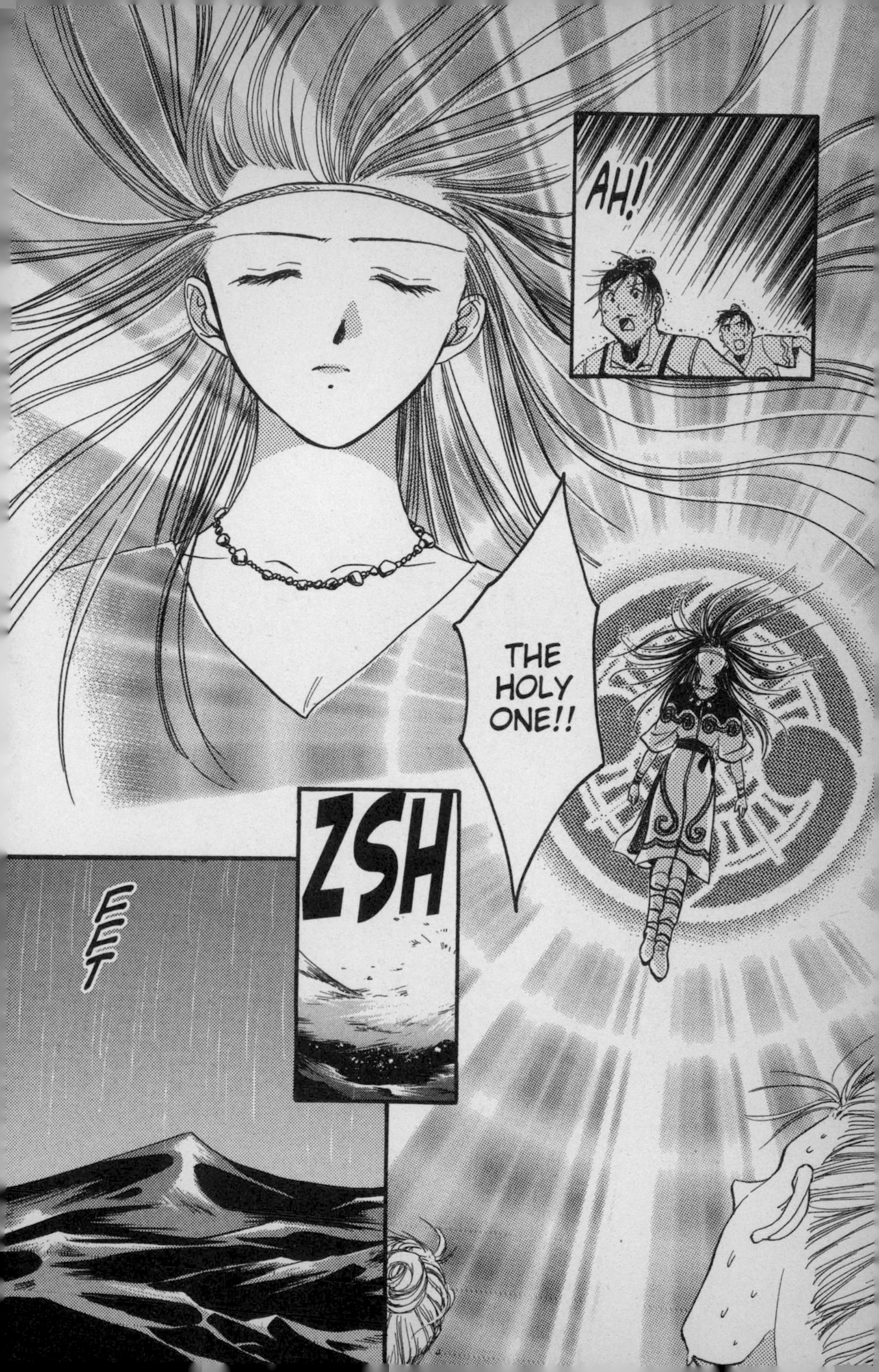
AH!
THE HOLY ONE!!
ZSH
FEET

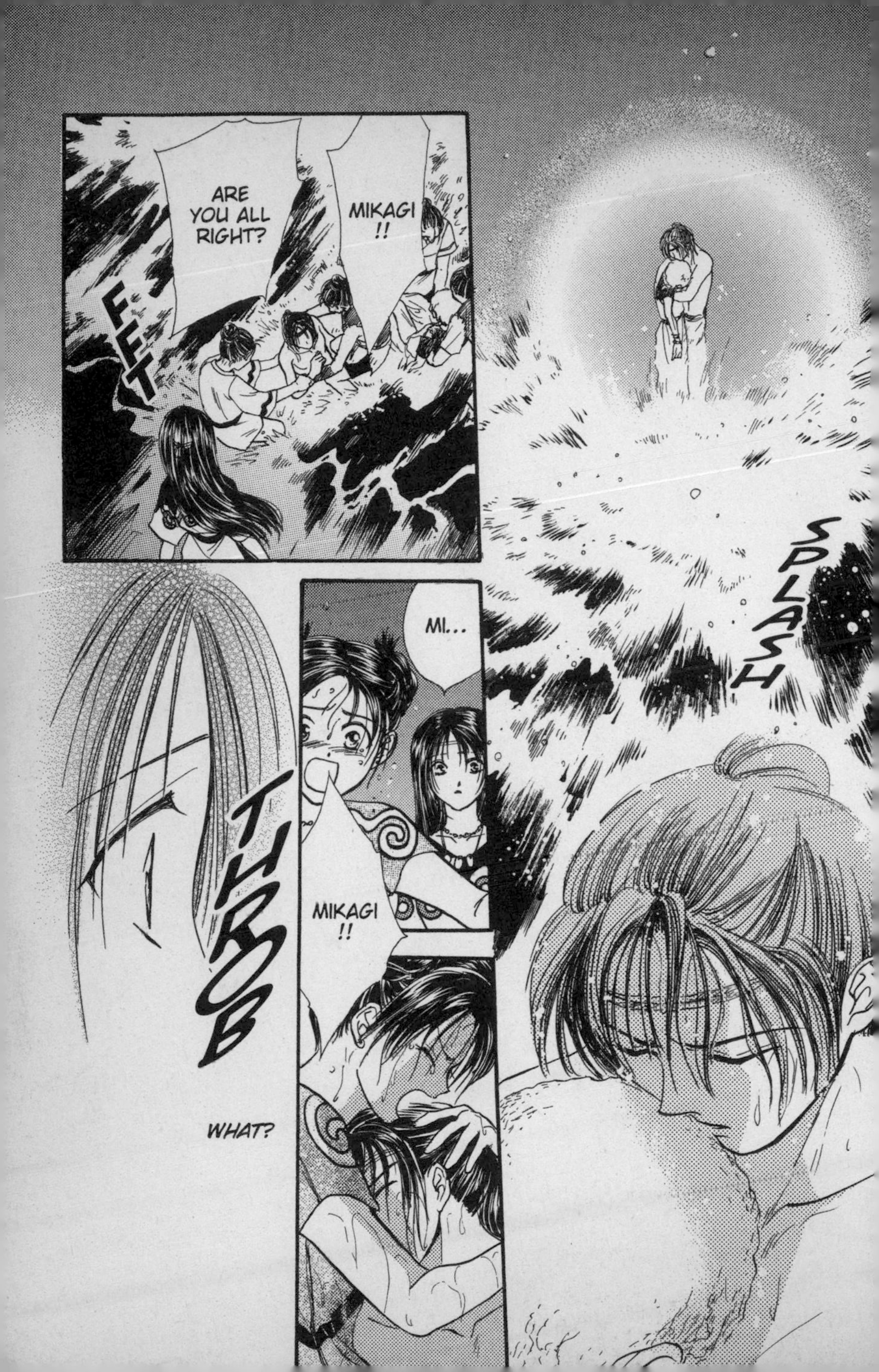
SPLASH
MIKAGI !!
ARE YOU ALL RIGHT?
FFT
MI...
MIKAGI !!
THROB
WHAT?

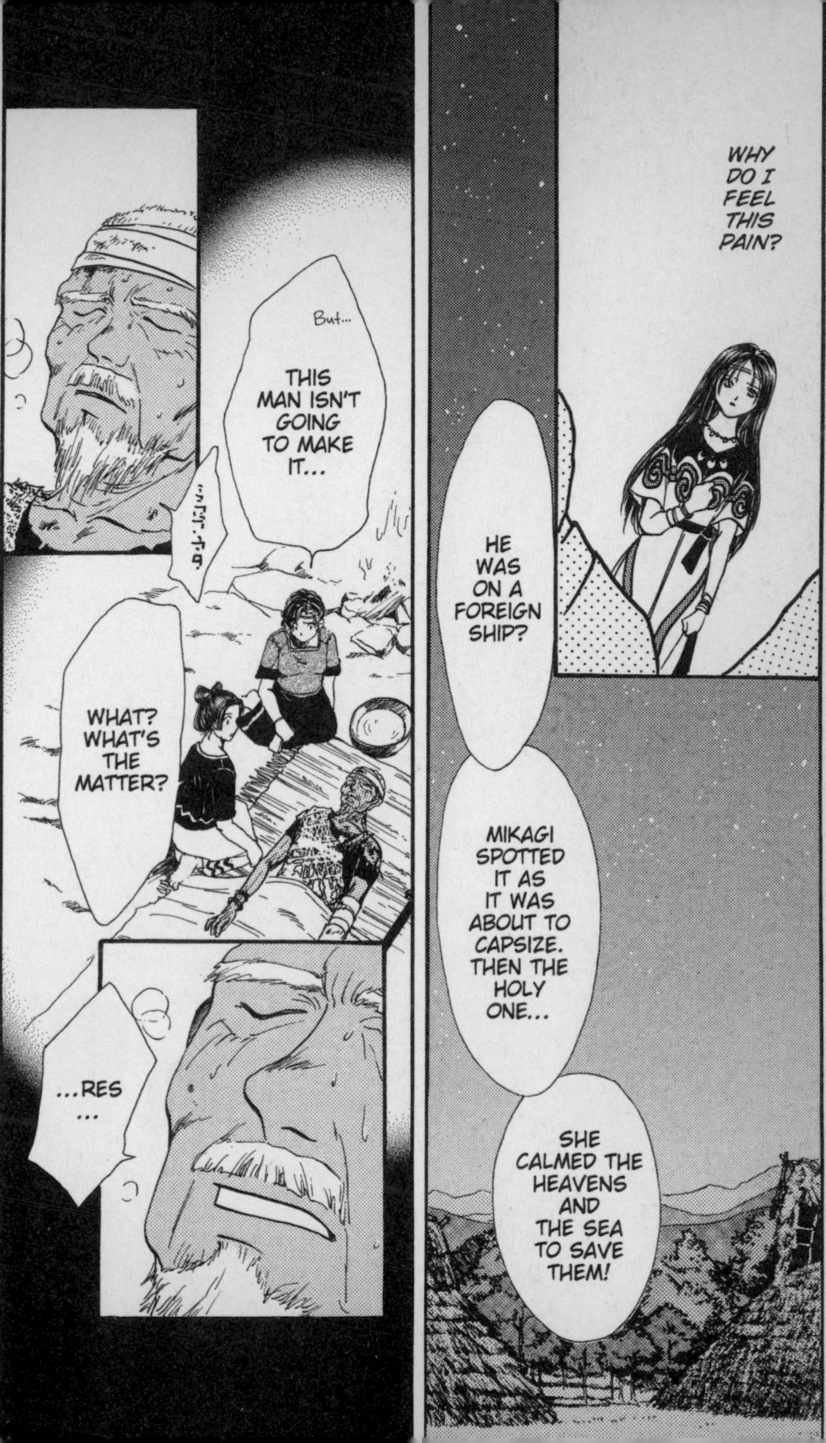
WHY DO I FEEL THIS PAIN?
HE WAS ON A FOREIGN SHIP?
MIKAGI SPOTTED IT AS IT WAS ABOUT TO CAPSIZE. THEN THE HOLY ONE...
SHE CALMED THE HEAVENS AND THE SEA TO SAVE THEM!
But...
THIS MAN ISN'T GOING TO MAKE IT...
WHAT? WHAT'S THE MATTER?
...RES ...

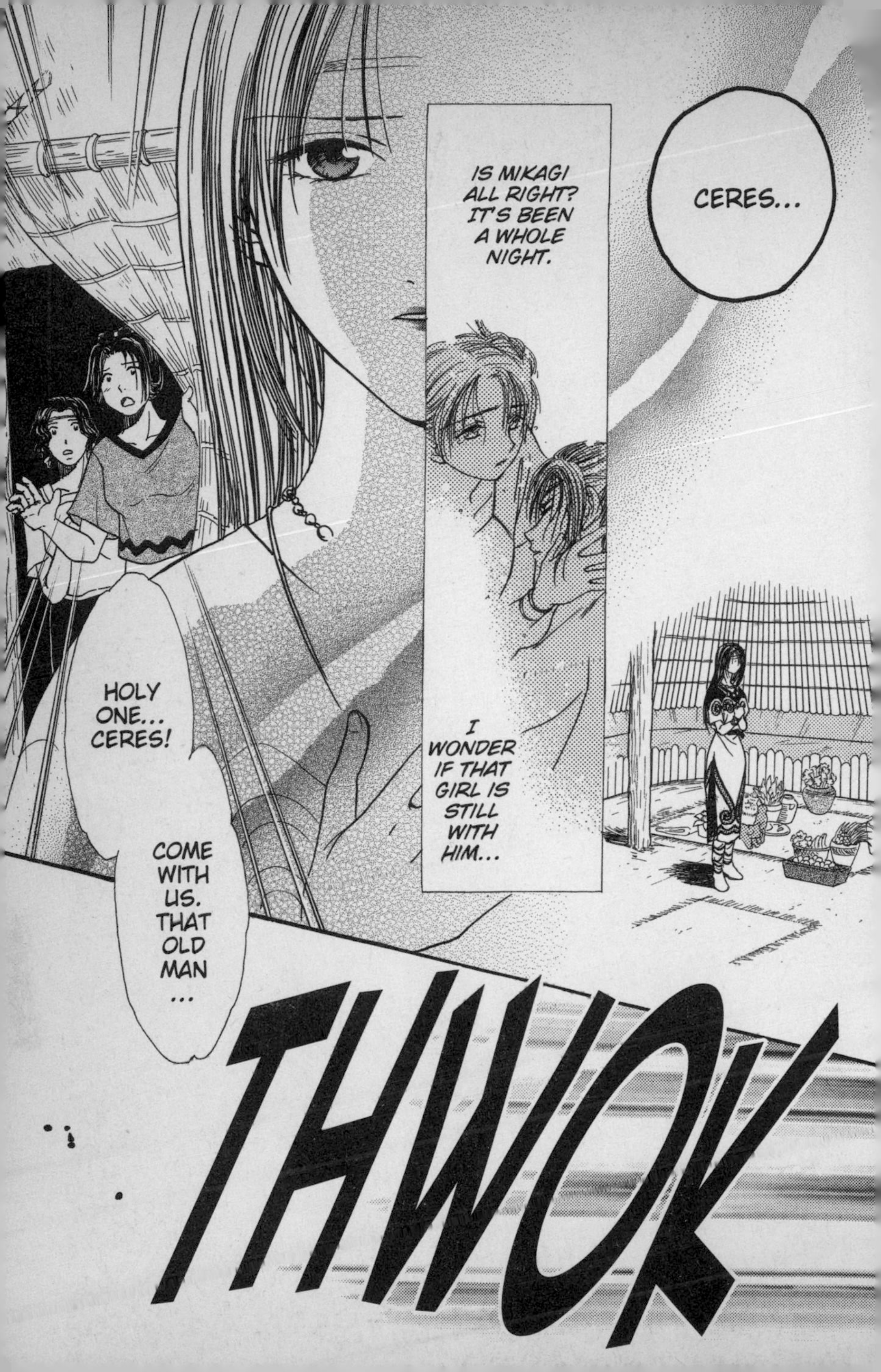
CERES...
IS MIKAGI ALL RIGHT? IT'S BEEN A WHOLE NIGHT.
I WONDER IF THAT GIRL IS STILL WITH HIM...
HOLY ONE... CERES!
COME WITH US. THAT OLD MAN...
THWOK

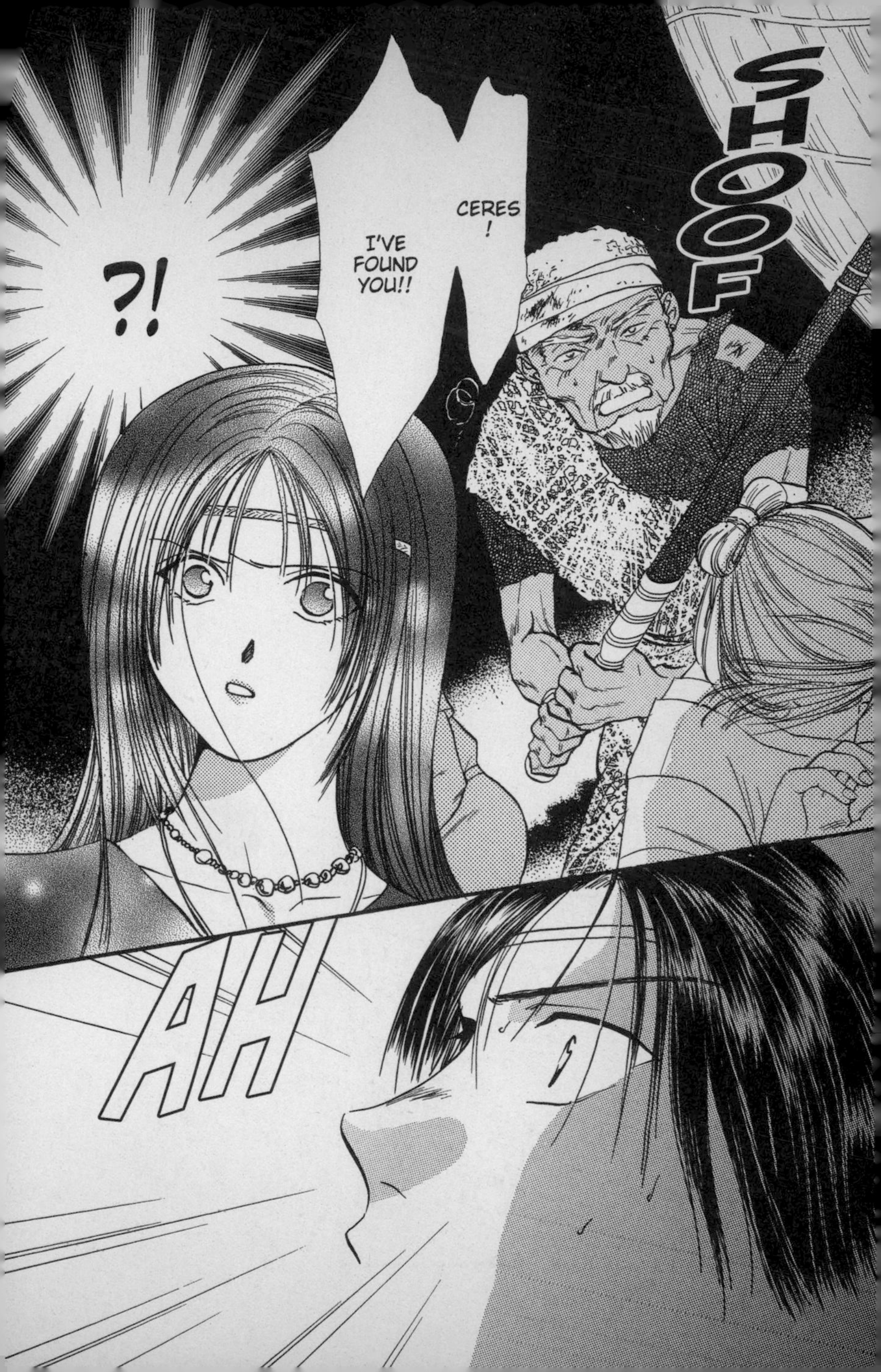
SHOOF
CERES!
I'VE FOUND YOU!!
?!
AH

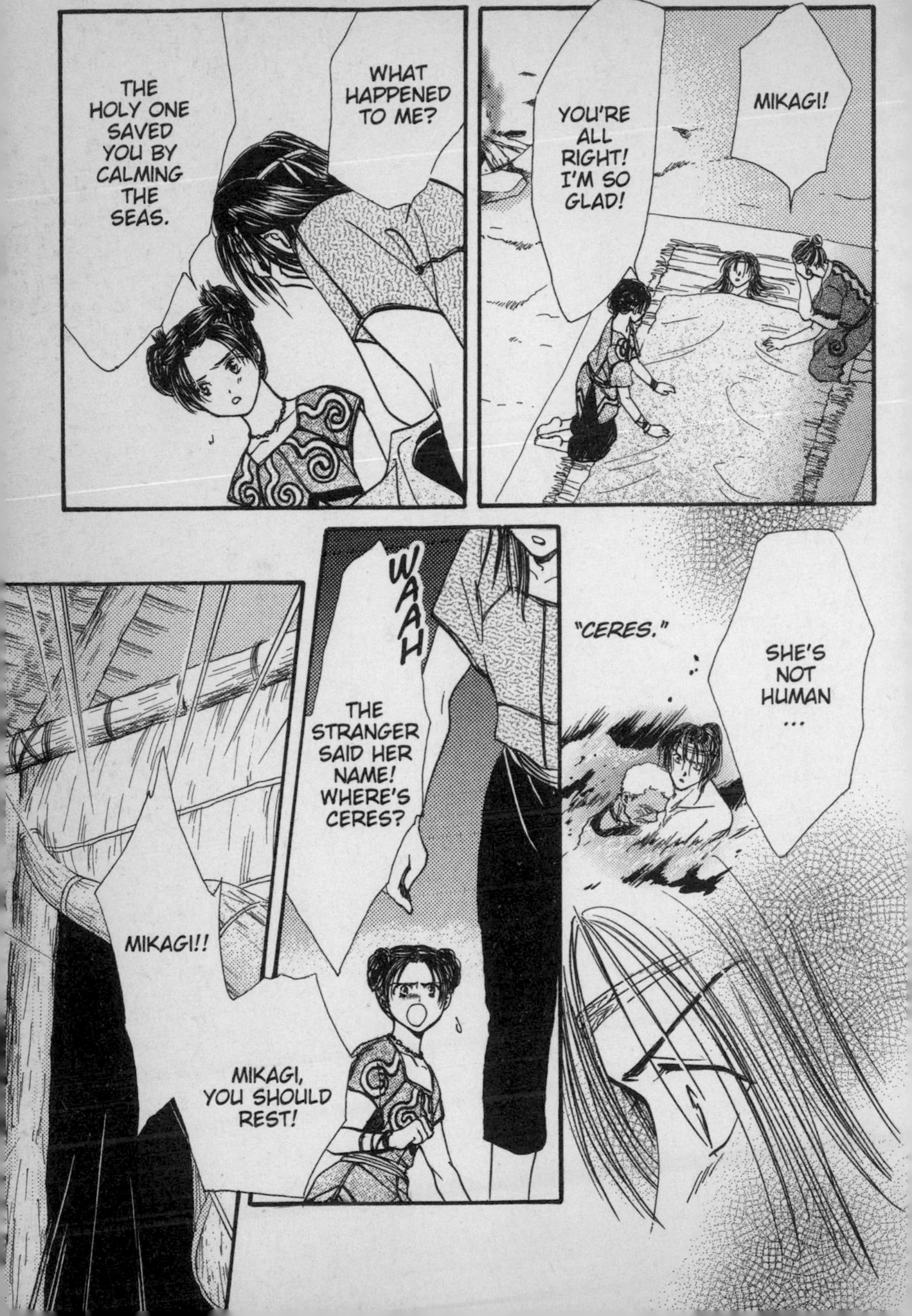
MIKAGI!
YOU'RE ALL RIGHT! I'M SO GLAD!
WHAT HAPPENED TO ME?
THE HOLY ONE SAVED YOU BY CALMING THE SEAS.
SHE'S NOT HUMAN ...
"CERES."
WAAH
THE STRANGER SAID HER NAME! WHERE'S CERES?
MIKAGI, YOU SHOULD REST!
MIKAGI!!

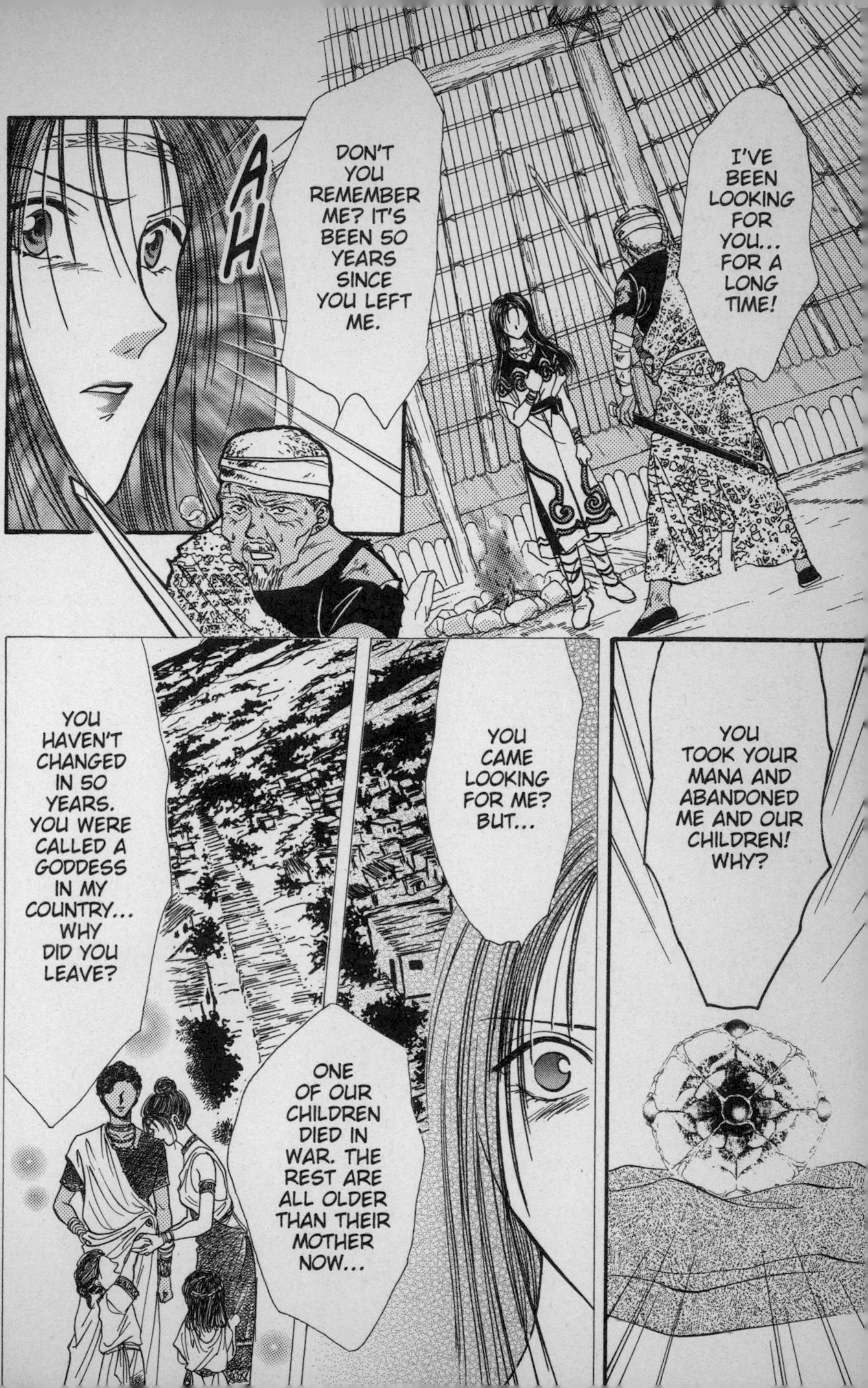
I'VE BEEN LOOKING FOR YOU... FOR A LONG TIME!
AH
DON'T YOU REMEMBER ME? IT'S BEEN 50 YEARS SINCE YOU LEFT ME.
YOU TOOK YOUR MANA AND ABANDONED ME AND OUR CHILDREN! WHY?
YOU CAME LOOKING FOR ME? BUT...
YOU HAVEN'T CHANGED IN 50 YEARS. YOU WERE CALLED A GODDESS IN MY COUNTRY... WHY DID YOU LEAVE?
ONE OF OUR CHILDREN DIED IN WAR. THE REST ARE ALL OLDER THAN THEIR MOTHER NOW...

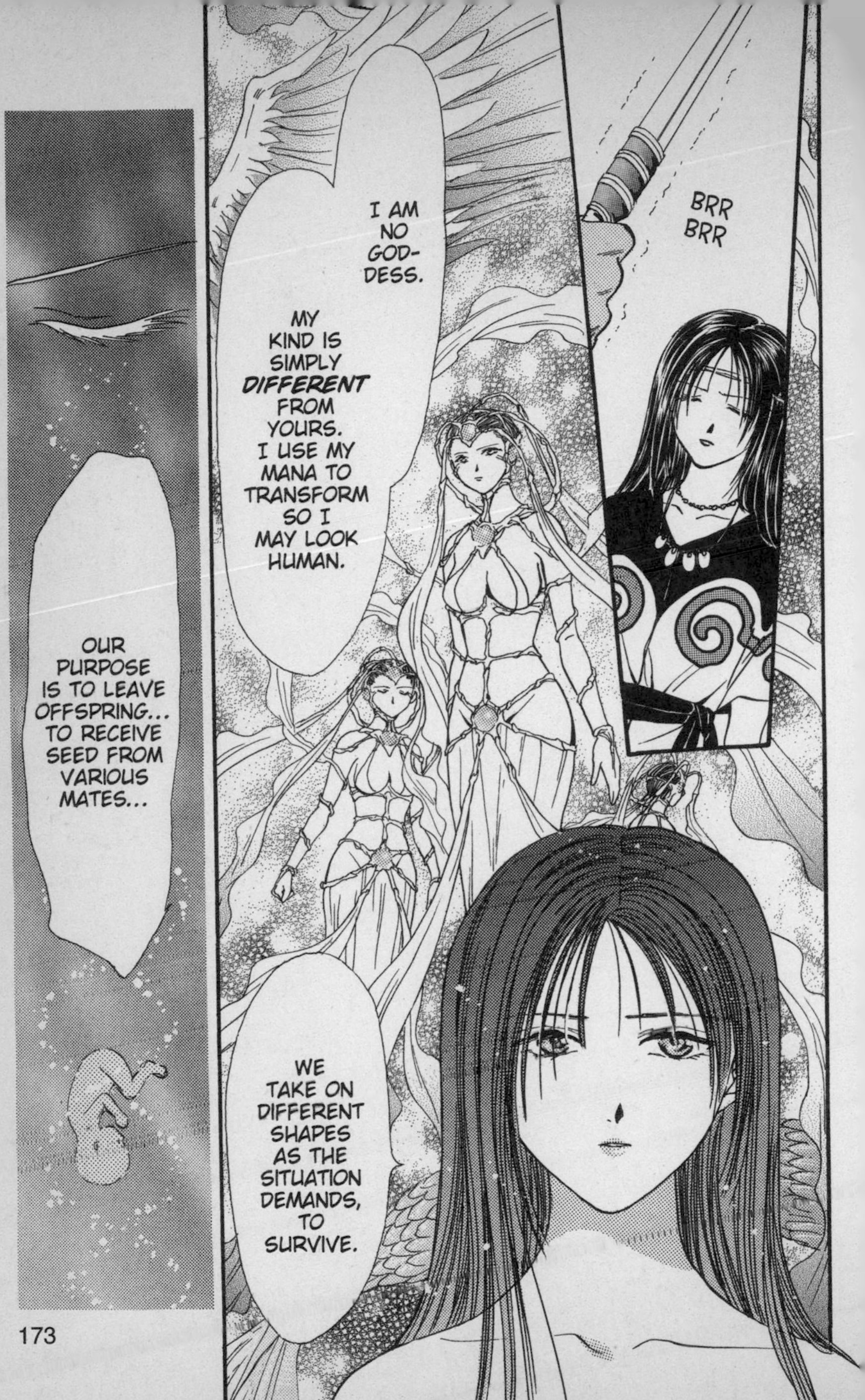
BRR BRR
I AM NO GOD-DESS.
MY KIND IS SIMPLY *DIFFERENT* FROM YOURS. I USE MY MANA TO TRANSFORM SO I MAY LOOK HUMAN.
WE TAKE ON DIFFERENT SHAPES AS THE SITUATION DEMANDS, TO SURVIVE.
OUR PURPOSE IS TO LEAVE OFFSPRING... TO RECEIVE SEED FROM VARIOUS MATES...

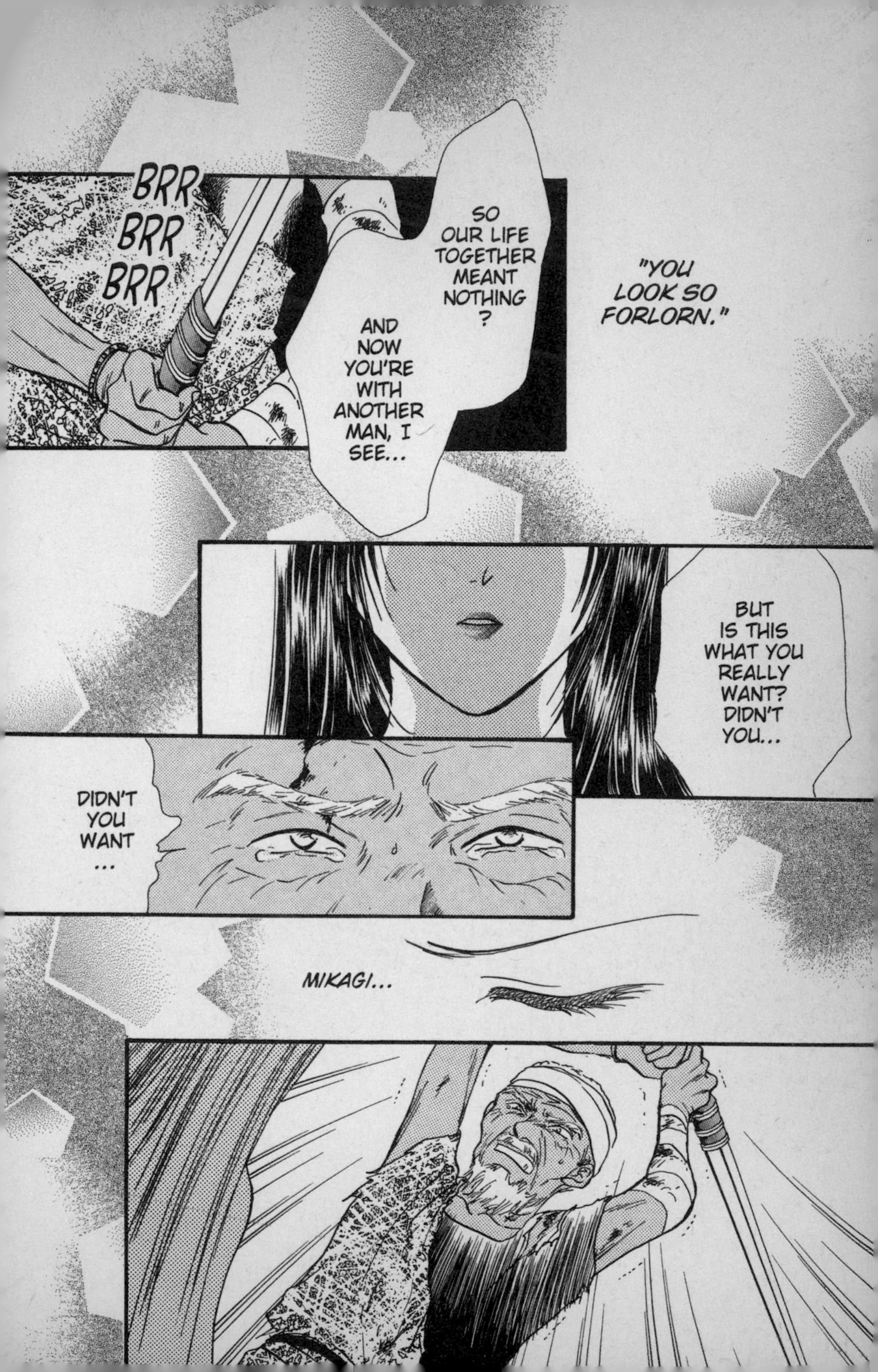
"YOU LOOK SO FORLORN."
SO OUR LIFE TOGETHER MEANT NOTHING?
AND NOW YOU'RE WITH ANOTHER MAN, I SEE...
BRR BRR BRR
BUT IS THIS WHAT YOU REALLY WANT? DIDN'T YOU...
DIDN'T YOU WANT...
MIKAGI...

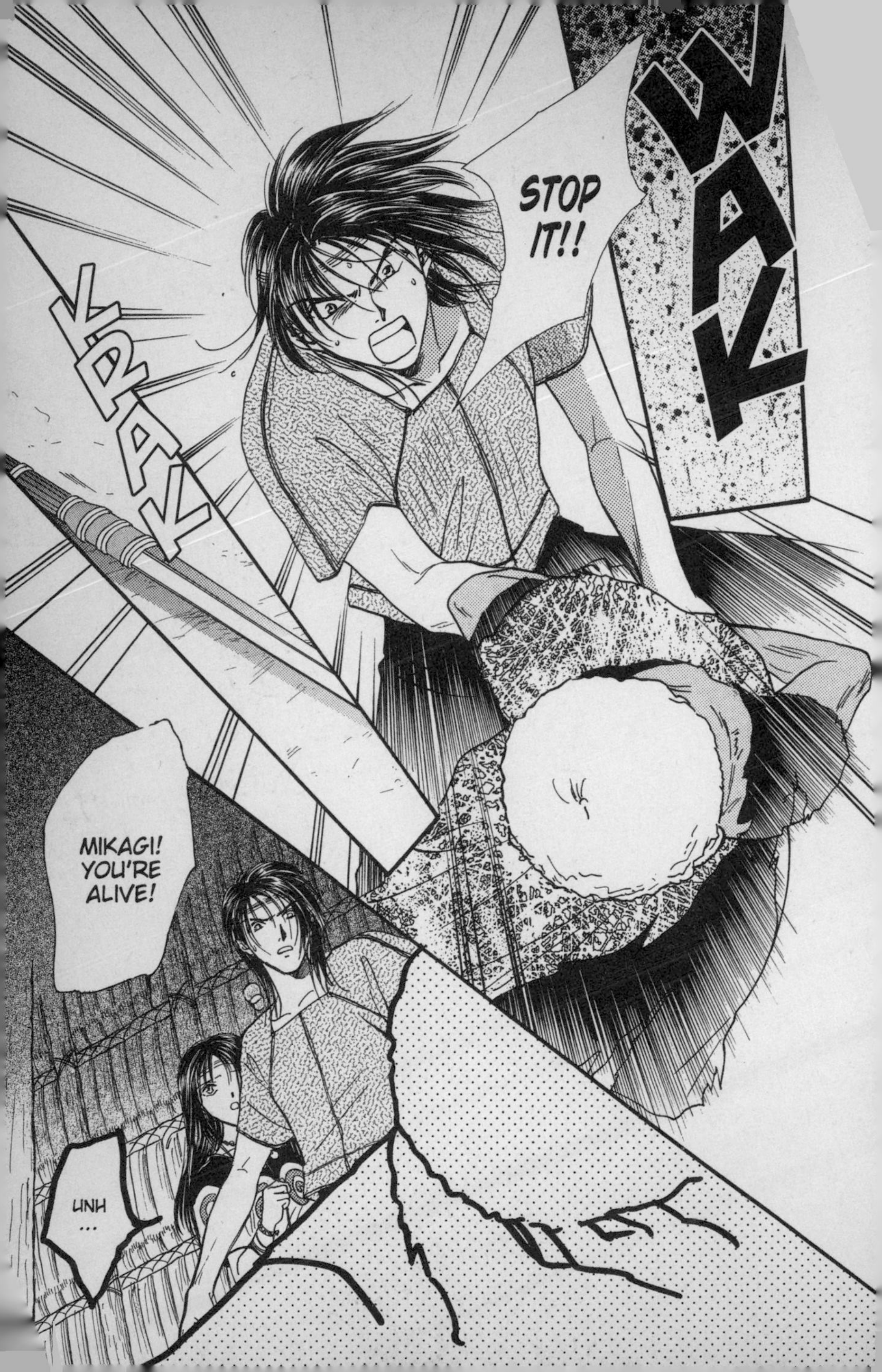
WAK
STOP IT!!
KRAK
MIKAGI! YOU'RE ALIVE!
UNH ...

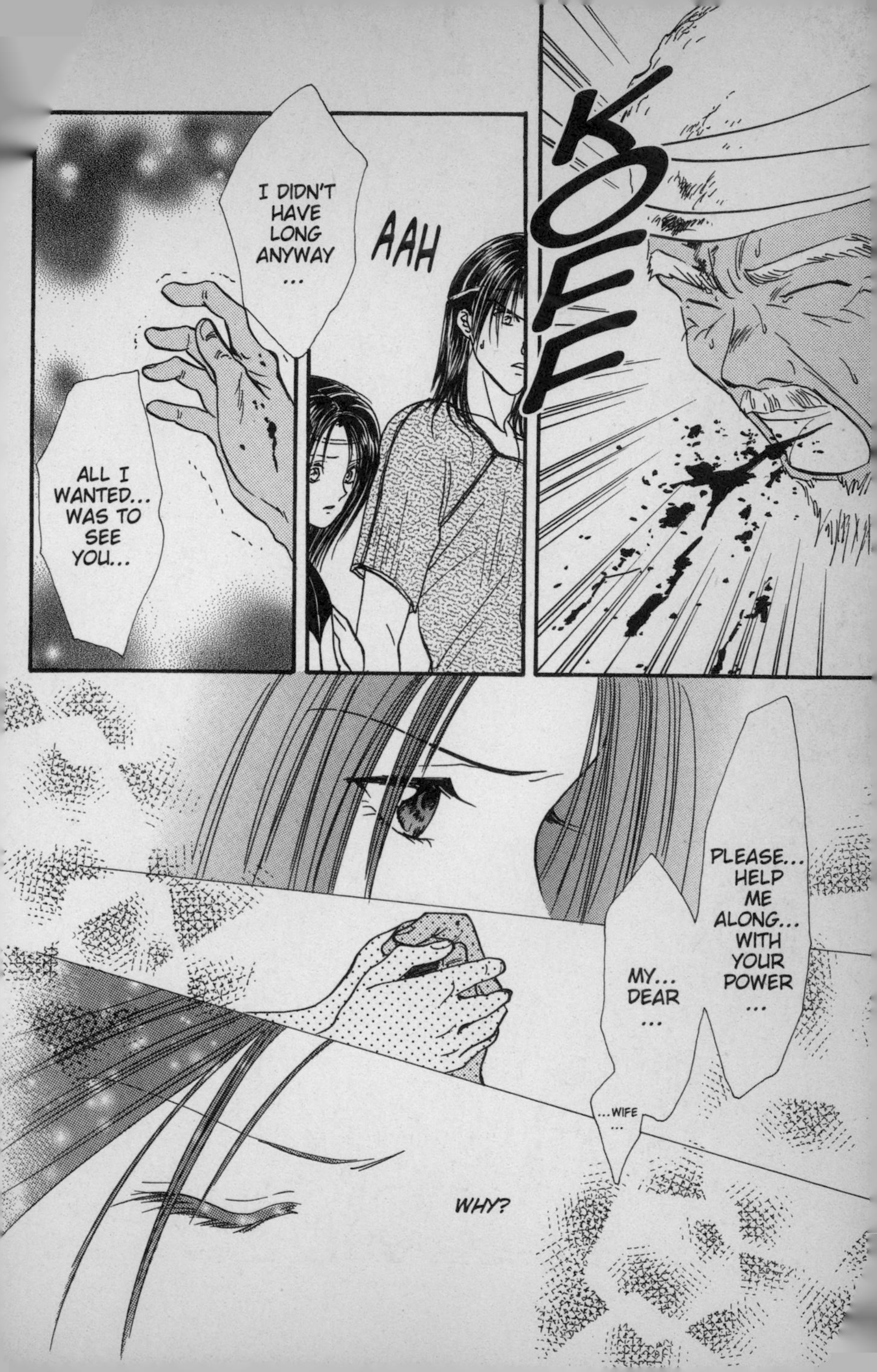
KOFF
AAH
I DIDN'T HAVE LONG ANYWAY ...
ALL I WANTED... WAS TO SEE YOU...
PLEASE... HELP ME ALONG... WITH YOUR POWER ...
MY... DEAR ...
...WIFE ...
WHY?

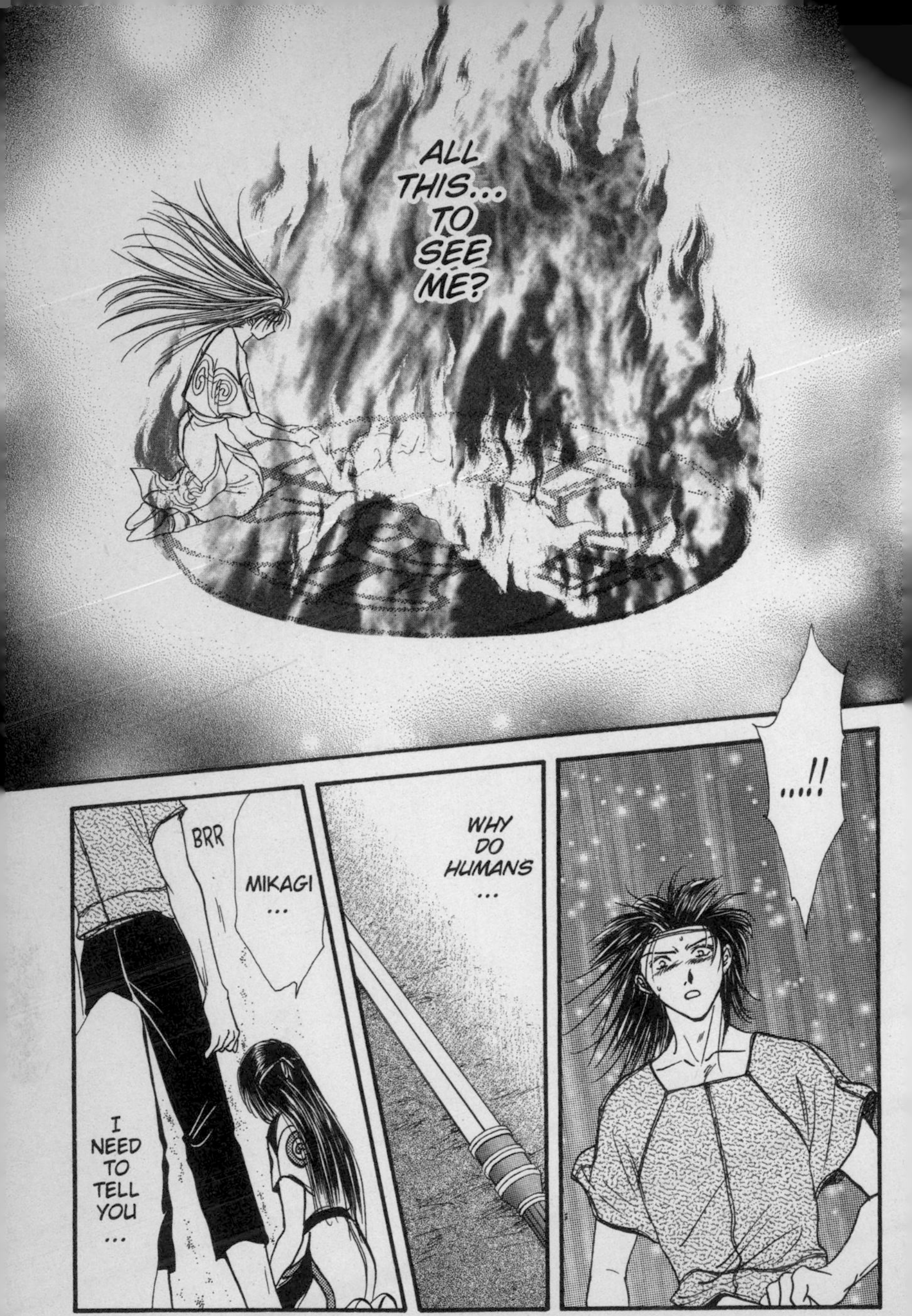
ALL THIS... TO SEE ME?
...!!
WHY DO HUMANS ...
BRR
MIKAGI ...
I NEED TO TELL YOU ...

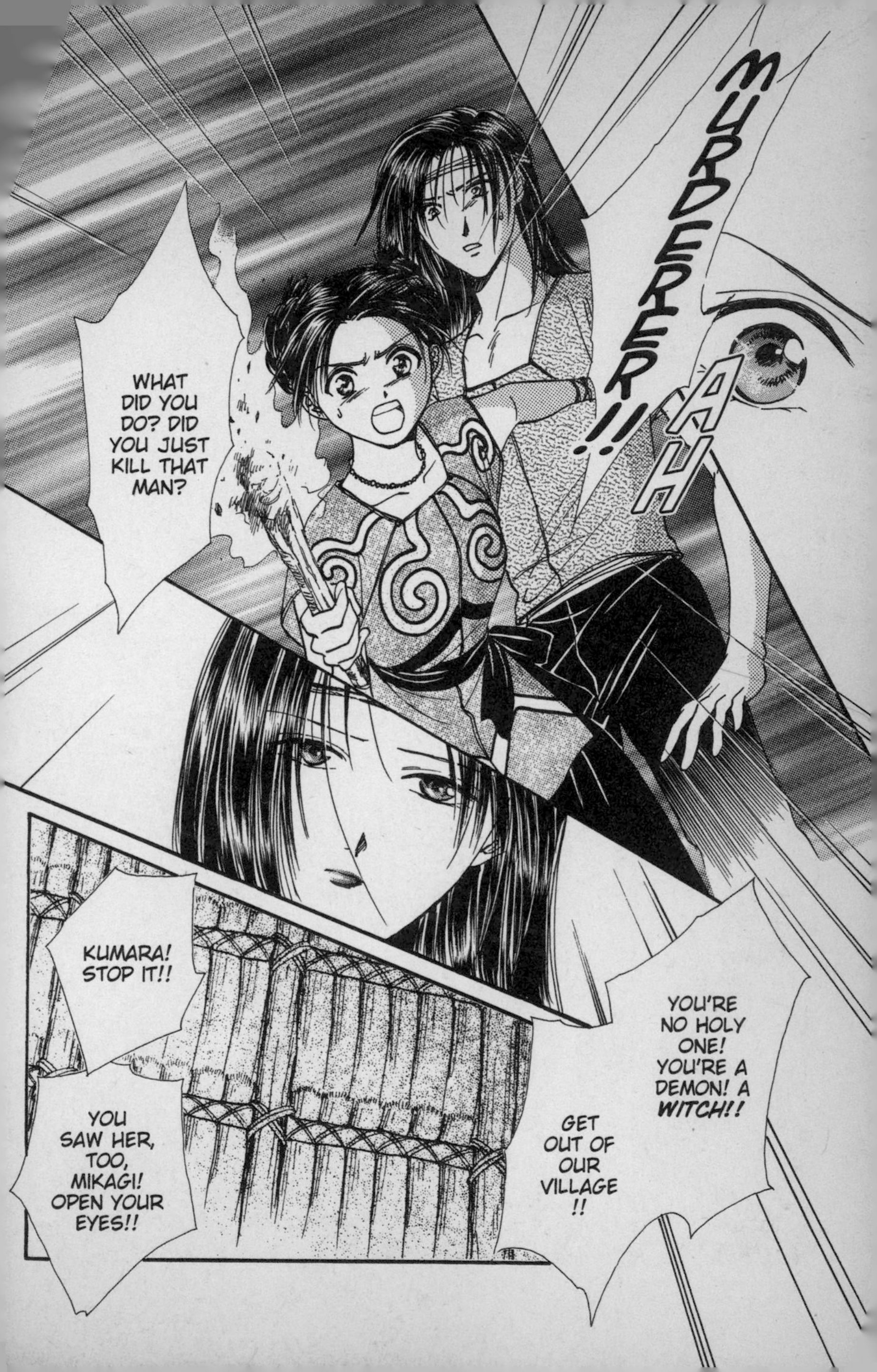
MURDERER!!
AH
WHAT DID YOU DO? DID YOU JUST KILL THAT MAN?
YOU'RE NO HOLY ONE! YOU'RE A DEMON! A WITCH!!
GET OUT OF OUR VILLAGE !!
KUMARA! STOP IT!!
YOU SAW HER, TOO, MIKAGI! OPEN YOUR EYES!!

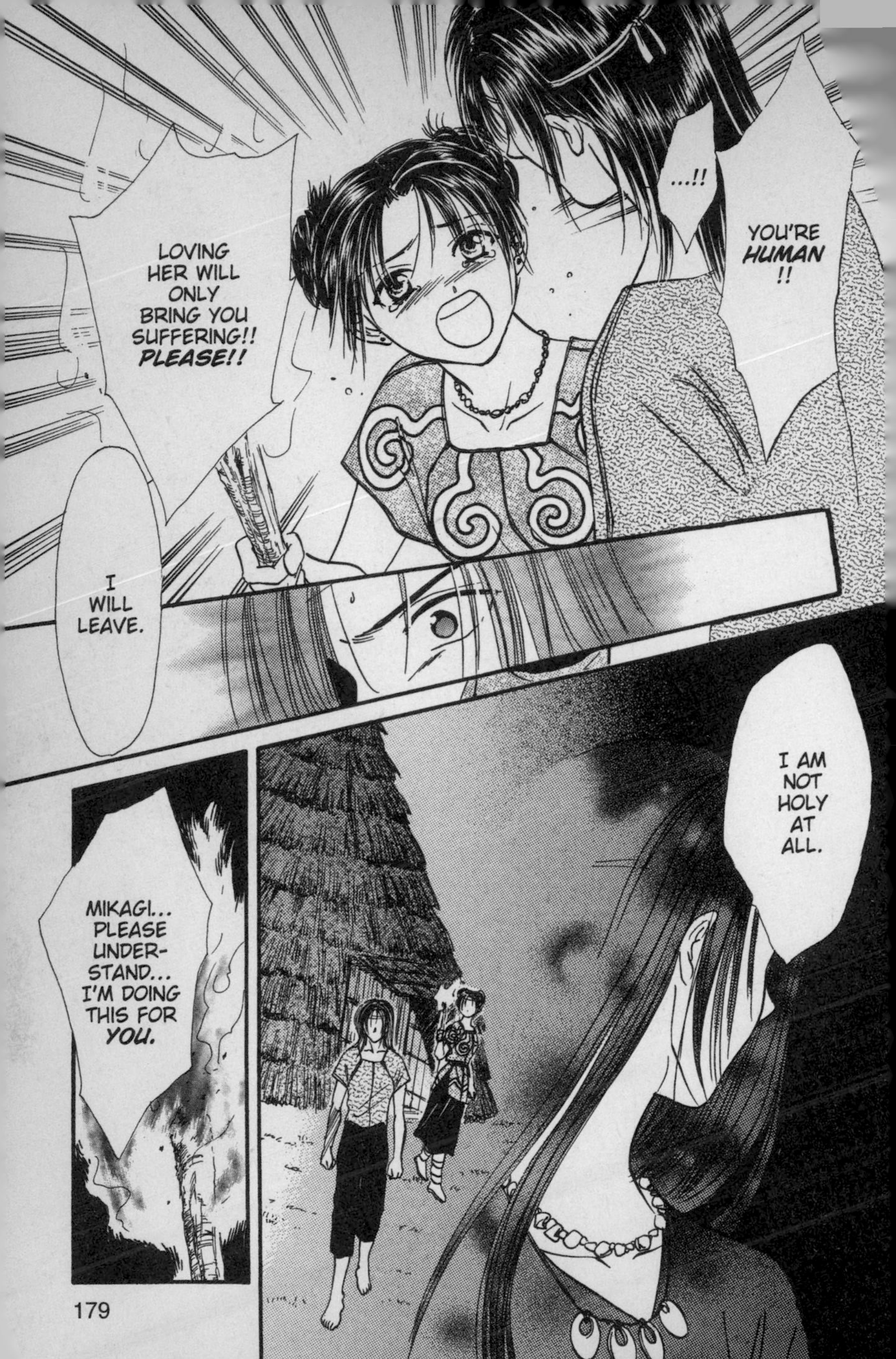
YOU'RE *HUMAN* !!
...!!
LOVING HER WILL ONLY BRING YOU SUFFERING!! *PLEASE!!*
I WILL LEAVE.
I AM NOT HOLY AT ALL.
MIKAGI... PLEASE UNDER-STAND... I'M DOING THIS FOR *YOU.*

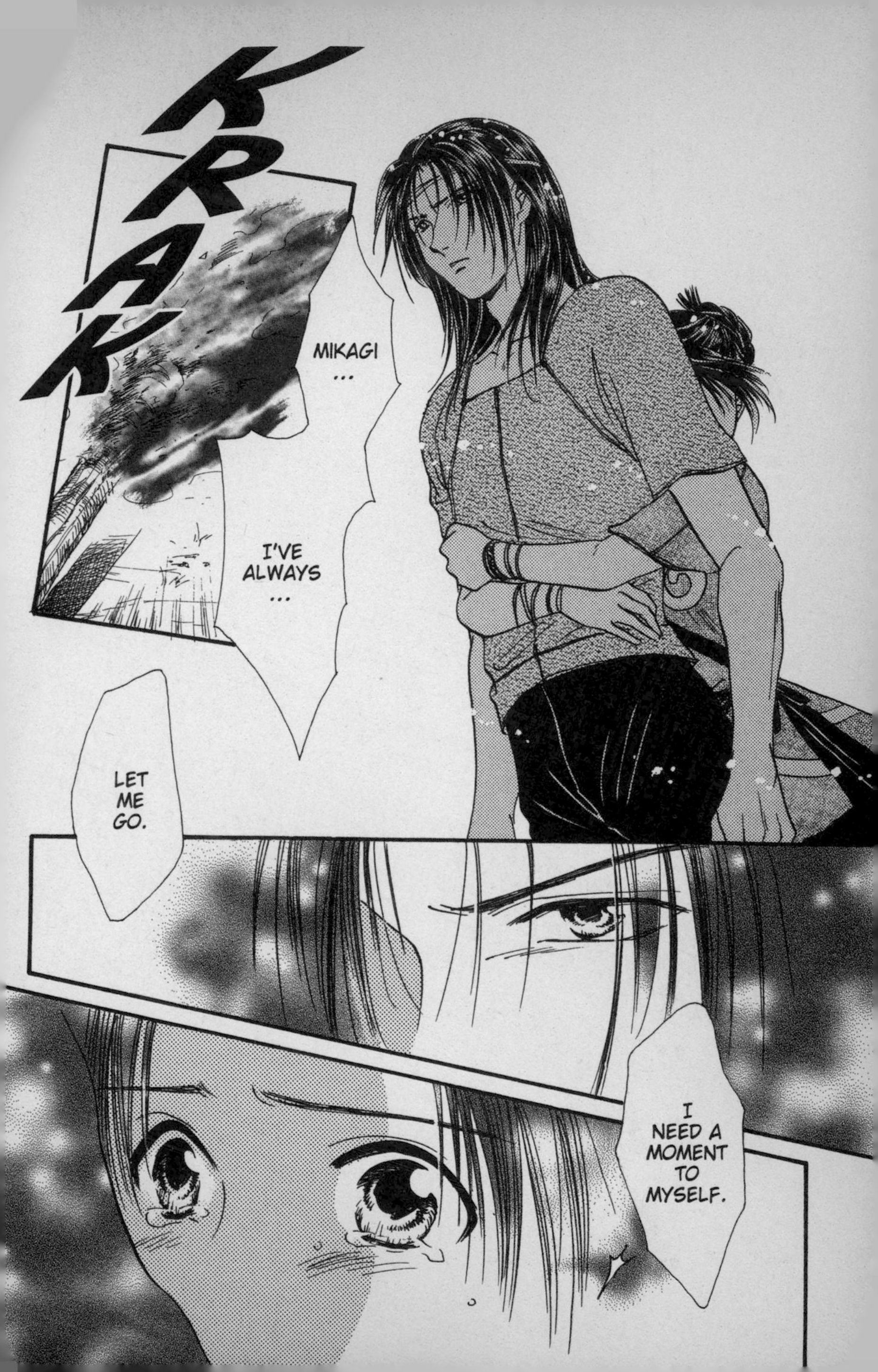
MIKAGI ...
I'VE ALWAYS ...
KRAK
LET ME GO.
I NEED A MOMENT TO MYSELF.

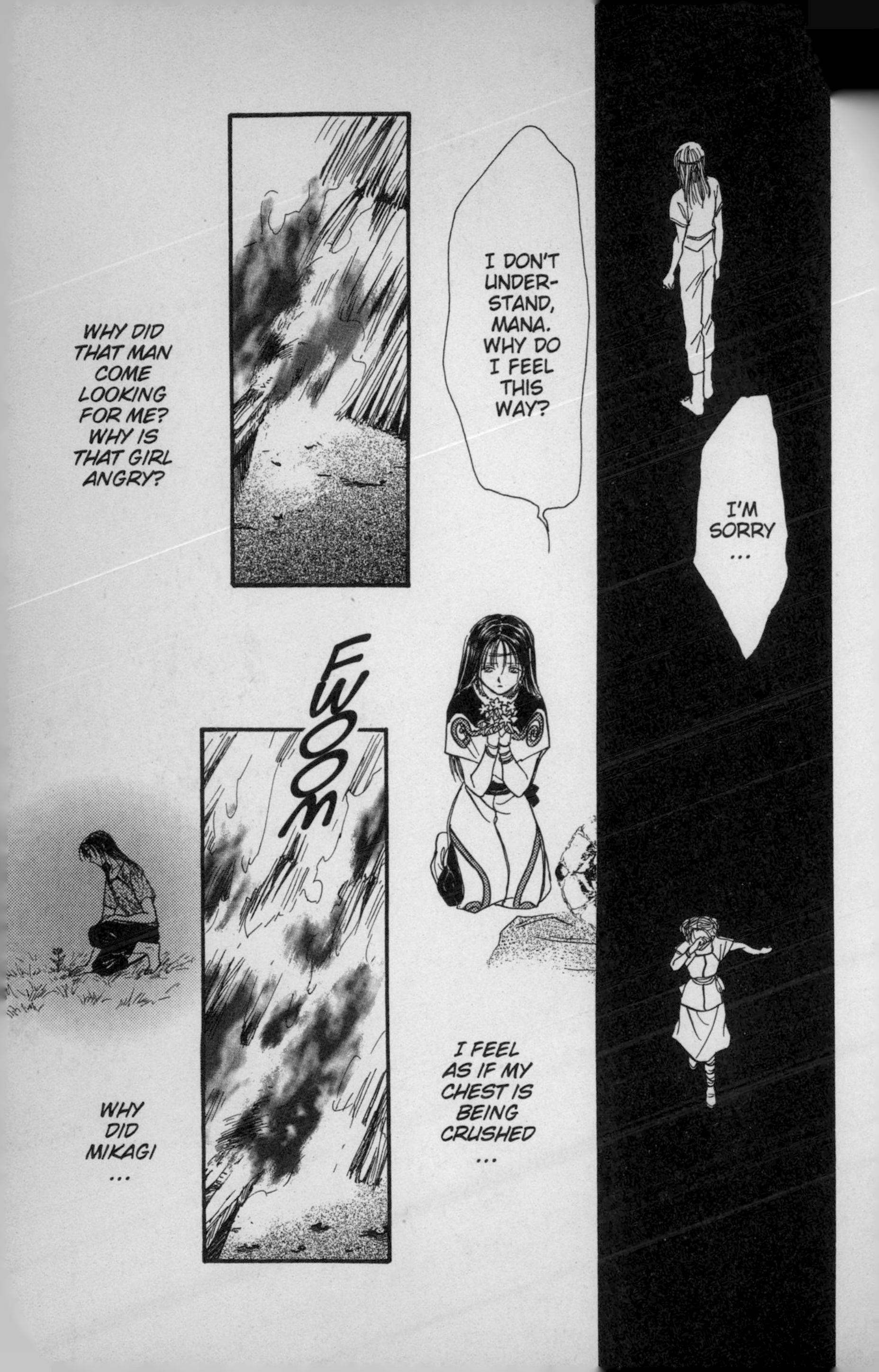
I'M SORRY...
I DON'T UNDER-STAND, MANA. WHY DO I FEEL THIS WAY?
WHY DID THAT MAN COME LOOKING FOR ME? WHY IS THAT GIRL ANGRY?
FWOOM
I FEEL AS IF MY CHEST IS BEING CRUSHED...
WHY DID MIKAGI...

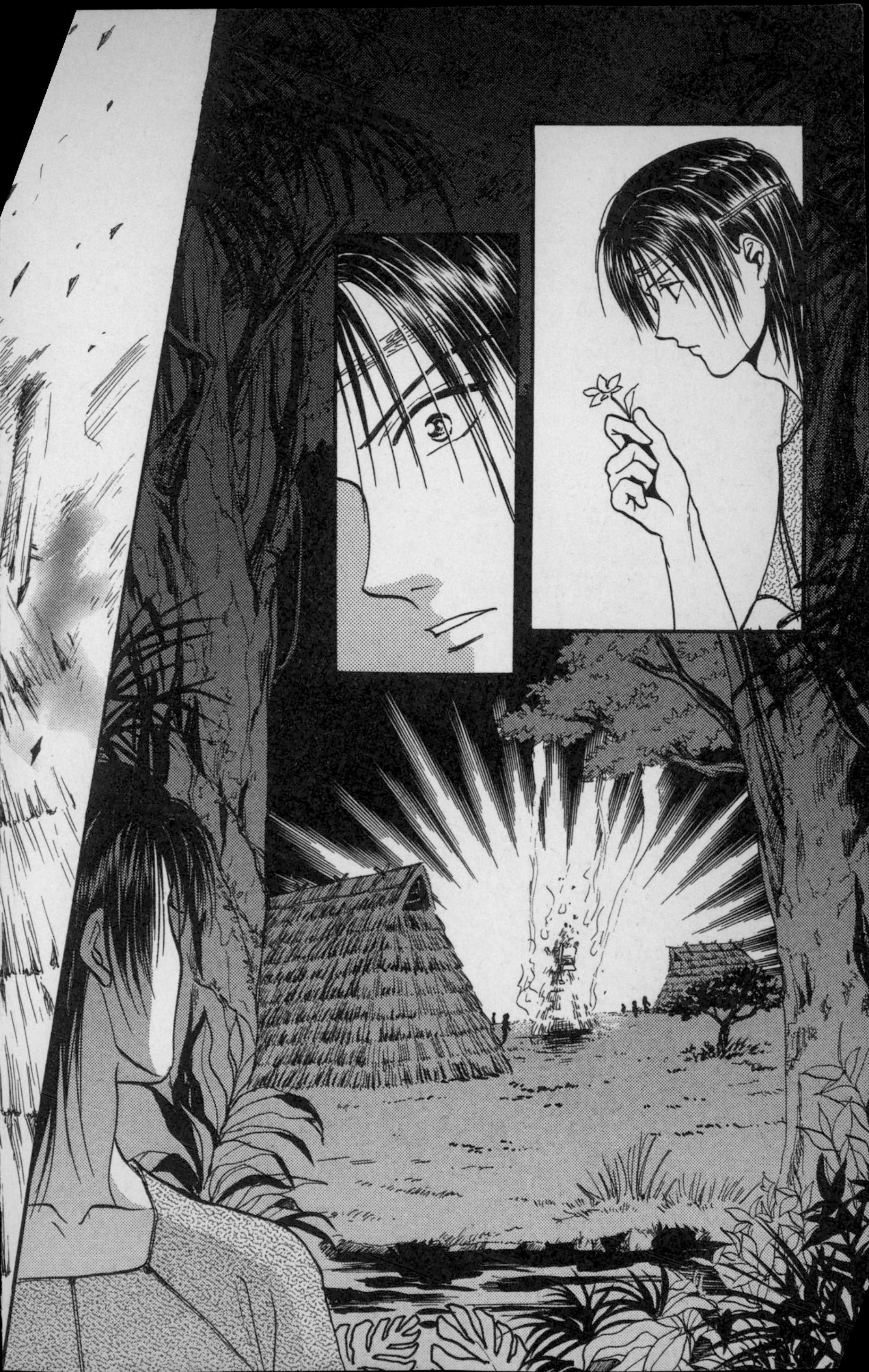

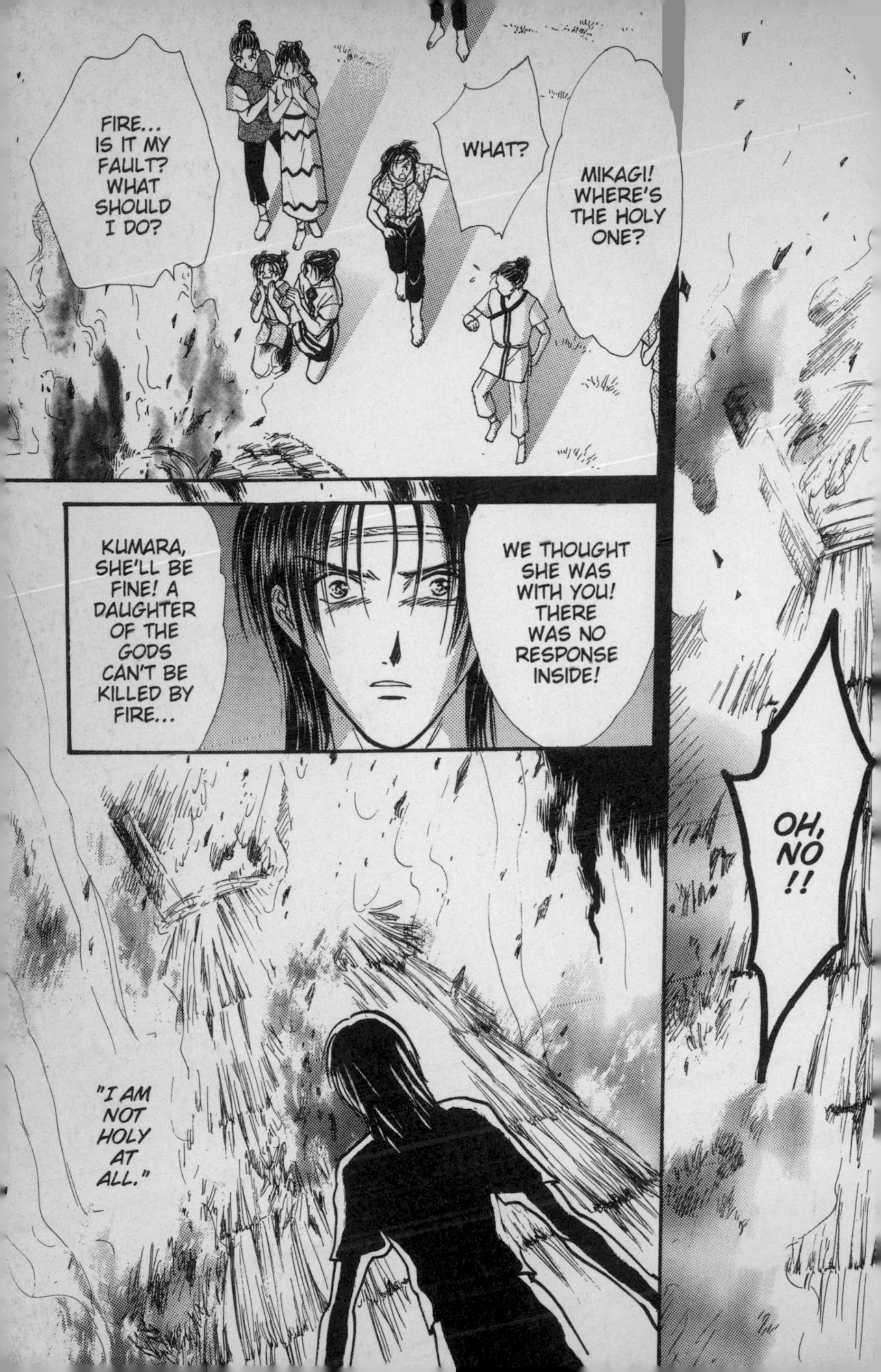
OH, NO!!
MIKAGI! WHERE'S THE HOLY ONE?
WHAT?
FIRE... IS IT MY FAULT? WHAT SHOULD I DO?
WE THOUGHT SHE WAS WITH YOU! THERE WAS NO RESPONSE INSIDE!
KUMARA, SHE'LL BE FINE! A DAUGHTER OF THE GODS CAN'T BE KILLED BY FIRE...
"I AM NOT HOLY AT ALL."

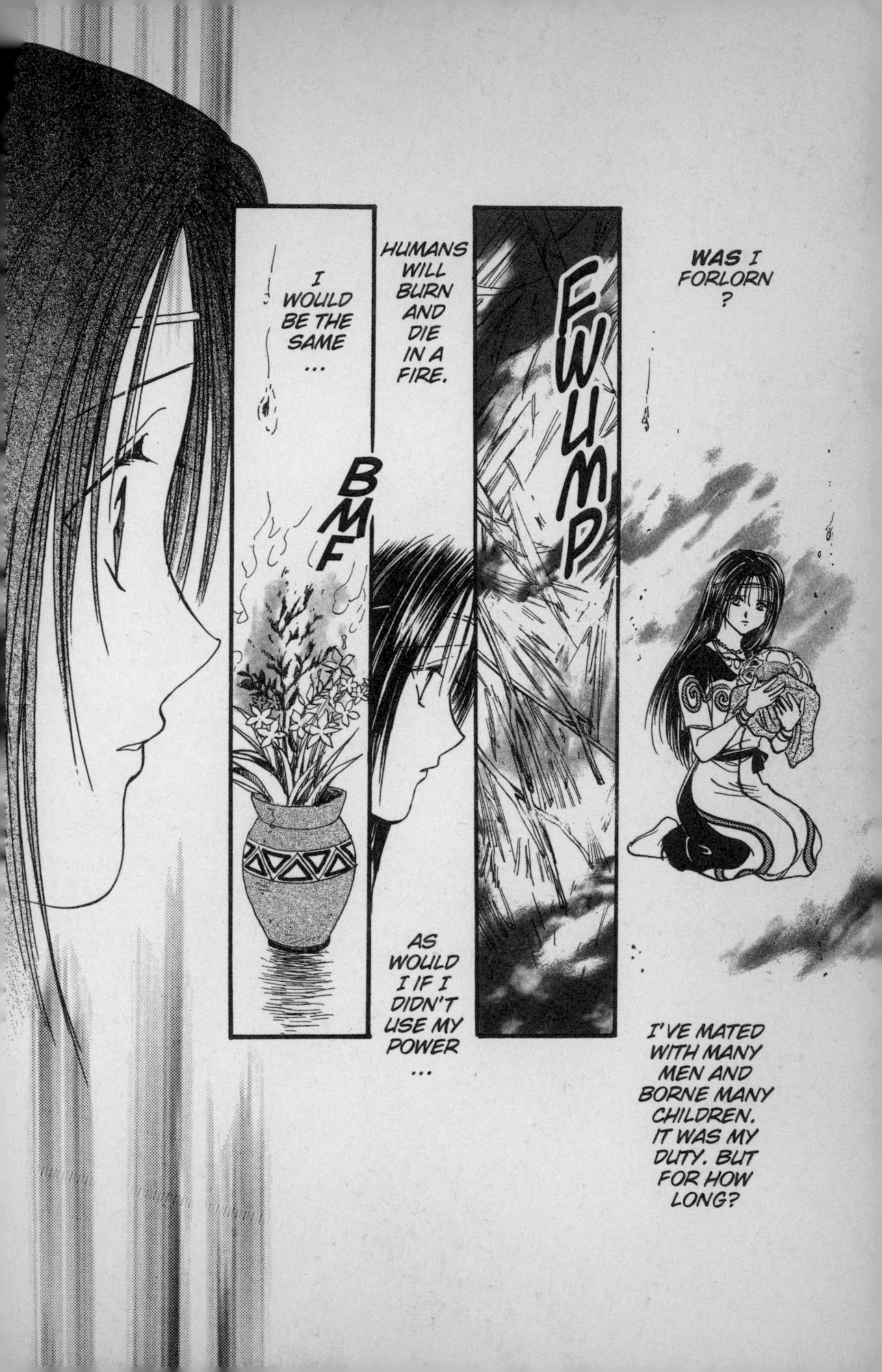
WAS I FORLORN ?
I'VE MATED WITH MANY MEN AND BORNE MANY CHILDREN. IT WAS MY DUTY. BUT FOR HOW LONG?
FWUMP
HUMANS WILL BURN AND DIE IN A FIRE.
AS WOULD I IF I DIDN'T USE MY POWER ...
BMF
I WOULD BE THE SAME ...

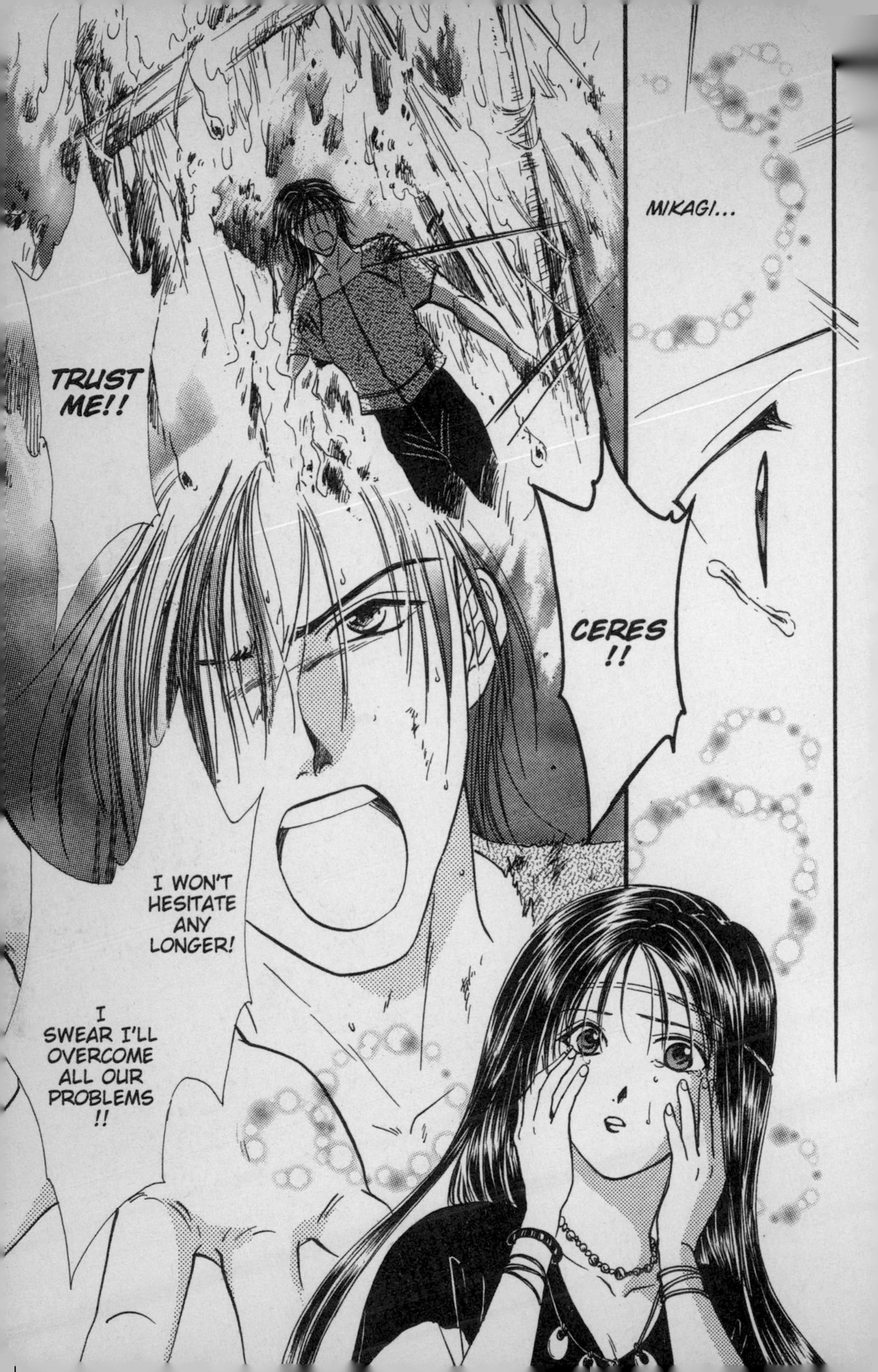
MIKAGI...
CERES !!
TRUST ME!!
I WON'T HESITATE ANY LONGER!
I SWEAR I'LL OVERCOME ALL OUR PROBLEMS !!

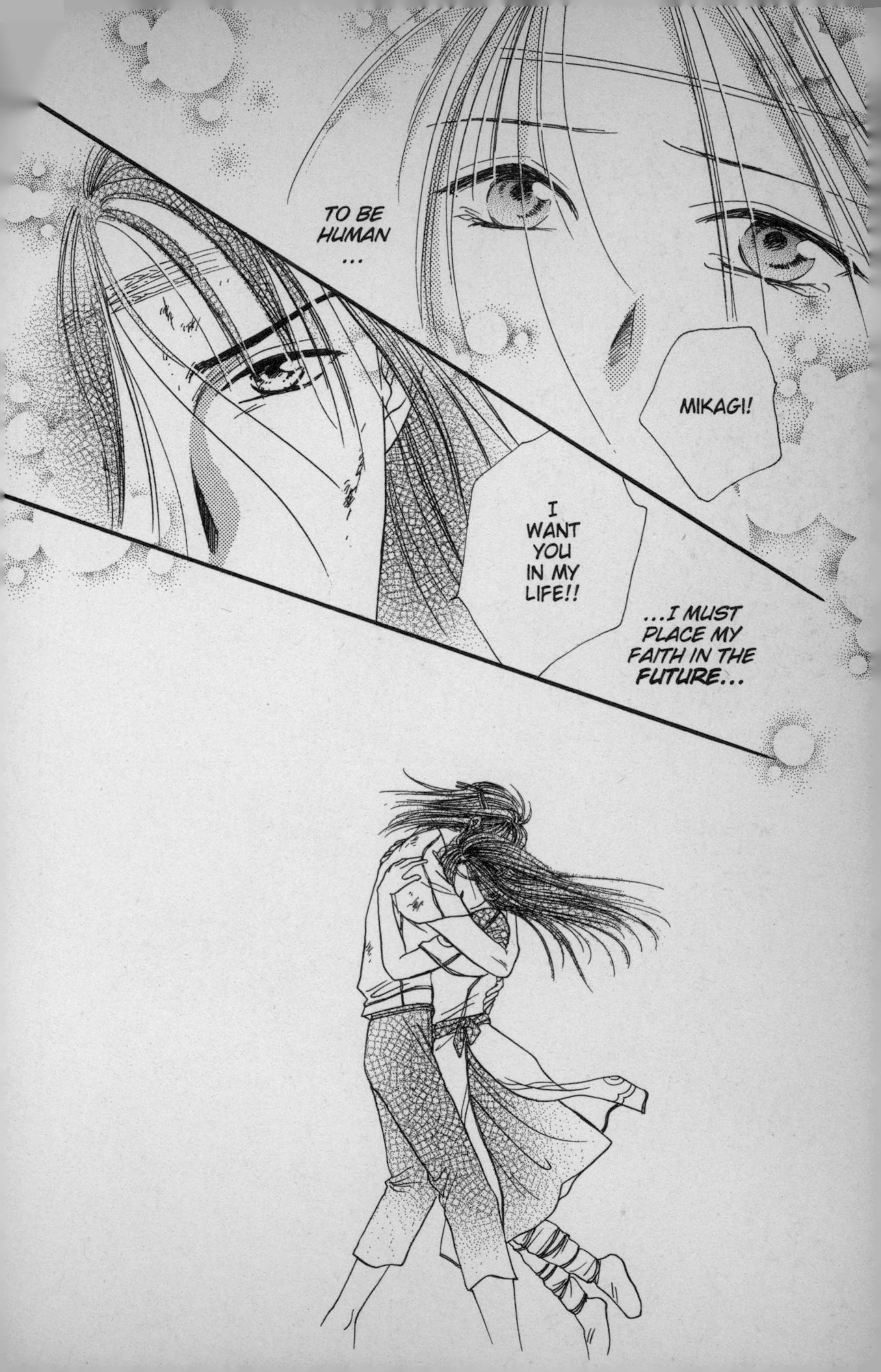
MIKAGI!
TO BE HUMAN ...
I WANT YOU IN MY LIFE!!
...I MUST PLACE MY FAITH IN THE FUTURE...

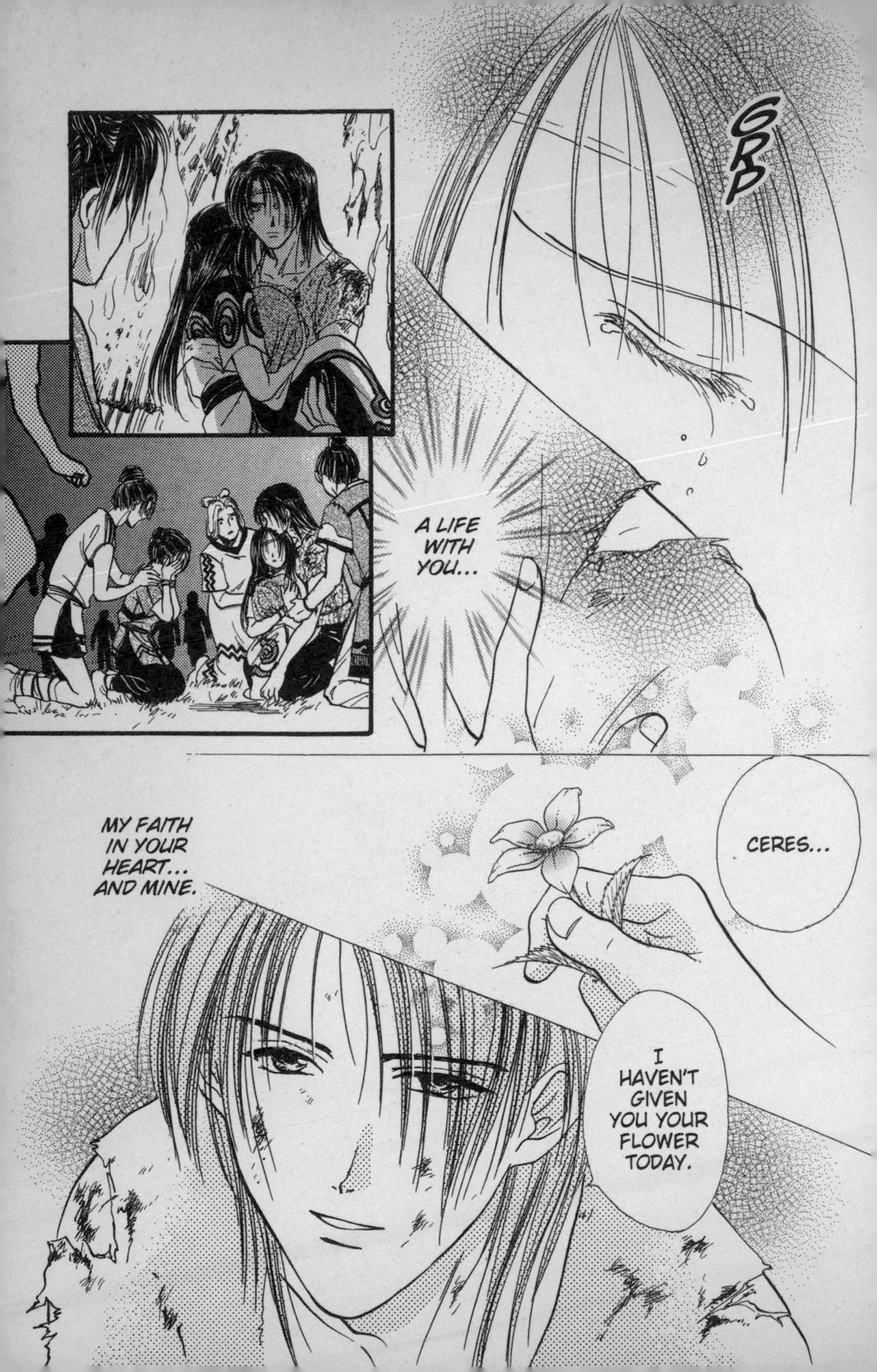
GRP
A LIFE WITH YOU...
CERES...
I HAVEN'T GIVEN YOU YOUR FLOWER TODAY.
MY FAITH IN YOUR HEART... AND MINE.

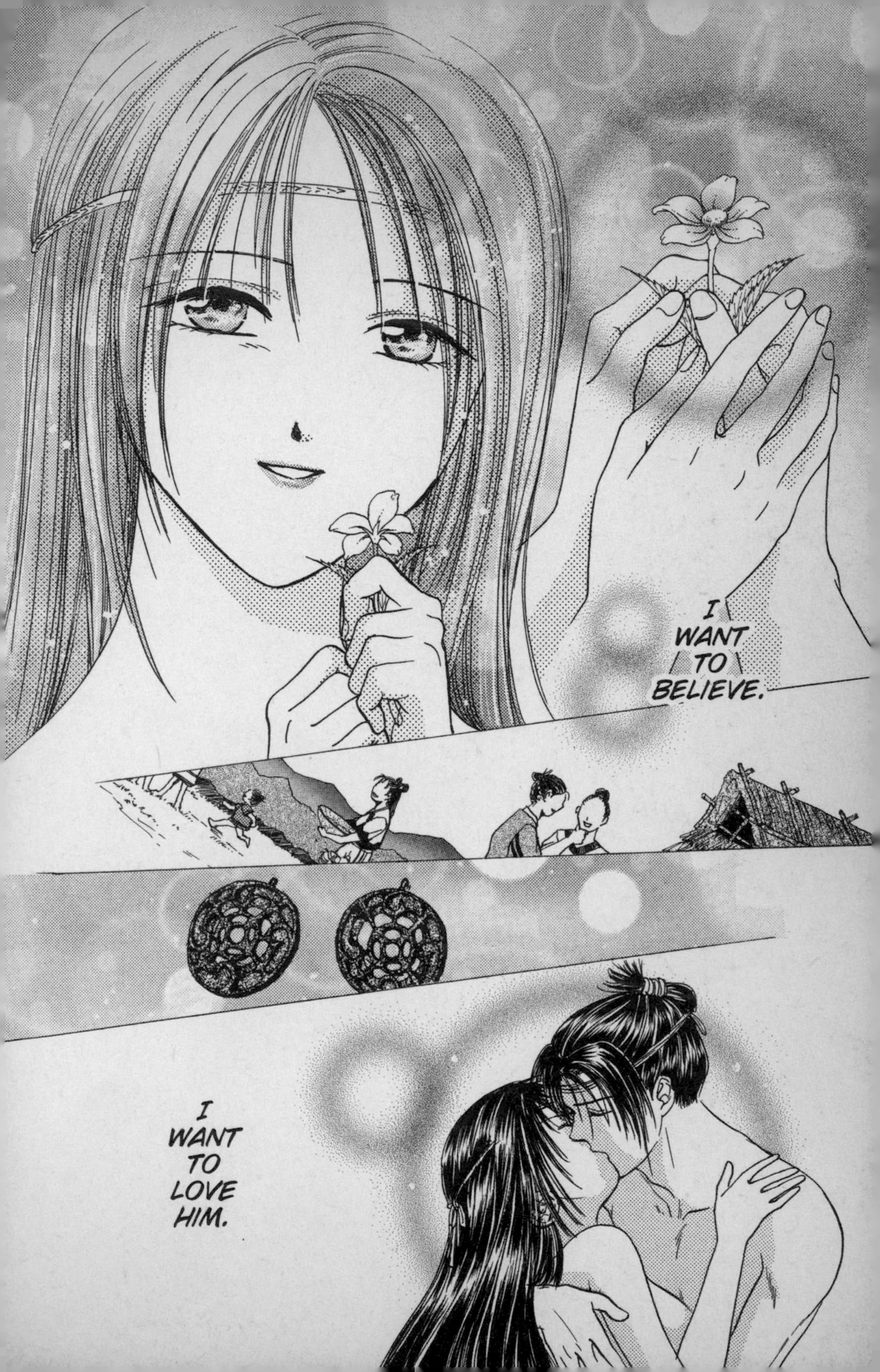
I WANT TO BELIEVE.
I WANT TO LOVE HIM.

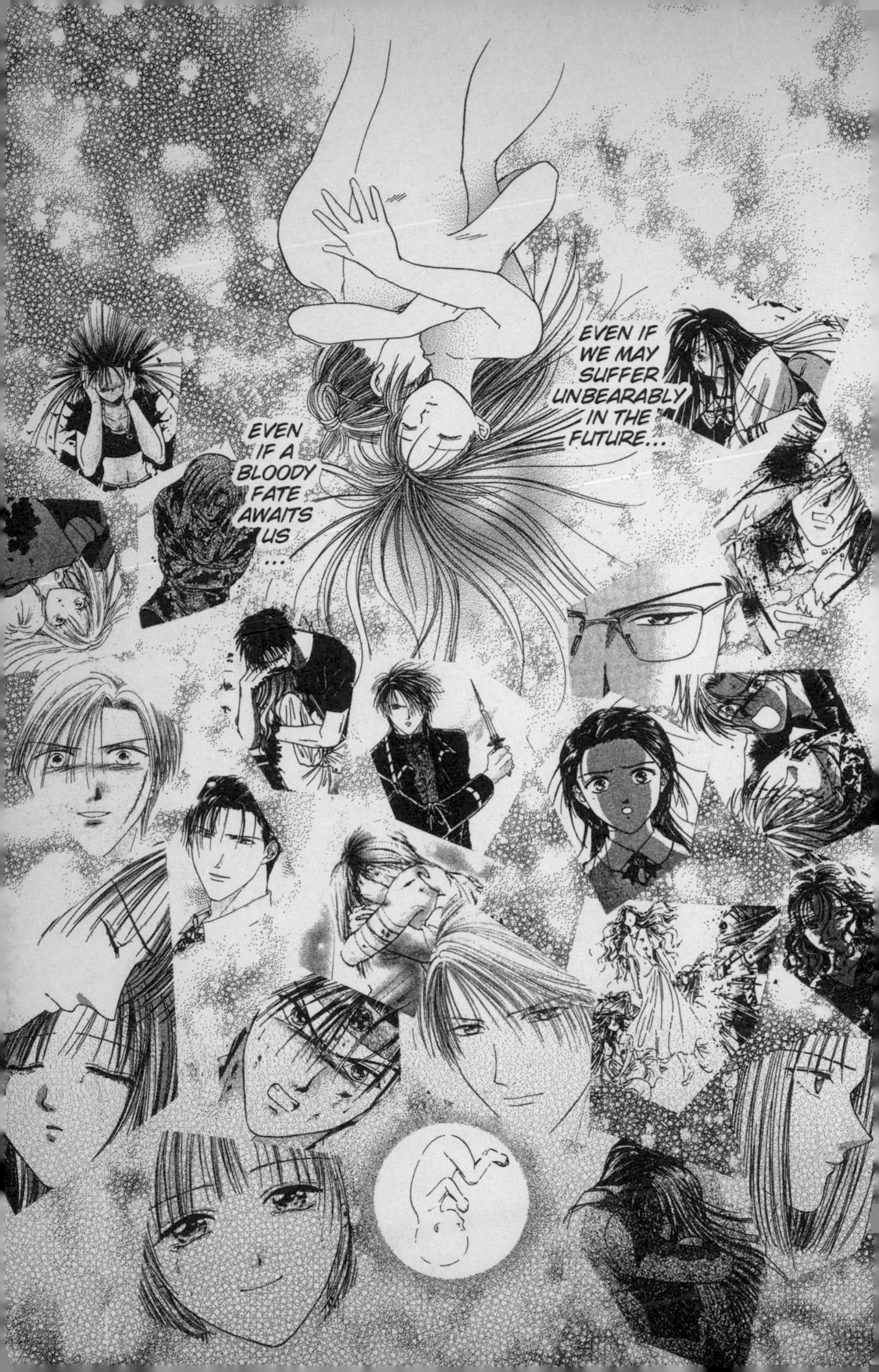
EVEN IF WE MAY SUFFER UNBEARABLY IN THE FUTURE...
EVEN IF A BLOODY FATE AWAITS US ...

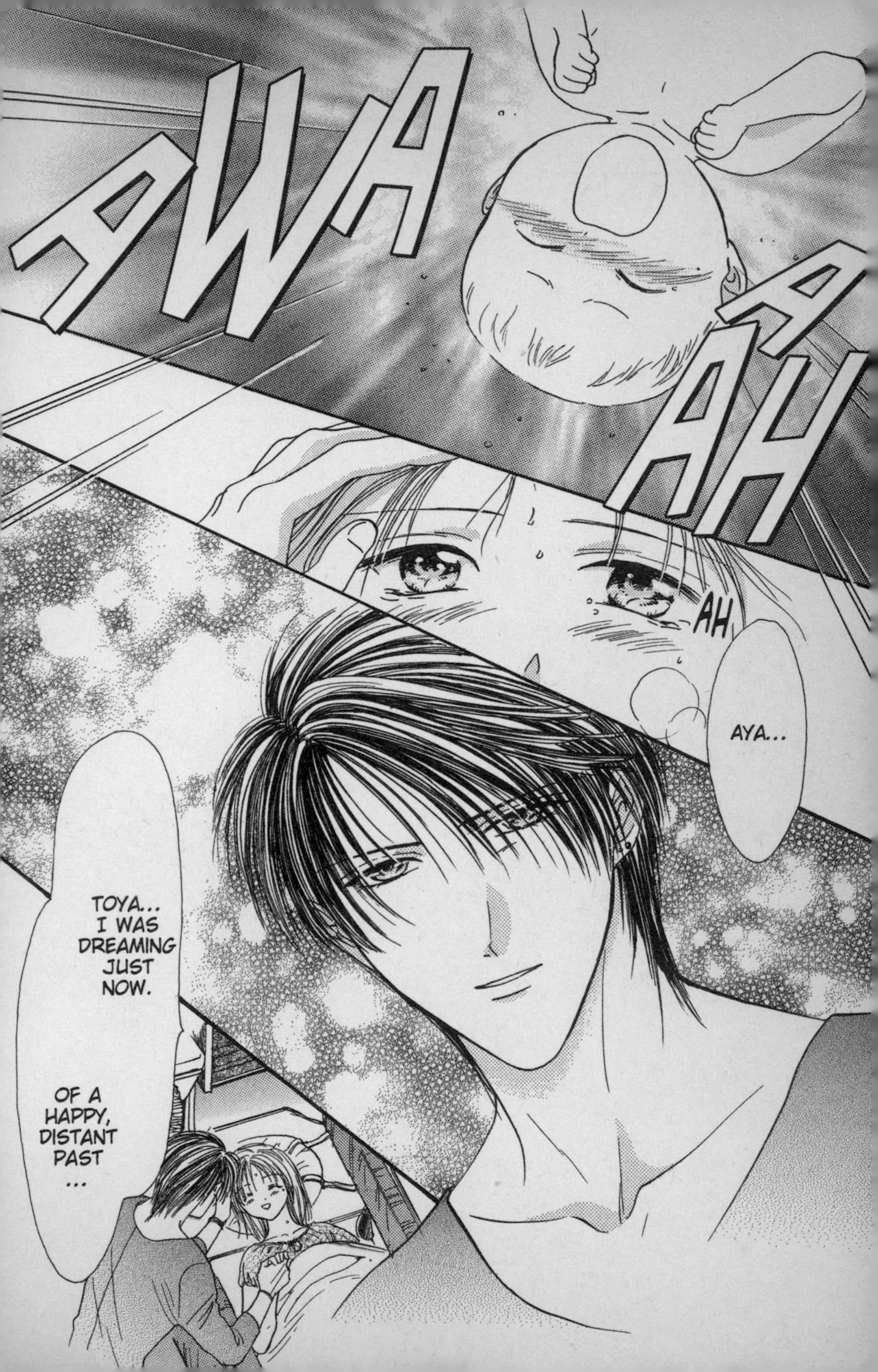
AAH
AWA
AH
AYA...
TOYA... I WAS DREAMING JUST NOW.
OF A HAPPY, DISTANT PAST ...

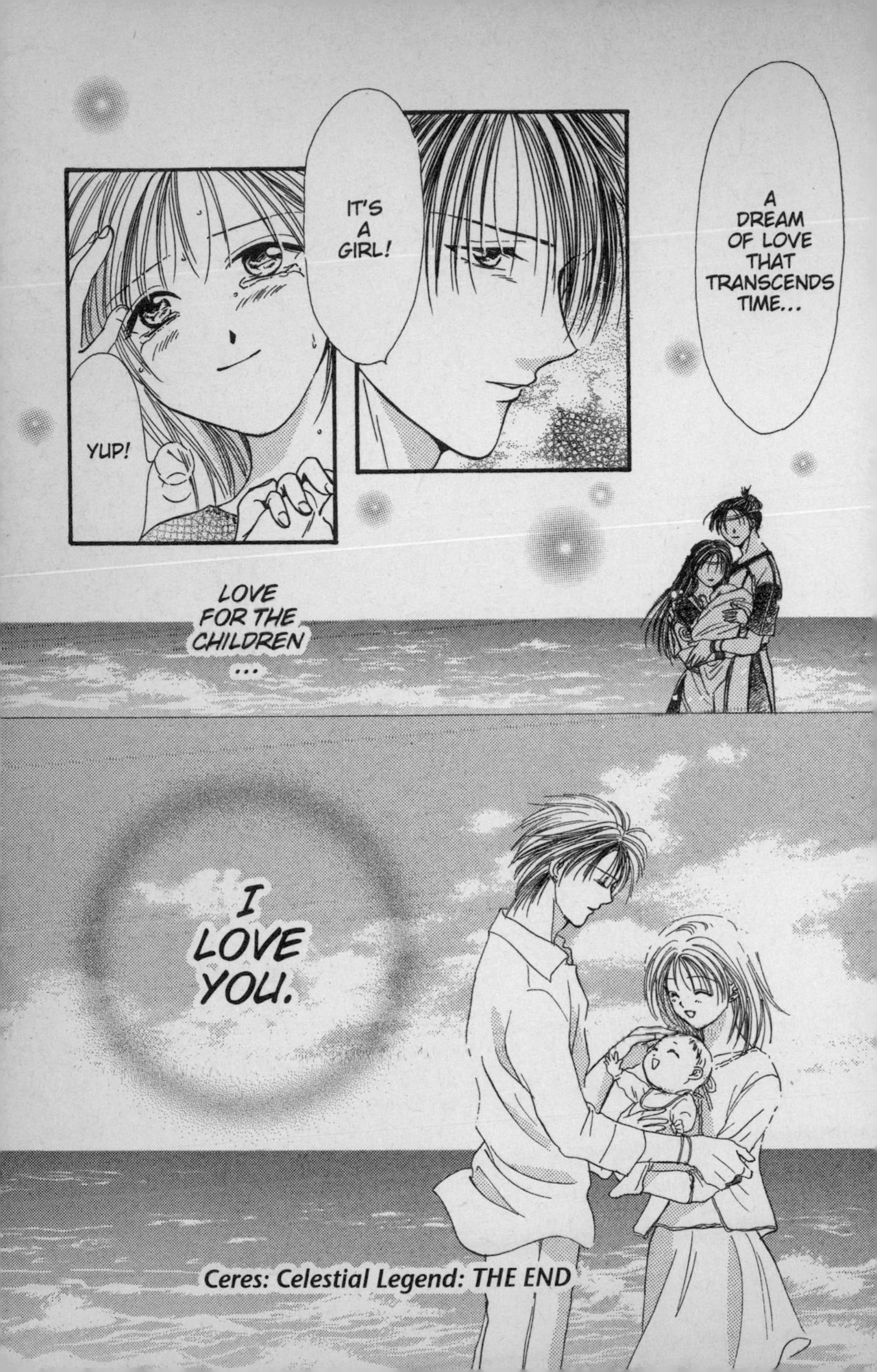
A DREAM OF LOVE THAT TRANSCENDS TIME...
IT'S A GIRL!
YUP!
LOVE FOR THE CHILDREN ...
I LOVE YOU.
Ceres: Celestial Legend: THE END

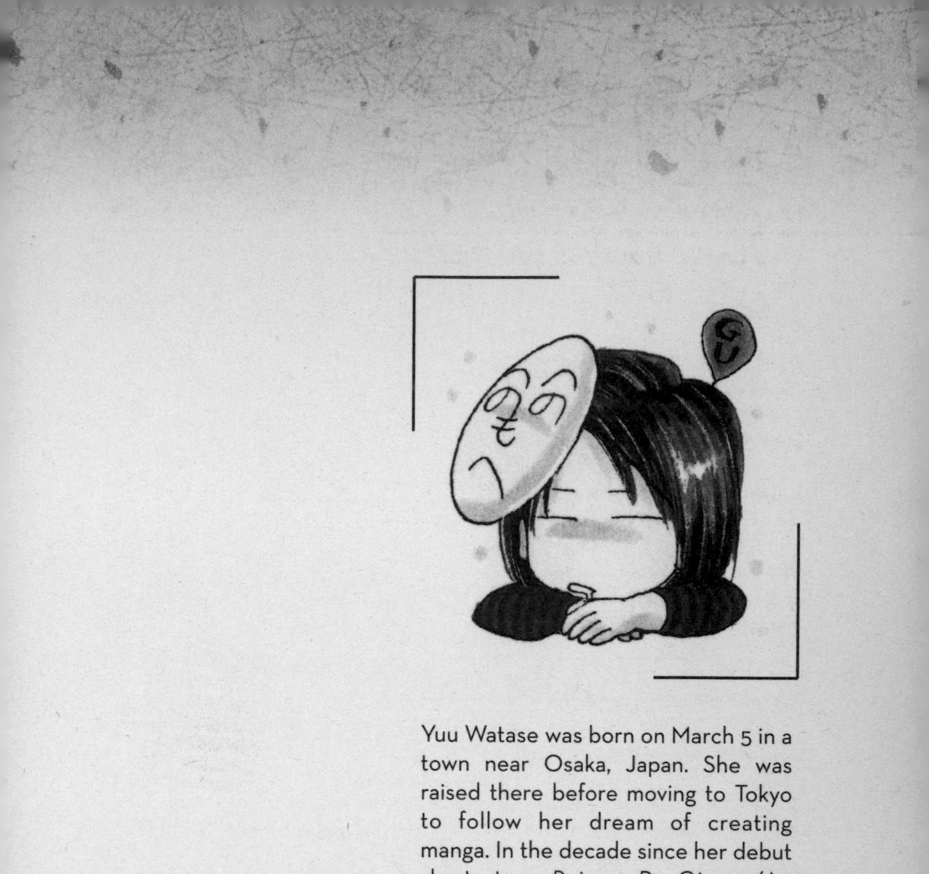
GU

Yuu Watase was born on March 5 in a town near Osaka, Japan. She was raised there before moving to Tokyo to follow her dream of creating manga. In the decade since her debut short story, *Pajama De Ojama* (An Intrusion in Pajamas), she has produced more than 50 volumes of short stories and continuing series. Her latest work, *Absolute Boyfriend*, appeared in Japan in the anthology magazine *Shôjo Comic* and is currently serialized in English in *Shojo Beat* magazine. Watase's other beloved series, *Alice 19th*, *Imadoki!*, and *Ceres: Celestial Legend*, are available in North America in English editions published by VIZ Media.

Fushigi Yûgi: Genbu Kaiden Vol. 6

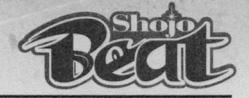

The Shojo Beat Manga Edition

STORY AND ART BY
YUU WATASE

Translation/Lillian Olsen
Touch-up Art & Lettering/Rina Mapa
Design/Izumi Hirayama
Editor/Shaenon K. Garrity

Editor in Chief, Books/Alvin Lu
Editor in Chief, Magazines/Marc Weidenbaum
VP of Publishing Licensing/Rika Inouye
VP of Sales/Gonzalo Ferreyra
Sr. VP of Marketing/Liza Coppola
Publisher/Hyoe Narita

Printed in Canada

Published by VIZ Media, LLC
P.O. Box 77010
San Francisco, CA 94107

Shojo Beat Manga Edition
10 9 8 7 6 5 4 3 2 1
First printing, February 2008

www.viz.com

RATED T+ FOR OLDER TEEN

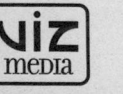

PARENTAL ADVISORY
FUSHIGI YÜGI: GENBU KAIDEN is rated T+ for Older Teen and is recommended for ages 16 and up. Contains nudity, strong language, sexual themes, and realistic and fantasy violence.
ratings.viz.com

store.viz.com

Tell us what you think about Shojo Beat Manga!

Our survey is now available online. Go to:

shojobeat.com/mangasurvey

Help us make our product offerings better!

viz media™

Shojo Beat
MANGA from the HEART

THE REAL DRAMA BEGINS IN...